# An Objective Approach to English Literature

# An Objective Approach to English Literature

## For NET, JRF, SLET and Pre-Ph.D. Registration Test

Ivan K. Masih

K.K. Narayan
Pandey Om Prakash
Rahmat Jahan
Neeraj Kumar

ATLANTIC

PUBLISHERS & DISTRIBUTORS (P) LTD

Published by

**ATLANTIC**

**PUBLISHERS & DISTRIBUTORS (P) LTD**

7/22, Ansari Road, Darya Ganj, New Delhi-110002
Phones : +91-11-40775252, 40775214, 23273880, 23275880
Fax : +91-11-23285873
Web : www.atlanticbooks.com
E-mail : orders@atlanticbooks.com

**Branch Office: Chennai**
Phones : +91-44-48531784, 28291383
E-mail : chennai@atlanticbooks.com



Reprint 2009, 2011, 2012, 2013, 2014, 2016, 2017, 2018, 2019, 2020



Printed & bound in India by Atlantic Print Services

# Preface

This book has been planned to fulfill the need of the students by providing an authentic source of multiple choice questions and answers on English literature. It is this requirement of the students which prompted me to undertake preparation of this book. The idea of writing such a book was dormant in me for quite some time. But Dr. Neeraj Kumar's persistence and the enthusiasm of Dr. K.K. Narayan, Dr. Pandey Om Prakash and Dr. Rahmat Jahan helped me to resolve to embark on this not so brief a voyage. The result is a book of objective questions and answers on English Literature which I am sure will be welcomed by the students of different levels preparing for various examinations and those who wish to know English Literature all the better.

The desirability for clarity and authenticity determined the pattern of the book. At the same time an attempt has been made to make it exhaustive, informative and useful. Primarily the book has been divided into Sections, Units and Sub-units representing a historical period or an area of literary activity. Exclusive Sections have been devoted to American Literature, Commonwealth Literature, Indian Writing in English and Classics of World Literature. Each of the Sections has detailed questions on the historical background for better understanding of literary works. The answers to all questions are provided chapter-wise at the end of the book so as to facilitate self-assessment by the reader. The Contents are exhaustive for easy reference. The area of literature is wide and deep; therefore, selection was necessary, and a selection howsoever judiciously made leaves behind something worthwhile. I only hope that nothing has been left which a keen student may look for. Finally, I concede that any such endeavour leaves scope for further addition and improvement. Any suggestions that would enhance the quality of the book or enrich its contents would be highly appreciated.

I am thankful to my daughter-in-law Ms. Meenul and to my son Rahul for their great help and cooperation in completing this book. I also acknowledge Sri Arif Mullick and Mr. Sylvestor George for their unstinting support in the final preparation of the book. Dr. Humair Ahmad was one person who had great faith in the success of this work and has rendered his unequivocal support to it. I am grateful to each one of them.

I also appreciate my wife, Mrs. Rita Masih's unceasing support to me during writing of this book. Above all, it is my US based interior architect daughter, Ms. Rina Naik who brought to me the power and joy of prayer which changed my world view. My thanks and blessings to her.

**IVAN K. MASIH**

# Contents

9. *Gone with the Wind* (Mitchell)
10. *The Good Earth* (Pearl S. Buck)
11. *Kim* (Kipling)
12. *The Second Sex* (Simone De Beauvoir)
13. *Lolita* (Nabokov)
14. *A Doll's House* (Ibsen)
15. *Tropics of Capricon* (Henry Miller)
16. *Faust* (Goethe)
17. *The Cherry Orchard* (Chekhov)
18. *Magic Mountain* (Thomas Mann)

# Early Period (Beginning to 1550)

# 1

## UNIT A: HISTORICAL PERSPECTIVE AND BACKGROUND

1. Who defined literature as "the humanization of the whole world"?
   (a) Chaucer (b) Plato
   (c) Goethe (d) Shakespeare
2. The Romans, trying to hold their empire together against barbarian invaders, withdrew from England in A.D.
   (a) 390 (b) 400 (c) 410 (d) 420
3. Anglo-Saxon literature, broadly speaking ranges from
   (a) 7th to 11th centuries (b) 6th to 10th centuries
   (c) 8th to 12th centuries (d) 5th to 9th centuries
4. Athelstan, King of Wessex and Mercia defeated the Scots at Brunanburh in
   (a) 917 (b) 927 (c) 937 (d) 947
5. The year of Norman Conquest of England in the Battle of Hastings was
   (a) 1066 (b) 1068 (c) 1070 (d) 1072
6. The year of the Battle of Lewes is
   (a) 1264 (b) 1364 (c) 1464 (d) 1564
7. The reign of Henry II covers the period from
   (a) 1144-89 (b) 1134-79 (c) 1144-79 (d) 1154-89
8. The reign of Edward I covers the period from
   (a) 1279-1307 (b) 1284-1311
   (c) 1289-1315 (d) 1293-1319

9. Edward III defeated the French at the Battle of Poitiers and the Battle of Crecy respectively in
   (a) 1336 and 1346 (b) 1338 and 1348
   (c) 1340 and 1350 (d) 1342 and 1352
10. Laurence Minot, the patriotic versifier belongs to the
   (a) 13th century (b) 12th century
   (c) 14th century (d) 15th century
11. Winchester College, the first great public school was established in
   (a) 1371 (b) 1372 (c) 1373 (d) 1374
12. Peasant Rebellion took place in
   (a) 1380 (b) 1381 (c) 1382 (d) 1383
13. Black Death is the name given to
   (a) the great Famine (b) the Epidemic of Plague
   (c) the Epidemic of Cholera (d) none of the above
14. Identify the year that marked the fall of Constantinople
   (a) 1405 (b) 1483 (c) 1453 (d) 1473
15. In which year did the Hundred Years' War with France begin?
   (a) 1358 (b) 1348 (c) 1338 (d) 1368
16. What was the year of the Battle of Crecy?
   (a) 1346 (b) 1348 (c) 1347 (d) 1349
17. The period of the Black Death was
   (a) 1348-49 (b) 1347-48 (c) 1349-50 (d) 1350-51
18. Henry IV ascended the throne in
   (a) 1398 (b) 1399 (c) 1400 (d) 1401
19. Edward III died in
   (a) 1376 (b) 1377 (c) 1378 (d) 1379
20. The War of Roses began in
   (a) 1450 (b) 1455 (c) 1460 (d) 1465
21. Which period of English history after the death of Chaucer was known as Post-Chaucerian age?
   (a) 1450-1480 (b) 1400-1450
   (c) 1490-1530 (d) 1401-1440

22. Edward III came to the throne in
    (a) 1317 (b) 1322 (c) 1327 (d) 1332
23. Richard II came to the throne in
    (a) 1375 (b) 1377 (c) 1379 (d) 1381
24. Which dialect became the standard English (King's English) by the time of Chaucer?
    (a) east-midland dialect (b) northern dialect
    (c) southern dialect (d) west-midland dialect
25. Henry IV addressed Parliament in English for the first time in
    (a) 1397 (b) 1398 (c) 1399 (d) 1400
26. Henry IV died in
    (a) 1413 (b) 1414 (c) 1415 (d) 1416
27. Henry VII came to the throne in
    (a) 1470 (b) 1475 (c) 1480 (d) 1485
28. The War of Roses was fought between
    (a) Richard II and Henry IV (b) Edward II and Richard II
    (c) Edward III and Henry IV (d) The House of York and the House of Lancaster
29. St. Paul's School was established in 1504 to serve as a model school for the teaching of
    (a) Latin (b) French
    (c) Greek (d) Latin and Greek
30. Joan of Arc headed the French army during the reign of
    (a) Richard II (b) Henry V
    (c) Henry VI (d) Henry VII
31. The medieval feudal system came to an end with the coming of the rule of
    (a) Henry VI (b) Henry VII
    (c) Henry V (d) Richard II
32. In The War of Roses, 'Roses' stands for
    (a) flowers (b) girls
    (c) houses (d) places

33. Giraldus Cambrensis wrote *Gemma Ecclesiastica* at the end of the
    (a) 11th century (b) 12th century
    (c) 13th century (d) 14th century
34. Henry VII married Anne Boleyn in
    (a) 1531 (b) 1532 (c) 1533 (d) 1534
35. The Reformation began during the reign of
    (a) Henry VII (b) Henry VIII
    (c) Edward VI (d) Queen Mary
36. Which King won for him the title of 'the Defender of the faith'?
    (a) Henry VIII (b) Henry VII
    (c) Edward VI (d) Edward III
37. Which language became the official language in England after Norman Conquest?
    (a) English (b) Latin (c) German (d) French
38. The Hundred Years' War was fought between ......... in 1338.
    (a) England and Italy (b) The Romans and the Saxons
    (c) England and France (d) The Greeks and the Romans

## UNIT B: THE ANGLO-SAXON PERIOD (650–1066)

39. Which is the oldest Anglo-Saxon biblical poem?
    (a) "Exodus" (b) "Daniel"
    (c) "Genesis" (d) "Christ"
40. Which is the earliest poem in our literature?
    (a) "Widsith" (b) "Deor"
    (c) "Beowulf" (d) "The Seafarer"
41. "Beowulf" is
    (a) an epic (b) a collection of ballads
    (c) a romance (d) a history of the Anglo-Saxon period

42. "Beowulf" was composed in Northumbria by a Christian poet working on pagan material in
(a) early 6th century (b) end of the 4th century
(c) end of the 7th century (d) beginning of 3rd century

43. Who is the author of "Beowulf"?
(a) Caedmon (b) Cynewulf
(c) John Gower (d) None of these

44. "Beowulf" consists of .... successive narratives
(a) two (b) three (c) four (d) five

45. Which poem depicts most vividly the tribal life and rites of ancient days?
(a) "Beowulf" (b) "The Seafarer"
(c) "Widsith" (d) None of the above

46. The oldest epic in Germanic literature is
(a) "The Wanderer" (b) "The Seafarer"
(c) "Beowulf" (d) "The Wife's Complaint"

47. The line 'Came on the dark night gliding, the shadowy prowler' has been taken from
(a) "Widsith" (b) "Beowulf"
(c) "Morte d' Arthur" (d) None of the above

48. The character of Heorrenda appears in
(a) "Beowulf" (b) "The Wanderer"
(c) "Deor" (d) "The Seafarer"

49. Who is called the father of English learning?
(a) Bede (b) Caedmon
(c) Cynewulf (d) Alfred

50. Bede, the famous Christian writer of the Anglo-Saxon period, wrote mostly in which language?
(a) Latin (b) English (c) French (d) German

51. The life span of Bede is
(a) 673-735 (b) 683-745 (c) 678-749 (d) 688-750

52. Bede, the great English ecclesiastical historian and scholar lived from
(a) 673-735 (b) 683-740 (c) 688-745 (d) 693-750

53. *Ecclesiastical History of the English People* was written by
    (a) Bede (b) Malory
    (c) Langland (d) None of these
54. Bede wrote his *Ecclesiastical History* in
    (a) French (b) Latin (c) Greek (d) English
55. Caedmon is a writer of
    (a) 5th century (b) 6th century
    (c) 7th century (d) 8th century
56. Who is known as 'the Anglo-Saxon Milton'?
    (a) Bede (b) Cynewulf
    (c) Caedmon (d) None
57. The poem "The Fates of the Apostles" has been written by
    (a) Cynewulf (b) Caedmon
    (c) Bede (d) Gower
58. Caedmon and Cynewulf were two poets. They were
    (a) Chaucer's contemporaries (b) Chaucer's predecessors
    (c) Chaucer's successors (d) not definitely known
59. One of the following poems was not written by Caedmon
    (a) "The Christ" (b) "The Judith"
    (c) "Dream of the Road" (d) "Beowulf"
60. The poem "The Christ" is written by
    (a) Chaucer (b) Langland
    (c) Cynewulf (d) Gower
61. Besides being a poet, Alfred is a great
    (a) novelist (b) playwright
    (c) essayist (d) translator
62. Alfred, King of Wessex died in
    (a) 900 A.D. (b) 901 A.D.
    (c) 902 A.D. (d) 903 A.D.
63. The last known poem of the Anglo-Saxon period "The Battle of Maldon" was written in
    (a) 990 A.D. (b) 991 A.D.
    (c) 992 A.D. (d) 993 A.D.

64. "The Battle of Maldon" shows a revival of the heroic spirit. The poem is attributed to
(a) Marlowe (b) Boethius
(c) Cynewulf (d) anonymous

65. Alexander Neckham wrote a Treatise on science in
(a) Latin (b) French (c) English (d) Spanish

66. "The Ruined Burg" is a fine
(a) elegy (b) ode (c) lyric (d) ballad

67. Aldhelm, Bede and Alcuin are renowned names in
(a) Latin literature (b) French literature
(c) Greek literature (d) English literature

68. "Praise of Virginity" has been written by
(a) Bede (b) Aldhelm
(c) Alcuin (d) None of the above

69. Which of the following poems was not written by Cynewulf?
(a) "Christ" (b) "Juliana"
(c) "The Fates of the Apostles" (d) "Beowulf"

70. Which is the oldest surviving English poem in the form of a dream?
(a) "Elene" (b) "Andreas"
(c) "The Dream of the Rood" (d) "Satan"

71. One of the following poems deals with contemporary history
(a) "The Ruin" (b) "The Wife's Lament"
(c) "The Battle of Brunanburh" (d) "The Husband's Message"

72. The translation of the *Cura Pastoralis* was done by
(a) Alfred (b) Bede
(c) Malory (d) None of the above

73. Alfred's translation of *Boethius, De Consolatione Philosophiae* is a work of
(a) literature (b) history
(c) science (d) philosophy

## UNIT C: THE ANGLO-NORMAN PERIOD (1066–1350)

### 1. French Writers

74. "Sir Gawayne and the Grene Knight" was written by
    (a) Langland (b) Chaucer
    (c) An unknown poet (d) Geoffrey of Monmouth
75. *History of Britain* has been written by
    (a) Chaucer (b) Gower
    (c) Langland (d) Geoffrey Monmouth
76. Which work originated the dream convention in English?
    (a) "Beowulf" (b) "Romance of the Rose"
    (c) "The Owl and the Nightingale" (d) None of the above
77. "The Romance of the Rose" has been written by
    (a) Chaucer (b) Langland
    (c) Malory (d) none of the above
78. "The Romance of the Rose" was originally written by
    (a) Flaubert (b) Maupassant
    (c) Zola (d) De Lorris & De Meung
79. "Chanson de Roland" was a famous epic in
    (a) French (b) Latin (c) German (d) English
80. *Historia Regum Britanniae* of Geoffrey of Monmouth was written in
    (a) English (b) French (c) Latin (d) Spanish
81. "The legend of King Arthur and His Knights of the Round Table" was first related in
    (a) Malory's *Morte de Arthur* (b) Geoffrey's *Historia*
    (c) Layamon's *Brut* (d) Tennyson's *Idylls of the King*
82. "Fabliau", a short narrative poem, is of..... origin.
    (a) French (b) English (c) Latin (d) Spanish
83. Fable, a popular medieval literary form, came to the Middle Ages from
    (a) French sources (b) Greek sources
    (c) Indian sources (d) Greek and Indian sources

84. *Roman de Renart*, a collection of beast stories, is in which language?
(a) English (b) Latin (c) French (d) Greek

**2. Metrical Romances**

85. Which of the four poems belongs to the romance of chivalry?
(a) "Pearl" (b) "Patience"
(c) "Cleanness" (d) "Sir Gawayne and the Grene Knight"

86. Which of the following anonymous poems is a romance?
(a) "Sir Gawayne and the Grene Knight" (b) "Patience"
(c) "Pearl" (d) "Purity"

87. "Patience", "Pearl" and "Purity" – these anonymous poems have been written in
(a) southern dialect (b) northern dialect
(c) east-midland dialect (d) west-midland dialect

88. In the poem "Pearl", pearl is the name of a
(a) diamond (b) girl (c) place (d) gem

89. The poem "The Pearl" is
(a) an elegy (b) an allegory
(c) a lyric (d) a satire

90. The poems "Pearl", "Patience" and "Purity", have been written by
(a) Gower (b) Langland
(c) Walter Hilton (d) None of the above

**3. Miscellaneous Poems**

91. *Scale of Perfection* has been written by
(a) John Wyclif (b) Walter Hilton
(c) Malory (d) None of the above

92. The only political poem in English which has survived in complete form is
(a) "Song of Lewes" (b) "The Seafarer"
(c) "The Wanderer" (d) "The Owl and the Nightingale"

93. Macaronic poem is one where.... and .... are used together.
    (a) French and English (b) Latin and English
    (c) French and Latin (d) English and Spanish
94. *Meditation of the Passion* has been written by
    (a) Richard Rolle (b) Walter Hilton
    (c) Julian of Norwich (d) Wyclif
95. "The Owl and the Nightingale" was written about
    (a) 1210 (b) 1215 (c) 1220 (d) 1225
96. The earliest of the religious work *The Poema Morale* dates from about
    (a) 1170 (b) 1172 (c) 1174 (d) 1176
97. "The Ormulum" consisting of metrical paraphrases of the Gospel was written about
    (a) 1198 (b) 1200 (c) 1205 (d) 1210
98. "Havelok" and "Horn", the two romances based on Scandinavian originals were written at the end of the
    (a) 11th century (b) 12th century
    (c) 13th century (d) 14th century
99. Princess Goldburgh is a character in
    (a) "Horn" (b) "Havelok"
    (c) "The Owl and the Nightingale" (d) None of the above

## UNIT D: THE AGE OF CHAUCER (1350–1400)

### 1. Geoffrey Chaucer

100. In which tale of Chaucer, a daughter is killed by her father?
    (a) "The Monk's Tale" (b) "The Physician's Tale"
    (c) "The Friar's Tale" (d) "The Clerk's Tale"
101. In Chaucer's "The Canterbury Tales" which tale deals with two young Theban warriors?
    (a) "The Knight's Tale" (b) "The Squire's Tale"
    (c) "The Miller's Tale" (d) "The Friar's Tale"

102. Chaucer's .... is based in part on a notable French sermon of Friar Laurens.
(a) "Parson's Tale" (b) "Pardoner's Tale"
(c) "Friar's Tale" (d) "Monk's Tale"

103. The writer who gave the first full expression of 'the English sense of humour' was
(a) Langland (b) Gower
(c) Chaucer (d) Wyclif

104. Who translated *Romance of the Rose*, a French work into English?
(a) Chaucer (b) Malory
(c) Langland (d) Gower

105. Who has been called 'the Morning Star of the Renaissance'?
(a) Langland (b) Gower
(c) Chaucer (d) Wyclif

106. Which of the following works of Chaucer does not belong to Chaucer's 'Italian Period'?
(a) *The Hous of Fame* (b) *Legende of Good Women*
(c) *Canterbury Tales* (d) *Troilus and Cryseyde*

107. Which work of Chaucer was an allegory on the death of Blanche, the wife of his patron?
(a) *The Hous of Fame* (b) *The Parliament of Fouls*
(c) *The Book of the Duchess* (d) *Legende of Good Women*

108. How many pilgrims in the *Prologue to the Canterbury Tales* represent the military profession?
(a) 1 (b) 2 (c) 3 (d) 4

109. To which shrine are the pilgrims going?
(a) shrine of St. Agnes at Canterbury (b) shrine of St. Lucas of Jerusalem
(c) shrine of St. Thomas at Canterbury (d) shrine of St. Mark in Southwark

110. In whose story, the character of Griselda appears?
(a) "The Clerk's Tale" (b) "The Reeve's Tale"
(c) "The Miller's Tale" (d) "The Friar's Tale"

111. Who tells the story of January and May in Chaucer's *Prologue to The Canterbury Tales*?
(a) the Wife of Bath (b) the Friar
(c) the Clerk (d) the Merchant

112. Which of Chaucer's work has the Trojan War as its background?
(a) *The Parliament of Fowls* (b) *Troilus and Cryseyde*
(c) *The Book of the Duchess* (d) *The Hous of Fame*

113. Pandare, who is a Chaucerian character appears in
(a) *Troilus and Cryseyde* (b) *The Hous of Fame*
(c) *The Canterbury Tales* (d) None of the above

114. Who has uttered these lines?
'No hadde I er now, my swete herte deere,
Ben yold, ywis, I were now nought heere'!
(a) Cryseyde (b) Troilus
(c) Diomede (d) None of the above

115. "Miller's" and "Reeve's Tales" are the examples of
(a) fable (b) sermon
(c) fabliau (d) romance

116. One of the portraits in the *Prologue* is that of Wife of Bath. 'Bath' is
(a) the Christian name of the lady (b) the surname of the lady
(c) the name of her husband (d) the name of the town

117. 'He was as fresh as the month of May.' This line occurs in the *Prologue*. Whom does this line refer to?
(a) Friar (b) Franklin
(c) Doctor of Physic (d) Squire

118. Which of the following tales in Chaucer's *Canterbury Tales* is in prose?
(a) "The Pardoner's Tale" (b) "The Parson's Tale"
(c) "The Monk's Tale" (d) "The Knight's Tale"

119. Which of the following is not a work of Chaucer?
(a) *The Hous of Fame* (b) *The Owl and The Nightingale*
(c) *The Legende of Good Women* (d) *Romaunt of the Rose*

120. Chaucer went on diplomatic missions abroad
(a) from 1365 to 1373 (b) from 1370 to 1378
(c) from 1375 to 1383 (d) from 1380 to 1388

121. The *Prologue to the Canterbury Tales* is supposed to have been written in
(a) 1386 (b) 1387 (c) 1388 (d) 1389

122. "His voice was merrier than the organ's tone.
In Church on solemn mass days loudly blown."
These lines have been taken from
(a) "Pardoner's Tale" (b) "Nun's Priest's Tale"
(c) "Friar's Tale" (d) "Monk's Tale"

123. Which work of Chaucer is considered to be the epitome of 14th century England?
(a) *The Canterbury Tales* (b) *The Hous of Fame*
(c) *The Book of the Duchess* (d) None of the above

124. 'He found English a dialect and left it a language.' Here 'he' stands for
(a) Chaucer (b) Gower
(c) Langland (d) Mandeville

125. Pandarus, the first great comic character in English literature has been depicted by
(a) Joher Barbour (b) Chaucer
(c) Wyclif (d) Langland

126. Which is the first English novel in verse?
(a) *Troilus and Cryseyde* (b) *The Hous of Fame*
(c) *The Book of the Duchess* (d) None of the above

127. The idea of which work of Chaucer has been taken from Boccaccio's *Decamenon*?
(a) *The Parliament of Fouls* (b) *Legende of Good Women*
(c) *The Canterbury Tales* (d) *The Book of the Duchess*

128. Which work of Chaucer bears close resemblance to Dante's *Divine Comedy*?
(a) *The Hous of Fame* (b) *The Parliament of Fouls*
(c) *The Legend of Good Women* (d) *The Canterbury Tales*

129. In which work Chaucer has first used the heroic couplet?
(a) *Troilus and Cryseyde* (b) *The Hous of Fame*
(c) *The Canterbury Tales* (d) *Legende of Good Women*

130. Which work of Chaucer entitles him to the claim of being called 'the Father of English Poetry'?
(a) *The Book of the Duchess* (b) *The Canterbury Tales*
(c) *The Parliament of Fouls* (d) *The Hous of Fame*

131. In the *Prologue* which character has a forked beard?
(a) Merchant (b) Friar
(c) Monk (d) Squire

132. The Wife of Bath was
(a) lame (b) deaf
(c) blind (d) none of the above

133. In the *Prologue* children were afraid of whose face
(a) Miller (b) Ploughman
(c) Summoner (d) Carpenter

134. In *Nun's Priest's Tale*, the poor widow had ..... sons.
(a) two (b) three (c) four (d) five

135. Chanticleer was the name of the
(a) cock (b) sow (c) sheep (d) cow

136. The character Pertelote appears in
(a) "Canterbury Tales" (b) "Pardoner's Tale"
(c) "Friar's Tale" (d) "Nun's Priest's Tale"

137. Kenelphus, the noble king of Mercia, has been referred to in
(a) "Pardoner's Tale" (b) "Nun's Priest's Tale"
(c) "Monk's Tale" (d) None of the above

138. Andromache was the wife of
(a) Hector (b) Kenelphus
(c) Croesus (d) Macrobius

139. In the first line of the *Prologue* which month has been referred to by Chaucer?
(a) March (b) April (c) May (d) June

140. Chaucer begins his story with the description of
(a) the Knight (b) a Nun
(c) a Monk (d) a Merchant

141. The Squire was the son of
(a) the Merchant (b) the Friar
(c) the Monk (d) none of the above

142. The Yeoman used to wear coat of which colour
(a) red (b) blue (c) green (d) yellow

143. In the *Prologue* which character is fond of hunting and riding?
(a) Monk (b) Squire (c) Friar (d) Yeoman

144. Whose favourite dish was a fat roastede swan?
(a) Nun (b) Monk
(c) Friar (d) None of the above

145. Chaucer's *The Book of the Duchess* was written at the end of
(a) 1366 (b) 1367 (c) 1368 (d) 1369

146. The influence of Dante's *Divine Commedia* is apparent in which of Chaucer's works?
(a) *The Hous of Fame* (b) *The Parliament of Fouls*
(c) *The Book of Duchess* (d) *Troilus and Cryseyde*

147. Which of Chaucer's works celebrates Saint Valentine's Day?
(a) *The Canterbury Tales* (b) *The Book of the Duchess*
(c) *The Hous of Fame* (d) *The Parliament of Fouls*

148. Name Chaucer's work in which a love story has been told with a delicacy of psychological awareness.
(a) *The Book of the Duchess* (b) *Troilus and Cryseyde*
(c) *The Parliament of Fouls* (d) None of the above

149. Pandare is a character which appears in Chaucer's work
(a) *Troilus and Cryseyde* (b) *The Canterbury Tales*
(c) *The Hous of Fame* (d) None of the above

150. Which of Chaucer's work is a superb satire on human marital relationships?
(a) "The Pardoner's Tale" (b) "The Franklin's Tale"
(c) "Nun's Priest's Tale" (d) "The Clerk's Tale"

151. Chaucer's early period (French Period) ranges from
(a) 1360-1370 (b) 1365-1375
(c) 1375-1385 (d) None of the above

152. Chaucer's middle or Italian period ranges from
(a) 1370-1385 (b) 1375-1390
(c) 1380-1395 (d) 1385-1400

153. Chaucer was elected a knight of the shire for Kent in
(a) 1385 (b) 1386 (c) 1387 (d) 1388

154. Chaucer's *Boke of Blanche the Duchesse* was written to commemorate the death of Blanche of Lancaster, first wife of John of Gaunt in
(a) 1369 (b) 1370 (c) 1371 (d) 1372

155. Chaucer celebrated some princely betrothal in which of his work?
(a) *The Parliament of Fouls* (b) *Legende of Good Women*
(c) *The Hous of Fame* (d) None of the above

156. For his *Troilus and Cryseyde*, Chaucer owes to
(a) Dante (b) Petrarch
(c) Boccaccio (d) None of the above

157. Who is called the Father of English poetry?
(a) Shakespeare (b) Jonson
(c) Chaucer (d) Langland

158. Which language had an indelible impact on Chaucer?
(a) Latin (b) Greek (c) French (d) Roman

159. *Troilus and Cryseyde* is written by
(a) Shakespeare (b) Chaucer
(c) Virgil (d) Langland

160. The life span of Geoffrey Chaucer is
(a) 1330-1400 (b) 1340-1400
(c) 1350-1410 (d) 1330-1410

161. Chaucer lived during the reigns of
(a) Edward III and Richard II (b) Edward III and Henry IV
(c) Richard II and Henry IV (d) Edward III, Richard II and Henry IV

162. *The Canterbury Tales* is
(a) lyrical (b) mythical
(c) allegorical (d) ironical

163. The rocks of Britanny feature in Chaucer's
(a) "Miller's Tale" (b) "Franklin's Tale"
(c) "Wife of Bath's Tale" (d) "Parson's Tale"

164. The verse in *The Canterbury Tales* consists of
(a) alliterative lines (b) rhymed couplets
(c) unrhymed couplets (d) alternative lines rhyming

165. How many pilgrims are going on the pilgrimage in Chaucer's *Canterbury Tales*?
(a) 27 (b) 29 (c) 31 (d) 33

166. How many women characters figure in the *Prologue*?
(a) 1 (b) 2 (c) 3 (d) 4

167. Chaucer visited Italy in
(a) 1372-73 (b) 1374-75 (c) 1375-76 (d) 1376-77

168. While Chaucer was in Italy he came into contact with the work of
(a) Dante (b) Boccaccio (c) Petrarch (d) all

169. In which month did Chaucer's pilgrims go on the pilgrimage?
(a) January (b) February (c) March (d) April

170. *The Book of the Duchess* is a/an
(a) epic (b) allegory (c) satire (d) ballad

171. *The Hous of Fame* is written by
(a) Chaucer (b) Malory (c) Langland (d) Wyclif

172. *Legende of Good Women* is written in
(a) 1385 (b) 1375 (c) 1365 (d) 1395

173. How many ecclesiastical characters are portrayed in the *Prologue*?
(a) 5 (b) 6 (c) 7 (d) 8

174. Name the inn where the pilgrims assemble for the night
(a) Temple Inn (b) Tabard Inn
(c) Southwark Inn (d) St. Becket Inn

175. Which of the following is Chaucer's prose work?
(a) *Troilus and Cryseyde* (b) *Legende of Good Women*
(c) *Treatise on the Astrolabe* (d) *The Hous of Fame*

176. Chaucer was not indebted for his sources to one of the following. Identify him.
(a) Homer (b) Virgil (c) Dante (d) Ovid

177. Chaucer's earliest work is
(a) *The Book of the Duchess* (b) *Troilus and Cryseyde*
(c) *Prologue to the Canterbury Tales* (d) Nun's Priest's Tale

178. There is a reference of Goddess Venus in
(a) *Legende of Good Women* (b) *The Parliament of Fouls*
(c) *The Hous of Fame* (d) *Troilus and Cryseyde*

179. Which work of Chaucer is called 'a psychological novel'?
(a) *The Canterbury Tales* (b) *Troilus and Cryseyde*
(c) *Legende of Good Women* (d) *The Hous of Fame*

180. The 'Rhyme Royal' is used by
(a) Langland (b) Chaucer
(c) Malory (d) None of the above

181. Chaucer has used the technique of mock-heroic in
(a) *The Canterbury Tales* (b) *The Hous of Fame*
(c) *Nun's Priest's Tale* (d) *Pardoner's Tale*

**2. William Langland**

182. Who is the author of *Piers the Plowman*?
(a) Chaucer (b) Langland
(c) Lydgate (d) None of the above

183. William Langland was born in
(a) 1331 (b) 1332 (c) 1333 (d) 1334

184. The correct title of William Langland's whole poem is
(a) *The Piers Plowman* (b) *Piers the Plowman*
(c) *The Vision of Piers the Plowman* (d) *The Books of Piers the Plowman*

185. There is a reference of Malvern Hills in
(a) *Piers the Plowman* (b) *Morte d' Arthur*
(c) *The Canterbury Tales* (d) *The Christ*

186. The chief weapon of Langland's allegory is
(a) irony (b) sarcasm (c) satire (d) all

187. The First version of Langland's *Piers the Plowman* was written in
(a) 1361 (b) 1362 (c) 1363 (d) 1364

188. A beautiful lady, Holy Church appears in which work?
(a) Chaucer's *Nun's Priest's Tale* (b) Gower's *Confessio Amantis*
(c) Langland's *Piers the Plowman* (d) None of the above

189. In *Piers the Plowman* Langland saw a series of visions. What was the first vision that he saw?
(a) The vision of Seven Deadly Sins
(b) The vision of a Field Full of Folks
(c) The vision of Lady Bribery
(d) The vision of Man's Moral and Spiritual Life

190. The expression 'a faire felde ful of folke' appears in
(a) *The Canterbury Tales* (b) *Piers the Plowman*
(c) *Morte d' Arthur* (d) *Pardoner's Tale*

191. In Langland's *Piers the Plowman*, Piers plowman first appears in
(a) Passus IV (b) Passus V
(c) Passus VI (d) Passus VII

192. *Richard, the Redeless* was written by
(a) Langland (b) Chaucer
(c) Malory (d) Gower

193. "In a somer seson, whon soft was the sonne,
I shope me in shroudes, as I a shepe were."
These lines have been taken from
(a) *Piers the Plowman* (b) *Pardoner's Tale*
(c) *Beowulf* (d) *Parliament of Fouls*

194. How many cantos are there in Langland's *Piers the Plowman*?
(a) five (b) six (c) seven (d) eight

195. The first canto of *Piers the Plowman* deals with
(a) the vision of Holy Church (b) lady Meed
(c) falsehood (d) seven deadly sins

196. 'In whose hands is wickedness: and their right hand is full of gifts.'
The line has been taken from
(a) *Piers the Plowman* (b) *The Canterbury Tales*
(c) *Pardoner's Tale* (d) *Morte d' Arthur*

197. John Barbour's "Bruce" a poem which deal with the sheme
(a) social (b) political (c) national (d) moral

**3. John Gower**

198. Gower was a contemporary of
(a) Spenser (b) Shakespeare
(c) Chaucer (d) Marlowe

199. The life span of Gower is
(a) 1325-1408 (b) 1330-1405
(c) 1335-1410 (d) 1332-1408

200. *Confessio Amantis* is a great English work written by
(a) John Gower (b) Geoffrey Chaucer
(c) William Langland (d) None of the above

201. *Miroir de l' Homme*, a French work was written by
(a) Langland (b) Gower
(c) Chaucer (d) None of the above

202. Which work deals with the Peasants' Revolt of 1381?
(a) *Vox Clamantis* (b) *Confessio Amantis*
(c) *The Hous of Fame* (d) *Legende of Good Women*

203. The lines—'Under an hill there is a cave, which of the sonne mai noght have...' have been taken from
(a) *Confessio Amantis* (b) *The Parliament of Fouls*
(c) *The Canterbury Tales* (d) None of the above

204. *Speculum Meditantis*, a French work has been written by
(a) John Lydgate (b) Thomas Occleve
(c) John Gower (d) John Skelton

205. Which work of John Gower is inspired by the Peasant's Revolt of 1881?
(a) *Confessio Amantis* (b) *Vox Clamantis*
(c) *Speculum Meditantis* (d) None of the above

206. John Gower died in the year
(a) 1407 (b) 1408 (c) 1400 (d) 1410

207. *Vox Clamantis* has been written by
(a) Chaucer (b) Langland (c) Malory (d) Gower

208. *Vox Clamantis* is a dream allegory written in which language?
(a) French (b) English (c) Latin (d) Spanish

209. *Confessio Amantis* is a collection of tales in
(a) English octosyllabic couplets (b) French octosyllabic couplets
(c) English monosyllabic couplets (d) French monosyllabic couplets

210. *Speculum Hominis*, a work in French has been written by
(a) John Gower (b) Chaucer
(c) Langland (d) None of the above

211. Gower's *Vox Clamantis* consists of ...... books.
(a) five (b) six (c) seven (d) eight

212. In *Vox Clamantis*, the author divides people into three classes
(a) doctor, soldier and clerk (b) clerk, soldier, ploughman
(c) clerk, soldier and businessman (d) soldier, teacher, clerk

213. Gower's last writing *Traite*, dealing with the theme of love and marriage was written about
(a) 1397 (b) 1398 (c) 1399 (d) 1400

**4. John Wyclif**

214. Who translated Higden's *Polychronicon*?
(a) John Wyclif (b) John of Trevisa
(c) Langland (d) Gower

215. *The Voyage and Travels of Sir John Mandeville* was written in
(a) 1354 (b) 1355 (c) 1356 (d) 1377

216. *The Voyage and Travels of Sir John Mandeville* was originally written in
(a) Latin (b) French (c) English (d) Spanish

217. Wyclif and the Lollards began Reformation in England in
(a) 1377 (b) 1477 (c) 1378 (d) 1478

218. One of the first Englishmen to challenge the authority of the Catholic Church was
(a) John Wyclif (b) Chaucer
(c) Malory (d) None of the above

219. Who is known as 'father of English prose'?
(a) John Gower (b) John Wyclif
(c) Chaucer (d) Langland

220. The first theologian to distribute leaflets and pamphlets to the people was
(a) John Bunyan (b) William Langland
(c) John Wyclif (d) Hilton

221. Who is known as 'Morning Star of Reformation'?
(a) John Wyclif (b) Langland
(c) Chaucer (d) Malory

222. What was the period of John Wyclif?
(a) 1400-1440 (b) 1324-1384
(c) 1390-1445 (d) 1290-1340

223. Who were Lollards?
(a) Poor priests of the Church of England
(b) Poor priests of the Roman Catholic Church
(c) The followers of Wyclif
(d) The pilgrims of Chaucer's Age

224. Wyclif's *The Bible* is a translation of
(a) Greek Texts (b) Latin Texts
(c) Hebrew Texts (d) Arabic Texts

225. Which year John Wyclif rendered the *Bible* into English?
(a) 1280 (b) 1380 (c) 1400 (d) 1480

## UNIT E: THE REVIVAL OF LEARNING (1400–1550)

### 1. English Chaucerians

226. The life span of Thomas Occleve, a consistent follower of Chaucer is
(a) 1360-1440 (b) 1370-1450
(c) 1350-1430 (d) 1380-1440

227. *Regement of Princes* is a work of
(a) John Lydgate (b) Thomas Occleve
(c) John Walton (d) Alexander Barclay

228. Who of the following poets wrote a famous poem mourning the death of Chaucer?
(a) Occleve in "The Governail of Princes"
(b) Lydgate in "Falles of Princes"
(c) James I of Scotland in "The King's Quair"
(d) William Dunbar in The "Thistle and the Rose"

229. The life span of Alexander Barclay is
(a) 1475-1552 (b) 1470-1547
(c) 1465-1550 (d) 1480-1555

230. The use of the pastoral of satire for court life, etc. was first used by
(a) Barclay (b) Stephen Hawes
(c) John Skelton (d) None

231. Who translated the work of the German poet Sebastian Brant entitled *The Ship of Fools*?
(a) Alexander Barclay (b) Thomas Occleve
(c) John Skelton (d) None of the above

232. Which poet introduced 'Eclogues' (pastoral poems) to England?
(a) Alexander Barclay (b) John Skelton
(c) Gawin Douglas (d) Robert Henryson

233. Who was the first English poet to choose a German subject?
(a) Stephen Hawes (b) John Skelton
(c) Alexander Barclay (d) None of the above

234. *The Ship of Fools*, a translation from German has been written by
(a) Robert Henryson (b) Alexander Barclay
(c) Stephen Hawes (d) Thomas Occleve

235. *Example of Virtue* has been written by
(a) William Nevill (b) Stephen Hawes
(c) William Caxton (d) Alexander Barclay

236. Which English Chaucerian has written *The Pastime of Pleasure*?
(a) Stephen Hawes (b) Thomas Occleve
(c) John Skelton (d) Alexander Barclay

237. *The Fall of Princes* has been written by
(a) John Skelton (b) Occleve
(c) John Lydgate (d) Alexander Barclay

238. Who made frequent use of tag phrases (like 'sothly to telle) in his work?
(a) John Skelton (b) Stephen Hawes
(c) William Dunbar (d) John Lydgate

239. Who has the credit of being the most voluminous poet of medieval England?
(a) John Lydgate (b) Thomas Occleve
(c) Stephen Hawes (d) Alexander Barclay

240. The life span of John Skelton is
(a) 1450-1519 (b) 1455-1524
(c) 1460-1529 (d) 1465-1534

241. "The Bowge of Court" has been written by
(a) Lydgate (b) John Skelton
(c) Alexander Barclay (d) Hawes

242. Which work of Skelton is an elaborate set piece in praise of himself?
(a) "Magnificence" (b) "Garland of Laurel"
(c) "The Book of Philip Sparrow" (d) "The Bowge of Court"

243. "The Court of Sapience" which dates from about 1470 has been written by
(a) Lydgate (b) Anonymous author
(c) Dunbar (d) Occleve

244. William Nevill's "Castell of Pleasure" was published in
(a) 1516 (b) 1517 (c) 1518 (d) 1519

**2. Scottish Chaucerians**

245. Robert Henryson is a Scottish poet of the
(a) 13th century (b) 14th century
(c) 15th century (d) 16th century

246. Who wrote "King's Quair"?
(a) Robert Henryson (b) William Dunbar
(c) Gavin Douglas (d) James I of Scotland

247. Who is known as the Chaucer of Scotland?
(a) William Dunbar (b) Robert Henryson
(c) John Lydgate (d) Gavin Douglas

248. Who is considered to be the greatest of the Scottish Chaucerians?
(a) Gavin Douglas (b) William Dunbar
(c) Robert Henryson (d) King James I

249. Which work of Dunbar deals with the union of two countries – England and Scotland?
(a) "The Golden Targe" (b) "The Thistle and the Rose"
(c) "The Dance of the Seven Deadly Sins" (d) "The Two Married Women and the Widow"

250. Which work of the Scottish Chaucerian imitates Chaucer's *Hous of Fame*?
(a) Douglas' "King Hart" (b) Douglas' "The Palace of Honour"
(c) Dunbar's "The Thistle and the Rose" (d) Henryson's "Treatment of Cresseid"

251. Which poem by the Scottish Chauceriand was inspired by Chaucer's *Hous of Fame*?
(a) Douglas's "The Palace of Honour" (b) Dunbar's "The Golden Targe"
(c) James' "The Kings Quair" (d) Henryson's "Robene and Makyne"

252. Who was the first Chaucerian to translate the whole of Virgil into English verse?
(a) King James I (b) Gavin Douglas
(c) William Dunbar (d) Robert Henryson

253. The poem "The Cuckoo and the Nightingale" has been written by
(a) William Dunbar (b) John Skelton
(c) Stephen Hawes (d) An anonymous writer

254. In the poem "The Flower and the Leaf" the flower stands for
(a) sweet smell (b) pleasures of life
(c) happiness (d) colour

### 3. Folk Poetry

255. "Lord Randal" is a famous
(a) lyric (b) allegory (c) ballad (d) epic

256. The word 'Ballad' is derived from the word..... which means 'to dance'.
(a) ballare (b) ballere (c) ballade (d) balled

257. "The Nut Brown Maid" is a well known
(a) satire (b) lyric (c) ballad (d) sonnet

### 4. Prose

258. John Fortescue mainly wrote in
(a) Latin (b) English (c) French (d) Spanish

259. Fortescue praises the constitution of his country in
(a) "De Natura Lagis Naturae" (b) "The Governance of England"
(c) "De Laudibus Legum Anliae" (d) None of the above

260. Name the first English printer?
(a) William Caxton (b) Holinshed
(c) John Dewey (d) None of the above

261. Caxton's printing press was set up in
(a) 1475 (b) 1476 (c) 1477 (d) 1478

262. William Caxton who invented the printing press was basically a
(a) writer (b) merchant
(c) businessman (d) doctor

263. The printing press fixed forever the ... as the national language of England.
(a) northern dialect (b) southern dialect
(c) east-midland dialect (d) west-midland dialect

264. Which was the first printed English book?
(a) *The Boke of Historyes of Jason* (b) *The Recuyell of the Historye of Troye*
(c) *Morte d' Arthur* (d) *The Foure Sonnes of Aymon*

265. Which book, published by Caxton, had the largest circulation of all his publications?
(a) *Translation of the Golden Legend* (b) *The Lyf of Charles the Gredte*
(c) *The Historye of Reynart the Foxe* (d) *Morte d' Arthur*

266. Sir Thomas Malory wrote *Morte d' Arthur* in
(a) 1470 (b) 1485 (c) 1490 (d) 1495

267. Who has written most of his stories in prison?
(a) Chaucer (b) Langland (c) Malory (d) Skelton

268. Guenevere is the name of a character who appears in
(a) *Morte d' Arthur* (b) *Piers the Plowman*
(c) *The Canterbury Tales* (d) *Vox Clamantis*

269. Which is the first book in English in poetic prose?
(a) *Confessio Amantis* (b) *Nun's Priest's Tale*
(c) *Morte d' Arthur* (d) *Vox Clamantis*

## 5. The Educationists

270. "Praise of Folly" is a famous piece of satire written by
(a) Desiderius Erasmus (b) Roger Ascham
(c) Sir Thomas More (d) William Tyndale

271. In Cambridge, the teaching of Greek was given impetus by
(a) Desiderius Erasmus (b) William Latimer
(c) John Colet (d) Richard Croke

272. Which work is considered to be 'the true prologue to the Renaissance'?
(a) Tottel's *Miscellany* (b) More's *Utopia*
(c) Aschem's *The Schoolmaster* (d) None of the above

273. Sir Thomas More's *Utopia* (the Kingdom of Nowhere) was originally written in
(a) English (b) French (c) Latin (d) Spanish

274. *The Schoolmaster* is a well known work written by
(a) Roger Ascham (b) William Tyndale
(c) Sir Thomas More (d) Desiderius Erasmus

### 6. The Religious Reformers

275. *English Prayer Book* which was adopted as the official prayer book in 1549 was written by
(a) Tyndale (b) Roger Ascham
(c) Thomas Cranner (d) None of the above

276. Which of the following is the earliest version of *Bible*?
(a) William Tyndale's *English New Testament*
(b) Miles Coverdales's *English Bible*
(c) Cromwell's *Great Bible*
(d) King James' *Authorised Version of the Bible*

### 7. Earliest Poetry

277. Sir Thomas Wyatt, a young courtier of the court of Henry VIII was deeply influenced by
(a) French tradition (b) Latin tradition
(c) Italian tradition (d) English tradition

278. The vogue of the lyric was inaugurated by
(a) Wyatt (b) Henry Howard
(c) Thomas Sackville (d) Sir Thomas Moore

279. Henry Howard, Earl of Surrey divided his sonnet into
(a) three quatrains and a couplet (b) an octave and a sestet
(c) two quatrains and a sestet (d) an octave and three couplets

280. Who is known as the connecting link between Chaucer and Spenser?
(a) Henry Howard (b) Thomas Sackville
(c) Roger Ascham (d) Sir Thomas Wyatt

281. The works of Wyatt and Surrey were published in Tottel's *Miscellany* in
(a) 1553 (b) 1558 (c) 1563 (d) 1568

**8. English Drama**

282. The Licensing Act for closing of all theatres except Drury Lane and Covent Garden was passed in
(a) 1734 (b) 1735 (c) 1736 (d) 1737

283. The characters represent abstract qualities in
(a) Morality plays (b) Mystery plays
(c) Miracle plays (d) Interludes

284. In subject the miracle plays were essentially
(a) historical (b) social
(c) theological (d) political

285. *The Betraying of Christ* is a
(a) miracle play (b) morality play
(c) social play (d) political play

286. *The Castle of Perseverance* is a significant
(a) morality play (b) interlude
(c) miracle play (d) none of the above

287. The morality play *Everyman* belongs to the
(a) 14th century (b) 13th century
(c) 15th Century (d) 16th century

288. John Rastell is a famous writer of
(a) interludes (b) miracle plays
(c) morality plays (d) none of the above

289. *The Merry Play* is written by
(a) John Heywood (b) John Rastell
(c) Sir Thomas Moore (d) None of the above

290. Miracle plays were based on
(a) stories from the *Bible* (b) stories from the lives of the Saints
(c) concepts of Christian Theology (d) none of these

291. Blank verse is used for the first time for dramatic purposes in
(a) *Jocasta* (b) *Gorboduc*
(c) *Spanish Tragedy* (d) None of the above

292. The first English playhouse called 'The Theatre' was founded in
(a) 1574 (b) 1575 (c) 1576 (d) 1577

293. *Ralph Roister Doister*, the first regular comedy in English was written by
(a) Nicholas Udall (b) Thomas Norton
(c) Geoffrey of Monmouth (d) John Heywood

294. *Gorboduc*, the first regular tragedy in English was written by
(a) Thomas Sackville (b) John Heywood
(c) Thomas Norton (d) Sackville and Norton

295. The book *Revelations of Divine Love* has been written by
(a) Julian of Norwich (b) Richard Rolle
(c) William Langland (d) John Gower

296. *The Birth of Jesus* is a famous
(a) morality play (b) miracle play
(c) mystery play (d) interlude

297. *The Play of the Sacrament* is a well known
(a) miracle play (b) interlude
(c) morality play (d) mystery play

298. The earliest known religious play is
(a) *Noah* (b) *Nativity*
(c) *Adam* (d) None of the above

299. *The Four Elements*, a well known morality play has been written by
(a) Sir John Lyndsay (b) John Skelton
(c) John Bales (d) None of the above

300. In Lyndsay's morality play *The Satire of the Three Estates*, three estates are
    (a) king, minister and clergy
    (b) the clergy, bishop and the King
    (c) the nobility, the clergy and the merchants
    (d) the nobility, the clergy and the bishop
301. Real and allegorical characters mingled freely for the first time in
    (a) *King Jehan*
    (b) *Magnificence*
    (c) *The Four Elements*
    (d) *The Satire of the Three Estates*

## ANSWERS

### Unit A

| | | | | | | | |
|---|---|---|---|---|---|---|---|
| 1. | (c) | 2. | (c) | 3. | (a) | 4. | (c) |
| 5. | (a) | 6. | (a) | 7. | (d) | 8. | (a) |
| 9. | (a) | 10. | (c) | 11. | (c) | 12. | (b) |
| 13. | (b) | 14. | (c) | 15. | (c) | 16. | (a) |
| 17. | (a) | 18. | (b) | 19. | (b) | 20. | (b) |
| 21. | (b) | 22. | (c) | 23. | (b) | 24. | (a) |
| 25. | (c) | 26. | (a) | 27. | (d) | 28. | (d) |
| 29. | (d) | 30. | (c) | 31. | (b) | 32. | (c) |
| 33. | (c) | 34. | (c) | 35. | (b) | 36. | (b) |
| 37. | (d) | 38. | (c) | | | | |

### Unit B

| | | | | | | | |
|---|---|---|---|---|---|---|---|
| 39. | (a) | 40. | (c) | 41. | (a) | 42. | (c) |
| 43. | (d) | 44. | (b) | 45. | (a) | 46. | (c) |
| 47. | (b) | 48. | (c) | 49. | (a) | 50. | (a) |
| 51. | (a) | 52. | (a) | 53. | (a) | 54. | (b) |
| 55. | (c) | 56. | (c) | 57. | (a) | 58. | (b) |
| 59. | (a) | 60. | (c) | 61. | (d) | 62. | (b) |
| 63. | (b) | 64. | (d) | 65. | (a) | 66. | (a) |
| 67. | (a) | 68. | (b) | 69. | (d) | 70. | (c) |
| 71. | (c) | 72. | (a) | 73. | (d) | | |

**Unit C**

| | | | | | | | |
|---|---|---|---|---|---|---|---|
| 74. | (c) | 75. | (a) | 76. | (b) | 77. | (d) |
| 78. | (d) | 79. | (a) | 80. | (c) | 81. | (c) |
| 82. | (a) | 83. | (d) | 84. | (c) | 85. | (a) |
| 86. | (a) | 87. | (b) | 88. | (b) | 89. | (a) |
| 90. | (d) | 91. | (b) | 92. | (a) | 93. | (b) |
| 94. | (a) | 95. | (c) | 96. | (a) | 97. | (b) |
| 98. | (c) | 99. | (b) | | | | |

**Unit D**

| | | | | | | | |
|---|---|---|---|---|---|---|---|
| 100. | (b) | 101. | (a) | 102. | (a) | 103. | (c) |
| 104. | (c) | 105. | (a) | 106. | (c) | 107. | (c) |
| 108. | (c) | 109. | (a) | 110. | (a) | 111. | (d) |
| 112. | (b) | 113. | (a) | 114. | (a) | 115. | (c) |
| 116. | (d) | 117. | (d) | 118. | (b) | 119. | (b) |
| 120. | (b) | 121. | (c) | 122. | (b) | 123. | (a) |
| 124. | (a) | 125. | (b) | 126. | (a) | 127. | (c) |
| 128. | (a) | 129. | (d) | 130. | (b) | 131. | (a) |
| 132. | (b) | 133. | (c) | 134. | (b) | 135. | (a) |
| 136. | (d) | 137. | (b) | 138. | (a) | 139. | (b) |
| 140. | (a) | 141. | (d) | 142. | (c) | 143. | (a) |
| 144. | (b) | 145. | (d) | 146. | (a) | 147. | (d) |
| 148. | (a) | 149. | (a) | 150. | (c) | 151. | (a) |
| 152. | (a) | 153. | (b) | 154. | (a) | 155. | (a) |
| 156. | (c) | 157. | (c) | 158. | (a) | 159. | (b) |
| 160. | (b) | 161. | (d) | 162. | (c) | 163. | (b) |
| 164. | (b) | 165. | (b) | 166. | (c) | 167. | (a) |
| 168. | (d) | 169. | (d) | 170. | (b) | 171. | (a) |
| 172. | (a) | 173. | (d) | 174. | (b) | 175. | (c) |
| 176. | (a) | 177. | (a) | 178. | (b) | 179. | (b) |
| 180. | (b) | 181. | (c) | 182. | (b) | 183. | (b) |
| 184. | (c) | 185. | (a) | 186. | (a) | 187. | (b) |

| | | | | | | | |
|---|---|---|---|---|---|---|---|
| 188. | (c) | 189. | (b) | 190. | (b) | 191. | (b) |
| 192. | (a) | 193. | (a) | 194. | (c) | 195. | (a) |
| 196. | (a) | 197. | (c) | 198. | (c) | 199. | (a) |
| 200. | (a) | 201. | (b) | 202. | (a) | 203. | (a) |
| 204. | (c) | 205. | (b) | 206. | (b) | 207. | (d) |
| 208. | (c) | 209. | (a) | 210. | (a) | 211. | (a) |
| 212. | (b) | 213. | (a) | 214. | (b) | 215. | (d) |
| 216. | (b) | 217. | (a) | 218. | (a) | 219. | (b) |
| 220. | (c) | 221. | (a) | 222. | (b) | 223. | (c) |
| 224. | (b) | 225. | (b) | | | | |

## Unit E

| | | | | | | | |
|---|---|---|---|---|---|---|---|
| 226. | (b) | 227. | (b) | 228. | (a) | 229. | (a) |
| 230. | (a) | 231. | (a) | 232. | (a) | 233. | (c) |
| 234. | (b) | 235. | (c) | 236. | (a) | 237. | (c) |
| 238. | (d) | 239. | (a) | 240. | (c) | 241. | (b) |
| 242. | (b) | 243. | (b) | 244. | (c) | 245. | (c) |
| 246. | (d) | 247. | (a) | 248. | (b) | 249. | (b) |
| 250. | (b) | 251. | (a) | 252. | (b) | 253. | (d) |
| 254. | (b) | 255. | (c) | 256. | (a) | 257. | (c) |
| 258. | (a) | 259. | (c) | 260. | (a) | 261. | (b) |
| 262. | (b) | 263. | (c) | 264. | (b) | 265. | (a) |
| 266. | (a) | 267. | (c) | 268. | (a) | 269. | (c) |
| 270. | (a) | 271. | (a) | 272. | (b) | 273. | (c) |
| 274. | (a) | 275. | (c) | 276. | (a) | 277. | (c) |
| 278. | (a) | 279. | (a) | 280. | (b) | 281. | (b) |
| 282. | (d) | 283. | (a) | 284. | (c) | 285. | (b) |
| 286. | (a) | 287. | (c) | 288. | (a) | 289. | (a) |
| 290. | (a) | 291. | (b) | 292. | (c) | 293. | (a) |
| 294. | (d) | 295. | (a) | 296. | (b) | 297. | (a) |
| 298. | (c) | 299. | (d) | 300. | (c) | 301. | (a) |

# The Renaissance Period (1550–1660)

# 2

## UNIT A: HISTORICAL PERSPECTIVE AND BACKGROUND

1. The first tragedy written in English
   (a) *King Lear* (b) *Edward II*
   (c) *Hamlet* (d) *Gorboduc*
2. *Gorboduc* was written in
   (a) 1561 (b) 1555 (c) 1540 (d) 1562
3. Queen Elizabeth had been reigning nearly ......... years when Shakespeare was born.
   (a) six (b) eight (c) ten (d) twelve
4. John Shakespeare (Shakespeare's father) married Mary Arden in
   (a) 1507 (b) 1515 (c) 1520 (d) 1557
5. Edmund Burke's *Reflection on the French Revolution* resulted in
   (a) War with France (b) French victory
   (c) Puritan dominance (d) Spiritual death of the English
6. The Royalist's spirit towards the Puritan was expressed in
   (a) *Pilgrim's Progress* (b) *Brut*
   (c) *Hudibras* (d) *Euphues*
7. Which year saw the publication of *Principia*?
   (a) 1680 (b) 1681 (c) 1687 (d) 1666
8. When were Theatres closed in England?
   (a) 1623 (b) 1642 (c) 1616 (d) 1650

9. The year .......... saw the publication of Ottways' *Venice Preserved.*
   (a) 1682 (b) 1688 (c) 1678 (d) 1675
10. Which is the first periodical, manuscript, newspaper that figured in Europe?
    (a) *Gazetta* (b) *The Rambler*
    (c) *Times Supplement* (d) *Paston Letters*
11. Marston, Chapman and Webster died in the year
    (a) 1647 (b) 1634 (c) 1643 (d) 1641
12. Shakespeare died during the reign of
    (a) Mary (b) James II (c) Charles II (d) Elizabeth
13. Roger Ascham was .......... to Elizabeth.
    (a) court poet (b) tutor
    (c) friend (d) admirer
14. When did the Great fire of London take place?
    (a) 1610 (b) 1606 (c) 1640 (d) 1666
15. The Empire of Babylon was at the Zenith
    (a) 2500 years ago (b) 1000 years ago
    (c) 1500 years ago (d) 3000 years ago
16. Baccaccio first attempted prose adventure *The Decameron* in
    (a) Italy (b) France (c) Paris (d) Greece

## UNIT B: NON-DRAMATIC POETS OF THE ELIZABETHAN AGE

### 1. Edmund Spenser

17. Spenser's "The Shepherd's Calendar" was written in
    (a) 1579 (b) 1660 (c) 1597 (c) 1507
18. Who is at once the child of the Renaissance and the Reformation?
    (a) Spenser (b) Sidney (c) Kyd (d) Nashe
19. "The Shepherd's Calendar" was published in
    (a) 1579 (b) 1570 (c) 1560 (d) 1550

20. Spenser's autobiographical poem is
    (a) "Fairie Queene" (b) "Cynthia"
    (c) "The Shepherd's Calendar" (d) "Colin Clouts Come Home Again"
21. Who has been called the poet's poet?
    (a) Sidney (b) Shakespeare
    (c) Spenser (d) Ben Jonson
22. "The Shepherd's Calendar" was inspired by
    (a) Beaumont and Fletcher (b) Virgil and Theocritus
    (c) Sackville and Norton (d) None
23. The word 'sonnet' is derived from .......... word 'sonetto'.
    (a) English (b) Greek (c) Latin (d) Italian

**2. Thomas Sackville**

24. The first English tragedy written by Thomas Sackville and Thomas Morton was
    (a) *Gorboduc* (b) *Everyman*
    (c) *New Custom* (d) *King John*
25. Of the five acts of *Gorboduc*, Thomas Sackville wrote the
    (a) first and second (b) second and third
    (c) third and fourth (d) fourth and fifth
26. Sackville's *Gorboduc* treats of an episode in
    (a) national history (b) philosophy
    (c) witchcraft (d) politics

**3. George Chapman**

27. Who dedicated some of his plays to the Earl of Essex?
    (a) Chapman (b) Marston
    (c) Webster (d) Heywood
28. Who was the scholarly translator of *Iliad*, *Odyssey* and *Hymns*?
    (a) Massinger (b) Webster
    (c) Chapman (d) Middleton
29. Chapman's comedy *All Fools* was written in
    (a) 1599 (b) 1600 (c) 1601 (d) 1602

30. Chapman's *The Admiral of France* was
    (a) a comedy (b) a satire
    (c) a burlesque (d) a French tragedy

**4. Michael Drayton**

31. "A Parting" has been written by
    (a) Drayton (b) Lodge (c) Hall (d) Donne
32. Drayton's literary life opens in
    (a) 1580 (b) 1581 (c) 1590 (d) 1591
33. Drayton's "Shepherd's Garland" is an experiment in
    (a) pastoral verse (b) sacred verse
    (c) allegorical verse (d) Italian sonnet
34. The well-known historical poem of Michael Drayton is
    (a) "Harmony of the Church" (b) "Shepherd's Garland"
    (c) "Ballad of Agincourt" (d) "Nymphidia"
35. Drayton's "The Owl and The Man in the Moon" is an illustration of
    (a) fantasy (b) satire
    (c) historical verse (d) sacred verse

## UNIT C: ORIGIN OF THE DRAMA

**1. Miracle Plays**

36. The Miracles were well established by
    (a) 16th century (b) 15th century
    (c) 17th century (d) 18th century
37. The York Collection consists of
    (a) 40 plays (b) 42 plays (c) 35 plays (d) 48 plays
38. A good example of pathos in miracles is in the play of *Abraham and Isaac* in which Abraham offers to sacrifice his
    (a) brother (b) son (c) wife (d) daughter
39. The earliest example of miracle plays *St. Nicholas* was written in
    (a) Greek (b) French
    (c) Old English (d) Latin

40. The York plays are written in
    (a) Scandinavian (b) Northumbrian
    (c) Latin (d) Greek

**2. Morality Plays**

41. The earliest morality play was
    (a) *The Castle of Perseverance* (b) *Everyman*
    (c) *The Trial of Treasure* (d) *New Custom*

42. Of all morality plays, the only one which was so good that it was revived on modern stage in both England and America, is
    (a) *Mankind* (b) *Hickscorner*
    (c) *Everyman* (d) *The Castle of Perseverance*

**3. Interludes**

43. Skelton's *Magnificence*, the earliest secular morality was aimed at the extravagance of
    (a) Henry V (b) Henry VI
    (c) Henry VIII (d) Henry VII

44. The most prolific writer of interludes, John Heywood was a .......... in the court of Henry VIII.
    (a) jester (b) musician
    (c) singer (d) poet

45. In Heywood's *The Four P's*, a Palmer, a Pardoner, a Potycary and a Pedlar dispute as to which of them can tell the biggest
    (a) joke (b) story (c) lie (d) event

46. Heywood substituted the abstractions of the moralities with
    (a) human characters (b) supernatural characters
    (c) natural characters (d) sub-human characters

47. Heywood's *The Mery Play between the Pardoner and the Frere* was printed in
    (a) 1513 (b) 1520 (c) 1525 (d) 1533

## UNIT D: SHAKESPEARE'S PREDECESSORS

### 1. Christopher Marlowe

48. Who completed Marlowe's *Hero and Leander?*
    (a) Shakespeare (b) Chapman
    (c) Ben Jonson (d) Heywood
49. *Tamburlaine the Great* was first produced in
    (a) 1587-88 (b) 1560-61 (c) 1554-55 (d) 1540-41
50. *Tamburlaine* is the story of
    (a) a sailor (b) a French soldier
    (c) a Roman soldier (d) a Scythian shepherd
51. The resounding use of exotic place in *Paradise Lost* has its origin in
    (a) *Tamburlaine* (b) *Arden of Feversham*
    (c) *The Spanish Tragedy* (d) None
52. *Tamburlaine* is the perfect illustration of the view maintained in
    (a) Hobbes' *Leviathan* (b) Milton's *Paradise Lost*
    (c) Kyd's *The Spanish Tragedy* (d) Marlowe's *Tamburlaine*
53. 'Marlowe's mighty lines' first came into Elizabethan drama with
    (a) Tamburlaine (b) Edward II
    (c) Dr. Faustus (d) None
54. The most celebrated and the most successful of Marlowe's character's speech was by
    (a) Dr. Faustus (b) Edward II
    (c) Gaveston (d) Helen of Troy
55. Marlowe's *The Jew of Malta* is a dramatic presentation of
    (a) a king (b) a duke
    (c) a scholar (d) Machiavillian man

### 2. Thomas Kyd

56. Thomas Kyd was the founder of
    (a) romantic comedy (b) romantic tragedy
    (c) satire (d) dramatic romance

57. Thomas Kyd was the son of a
    (a) wine merchant (b) London notary
    (c) writer (d) dramatist
58. The most popular of Kyd's plays is
    (a) *Cornelia* (b) *Jeronimo*
    (c) *The Spanish Tragedy* (d) *Solyman and Perseda*
59. Kyd's *The Spanish Tragedy* was translated into German and Dutch and one of the Elizabethan dramatists is supposed to have collaborated with him. Who was he?
    (a) Beaumont (b) Fletcher
    (c) Middleton (d) Ben Jonson
60. Who gave the name 'Sporting Kyd' to Thomas Kyd?
    (a) Shakespeare (b) Ben Jonson
    (c) Marlowe (d) John Lyly
61. Thomas Kyd is popularly known for his adherence to the
    (a) Romantic School (b) Senecan School
    (c) Medieval School (d) Primitive School
62. The 'blood and thunder' element of Thomas Kyd's drama proved one of the ......... of Pre-Shakespearean drama.
    (a) nemesis (b) attractive features
    (c) weaknesses (d) experiments

**3. Thomas Nash**

63. Thomas Nash distinguished himself as a
    (a) satirist (b) humorist
    (c) playwright (d) allegorist
64. Nash's *The Unfortunate Traveller* was published in
    (a) 1504 (b) 1540 (c) 1590 (d) 1594
65. Nash died at the age of
    (a) 25 (b) 30 (c) 33 (d) 40
66. Thomas Nash had a rich fund of humour that resembles that of
    (a) Dryden (b) Swift (c) Rabelais (d) None

67. Who was the first great realist who graphically depicted contemporary London life and its manners?
(a) Thomas Nash (b) Thomas Deloney
(c) Robert Greene (d) Thomas Sackville

68. Which work of Nash is a study of the superstition of the age?
(a) *Terrors of Night* (b) *Anatomy of Absurdity*
(c) *The Unfortunate Traveller* (d) *Christ's Tears over Jerusalem*

69. The first picaresque novel is
(a) *The Life of Jack Wilton* (b) *Terrors of Night*
(c) *Anatomy of Absurdity* (d) None of these

70. Nash's *The Life of Jack Wilton* is
(a) romance (b) tragedy
(c) comedy (d) both tragedy and comedy

71. Nash's *The Unfortunate Traveller* is the first Elizabethan
(a) novel (b) romance (c) tragedy (d) comedy

72. Which Elizabethan fiction writer writes more like eighteenth century novel?
(a) Nash (b) Lyly (c) Deloney (d) Greene

### 4. John Lyly

73. John Lyly was born in
(a) 1554 (b) 1540 (c) 1544 (d) 1560

74. John Lyly wrote his *Euphues* when he was in
(a) B.A. (b) M.A.
(c) Matriculation (c) Higher Secondary

75. John Lyly wrote some Latin verses in praise of the Queen in
(a) 1570 (b) 1580 (c) 1590 (d) 1597

76. Lyly's *The Golden Book of Marcus Aurelius* was translated by
(a) Thomas North (b) John Foxe
(c) Francis Bacon (d) Richard Hooker

77. Which Lyly's comedy stands apart from his other plays being in the tradition of Plautus and Terence?
(a) *Mother Bombie* (b) *Euphues*
(c) *Sapho and Phao* (d) *Midas*

**5. George Peele**

78. George Peele was born about
(a) 1500 (b) 1520 (c) 1530 (d) 1558

79. *The Arraignment of Paris*, *Edward I*, *The Battle of Alcazar* and *The Old Wives Tale* are authored by
(a) Thomas Kyd (b) Thomas Nash
(c) John Lyly (d) George Peele

80. *The Arraignment of Paris* contains an elaborate tribute to the
(a) Queen Elizabeth (b) Charles I
(c) James I (d) James II

81. *David and Fair Bathsheba* was written by George Peele in
(a) 1590 (b) 1595 (c) 1596 (d) 1599

**6. Robert Greene**

82. The first work of Robert Greene was
(a) *Mamillia* (b) *Orlando Furioso*
(c) *Friar Bacon and Friar Bungay* (d) *Pandosto*

83. Robert Greene's *Looking Glass for London and England* was written in collaboration with
(a) Thomas Lodge (b) Thomas Nash
(c) John Lyly (d) George Peele

84. Which work of Robert Greene gave the plot to Shakespeare's *The Winter's Tale*?
(a) *Groat's Worth of Wit* (b) *Pandosto*
(c) *Orlando Furioso* (d) *Friar Bacon*

85. Robert Greene entered St. John's College Cambridge at the age of
(a) 16 (b) 15 (c) 17 (d) 18

86. Which work of Robert Greene is best known for its early reference to Shakespeare?
    (a) *Pandosto* (b) *Menaphon*
    (c) *Groatsworth of Wit Bought with a million of Repentance* (d) None

87. As a writer of prose romance, Greene is remembered for
    (a) *Pandosto* (b) *Mamilia*
    (c) *Menaphon* (d) *Never too Late*

88. Greene's *Pandosto* supplied plot to Shakespeare's
    (a) *The Tempest* (b) *The Winter's Tale*
    (c) *King Lear* (d) *Pericles*

## UNIT E: ELIZABETHAN DRAMA

### 1. William Shakespeare

89. Holinshed's *Chronicle* was used by which Elizabethan dramatist?
    (a) Shakespeare (b) Marlowe
    (c) Heywood (d) Dekker

90. Shakespeare took hint from *Spanish Tragedy* in his
    (a) *Macbeth* (b) *Othello* (c) *Hamlet* (d) *King Lear*

91. Shakespeare was born in
    (a) 1550 (b) 1505 (c) 1510 (d) 1564

92. *Venus and Adonais* and *The Rape of Lucrece* are
    (a) love poems (b) tragedies
    (c) comedies (d) novels

93. Shakespeare died in
    (a) 1600 (b) 1601 (c) 1610 (d) 1616

94. *Life of Shakespeare* is written by
    (a) Sidney Lee (b) Philip Sidney
    (c) Marlowe (d) Spenser

95. Out of Shakespeare's 37 plays .......... plays were published in quarto form.
    (a) 12 (b) 15 (c) 20 (d) 16

96. Shakespeare's First Folio was published in
    (a) 1600 (b) 1610 (c) 1620 (d) 1623
97. Who spoke?
    "The lunatic, the lover and the poet,/ Are of imagination all compact."
    (a) Theseus (b) Bottom (c) Pyramus (d) Thisbey
98. Shakespeare wrote *Merry Wives* at the behest of
    (a) his father (b) his friend
    (c) his beloved (d) Queen Elizabeth
99. Benedick and Beatrice appear in
    (a) *Much Ado About Nothing* (b) *The Winter's Tale*
    (c) *The Tempest* (d) *Pericles*
100. The famous song, 'Take, O take those lips away' occurs in
    (a) *As You Like It* (b) *Merchant of Venice*
    (c) *Much Ado About Nothing* (d) *Measure for Measure*
101. Falstaff is a character in Shakespeare's
    (a) *Henry I* (b) *Henry VIII*
    (c) *Henry IV* (d) *Henry V*
102. Which Shakespeare's tragedy is a tragedy of misanthropy
    (a) *Hamlet* (b) *King Lear*
    (c) *Othello* (d) *Timon of Athens*
103. Imogen is a character in
    (a) *Pericles* (b) *Coriolanus*
    (c) *Tempest* (d) *Cymbeline*
104. Last plays of Shakespeare are tragic-comedies and also known as
    (a) comedies (b) farces
    (c) tragedies (d) romances
105. Which play by Shakespeare is considered autobiographical?
    (a) *The Winter's Tale* (b) *Cymbeline*
    (c) *Pericles* (d) *The Tempest*
106. Who said?
    'It is the stars,
    The stars above us, govern our conditions.'
    (a) King Lear (b) Edgar (c) Kent (d) Fool

107. The lines: 'The fault, dear Brutus, is not in our stars. But in ourselves that we are underlings' are said by
(a) Brutus (b) Cassius (c) Ceasar (d) None

108. Which play of Shakespeare is a dramatisation of a story told by Chaucer in "Knight's Tale"?
(a) *The Merchant of Venice* (b) *As You Like It*
(c) *The Two Noble Kinsmen* (d) *The Tempest*

109. In which Shakespearean play all are guilty?
(a) *Measure for Measure* (b) *Twelfth Night*
(c) *As You Like It* (d) *All's Well That Ends Well*

110. Mythology, folklore and magic find their way into Shakespeare's
(a) tragedies (b) comedies (c) last plays (d) none

111. Which play of Shakespeare ends without a climax?
(a) *Troilus and Cressida* (b) *Antony and Cleopatra*
(c) *All's Well That Ends Well* (d) *Twelfth Night*

112. Boccaccio's *Decamenon* is echoed in Shakespeare's
(a) *All's Well That Ends Well* (b) *Troilus and Cressida*
(c) *As You Like It* (d) *Twelfth Night*

113. Which comic character of Shakespeare is known more for his wisdom?
(a) Feste (b) Fool
(c) Bottom (d) Puck

114. Sidney's *Arcadia* is drawn by Shakespeare in
(a) *King Lear* (b) *Macbeth*
(c) *The Winter's Tale* (d) *The Tempest*

**2. Ben Jonson**

115. Whose words are these?
'Drink to me only with thine eyes'
(a) Shakespeare (b) Ben Jonson
(c) Milton (d) Marlowe

116. Jonson's first important and successful play was
(a) *Volpone* (b) *The Silent Woman*
(c) *Everyman in His Humour* (d) *Everyman Out of His Humour*

117. *Cynthia's Revels* was first acted in
(a) 1600 (b) 1605 (c) 1620 (d) 1650

118. *The Fox* is the sub-title of
(a) *The Alchemist* (b) *Volpone*
(c) *Everyman in His Humour* (d) None

119. Mosca is a character found in
(a) *Volpone* (b) *The Alchemist*
(c) *The Poetaster* (d) None

120. Ben Jonson's *The Poetaster* was directed against
(a) Marston (b) Deloney (c) Nashe (d) Kyd

121. Which drama of Ben Jonson was analysed by Dryden?
(a) *The Alchemist* (b) *Volpone*
(c) *Bartholomew Fair* (d) *Epicoene*

122. Face and Subtle are the characters of
(a) *The Alchemist* (b) *Volpone*
(c) *The Poetaster* (d) *Epicoene*

123. Which play of Ben Jonson is the most expansive of mature satiric comedies?
(a) *Bartholomew Fair* (b) *Volpone*
(c) *The Silent Woman* (d) *The Poetaster*

124. Jonson's *Sejanus* and *Catiline* are moved by Shakespeare's
(a) *Julius Ceaser* (b) *Romeo and Juliet*
(c) *As You Like It* (d) *The Taming of a Shrew*

125. *Sejanus* of Jonson was written in
(a) 1600 (b) 1599 (c) 1610 (d) 1603

126. *Catiline* of Jonson was written in
(a) 1610 (b) 1609 (c) 1600 (d) 1611

127. Which Jonson's play is a more regular play complete with ghosts and chorus?
(a) *Catiline* (b) *Sejanus*
(c) *Volpone* (d) None of these

128. Jonson's drama which is an unfinished pastoral drama-is
(a) *The Sad Shepherd* (b) *The Tale of a Tub*
(c) *The Staple of News* (d) *The New Inn*

129. A play jointly written by Jonson, Marston and Chapman is
(a) *Eastward Hoe* (b) *The Silent Woman*
(c) *Volpone* (d) *The Poetaster*

130. In which year was Ben Jonson made poet to King James I?
(a) 1657 (b) 1624 (c) 1630 (d) 1614

### 3. Beaumont and Fletcher

131. John Fletcher was senior to Beaumont by
(a) 5 yrs. (b) 10 yrs. (c) 15 yrs. (d) 20 yrs.

132. John Fletcher died of
(a) cholera (b) plague
(c) tuberculosis (d) fever

133. How many plays are assigned to Beaumont and Fletcher alone and in collaboration?
(a) 30 (b) 40 (c) 45 (d) 52

134. Francis Beaumont wrote *The Woman Hater* in
(a) 1600 (b) 1603 (c) 1607 (d) 1610

135. John Fletcher's *The Wild Goose Chase* is a kind of Elizabethan version of Shaw's
(a) *Man and Superman* (b) *Candida*
(c) *Arms and the Man* (d) *Pygmalion*

136. Beaumont and Fletcher's *Philaster* is a fine study in
(a) romance (b) supernaturalism
(c) jealousy (d) human psychology

137. Fletcher did not collaborate with Beaumont in
(a) *The City Madam* (b) *The Scornful Lady*
(c) *Faithful Shepherdess* (d) *A King and No King*

138. *The Woman Hater* was written by
(a) Beaumont (b) Fletcher
(c) Shakespeare (d) Marlowe

### 4. John Webster

139. John Webster followed the trade of a ......... as a means of livelihood.
(a) barber (b) tailor (c) carpenter (d) blacksmith

140. In *The Malcontent* Webster collaborated with
    (a) Middleton (b) Marston
    (c) Dekker (d) Massinger
141. Webster's *The White Devil* was published in
    (a) 1600 (b) 1605 (c) 1608 (d) 1610
142. Webster's *The White Devil* is founded on Italian history and dramatises events that took place in
    (a) 1500 (b) 1550 (c) 1570 (d) 1580
143. The white devil in *The White Devil* is
    (a) satan (b) villain (c) courtesan (d) ghost
144. The only one of the plays of John Webster presented on the modern stage was
    (a) *The White Devil* (b) *The Duchess of Malfi*
    (c) *The Devil's Law Case* (d) *Appuis and Virginia*
145. The style and treatment of the subject in the story of *The Duchess of Malfi* has been inspired by
    (a) Shakespeare (b) Sidney
    (c) Shelley (d) Keats
146. Which play is widely recognized as Webster's masterpiece?
    (a) *The Duchess of Malfi* (b) *The Malcontent*
    (c) *The White Devil* (d) *The Devil's Law Case*

**5. Thomas Middleton**

147. Which play of Middleton landed him in trouble?
    (a) *A Game of Chess* (b) *The Changeling*
    (c) *The Old Law* (d) *A Faire Quarrel*
148. In which play Middleton collaborated with Thomas Dekker?
    (a) *The Changeling* (b) *A Game of Chess*
    (c) *The Mayor of Quinborough* (d) *The Roaring Girl*
149. Which play of Middleton is remembered more for its association with *Macbeth* than for its merit?
    (a) *Witch* (b) *The Old Law*
    (c) *The Changeling* (d) *A Trick to Catch the Old One*

150. Middleton's *A Trick to Catch the Old One* and *A Chaste Maid in Cheapside* are
(a) tragic comedies (b) comedies
(c) tragedies (d) satirical comedies

151. The famous tragi-comedy of Middleton is
(a) *The Family of Love* (b) *Anything for a Quiet life*
(c) *A Trick to Catch the Old One* (d) *The Changeling*

**6. Thomas Heywood**

152. Who described Thomas Heywood as a sort of prose Shakespeare?
(a) Charles Lamb (b) Johnson
(c) Coleridge (d) Middleton

153. The most remarkable work of Thomas Heywood is
(a) *Fair Maid of the West* (b) *The English Traveller*
(c) *The Woman Killed with Kindness* (d) *Arden of Feversham*

154. In *A Woman Killed with Kindness* Heywood sounds a .......... note.
(a) lyrical (b) domestic (c) satirical (d) comical

155. The title of the play *A Woman Killed with Kindness* is taken from a proverb quoted in
(a) *King Lear* (b) *The Tempest*
(c) *Macbeth* (d) *The Taming of the Shrew*

156. John Webster's chronicle plays are written to appeal to the
(a) gallants (b) groundlings
(c) contemporary society (d) aristocrats

**7. Philip Massinger**

157. Massinger collaborated with Dekker in
(a) *The Virgin Martyr* (b) *The City Madam*
(c) *The Unnatural Combat* (d) *Empire of the East*

158. Philip Massinger was born in
(a) 1503 (b) 1530 (c) 1533 (d) 1583

159. Philip Massinger died in
(a) 1600 (b) 1604 (c) 1640 (d) 1650

160. Nearly all the weaknesses of Shakespearean school are seen in Massinger's
(a) *The Unnatural Combat* (b) *The Virgin Martyr*
(c) *The Roman Actor* (d) *The Duke of Milan*

**8. John Ford**

161. John Ford's *'Tis a Pity She's a Whore* has ...... for its theme.
(a) revenge (b) jealousy
(c) incest (d) over-ambition

162. Ford's *The Broken Heart* was published in
(a) 1607 (b) 1619 (c) 1620 (d) 1629

163. Ford's *'Tis Pity She's a Whore* has the same theme as Beaumont and Fletcher's
(a) *A King and No King* (b) *The Maid's Tragedy*
(c) *Philaster* (d) *The Knight of the Burning Pestle*

**9. James Shirley**

164. James Shirley was born in London in
(a) 1506 (b) 1560 (c) 1566 (d) 1596

165. In 1636, James Shirley settled in
(a) London (b) Italy (c) Paris (d) Dublin

166. Shirley wrote *The Gamester* and *The Lady of Pleasure* in
(a) London (b) Dublin (c) Italy (d) France

167. *The Duke's Mistress, The Contention for Honour and Riches* are James Shirley's
(a) comedies (b) tragedies (c) satires (d) masques

168. Of Shirley's plays, the best known is
(a) *The Wedding* (b) *The Grateful Servant*
(c) *The Witty Fair One* (d) *The Maid's Revenge*

169. James Shirley forms a link between the
(a) Elizabethan and Restoration drama (b) Elizabethan and Post-Elizabethan drama
(c) Elizabethan and Classical drama (d) Elizabethan and Jacobean drama

### 10. Thomas Dekker

170. Which work of Dekker is a graphic picture of London smitten by plague?
(a) *The Wonderful Year* (b) *The Shoemaker's Holiday*
(c) *The Gull's Hornbook* (d) *The Seven Deadly Sins of London*

171. *Old Fortunatus* is a morality play based on .......... legend.
(a) German (b) Russian (c) French (d) Italian

172. The first part of Thomas Dekker's *The Honest Whore* is thought to be influenced by
(a) Shakespeare (b) Middleton
(c) Marston (d) Heywood

173. *The Shoemaker's Holiday* was written by
(a) Heywood (b) Marston
(c) Dekker (d) Ben Jonson

174. *The Shoemaker's Holiday* was written in
(a) 1550 (b) 1610 (c) 1600 (d) 1616

175. Simon Eyre is a character of
(a) *Eastward Ho* (b) *Poetaster*
(c) *The Shoemaker's Holiday* (d) None

## UNIT F: ELIZABETHAN PROSE

### 1. Francis Bacon

176. Francis Bacon was born in
(a) 1561 (b) 1565 (c) 1550 (d) 1500

177. Bacon became a member of Parliament in
(a) 1500 (b) 1584 (c) 1561 (d) 1556

178. Which essayist wrote both in Latin and English?
(a) Raleigh (b) Foxe
(c) Bacon (d) Raphael Holinshed

179. Bacon's *The Advancement of Learning* is embodied in his
(a) *De Augmentis Scientarium* (b) *Novum Organum*
(c) *Scala Intellectus* (d) *Prodromi*

180. Bacon's *The Advancement of Learning* appeared in
(a) 1600 (b) 1660 (c) 1601 (d) 1605

181. Bacon's *History of Henry VII* appeared in
(a) 1600 (b) 1620 (c) 1622 (d) 1559

182. *New Atlantis* is modelled on
(a) More's *Utopia* (b) Jonson's *Epigramme*
(c) Marlowe's *Hero and Leander* (d) None

183. Which work of Bacon was left incomplete due to his sudden death?
(a) *Sylva Sylvarum* (b) *Novum Organum*
(c) *New Atlantis* (d) None

184. Who called Bacon the first essayist, as he remains for sheer mass and weight of genius?
(a) Dr. Johnson (b) Ben Jonson
(c) Hugh Walker (d) Shakespeare

185. Bacon's general conception of essay was borrowed from
(a) Seneca (b) Montaigne
(c) Hugh Walker (d) Hooker

186. Who called Bacon's style an index of the emergence of the modern world?
(a) Dryden (b) Johnson
(c) Pope (d) L.C. Knights

187. Which writing of Bacon is philosophical?
(a) *Essays* (b) *The Advancement of Learning*
(c) *New Atlantis* (d) None

188. Where does Bacon advise one to 'divide with the reason between self-love and society'?
(a) "Of Death" (b) "Wisdom for a Man's self"
(c) "Of Ambition" (d) "Essay of Empire"

189. *Counsels, civil and moral* is the subtitle given to
(a) Bacon's essays (b) Hooker's pamphlet
(c) Montaigne's essays (d) Nashe's novel

190. Bacon's essays in first edition are .......... in number.
(a) 20 (b) 15 (c) 10 (d) 12

191. The first edition of Bacon's essays were published in
(a) 1509 (b) 1519 (c) 1590 (d) 1597

192. Who said?
'Reading maketh a full man, conference a ready man and writing an exact man.'
(a) Bacon (b) Deloney
(c) Montaigne (d) Lodge

193. The only essay of Bacon which is personal is
(a) Of Death (b) Of Superstition
(c) Of Ambition (d) Of Gardens

194. Which work of Bacon is another *Utopia*?
(a) *Advancement of Learning* (b) *New Atlantis*
(c) *Novum Organum* (d) None

**2. Richard Hooker**

195. *Of the Laws of Ecclesiastical Polity* is a monumental book by
(a) Hooker (b) Bacon (c) Deloney (d) Nashe

196. Hooker's book is an object lesson in
(a) religion controversy (b) Puritanism
(c) episcopacy (d) capitalism

**3. Sir Philip Sidney**

197. Sidney's *Arcadia* is a
(a) romance (b) tragedy (c) masque (d) satire

198. *Arcadia* was written in
(a) 1590 (b) 1500 (c) 1550 (d) 1540

199. Sidney wrote *Arcadia* to entertain
(a) Earl of Warwickshire (b) Earl of Southampton
(c) Duke of Wales (d) Countess of Pembroke

200. The most important critical work of Elizabethan period is
(a) *Apologie for Poetrie* (b) *The School of Abuse*
(c) *Defence of Rhyme* (d) *Arcadia*

201. In his general attitude to literature, Sidney is a
(a) romantic (b) classicist (c) both (d) none

**4. Sir Walter Raleigh**

202. Walter Raleigh was knighted in
(a) 1504 (b) 1514 (c) 1540 (d) 1584

203. Walter Raleigh was appointed Lord Warden of the Stannaries in
(a) 1575 (b) 1580 (c) 1582 (d) 1585

204. During imprisonment in Tower, Walter Raleigh wrote
(a) *History of the World* (b) *Discovery of Guiana*
(c) *The Discoveries* (d) *The Pilgrimage*

## UNIT G: THE TRANSITION POETS

**1. Giles Fletcher**

205. Giles Fletcher was born in
(a) 1505 (b) 1515 (c) 1525 (d) 1585

206. Giles Fletcher's *Christ's Victory and Triumph* shows a remarkable influence of
(a) Shakespeare (b) Ben Jonson
(c) Spenser (d) None

**2. George Wither**

207. George Wither was a student of
(a) medicine (b) law
(c) political science (d) philosophy

208. George Wither was imprisoned for his
(a) "Juvenilia" (b) "Abuses Stript and Whipt"
(c) "The Manly Heart" (d) "Shall I Waste in Despair"

## UNIT H: THE METAPHYSICAL POETS

**1. John Donne**

209. John Donne revolted against the tradition of
(a) Shakespeare (b) Ben Jonson
(c) Spenser (d) Samuel Daniel

210. John Donne was imprisoned for his
(a) obscene writing (b) rebellious writing
(c) clandestine marriage (d) financial corruption

211. Which work of John Donne was highly approved by James I as a contribution to anti-Catholic controversy?
(a) *Pseudo Martyr* (b) *The Progress of the Soul*
(c) *An Anatomy of the World* (d) *Epithalamium*

212. Donne's poetry falls into ......... divisions.
(a) 5 (b) 6 (c) 3 (d) 4

213. Donne's *The Progress of the Soul* and *Metempsychosis* are illustrations of his
(a) amorous poems (b) metaphysical poems
(c) satirical poems (d) religious poems

214. With Donne, it may be said Caroline poetry
(a) flourishes (b) declines (c) begins (d) closes

**2. George Herbert**

215. George Herbert was educated at
(a) Oxford (b) Cambridge
(c) Harvard (d) None

216. Herbert died at the early age of
(a) 25 yrs. (b) 30 yrs. (c) 35 yrs. (d) 40 yrs.

217. Herbert's collection of religious poems *The Temple, Sacred Poems* and *Private Ejaculations* was published in
(a) 1620 (b) 1630 (c) 1633 (d) 1635

218. *A Priest to the Temple: or the Country Parson, his Character and Rule of Holy Life* is a ......... of George Herbert.
(a) prose work (b) religious poem
(c) metaphysical poem (d) cavalier poem

**3. Richard Crashaw**

219. Richard Crashaw was a
(a) Catholic priest (b) Catholic convert
(c) Protestant priest (d) None

220. Richard Crashaw was born in
(a) 1610 (b) 1612 (c) 1620 (d) 1625

221. Richard Crashaw was an eloquent
   (a) Catholic priest (b) Catholic convert
   (c) Puritan divine (d) Puritan poet

222. Crashaw was expelled from his Fellowship for
   (a) writing vulgar poems (b) blasphemy
   (c) for defying royal orders (d) refusing to sign the Solemn League and Covenant

223. Crashaw's secular poems were called
   (a) *Delights of The Muse* (b) *Steps to the Temple*
   (c) *The Flaming Heart* (d) *Wishes to his Unknown Mistress*

224. *Steps to the Temple* was the name given to his collection of
   (a) sacred poems (b) secular poems
   (c) lighter poems (d) love poems

**4. Abraham Cowley**

225. About Cowley's collection of poems *The Mistress*, who remarked that it had no power of seduction?
   (a) Dr. Johnson (b) Charles Lamb
   (c) Swinburne (d) Eliot

226. Cowley's imitations of Pindar set the style for the
   (a) pre-Raphaelites (b) neo-classicists
   (c) eighteenth century Pindaric ode (d) none

**5. Andrew Marvell**

227. Andrew Marvell was the son of
   (a) lawyer (b) Yorkshire clergyman
   (c) sailor (d) doctor

228. Marvell became Latin Secretary to Milton and Member of Parliament in
   (a) 1607 (b) 1617 (c) 1627 (d) 1657

229. Marvell's finest poem is the noble
   (a) "Growth of Popery" (b) "Affairs of State"
   (c) "The Nymph" (d) "Horation Ode"

230. 'Annihilating all that's made, To a green thought in a green shade.' These lines occur in Marvell's
(a) "Thoughts in a Garden" (b) "The Nymph"
(c) "Affairs of State" (d) "Growth of Popery and Arbitrary"

231. Marvell's political satires look forward to those of
(a) Pope (b) Dryden (c) Milton (d) Heywood

**6. Henry Vaughan**

232. Henry Vaughan regarded himself as a disciple of
(a) Richard Crashaw (b) George Herbert
(c) John Donne (d) Andrew Marvell

233. *Silex Scintillans* was a collection of Vaughan's
(a) religious poems (b) secular poems
(c) love poems (d) metaphysics

234. Vaughan's "The Retreat" has been compared to Wordsworth's
(a) "Daffodils" (b) "Lucy Poems"
(c) "Immortality Ode" (d) "The Solitary Reaper"

235. Henry Vaughan studied law and became a
(a) lawyer (b) physician
(c) philosopher (c) politician

236. A serious illness in ......... led to Vaughan's deep religious fervour.
(a) 1615 (b) 1625 (c) 1627 (d) 1651

237. Vaughan died in
(a) 1605 (b) 1650 (c) 1655 (d) 1695

238. Vaughan was at heart a
(a) romantic (b) mystic (c) satirist (d) classicist

## UNIT I: THE CAVALIER POETS

**1. Thomas Carew**

239. To whom did Carew pay the tribute as the poet who 'ruled as he thought fit/The universal monarchy of wit'?
(a) Donne (b) Herrick
(c) Crashaw (d) Henry Vaughan

240. Carew produced a mixture of classical influence of Jonson with the metaphysical influence of Donne suited to the atmosphere of the Court of
(a) James I (b) James II (c) Charles I (d) Charles II

**2. Sir John Suckling**

241. John Suckling was born in
(a) 1600 (b) 1605 (c) 1609 (d) 1610

242. John Suckling was educated at
(a) Oxford (b) Cambridge
(c) Harvard (d) London

243. Suckling died in
(a) London (b) Paris (c) Tower (d) Germany

**3. Sir Richard Lovelace**

244. Richard Lovelace was born in
(a) 1610 (b) 1615 (c) 1618 (d) 1620

245. Richard Lovelace suffered imprisonment
(a) twice (b) innocently
(c) for blasphemy (d) for royal disobedience

246. Which poem of Lovelace uses imagery that is as much Petrarchan as metaphysical?
(a) "To Althea from Prison" (b) "Lucasta"
(c) "On going to the Wars" (d) "The Grasshopper"

**4. Robert Herrick**

247. Robert Herrick served an apprenticeship as a
(a) lawyer (b) doctor
(c) blacksmith (d) goldsmith

248. The happiest expression of Herrick's powers may be found in his
(a) religious poems (b) love poems
(c) secular poems (d) nature poems

249. Robert Herrick turned to the classical lyric for
(a) inspiration (b) rejuvenation
(c) consolation (d) entertainment

## UNIT J: THE PURITAN POET

### 1. John Milton

250. How many books are there in "Paradise Lost"?
(a) 18 (b) 12 (c) 15 (d) 5

251. Christian struggle for salvation is the theme of
(a) "Pilgrim's progress" (b) "Prufrock"
(c) "On his Blindness" (d) "Fairie Queene"

252. *The Lady of Light* was the nickname of
(a) Milton (b) Donne (c) Vaughan (d) None

253. Which Milton's poem is based on patience
(a) "Paradise Regained" (b) "L'Allegro"
(c) "Paradise Lost" (d) "On his Blindness"

254. Which one is Milton's elegy on Edward King?
(a) "L'Allegro" (b) "On His Blindness"
(c) "Comus" (d) "Lycidas"

255. Milton's "On his Blindness" is a/an
(a) epic (b) elegy
(c) sonnet (d) blank verse

256. "Lycidas" of Milton is an/a
(a) epic (b) masque (c) comedy (d) elegy

257. In "Lycidas", the King has been presented as a
(a) poet (b) shepherd (c) priest (d) none

258. Which poet helped Milton in writing when he became blind?
(a) Andrew Marvell (b) Henry Vaughan
(c) Donne (d) None

259. Milton's "Comus" was published in
(a) 1634 (b) 1644
(c) 1654 (d) 1664

260. Puritanism has Milton as its
(a) singer (b) preacher
(c) playwright (d) priest

261. "Paradise Regained" and "Samson Agonistes" were published together in
(a) 1671 (b) 1617 (c) 1607 (d) 1610

262. "Comus" was published in 1637
(a) by Milton (b) by Spenser
(c) by Henry Lewes (d) anonymously

263. 'I was born in London of an honest family. I hardly ever left my studies or went to bed before midnight.' Milton said in
(a) "Paradise Lost" (b) "Comus"
(c) "Samson Agonistes" (d) "Second Defence of the English People"

264. Which Milton's work is without a trace of Puritanism?
(a) "L'Allegro" (b) "Pensereso"
(c) Both (d) None

## UNIT K: MID-SEVENTEENTH CENTURY PROSE

### 1. John Bunyan

265. John Bunyan wrote "Sighs from Hell", ........ years after his marriage.
(a) 3 (b) 8 (c) 5 (d) 6

266. John Bunyan was committed to prison for three months in
(a) 1660 (b) 1600 (c) 1610 (d) 1605

267. Bunyan was appointed as the minister of Baptists in
(a) 1671 (b) 1771 (c) 1660 (d) 1661

268. The most popular of Bunyan's works is
(a) *The Pilgrim's Progress* (b) *The Holy War*
(c) *The Holy City* (d) *The Life and Death of Mr. Badman*

269. Bunyan's style was influenced by
(a) *Bible* (b) *Faerie Queene*
(c) *Euphues* (d) *Pandosto*

270. John Bunyan's first work was
    (a) *Sighs from Hell* (b) *The Pilgrim's Progress*
    (c) *The Holy War* (d) *The Holy City*

**2. Robert Burton**

271. Robert Burton entered Christ Church as a
    (a) priest (b) student (c) rector (d) bishop
272. Burton's great and only literary achievement *The Anatomy of Melancholy* is
    (a) satirical (b) melancholic
    (c) religious (d) characteristic of time
273. Burton's *The Anatomy of Melancholy* is a ......... inspiration.
    (a) Shakespeare (b) metaphysics
    (c) Jacobean (d) post-Elizabethan

**3. Sir Thomas Browne**

274. By profession, Thomas Browne was a
    (a) sailor (b) politician (c) doctor (d) chemist
275. The bulkiest of Browne's works is
    (a) *Vulgar Errors* (b) *Religio Medici*
    (c) *A Letter to a Friend* (d) *The Garden of Cyrus*
276. Browne died in
    (a) 1660 (b) 1672 (c) 1678 (d) 1682
277. The masterpiece of Thomas Browne is
    (a) *Hydriotaphia* (b) *The Garden of Cyrus*
    (c) *Religio Medici* (d) *Vulgar Errors*
278. Browne wrote *Religio Medici* to defend doctors against the charge of
    (a) witchcraft (b) magic (c) astrology (d) atheism
279. Thomas Browne was the son of a
    (a) doctor (b) sailor
    (c) priest (d) London Merchant
280. Browne was born in
    (a) 1600 (b) 1610 (c) 1605 (d) 1650

281. Browne was knighted in
(a) 1611 (b) 1621 (c) 1617 (d) 1671

282. His idiosyncratic diction and his learned allusions make Browne
(a) popular (b) difficult
(c) enlightened (d) orthodox

### 4. Thomas Fuller

283. Thomas Fuller was born in
(a) 1600 (b) 1605 (c) 1608 (d) 1610

284. Fuller's most considerable work *The Worthies of England* was published by
(a) his son (b) his father
(c) his brother (d) his friend

285. Coleridge and Lamb were influenced by Fuller's
(a) satire (b) comedy
(c) antithetical humour (d) masque

### 5. Izaak Walton

286. Izaak Walton was born of a
(a) yeoman stork (b) trader
(c) tailor (d) priest

287. Walton's most famous work *The Complete Angler* was published in
(a) 1603 (b) 1623 (c) 1633 (d) 1653

### 6. *Bible*

288. "The Preacher" is the sub-title of
(a) "Ecclesiastical" (b) "Ezekiel"
(c) "Haggai" (d) "St. Matthew"

289. *The New Testament* opens with
(a) "St. Matthew" (b) "St. Mark"
(c) "Philemon" (d) "Hebrews"

290. Who told Job to 'curse God and die'?
(a) his wife (b) his neighbour
(c) his sons (d) satan

291. In "Genesis", Abel was a
(a) shepherd (b) farmer
(c) horse keeper (d) mason

292. In the beginning, God created Heaven and the
(a) earth (b) stars (c) sun (d) man

293. In "Genesis", God called the dry land
(a) desert (b) earth (c) air (d) mountains

294. God created man in His
(a) light (b) image (c) name (d) shadow

295. Job's friends sat on the ground with him seven days and seven nights and did not speak a word. Why?
(a) his grief was great (b) he was sick
(c) he was angry (d) he was excited

296. Elihu's wrath was kindled against his three friends because
(a) they foresook him (b) they cursed him
(c) they did not help him (d) they had condemned Job wrongly

297. In Chapter 38 of the *Book of Job*, the Lord answered out of the
(a) whirlwind (b) fire
(c) sky (d) sea

298. How many daughters was Job given in the end by God?
(a) 3 (b) 7 (c) 5 (d) 12

299. After regaining his blessings and children, he lived for
(a) 120 yrs. (b) 130 yrs. (c) 135 yrs. (d) 140 yrs.

300. Which Psalm is "A Prayer of David"?
(a) 80 (b) 75 (c) 17 (d) 65

301. A beast with seven heads and ten horns appears in Chapter 13 of
(a) "John" (b) "Colossias"
(c) "Revelation" (d) "Corinthians"

302. In Chapter 10 of Judges, the anger of the Lord was hot against
(a) Palestine (b) Israel (c) Philistine (d) Syria

303. How many books are there in the *Bible*?
(a) 66 (b) 60 (c) 50 (d) 46

304. Medieval Europe knew the *Bible* in
(a) Latin (b) French (c) Greek (d) English

305. William Tyndale translated the "New Testament" from
(a) Greek (b) Latin (c) French (d) English

306. James I of England appointed 47 scholars to produce an English version of the *Bible* in
(a) 1600 (b) 1610 (c) 1604 (d) 1620

307. *The Old Testament* was originally written in
(a) Hebrew (b) Latin (c) Greek (d) English

308. *The New Testament* was translated into Middle English in
(a) 16th century (b) 15th century
(c) 14th century (d) 12th century

309. The script of *The Old Testament* was
(a) Latin (b) French (c) Russian (d) Greek

## ANSWERS

### Unit A

| | | | |
|---|---|---|---|
| 1. (d) | 2. (a) | 3. (a) | 4. (d) |
| 5. (a) | 6. (c) | 7. (c) | 8. (b) |
| 9. (a) | 10. (a) | 11. (b) | 12. (d) |
| 13. (b) | 14. (d) | 15. (a) | 16. (a) |

### Unit B

| | | | |
|---|---|---|---|
| 17. (a) | 18. (a) | 19. (a) | 20. (d) |
| 21. (c) | 22. (a) | 23. (d) | 24. (a) |
| 25. (d) | 26. (a) | 27. (a) | 28. (c) |
| 29. (a) | 30. (d) | 31. (a) | 32. (d) |
| 33. (a) | 34. (c) | 35. (b) | |

### Unit C

| | | | |
|---|---|---|---|
| 36. (b) | 37. (d) | 38. (b) | 39. (d) |
| 40. (b) | 41. (a) | 42. (c) | 43. (c) |

| | | | | | | | |
|---|---|---|---|---|---|---|---|
| 44. | (b) | 45. | (c) | 46. | (a) | 47. | (d) |

## Unit D

| | | | | | | | |
|---|---|---|---|---|---|---|---|
| 48. | (b) | 49. | (a) | 50. | (d) | 51. | (a) |
| 52. | (a) | 53. | (a) | 54. | (a) | 55. | (d) |
| 56. | (a) | 57. | (b) | 58. | (c) | 59. | (d) |
| 60. | (b) | 61. | (b) | 62. | (b) | 63. | (a) |
| 64. | (d) | 65. | (c) | 66. | (c) | 67. | (a) |
| 68. | (a) | 69. | (a) | 70. | (d) | 71. | (a) |
| 72. | (a) | 73. | (a) | 74. | (b) | 75. | (d) |
| 76. | (a) | 77. | (a) | 78. | (c) | 79. | (d) |
| 80. | (a) | 81. | (d) | 82. | (a) | 83. | (a) |
| 84. | (b) | 85. | (b) | 86. | (c) | 87. | (a) |
| 88. | (b) | | | | | | |

## Unit E

| | | | | | | | |
|---|---|---|---|---|---|---|---|
| 89. | (a) | 90. | (c) | 91. | (d) | 92. | (a) |
| 93. | (d) | 94. | (a) | 95. | (d) | 96. | (d) |
| 97. | (a) | 98. | (d) | 99. | (a) | 100. | (d) |
| 101. | (c) | 102. | (d) | 103. | (d) | 104. | (d) |
| 105. | (d) | 106. | (a) | 107. | (b) | 108. | (c) |
| 109. | (a) | 110. | (c) | 111. | (a) | 112. | (a) |
| 113. | (b) | 114. | (a) | 115. | (b) | 116. | (c) |
| 117. | (a) | 118. | (b) | 119. | (a) | 120. | (a) |
| 121. | (d) | 122. | (a) | 123. | (a) | 124. | (a) |
| 125. | (d) | 126. | (d) | 127. | (a) | 128. | (a) |
| 129. | (a) | 130. | (b) | 131. | (a) | 132. | (b) |
| 133. | (d) | 134. | (c) | 135. | (a) | 136. | (c) |
| 137. | (a) | 138. | (a) | 139. | (b) | 140. | (b) |
| 141. | (c) | 142. | (d) | 143. | (c) | 144. | (b) |
| 145. | (b) | 146. | (c) | 147. | (a) | 148. | (d) |
| 149. | (a) | 150. | (d) | 151. | (d) | 152. | (a) |
| 153. | (c) | 154. | (b) | 155. | (d) | 156. | (b) |

| | | | | | | | |
|---|---|---|---|---|---|---|---|
| 157. | (a) | 158. | (d) | 159. | (c) | 160. | (a) |
| 161. | (c) | 162. | (d) | 163. | (a) | 164. | (d) |
| 165. | (d) | 166. | (b) | 167. | (d) | 168. | (d) |
| 169. | (a) | 170. | (a) | 171. | (a) | 172. | (b) |
| 173. | (c) | 174. | (c) | 175. | (c) | | |

**Unit F**

| | | | | | | | |
|---|---|---|---|---|---|---|---|
| 176. | (a) | 177. | (b) | 178. | (c) | 179. | (a) |
| 180. | (d) | 181. | (c) | 182. | (a) | 183. | (c) |
| 184. | (c) | 185. | (b) | 186. | (d) | 187. | (b) |
| 188. | (b) | 189. | (a) | 190. | (c) | 191. | (d) |
| 192. | (a) | 193. | (d) | 194. | (b) | 195. | (a) |
| 196. | (a) | 197. | (a) | 198. | (a) | 199. | (d) |
| 200. | (a) | 201. | (b) | 202. | (d) | 203. | (d) |
| 204. | (a) | | | | | | |

**Unit G**

| | | | | | | | |
|---|---|---|---|---|---|---|---|
| 205. | (d) | 206. | (c) | 207. | (b) | 208. | (b) |

**Unit H**

| | | | | | | | |
|---|---|---|---|---|---|---|---|
| 209. | (c) | 210. | (c) | 211. | (a) | 212. | (c) |
| 213. | (b) | 214. | (c) | 215. | (b) | 216. | (d) |
| 217. | (c) | 218. | (a) | 219. | (b) | 220. | (b) |
| 221. | (c) | 222. | (d) | 223. | (a) | 224. | (a) |
| 225. | (a) | 226. | (c) | 227. | (b) | 228. | (d) |
| 229. | (d) | 230. | (a) | 231. | (b) | 232. | (b) |
| 233. | (a) | 234. | (c) | 235. | (b) | 236. | (d) |
| 237. | (d) | 238. | (b) | | | | |

**Unit I**

| | | | | | | | |
|---|---|---|---|---|---|---|---|
| 239. | (a) | 240. | (c) | 241. | (c) | 242. | (b) |
| 243. | (b) | 244. | (c) | 245. | (a) | 246. | (a) |
| 247. | (d) | 248. | (b) | 249. | (a) | | |

## Unit J

| | | | |
|---|---|---|---|
| 250. (b) | 251. (a) | 252. (a) | 253. (d) |
| 254. (d) | 255. (c) | 256. (d) | 257. (b) |
| 258. (a) | 259. (a) | 260. (a) | 261. (a) |
| 262. (d) | 263. (d) | 264. (c) | |

## Unit K

| | | | |
|---|---|---|---|
| 265. (a) | 266. (a) | 267. (a) | 268. (a) |
| 269. (a) | 270. (a) | 271. (b) | 272. (d) |
| 273. (c) | 274. (a) | 275. (a) | 276. (d) |
| 277. (a) | 278. (d) | 279. (d) | 280. (c) |
| 281. (d) | 282. (b) | 283. (c) | 284. (a) |
| 285. (c) | 286. (a) | 287. (d) | 288. (a) |
| 289. (a) | 290. (a) | 291. (a) | 292. (a) |
| 293. (b) | 294. (b) | 295. (a) | 296. (d) |
| 297. (a) | 298. (a) | 299. (d) | 300. (c) |
| 301. (c) | 302. (b) | 303. (a) | 304. (a) |
| 305. (a) | 306. (c) | 307. (a) | 308. (c) |
| 309. (d) | | | |

# The Restoration Period (1660–1702)

# 3

## UNIT A: HISTORICAL PERSPECTIVE AND BACKGROUND

1. Who was restored to the throne of England in 1660?
   (a) Charles I (b) Charles II (c) James (d) Harold
2. Which puritan king ruled over England before Charles II?
   (a) Oliver Cromwell (b) Henry Crown
   (c) Elizabeth (d) Prince Charles
3. The Restoration of Charles II to the throne of England brought about a revolution in English literature. What was that revolution?
   (a) England became a highly industrialized country
   (b) there was agricultural revolution
   (c) with the Restoration there was a violent reaction against the Puritan restraints
   (d) none of these
4. What is the period of Oliver Cromwell's rule?
   (a) 1642 – 1660 (b) 1670 – 1700
   (c) 1618 – 1650 (d) 1620 – 1650
5. Which of the following statements is true about the rule of Oliver Cromwell?
   (a) Oliver Cromwell, a puritan, had suppressed too many natural impulses
   (b) Oliver Cromwell had brought about many economic reforms for the welfare of England

(c) Oliver Cromwell encouraged the English dramatists and he made significant contribution towards the development of English drama
(d) None of these

6. Which of the following statements may be wrong?
(a) with the end of the puritan rule of Oliver Cromwell, English society became a model of morality
(b) Oliver Cromwell had been too severe, he had suppressed too many natural impulses
(c) with the Restoration of Charles II to the English throne, there was a violent reaction against the Puritan restraints
(d) all the statements are ture

7. The period in English history after 1660 is called
(a) Restoration period (b) Elizabethan period
(c) Jacobean period (d) Victorian period

8. Which of the following statements is true about the Restoration period in England?
(a) Released from restraint, society abandoned the decencies of life and the reverence for law and plunged into excesses more unnatural than had been the restraints of Puritanism
(b) King Charles II imposed strict code of conduct on English Society
(c) King Charles II was a role model of social morality and human behaviour
(d) None of these

9. In the later part of the 17th century, England witnessed the rise of two political parties. What are these two political parties?
(a) the Whites and the Reds
(b) the Lords and the Commons
(c) the Whigs and the Tories
(d) the Communals and the Seculars

10. Charles II had no legitimate child and heir, it was certain that his brother James a catholic, would succeed to the

throne. Charles II wanted to exclude him from the throne by enthroning
(a) Prince Charles III, his-cousin
(b) Duke of Monmouth, his favourite and illegitimate son
(c) Oliver Cromwell
(d) John Dryden

11. Who succeeded the King Charles II in his attempt to exclude James from the English throne?
(a) the Earl of Shaftesbury (b) the Earl of Leicester
(c) the Duke of Montagua (d) none of these

12. Who ascended the English throne in 1685?
(a) James II (b) Charles II
(c) Oliver Cromwell (d) Shaftesbury

## UNIT B: RESTORATION SATIRE

### 1. John Dryden

13. The age of Dryden is called
(a) the Romantic Age (b) the Elizabethan Age
(c) the Victorian Age (d) the Augustan Age

14. Neo-Classical Age is also called
(a) the Romantic Age (b) the Elizabethan Age
(c) the Victorian Age (d) the Augustan Age

15. During Augustan Age ......... came to be regarded as an essential quality of English Literature.
(a) Classicism (b) Medievalism
(c) Romanticism (d) Imagism

16. The slogan "follow nature" can be applied to
(a) the Romantics (b) the Augustans
(c) the Jacobeans (d) the Gothic Writers

17. Dryden's *Mac Flecknoe* has been written in
(a) Blank verse (b) Free verse
(c) Heroic couplet (d) Spenserian stanza

18. "Mac Flecknoe" is a personal satire. It is dedicated against a fellow poet of his time
    (a) Thomas Shadwell (b) Alexander Pope
    (c) Shaftesbury (d) Dr. Johnson
19. "Mac Flecknoe" is a/an
    (a) mock-heroic poem (b) ballad
    (c) narrative poem (d) epic
20. Each line of a heroic couplet is
    (a) an Iambic pentameter (b) a trochaie pentameter
    (c) an Iambic tetrameter (d) an anapestic pentameter
21. The following lines occur in
    "All human things are subject to decay
    And, when fate summons, monarchs must obey"
    (a) "Absalo and Achitophel" (b) "The Medal"
    (c) "Mac Flecknoe" (d) "Religio Laici"
22. In this line taken from Dryden's "Mac Flecknoe", 'this aged Prince' refers to
    (a) Thomas Shadwell (b) Richard Flecknoe
    (c) Heywood (d) Shirley
23. In "Absalom & Achitophel" Dryden attacked
    (a) Duke of Monmouth (b) Thomas Shadwell
    (c) Richard Flecknoe (d) Charles II
24. In "Absalom & Achitophel" the character of Achitophel refers to
    (a) Shaftesbury (b) Monmouth
    (c) Charles II (d) James
25. In "Absalom & Achitophel" the character of Absalom refers to
    (a) Shaftesbury (b) Monmouth
    (c) Richard Flecknoe (d) Charles II
26. Which of the following is called the Father of English criticism?
    (a) Dr. Johnson (b) John Dryden
    (c) Longinus (d) Matthew Arnold

27. Which of the following statements may be true about 'satire'?
    (a) Satire is a union of denunciation and humour
    (b) Satire is a story with a moral lesson
    (c) Satire is a story with a tragic end
    (d) Satire is a story which has fun without any moral
28. In reference to Dryden's "Absalom & Achitophel" which of the following statements is true?
    (a) Absalom and Achitophel were avowed enemies
    (b) Achitophel supported the claims of Absalom
    (c) Absalom supported the claims of Achitophel
    (d) Absalom and Achitophel are two names of the same character
29. The author of "Absalom and Achitophel" aimed at
    (a) Upholding the legality and legitimacy of the Duke of York's succession to the throne of England and to condemn the case of whigs, particularly Shaftesbury
    (b) Upholding the legality and legitimacy of Shaftesbury's succession to the throne of England
    (c) Upholding King Charles II's stand on the Exclusion Bill
    (d) Upholding the Parliament against the crown
30. The following lines have been extracted from which of the following works of Dryden:

    "In pious times, ere priestcraft did begin,
    Before polygamy was made a sin;
    When man on many, multiplied his kind,
    Ere one to one was, cursedly confined."

    (a) "Mac Flecknoe" (b) "Absalom & Achitophel"
    (c) "Religio Laici" (d) "The Hind & the Panther"
31. In which of the following category will you keep Dryden's "Absalom & Achitophel"?
    (a) political Satire (b) religious Satire
    (c) literary Satire (d) personal Satire
32. The story of "Absalom & Achitophel" has been taken from
    (a) *The Bible* (b) the Roman History
    (c) Greek Legend (d) the English History

33. Which of the following has not been authored by Dryden?
(a) "Hudibras" (b) "Religio Laici"
(c) "The Hind and the Panther" (d) "The Medal"

34. Which of the following works has been authored by Dryden?
(a) "Annus Mirabilis" (b) "Religio Medici"
(c) "Hudibras" (d) "The Rape of the Lock"

35. The following lines have been taken from Dryden's"For as, when raging fevers boil the blood/The standing lake soon floats into a flood/And every hostile humour which before/Slept quiet in its channels bubbles o'er".
(a) "Mac Flecknoe" (b) "Absalom & Achitophel"
(c) "The Hind & the Panther" (d) "The Medal"

36. The mistress of Charles II who had given birth to James, the Duke of Monmouth was
(a) Catherine (b) Rebecca
(c) Mona Lisa (d) Lucy Waters

37. Regarding Dryden's "Absalom & Achitophel" which of the following statements is true?
(a) through a story taken from *The Bible*, Dryden preaches the importance of religion
(b) Dryden mocks at God
(c) under the cover of the Biblical story Dryden argues against the scheme of Shaftesbury for inducing Charles II to nominate his illegitimate son as successor to the throne, while Jame, the Duke of York was the legal claimant
(d) under the cover of the Biblical story Dryden argues against the claim of James, the Duke of York for the throne of England

38. James, the Duke of York was a/an
(a) Catholic (b) Protestant
(c) Anglican (d) atheist

39. Shaftesbury was not prepared to accept James, The Duke of York as the future King of England because
    (a) he was the illegal son of Chares II
    (b) he was a Catholic
    (c) he was corrupt
    (d) he was a Protestant
40. James, The Duke of York was the
    (a) brother of Charles II
    (b) son of Charles II
    (c) friend of Charles II
    (d) none of these
41. "Absalom & Achitophel" can be put in the category of
    (a) lyrical poem
    (b) a Romance
    (c) allegory
    (d) ballad
42. Which of the following statements is correct?
    (a) Shaftesbury was a Whig leader
    (b) Shaftesbury was a Tory leader
    (c) Shaftesbury was the son of Charles II
    (d) Shaftesbury was a friend of Charles II
43. Which of the following statements is correct?
    (a) The Whigs were in support of Charles II
    (b) The Whigs were trying to force King Charles II to exclude the Roman Catholic from the throne
    (c) The Tories were trying to force King Charles II to exclude the Roman Catholic from the throne
    (d) The Tories supported the claim of James, the Duke of Monmouth, for the throne of England
44. The story on which Dryden based his allegory, "Absalom & Achitophel" is found in
    (a) *New Testament*
    (b) Ten Commandments
    (c) Samuel Second of the *Old Testament*
    (d) None of these
45. Dryden's "Absalom & Achitophel" allegorically refers to
    (a) Shaftesbury and Monmouth
    (b) The Tory and The Whig parties
    (c) Dryden and Charles II
    (d) Shaftesbury and The Duke of York

46. Dryden's "Absalom & Achitophel" alludes to the Biblical story of
    (a) David & Goliath
    (b) *The Book of Job*
    (c) *The Ecclesiastes*
    (d) The historic quarrel between David, King of Israel and his son Absalom

47. In "Absalom & Achitophel" David in *Old Testament* allegorically refers to
    (a) Charles II
    (b) Oliver Cromwell
    (c) James, The Duke of York
    (d) James, The Duke of Monmouth

48. In "Absalom & Achitophel" the Biblical character Saul refers to
    (a) Charles II
    (b) Oliver Cromwell
    (c) James, The Duke of York
    (d) James, The Duke of Monmouth

49. In Dryden's "Mac Flecknoe" Mac means
    (a) father of
    (b) son of
    (c) teacher of
    (d) none of them

50. Which of the following statements is true about a mock-epic?
    (a) a mock epic mocks at an epic
    (b) in a mock epic trivial incidents are invested with dignified language in a kind of burlesque of the epic manner
    (c) in a mock-epic characters are super human beings
    (d) none of them

51. What was the relationship between Flecknoe and Shadwell?
    (a) Flecknoe was the natural father of Shadwell
    (b) Flecknoe was the intellectual father of Shadwell
    (c) Shadwell was the natural father of Flecknoe
    (d) Flecknoe and Shadwell are the same person

52. The line from Dryden's "Mac Flecknoe" "Shadwell never deviates into sense" means
    (a) Shadwell never talked nonsense
    (b) Shadwell was always nonsensical

(c) Shadwell was always intelligent
(d) Shadwell never committed a mistake

53. Which of the following statements is true?
(a) Richard Flecknoe is an imaginary character created by Dryden in "Mac Flecknoe"
(b) Richard Flecknoe was a poetaster of 17th century
(c) Richard Flecknoe was a friend of Dryden
(d) Richard Flecknoe in "Mac Flecknoe" is Dryden himself

54. Which of the following books was written by Shadwell?
(a) *The Medal* (b) "The Medal of John Bayes"
(c) "Mac Flecknoe" (d) None of them

55. What was the reason that induced Dryden to base the title of the poem "Mac Flecknoe" upon the obscure Irish writer Richard Flecknoe?
(a) Richard Flecknoe is the protagonist in this mock-epic
(b) for Dryden it was difficult to find a person more suitable to be the monarch of the Empire of dullness
(c) Dryden wanted to honour Mac Flecknoe
(d) Dryden wanted to satirise Mac Flecknoe

56. In Dryden's "Mac Flecknoe": "The mantle fell to the young prophet's part", 'young prophet' refers to
(a) Dryden (b) Richard Flecknoe
(c) Shadwell (d) Heywood

57. In Dryden's "Mac Flecknoe" "Shadwell alone my perfect image bears", here 'my' refers to
(a) Dryden (b) Richard Flecknoe
(c) Shadwell (d) Heywood

## UNIT C: RESTORATION COMEDY

### 1. William Congreve

58. The plays of William Congreve are known as
(a) comedy of humours (b) comedy of manners
(c) farce (d) comedy of errors

59. Millamant appears in which of the following comedies of Congreve?
    (a) *The Old Bachelor* (b) *Love for Love*
    (c) *The Way of the World* (d) *The Country Wife*

60. William Congreve was a
    (a) Restoration dramatist (b) Gothic novelist
    (c) Jacobean dramatist (d) Augustan satirist

61. The death of Oliver Cromwell in 1660 brought an end to the Puritanical rule and from here starts a period referred to in the history of English Literature as
    (a) Restoration Period (b) Elizabethan Period
    (c) Shakespearean Period (d) Medieval Period

62. The Restoration Period in the History of English Literature refers to the restoration of .......... brought into being with the accession of King Charles II to the throne of England in 1660.
    (a) democracy (b) monarchy
    (c) plutocracy (d) puritanism

63. *Essay of Dramatic Poesy* is written by
    (a) Congreve (b) Dryden
    (c) Shakespeare (d) Alexander Pope

64. Who speaks this line in *The Way of the World* "A wit should no more be sincere, than a woman constant"?
    (a) Witwoud (b) Millamant
    (c) Mirabel (d) Lady Wishfort

65. Who speaks this line in *The Way of the World* "Friendship without freedom is as dull as love without enjoyment"?
    (a) Witwoud (b) Millamant
    (c) Mirabel (d) Lady Wishfort

66. In Congreve's *The Way of the World* Millamant is loved by
    (a) Mr. Fainall (b) Petulant
    (c) Witwoud (d) Mirabel

67. In *The Way of the World* Mirabel is making pretensions of love towards
    (a) Lady Wishfort (b) Mrs. Fainall
    (c) Millamant (d) Mrs. Marwood
68. In Congreve's *The Way of the World* Lady Wishfort is the aunt of
    (a) Millamant (b) Mirabel
    (c) Mrs. Fainall (d) Marwood
69. Which of the following books has been written by William Congreve?
    (a) *A Midsummer Night's Dream* (b) *The Old Bachelor*
    (c) *She Would if She Could* (d) *The Country Wife*
70. Which of these has been authored by William Congreve?
    (a) *The Double Dealer* (b) *The Way of the World*
    (c) *The Constant Couple* (d) *Love for Love*
71. Which of the following statements is true?
    (a) Etherage is a restoration dramatist (b) Etherage is a restoration novelist
    (c) Etherage is a character in Congreve's play (d) Etherage is a contemporary of T.S. Eliot
72. Which of the following statements about a Restoration Comedy may be true?
    (a) it aimed at upholding the dignity of man
    (b) it dealt with supernatural elements like ghosts, fairies and witches
    (c) it presents a graphic picture of medieval times
    (d) the playwrights regarded portrayal of manners and depiction of characters the main aim of comedy.
73. "Plot in a comedy became a hotchpotch stuff, consisting of a series of entertaining scenes, loosely strung together, without any regard for unity of action." This statement may be applied to
    (a) Shakespearean tragedy (b) Shavian drama
    (c) Restoration comedy (d) the dramas of T.S. Eliot

74. The display of wit forms an important part of which of the following dramas?
    (a) Shakespearean comedy (b) Shakespearean Tragedy
    (c) Restoration Comedy (d) Jacobean Drama
75. *The Way of the World* opens in a chocolate house and Mirabell and Fainall are shown rising from a card-table. Mirabell has not been concentrating on the game because
    (a) Mirabell was losing the game
    (b) Mirabell had no more time for the game
    (c) Mirabell had to go to meet Mrs. Millamant
    (d) Mirabell was disappointed by the determined opposition of Lady Wishfort to his plan of marrying Millamant, her niece
76. Lady Wishfort hated Mirabell because
    (a) Mirabell was a depraved man
    (b) Mirabell had been pretending to love her (Lady Wishfort)
    (c) Mirabell's father had harmed her
    (d) Mirabell and Lady Wishfort belonged to two different political parties
77. Mirabell had been making false love to Lady Wishfort because
    (a) he was infatuated by her beauty
    (b) he wanted to seduce her
    (c) Mirabell flattered Lady Wishfort to be in her good books so that he could get her permission to marry her daughter
    (d) Mirabell flattered Lady Wishfort to be in her good books so that he could get her permission to marry her niece
78. The consent of Lady Wishfort is important to Mirabell, regarding his marriage with Mrs. Millamant because
    (a) Lady Wishfort has in her keeping six thousand pounds belonging to Millamant as her marriage portion. If Millamant marries against her wishes she stands to lose half of this inheritance

(b) Lady Wishfort has in her keeping ten thousand pounds belonging to Millamant
(c) Lady Wishfort has in her keeping four thousand pounds belonging to Millamant
(d) None of these

79. Mirabell's first plan to win Lady Wishfort has misfired because
(a) Mrs. Marwood, a young Lady who is after him but whose advances have been rejected by him in off-hand manner, warned the old lady of his real intentions, that is, of pleasing her simply, to get her consent to marry Millamant
(b) Lady Wishfort came to know the illicit relationship going on between Mirabell and Marwood
(c) Lady Wishfort had chosen someone else to be the husband of Millamant
(d) Lady Wishfort is an old woman and she wants an old man as her lover

80. When Mirabell's first plan to win Lady Wishfort's consent for his marriage with Millamant failed, he was working on the second plan. It was
(a) to elope with Millamant
(b) to murder Lady Wishfort
(c) to steal the marriage portion of Millamant
(d) that of compelling Lady Wishfort to agree to his proposal by involving her romantically with his man-servant, Waitwell

81. Which of the following statements is true regarding *The Way of the World*?
(a) Mirabell disguised himself as Sir Rowland.
(b) Waitwell disguised himself as Sir Rowland
(c) Witwoud disguised himself as Sir Rowland
(d) Mr. Fainall disguised himself as Sir Rowland

82. Waitwell had been secretly married to
(a) Mrs. Fainall (b) Marwood
(c) Lady Wishfort (d) Foible

83. Which of the following statements is wrong?
   (a) Fainall and Mrs. Fainall are not on good terms
   (b) Mrs. Fainall had a love affair with Mirabell
   (c) Fainall and Mrs. Fainall have been separated
   (d) Mr. Fainall ill-treats Mrs. Fainall
84. Which of the following statements is true?
   (a) Fainall and Mrs. Fainall intrigued to thwart the second plan of Mirabell
   (b) Fainall and Mrs. Marwood intrigued to thwart the second plan of Mirabell
   (c) Mrs. Fainall and Mrs. Marwood intrigued to thwart the second plan of Mirabell
   (d) Mrs. Fainall and Foible intrigued to thwart the second plan of Mirabell
85. About the character of Millamant which one of the following statements may be true?
   (a) Millamant is a true coquette
   (b) the coquettry of Millamant is a pretence. She wants to shorn Mirabell of some de-merits before marrying him
   (c) the love of Millamant for Mirabell is not real and constant, as there was no constancy in love in the Restoration society
   (d) Millamant wants to keep Mirabell engaged in the love-chase game simply for the sake of fun
86. Which of the following statements about *The Way of the World* is true?
   (a) Waitwell was disguised as Sir Rowland and he was to woo Lady Wishfort
   (b) Waitwell was disguised as Sir Rowland and he was to woo Foible
   (c) Mirabell disguised himself as Sir Rowland
   (d) Sir Rowland was sincerely in love with Lady Wishfort
87. These are the opening lines of Act IV, scene i, of *The Way of the World*

   "Out of my house, out of my house, thou viper, thou

serpent that I have fostered! Thou bosom traitress that I raised from nothing".

What is the context of these lines?

(a) The intrigue of Sir Rowland which was being played upon Lady Wishfort has been exposed and Lady Wishfort is speaking to Foible in anger
(b) Lady Wishfort is venting her wrath on her maid servant because she was caught in her bed
(c) Mr. Fainall is ill-treating Mrs. Fainall
(d) Millamant has turned Mirabell out of her house

88. Who was instrumental in exposing the intrigue which Mirabel was playing upon Lady Wishfort?
(a) Millamant (b) Mrs. Fainall
(c) Mrs. Marwood and Mr. Fainall (d) Marwood

89. 'The Proviso Scene' in *The Way of the World* refers to
(a) the scene of Sir Rowland and Lady Wishfort in the latter's chamber
(b) the scene of gambling between Mirabel and Mr. Fainall
(c) the scene of quarrel between Mr. and Mrs. Fainall
(d) the scene in which Mirabel and Millamant strike a bargain

90. Which of the following characters in *The Way of the World* was sent to prison at the end of the play?
(a) Waitwell (b) Mr. Fainall
(c) Mirabel (d) Witwoud

91. Which play of Congreve concludes with the following lines?

"From hence let those be warned, who mean to wed,
Lest mutual falsehood stain the bridal bed;
For each deceiver to his cost may find
That marriage frauds, too oft, are paid in kind."

(a) *The Way of the World* (b) *The Old Bachelor*
(c) *Love for Love* (d) *The Double Dealer*

92. In Congreve's *The Old Bachelor*, who is the old Bachelor?
(a) Mirabel (b) Witwoud (c) Fainall (d) Heartwell

93. Fondle wife is a character in which of the following plays of Congreve?
(a) *The Way of the World* (b) *Love for Love*
(c) *The Old Bachelor* (d) *The Double Dealer*

94. Valentine is a character in which of the following plays of Congreve?
(a) *Love for Love* (b) *The Way of The World*
(c) *The Old Bachelor* (d) *The Double Dealer*

95. The following lines have been taken from which play of Congreve?
"Since the Plain Dealer's scenes of manly rage/Not one has dare to lash his crying age."
(a) *Love for Love* (b) *The Way of the World*
(c) *The Old Bachelor* (d) *The Double Dealer*

96. The satire of Congreve is the mildest and he says about this in the epilogue of one of his plays: "Only shows its teeth, as if it smiled"
The above lines appears in the epilogue of which play?
(a) *Love for Love* (b) *The Double Dealer*
(c) *The Way of the World* (d) *The Old Bachelor*

**2. William Wycherley**

97. William Wycherley belonged to which of the following periods?
(a) Romantic Period (b) Victorian Period
(c) Restoration Period (d) Elizabethan Period

98. Who is the author of the play *The Country Wife*?
(a) William Congreve (b) William Wycherley
(c) William Shakespeare (d) Thomas Becket

99. Which of the following plays has been written by William Wycherley?
(a) *The Way of the World* (b) *She Stoops to Conquer*
(c) *The Plain Dealer* (d) *The Man of Mode*

100. In which play of Wycherley the character Blackacre appears?
(a) *The Plain Dealer* (b) *The Country Wife*
(c) *Love in a Wood* (d) *The Gentleman Dancing Master*

101. In which play of Wycherley the character Manly appears?
   (a) *The Plain Dealer* (b) *The Country Wife*
   (c) *Love in a Wood* (d) *The Gentleman Dancing Master*

102. Fidellia in Wycherley's *The Plain Dealer* is in love with which of the following characters?
   (a) Mirabel (b) Fainal
   (c) Manly (d) None of these

103. In Wycherley's *The Plain Dealer* who disguises as a boy to serve Manly?
   (a) Fidelia (b) Blackacre
   (c) Millamant (d) None of these

104. Olivia is a character in which of the following plays of Wycherley?
   (a) *The Plain Dealer* (b) *The Country Wife*
   (c) *Love in a Wood* (d) *The Gentleman Dancing Master*

105. "The main plot concerns the successive device of Mr. Horner to enable him to enjoy the favours of outwardly respectable and virtuous ladies with the consent of their husbands."
   To which play of Wycherley will you associate the above statement?
   (a) *The Plain Dealer* (b) *The Country Wife*
   (c) *The Gentleman Dancing Master* (d) *Love in a Wood*

106. In Wycherley's *The Country Wife* who proclaims himself to be an eunuch?
   (a) Manly (b) Mr. Horner
   (c) Mirabel (d) None of these

107. In Wycherley's *The Country Wife* which character has married the country girl and brought her to London?
   (a) Mr. Horner (b) Mr. Pinchwife
   (c) Mirabel (d) None of these

108. Which of the following characters in Wycherley's *The Plain Dealer* is the plain dealer?
(a) Manly (b) Fidelia
(c) Olivia (d) Mr. Pinchwife

### 3. George Farquhar

109. George Farquhar belonged to which of the following periods?
(a) Romantic Period (b) Victorian Period
(c) Restoration Period (d) Elizabethan Period

110. Which of the following plays has been written by Farquhar?
(a) *The Country Wife* (b) *The Man of Mode*
(c) *The Plain Dealer* (d) *The Beaux Stratagem*

111. Which of the following plays has not been written by Farquhar?
(a) *Love and a Bottle* (b) *The Constant Couple*
(c) *The Recruiting Officer* (d) *The Provoked Wife*

112. Which of the following is the last play written by Farquhar?
(a) *Love and a Bottle* (b) *The Constant Couple*
(c) *The Recruiting Officer* (d) *The Beaux Stratagem*

113. Silvia is a character in which of the following plays of Farquhar?
(a) *Love and a Bottle* (b) *The Constant Couple*
(c) *The Recruiting Officer* (d) *The Beaux Stratagem*

### 4. Sir George Etherage

114. George Etherage belonged to which of the following periods?
(a) Romantic Period (b) Victorian Period
(c) Restoration Period (d) Elizabethan Period

115. Which of the following can be said to be the first accomplished practitioner of the Restoration Comedy of manners?
(a) William Congreve (b) George Etherage
(c) William Wycherley (d) None

116. Which of the following is the first play written by George Etherage?
   (a) *The Comical Revenge* (b) *She Would if She Could*
   (c) *The Man of Mode* (d) *The Silent Woman*

117. In which play of Etherage, the character Dorimant appears?
   (a) *The Man of Mode* (b) *The Comical Revenge*
   (c) *She Would if She Could* (d) *The Silent Woman*

118. In which play of Etherage, the character Harriet appears?
   (a) *The Man of Mode* (b) *The Comical Revenge*
   (c) *She Would if She Could* (d) None

**5. Sir John Vanbrugh**

119. John Vanbrugh belonged to which of the following periods?
   (a) Romantic Period (b) Victorian Period
   (c) Restoration Period (d) Elizabethan Period

120. Who is the author of the play *The Provoked Wife*?
   (a) John Vanbrugh (b) William Congreve
   (c) William Wycherley (d) George Etherage

121. Which of the following plays has not been authored by John Vanbrugh?
   (a) *The Man of Mode* (b) *The Relapse*
   (c) *The Provoked Wife* (d) *The Confederacy*

122. In which play of Vanbrugh, Sir John and Lady Brute reveal their mutual antipathy?
   (a) *The Provoked Wife* (b) *The Relapse*
   (c) *The Confederacy* (d) *Journey to London*

123. "The plot of the play deals with a husband's adultery, as an act of sexual passion forced on him against his better judgement and against his genuine love for his wife."
   To which play of Vanbrugh will you associate the above statement?
   (a) *The Provoked Wife* (b) *The Relapse*
   (c) *The Confederacy* (d) *Journey to London*

## ANSWERS

### Unit A

| | | | | | | | |
|---|---|---|---|---|---|---|---|
| 1. | (b) | 2. | (a) | 3. | (c) | 4. | (a) |
| 5. | (a) | 6. | (a) | 7. | (a) | 8. | (a) |
| 9. | (c) | 10. | (b) | 11. | (a) | 12. | (a) |

### Unit B

| | | | | | | | |
|---|---|---|---|---|---|---|---|
| 13. | (d) | 14. | (d) | 15. | (a) | 16. | (b) |
| 17. | (c) | 18. | (a) | 19. | (a) | 20. | (a) |
| 21. | (c) | 22. | (b) | 23. | (a) | 24. | (a) |
| 25. | (b) | 26. | (b) | 27. | (a) | 28. | (b) |
| 29. | (a) | 30. | (b) | 31. | (a) | 32. | (a) |
| 33. | (a) | 34. | (a) | 35. | (b) | 36. | (d) |
| 37. | (c) | 38. | (a) | 39. | (b) | 40. | (a) |
| 41. | (c) | 42. | (a) | 43. | (b) | 44. | (c) |
| 45. | (a) | 46. | (d) | 47. | (a) | 48. | (b) |
| 49. | (b) | 50. | (b) | 51. | (b) | 52. | (b) |
| 53. | (b) | 54. | (b) | 55. | (b) | 56. | (c) |
| 57. | (b) | | | | | | |

### Unit C

| | | | | | | | |
|---|---|---|---|---|---|---|---|
| 58. | (b) | 59. | (c) | 60. | (a) | 61. | (a) |
| 62. | (b) | 63. | (b) | 64. | (a) | 65. | (a) |
| 66. | (d) | 67. | (a) | 68. | (a) | 69. | (b) |
| 70. | (b) | 71. | (a) | 72. | (d) | 73. | (c) |
| 74. | (c) | 75. | (d) | 76. | (b) | 77. | (d) |
| 78. | (a) | 79. | (a) | 80. | (d) | 81. | (b) |
| 82. | (d) | 83. | (c) | 84. | (b) | 85. | (b) |
| 86. | (a) | 87. | (a) | 88. | (c) | 89. | (d) |
| 90. | (a) | 91. | (a) | 92. | (d) | 93. | (c) |
| 94. | (a) | 95. | (a) | 96. | (a) | 97. | (c) |
| 98. | (b) | 99. | (c) | 100. | (a) | 101. | (a) |
| 102. | (c) | 103. | (a) | 104. | (a) | 105. | (b) |

| | | | | | | | |
|---|---|---|---|---|---|---|---|
| 106. | (b) | 107. | (b) | 108. | (a) | 109. | (c) |
| 110. | (d) | 111. | (d) | 112. | (d) | 113. | (c) |
| 114. | (c) | 115. | (b) | 116. | (a) | 117. | (a) |
| 118. | (a) | 119. | (c) | 120. | (a) | 121. | (a) |
| 122. | (a) | 123. | (b) | | | | |

# The Neo-Classical Age (1702–1740)

# 4

## UNIT A: HISTORICAL PERSPECTIVE AND BACKGROUND

1. The age of .......... is called the classical age of England.
   (a) Augustus (b) Queen Elizabeth
   (c) Queen Anne (d) Louis XIV
2. The Methodist Revival began in the .......... century.
   (a) 17th (b) 18th (c) 19th (d) 20th
3. The heroic tragedy was introduced by
   (a) Otway (b) Sir William Davenant
   (c) Corneille (d) Dryden
4. Who is known as 'ploughman poet'?
   (a) Arnold (b) Wordsworth
   (c) Thomson (d) Burns
5. What is meant by "the churchyard school of poets"?
   (a) the poetry that suffered from melancholic strain (b) the poetry about the church
   (c) both (d) none
6. Who wrote "Essay on Boswell's Life"?
   (a) Macaulay (b) T. S. Eliot
   (c) Goldsmith (d) None
7. The transitional poets replaced the Neo-classical Heroic couplet by
   (a) the four lined stanza (b) Spenserian stanza
   (c) the heroic quatrain (d) all these

8. The movement of return to nature has to do with
   (a) the Neo-Classical Age (b) the Romantic Age
   (c) the Pre-Romantic Age (d) none of these
9. The Tory party fell from power in the year
   (a) 1704 (b) 1702 (c) 1711 (d) 1702
10. What is the name of the first daily newspaper?
    (a) *Gazetta* (b) *The Daily Courant*
    (c) *The Tatler* (d) None of these
11. *The Daily Courant* the first daily newspaper came out in the year
    (a) 1642 (b) 1682 (c) 1700 (d) 1702
12. Who is considered to be the first literary philosopher?
    (a) George Berkeley (b) Arbuthnot
    (c) Addision (d) None
13. George II ascended to the throne in the year
    (a) 1727 (b) 1728 (c) 1729 (d) 1730
14. The picaresque novel *Gil Bilas* by Le Sage is
    (a) an English novel (b) a French novel
    (c) a Spanish novel (d) a Latin novel
15. *The Monk* is a gothic novel by
    (a) M.G. Lewis (b) Mrs. Shelley
    (c) Walpole (d) Clara Reeve
16. James Watt invents the steam engine in
    (a) 1836 (b) 1814 (c) 1784 (d) 1798
17. Louis XVI of France was executed by the revolutionaries in
    (a) 1799 (b) 1793 (c) 1765 (d) 1789
18. What is a picaresque novel?
    (a) a novel whose hero is a villain (b) a novel whose hero is a kinight
    (c) a novel whose hero is a wandering rogue (d) a novel whose hero is subordinate to the heroine
19. The Whig ministry in the parliament passed the Licensing Act in
    (a) 1747 (b) 1832 (c) 1742 (d) 1737

20. Who among the following were Jacobites?
    (a) The Tories (b) The Whigs
    (c) The Cavaliers (d) None
21. *Nightmare Abbey* is a novel by
    (a) Peacock (b) Walpole (c) Austen (d) None
22. Falkland is a character in
    (a) *Nightmare Abbey* (b) *Ruth*
    (c) *Caleb Williams* (d) None
23. God made the country and man made the town. This is suggestive of
    (a) neo-classics' preference for the human Nature and the town life
    (b) pre-Romantics' preference for the physical nature and the country life
    (c) the transition from neo-classicism to Romanticism
    (d) all these three
24. Queen Caroline died in the year
    (a) 1735 (b) 1737 (c) 1739 (d) 1741
25. Queen Anne succeeded to the throne in
    (a) 1702 (b) 1704 (c) 1706 (d) 1708

## UNIT B: ALEXANDER POPE

26. "What oft was thought but nev'er so well expressed" is an epigram which can be associated with
    (a) Alexander Pope (b) John Dryden
    (c) Dr. Johnson (d) Jonathan Swift
27. In Pope's "An Epistle to Dr. Arbuthnot" the character Atticus refers to
    (a) Jonathan Swift (b) John Dryden
    (c) Addison (d) Steele
28. In Pope's "An Epistle to Dr. Arbuthnot" the character Sporus refers to
    (a) Lord Hervey (b) Addison
    (c) Jonathan Swift (d) John Dryden

29. The age of Pope is called
    (a) Elizabethan Age (b) Victorian Age
    (c) Augustan Age (d) Georgian Age
30. In the age of Pope
    (a) poetry was inspired by passion and imagination
    (b) form was less important than the unrestrained expression of emotion
    (c) poetry was charged with artificiality of expression
    (d) attention came to be directed to correctness and neatness of expression and the critical rules of art
31. The term neo-classical in English literature means
    (a) a new kind of literature
    (b) an old and outdated literature
    (c) the work of the writers of classical antiquity presented to the poets and critics of the age the best of models and the ultimate standards of literary taste
    (d) literature of classical writers
32. "Essay on Criticism" is associated with which of the following authors?
    (a) John Dryden (b) Alexander Pope
    (c) Dr. Johnson (d) Matthew Arnold
33. The reason why 'Augustan' has been applied to the Age of Pope is
    (a) King Augustus ruled in England at that time
    (b) the poetry during this period was very holy
    (c) Augustus is the name of a poet
    (d) the Age of Augustus was the golden age of Latin literature and the age of Pope was regarded as the golden age of English literature
34. The literature during the age of Pope
    (a) was didactic and satirical
    (b) believed in arts for arts sake
    (c) was a literature of emotion and passion
    (d) had 'delight' as the main function

35. Epistle in Pope's "An Epistle to Dr. Arbuthnot" means
    (a) A short story written for Dr. Arbuthnot
    (b) An eulogy for Dr. Arbuthnot
    (c) A letter
    (d) A panegyric
36. The occasion for the publication of Pope's "An Epistle to Dr. Arbuthnot" was
    (a) he wanted to satirise Dr. Arbuthnot
    (b) he wanted to attack the Whig party
    (c) he wanted to make a reply to Dr. Arbuthnot's letter
    (d) he wanted to defend himself against criticism of his person and his morals by some persons
37. Which of the following statements about Pope's "An Epistle to Dr. Arbuthnot" is not correct—
    (a) Pope expresses his feeling of irritation and annoyance at the visits of a large number of poetasters who come with their verses to get his opinion about their poetic ability and to obtain help
    (b) Pope is bent upon exposing the stupidity of these poetasters through the Epistle
    (c) Pope defends himself against criticism
    (d) Pope was very sad about his criticism by some people and he expresses this sorrow to his friend Dr. Arbuthnot
38. Which of the following statements about Pope's 'Epistle' is true
    (a) "An Epistle to Dr. Arbuthnot" is a satire on contemporary society
    (b) "An Epistle to Dr. Arbuthnot" was written by its author in self-defence.
    (c) "An Epistle to Dr. Arbuthnot" is a mock-epic poem
    (d) "An Epistle to Dr. Arbuthnot" is an allegory
39. In the "Advertisement" which precedes the poem
    (a) Pope has advertised his poem
    (b) Pope has expressed his obligation towards the publication of this poem
    (c) Pope has made his comments about commercial advertisements

(d) Pope has explained the reason for the publication of this poem and the manner in which it had been composed

40. In "Advertisement" which precedes the poem "An Epistle to Dr. Arbuthnot", Pope refers to "the authors of verses to the Imitator of Horace and of an Epistle to a Doctor of Divinity from a Nobleman at Hampton Court". To whom does Pope refer by 'The authors'
    (a) the author of these poems were Lord Harvey and Lady Mary Montagu
    (b) the authors were Dryden and Shadwell
    (c) 'the authors' means Pope and his wife
    (d) the authors of these poems are imaginary
41. Which of the following statements about Pope's "Epistle" is true?
    (a) "An Epistle to Dr. Arbuthnot" is a criticism of Augustan society
    (b) "An Epistle to Dr. Arbuthnot" is a highly autobiographical poem
    (c) "An Epistle to Dr. Arbuthnot" expresses Pope's philosophy of life
    (d) "An Epistle to Dr. Arbuthnot" is a letter condemning Dr. Arbuthnot.
42. Which of the following poems has not been written by Pope?
    (a) "The Rape of the Lock" (b) "An Epistle to Dr. Arbuthnot"
    (c) "An Epistle to a Doctor of Divinity" (d) "The Essay on Criticism"
43. Which of the following poems has been written by Pope?
    (a) "The Medal" (b) "Mac Flecknoe"
    (c) "The Rime of the Ancient Mariner" (d) "The Dunciad"
44. Which of the following statements about Dr. Arbuthnot is true?
    (a) Dr. Arbuthnot was a great scholar in philosophy

(b) Dr. Arbuthnot was a physician who had treated Pope
(c) Dr. Arbuthnot is an imaginary character
(d) Dr. Arbuthnot is Pope himself

45. In the opening lines of "An Epistle to Dr. Arbuthnot" "Shut, shut the door, good John! Fatigued I said" 'I' refers to
(a) Dr. Arbuthnot (b) Alexander Pope
(c) a character who is afraid of ghosts (d) a character who is afraid of robbers

46. In the opening lines of "An Epistle to Dr. Arbuthnot" "Shut, shut the door, good John! fatigued I said" the speaker wants the door to be shut against
(a) robbers (b) ghosts
(c) poetasters (d) Dr. Arbuthnot

47. In the following lines from "An Epistle to Dr. Arbuthnot"

"All fly to Twit'nam, and in humble strain
Apply to me, to keep them mad or vain"

Twit'nam is Twickenham, what is this Twickenham
(a) the name of a river (b) the name of a bird
(c) it is the name of a place where the house of Pope was situated (d) the name of the writer's friend

48. Read the following lines from Pope's "An Epistle to Dr. Arbuthnot"
"Friend to my life (which did not you prolong,
The world had wanted many an idle song)"
'Friend' refers to
(a) Dr. Arbuthnot (b) Robert Walpole
(c) James (d) Alexander Pope

49. The following lines have been taken from which poem of Alexander Pope?
"Willing to wound, and yet afraid to strike,
Just hint a fault, and hesitate dislike"
(a) "The Rape of the Lock" (b) "The Dunciad"
(c) "An Epistle to Dr. Arbuthnot" (d) "The Essay on Man"

50. Read the following lines from "An Epistle to Dr. Arbuthnot"

"His life, tho' long, to sickness past unknown,
His death was instant, and without a groan"

'His' in the above lines refers to

(a) Alexander Pope's father (b) Dr. Arbuthnot
(c) Dr. Arbuthnot's father (d) Alexander Pope himself

51. Read the following lines from "An Epistle to Dr. Arbuthnot"

"Oh grant me thus to live, and thus to die!
Who sprung from Kings shall know less joy than I"

What kind of a life the poet desires, which would make him happier than people born in a royal family?

(a) The poet wants to be a very rich man
(b) The poet wants to pass a life without sickness as his father did
(c) The poet craves for fame
(d) The poet desires for a very humble life

52. There is a reference to Sporus in Pope's "An Epistle to Dr. Arbuthnot"

'Let Sporus tremble' –What ? that thing of silk,
"Sporus, that mere white curd of Ass's milk?
Satire or Sense alas! Can Sporus feel?"

Who was Sporus?

(a) Sporus was the name of a eunuch at the court of the ancient Roman emperor
(b) Sporus was a king of England
(c) Sporus was a Roman King
(d) Sporus was the name of a mythological animal

53. In Pope's "An Epistle to Dr. Arbuthnot" there is also reference of Jonathan Swift.'I found him close with Swift'. Which of the following statement is correct?

(a) Pope and Swift belong to different periods
(b) Pope and Swift were contemporary and they were at dagger's drawn
(c) Pope and Swift were contemporary and were good friends
(d) Pope criticized Swift in "An Epistle to Dr. Arbuthnot"

54. Read the following lines: "Proud, as Apollo on his forked hill/State full-blown Bufo, puffed by ev'ry quill;". Bufo in the above lines refers to
   (a) a common name
   (b) King ruling England at that time
   (c) Bufo is the name that Pope gives to man who claims to be a patron of poets and who therefore takes airs of importance
   (d) a critic who criticized Pope very bitterly
55. In the following line: "And he, whose Fustian's so sublimely bad". It refers to
   (a) oxymoron (b) antithesis
   (c) Euphemism (d) innuendo
56. Which of the following statements about Pope's "The Rape of the Lock" may be correct?
   (a) a girl has lost her locks (b) it is a mock heroic poem
   (c) it is an epic poem (d) it is an anti-sentimental comedy
57. Which of the following statements about Pope's "The Rape of the Lock" may be correct?
   (a) in "The Rape of the Lock", Pope mocks at the artificial social life of 18th century London
   (b) Pope wrote this to have his revenge on all those who had criticized, sometimes unjustly, his translations of Homer and his edition of Shakespeare
   (c) Pope satirises corruption in high places
   (d) none of these
58. Pope's "The Rape of the Lock" has been written in
   (a) spensarian Stanza (b) blank verse
   (c) free verse (d) heroic couplet
59. In Pope's "Dunciad" which of the following statements may be true?
   (a) Theobold, the noted Shakespearean scholar, was crowned the hero of Dunceland
   (b) Pope satirises the fashionable women of London
   (c) Pope satirises Dryden
   (d) One of these

60. "A Little learning is a dangerous thing", this line occurs in
    (a) "The Rape of the Lock" (b) "Essay on Criticism"
    (c) "Dunciad" (d) "Windsor Forest"
61. "To err is human to forgive divine", this line occurs in
    (a) "The Rape of the Lock" (b) "Essay on Criticism"
    (c) "Dunciad" (d) "Windsor Forest"
62. Who said this about Pope: "The Essay on Criticism" is one of Pope's greatest works, and if he had written nothing else, it would have placed him among the first critics and the first poets?
    (a) Dr. Johnson (b) John Dryden
    (c) Coleridge (d) Arnold
63. "Laugh where we must, be candid where we can/But vindicate the ways of God to man." This line has been taken from
    (a) "The Essay on Man" (b) "The Essay on Criticism"
    (c) "Dunciad" (d) "Windsor Forest"
64. "Moral Epistles" was written by
    (a) Pope (b) Swift
    (c) Goldsmith (d) Steele
65. Who is known as the high priest of a rationalistic and social age?
    (a) Johnson (b) Dryden
    (c) Goldsmith (d) Pope
66. Who asserted, "To copy nature is to copy them (the ancients)"
    (a) Pope (b) Swift (c) Johnson (d) Tennyson
67. The term 'bathos' was first used by
    (a) Pope (b) Shakespeare
    (c) Dryden (d) Arnold

## UNIT C: JONATHAN SWIFT

68. Which of the following prose works has not been authored by Swift?
    (a) *Gulliver's Travels* (b) *A Tale of a Tub*
    (c) *An Argument Against Abolishing Christianity* (d) *Tom Jones*

69. Which of the following prose works has been authored by Swift?
    (a) *Robinson Crusoe* (b) *The Pilgrim's Progress*
    (c) *Utopia* (d) *A Modest Proposal*

70. Jonathan Swift belongs to
    (a) age of Chaucer (b) Elizabethan age
    (c) age of Pope (d) modern age

71. In which of the following category would you put Swift's *Gulliver's Travels*?
    (a) Epic (b) Satire
    (c) Tragedy (d) Fairy Tale

72. In *Gulliver's Travels*, Gulliver sets out on
    (a) four voyages (b) five voyages
    (c) three voyages (d) six voyages

73. Which of the following voyages was undertaken by Gulliver in *Gulliver's Travels*?
    (a) voyage to Brobdingnag (b) voyage to Congo
    (c) voyage to the Malayan islands (d) voyage to Denmark

74. Which of the following voyages was not undertaken by Gulliver in *Gulliver's Travels*?
    (a) voyage to Lilliput (b) voyage to Brobdingnag
    (c) voyage to the Land Houyhnhnms (d) voyage to Congo

75. On reading Swift's *Gulliver's Travels* one may infer
    (a) nothing is big or small, it is only the way you look at it, relative perception
    (b) a man can be destroyed but not defeated

(c) happiness is but an occasional interlude in the general drama of life
(d) life is an adventure

76. In *Gulliver's Travels* Swifts yahoos may be taken as
(a) a symbol of low level to which humanity may degenerate into when the restraints of reason and society are removed
(b) a symbol of a man's yearning for freedom
(c) the unjustified ways of God to man
(d) a symbol of the English imperialistic attitude

77. In Swift's *Gulliver's Travels* Lilliput was threatened with an invasion from
(a) the island of Blefuscu (b) Brobdingnag
(c) Japan (d) Mildendo

78. In Swift's *Gulliver's Travels*, there is a reference to two parties in Liliput which are antagonistic to each other. These two parties are
(a) The blacks and the whites (b) Tory and Whig
(c) The democrats and the Republicans (d) Tracmecksan and Slamecksan

79. In *Gulliver's Travels* for the Man Mountain the Liliputian equivalents is
(a) Quinbus Flestrin (b) Skyris Bolgolam
(c) Limtoc Balonuff (d) Gulliver

80. The character in *Gulliver's Travels* who brought about an impeachment against Gulliver in Lilliput was
(a) Bolgolam (b) Blefuscu
(c) Mildendo (d) Flestrin

81. Which of the following is an article of impeachment against Gulliver in Lilliput?
(a) he had conspired to kill the king
(b) he was clandestinely in love with the queen
(c) he was planning to run away from Lilliput
(d) he had discharged urine within the precincts of the royal palace

82. Voyage to Lilliput is followed by which voyage in Swift's *Gulliver's Travels?*
(a) voyage to Brobdingnag (b) voyage to Laputa
(c) voyage to Houyhnhnms (d) voyage to Congo

83. Where does the following line occur? "Nothing is great or little, otherwise than by comparison"
(a) voyage to Lilliput (b) voyage to Brobdingnag
(c) voyage to Laputa (d) voyage to Houyhnhnms

84. What was the name given to Gulliver in his "A Voyage to Brobdingnag"?
(a) Bolgolam (b) Blefuscu (c) Mildendo (d) Grildrig

85. Lorbrulgrud is a metropolis in Gulliver's
(a) A Voyage to Lilliput (b) A Voyage to Brobdingnag
(c) A Voyage to Laputa (d) A Voyage to Houyhnhnms

86. Glumdalclitch is the name of a girl who looked after Gulliver in his
(a) voyage of Lilliput (b) voyage of Brobdingnag
(c) voyage of Laputa (d) voyage of Houyhnhnms

87. The following lines have been taken from which voyage of Gulliver?
"This made me reflect, how vain an attempt is for a man to endeavour doing himself honour among those who are out of all degree of equality or comparison with him."
(a) voyage to Lilliput (b) voyage to Brobdingnag
(c) voyage to Laputa (d) voyage of Houyhnhnms

88. 'My little friend Grildrig, you have made as most admirable panegyrick upon your country. You have clearly proved that ignorance, idleness and vice, are the proper ingredients for qualifying as a legislator.'
Who is the speaker of these lines?
(a) Gulliver (b) his Majesty in Gulliver's Voyage to Brobdingnag
(c) the King of England (d) his Majesty in Gulliver's Voyage to Lilliput

89. "I cannot but conclude the bulk of your natives, to be the most pernicious race of little odious vermin that nature ever suffered to crawl upon the surface of the earth."

    What does Swift want to say through these lines?

    (a) Swift through these lines has expressed his disgust for the human race
    (b) Swift was a human being, he cannot have antipathy for the human race
    (c) Swift is talking about dirty animals crawling upon the surface of the earth
    (d) None of these statement are true

90. How did Gulliver escape from Brobdingnag?
    (a) he ran away when his escort was sleeping
    (b) the box in which he was kept was lifted by an eagle and it chanced that the box was dropped in an ocean
    (c) Gulliver was allowed by the King of the land
    (d) England attacked Brobdingnag and Gulliver was freed

91. Lagado is the capital city in Gulliver's
    (a) voyage to Lilliput (b) voyage to Brobdingnag
    (c) voyage to Laputa (d) voyage to Houyhnhnms

92. Yahoos appear in which of the following voyages of Gulliver?
    (a) voyage to Lilliput (b) voyage to Brobdingnag
    (c) voyage to Laputa (d) voyage to Houyhnhnms

93. Which of the following statements may be true in the context of Swift's *Gulliver's Travels*?
    (a) Houyhnhnms is the name of a group of islands
    (b) Houyhnhnms is the name of a living thing
    (c) Houyhnhnms is the name of river
    (d) Houyhnhnms is the name of a mountain

94. Which of the following statements may be true in the context of Swift's *Gulliver's Travels*?
    (a) Houyhnhnms were the masters and Yahoos their servants
    (b) Yahoos were the master and Houyhnhnms their servants

(c) Houyhnhnms and Yahoos were friends
(d) Houyhnhnms and Yahoos were enemies of each other

95. Which of the following statements may be true in the context of Swift's *Gulliver's Travels*?
(a) Houyhnhnms were like human beings
(b) Yahoos were like human beings
(c) Gulliver was taken for a Houyhnhnms
(d) Yahoos were like horses

96. Swift has written in *Gulliver's Travels*: "And when I began to consider, that by copulating with one of the Yahoo species, I had become a parent of more; it struck me with the utmost shame, confusion and horror". Which of the following statements are true?
(a) the speaker is guilty for copulating
(b) the speaker is disgusted with the morally depraved condition of the Yahoos
(c) the speaker is not feeling guilty about anything
(d) the speaker wanted to live like a hermit, meditating in a forest.

97. In which of the voyages of Gulliver, Swift's misanthropy appears the most poignant?
(a) voyage to Lilliput (b) voyage to Brobdingnag
(c) voyage to Laputa (d) voyage to the Houyhnhnms

98. Which of the following books by Swift contains the tale of three sons Peter, Martin and Jack?
(a) *The Battle of the Books* (b) *A Tale of a Tub*
(c) *A Modest Proposal* (d) *Gulliver's Travels*

99. Which of the following statements is true?
(a) The Three Sons Peter, Martin and Jack represent the three periods–Classical, Medieval and Modern, respectively
(b) Peter, Martin and Jack are three brothers quarrelling among themselves for a coat
(c) Peter, Martin and Jack represent respectively the Roman Catholic Church, the Church of England and the Protestant dissenters
(d) None of these

100. In Swift's *A Modest Proposal*
(a) Swift's proposal is simply that both parents and children would suffer infinitely less than they do at present if young children were fattened and sold for food
(b) Swift's proposal is to get rid of all the books written by the ancients
(c) Swift's proposal is to get rid of all the books written by the moderns
(d) None of these

101. The following line ocurrs in: 'Whoever has an ambition to be heard in a crowd, must press, and squeeze and thrust, and climb, with indefatigable pains"
(a) *A Tale of a Tub* (b) *The Battle of the Books*
(c) *A Modest Proposal* (d) *Gulliver's Travels*

102. Which of the following works of Swift is a satire on the famous controversy regarding the relative merits of the ancients and the moderns?
(a) *A Modest Proposal* (b) *Polite Conversation*
(c) *The Battle of the Books* (d) *Gulliver's Travels*

103. Which of the following was a patron of Jonathan Swift?
(a) William Wolton (b) William Temple
(c) Queen Anne (d) James I

104. Which of the following works of Swift is a religious allegory?
(a) *Gulliver's Travels* (b) *Journal to Stella*
(c) *Polite Conversation* (d) *A Tale of a Tub*

105. Which of the following statements is true?
(a) Swift has vehemently criticized William Temple
(b) Swift sides with his patron, William Temple and defends the ancients and condemns the moderns
(c) Swift defends the moderns and condemns the ancients
(d) None of these

106. In Swift's *The Battle of the Books* a dispute arises between a spider living in the corner of the library and a bee that gets caught in the spider's web.

Which of the following statements in this context is true?

(a) spider is a symbol of divine will
(b) spider represents the ancients and the bee the moderns
(c) the bee is like the ancients who go to nature for their honey
(d) none of these

107. In Swift's *The Battle of the Books* who is the commander of the ancients?
(a) Dryden (b) Milton
(c) Hobbes (d) William Temple

108. Who said, "I heartily hate and detest that animal called man"?
(a) Orwell (b) Swift (c) Eliot (d) Pope

## UNIT D: DANIEL DEFOE

109. Who is the author of *Mall Flanders?*
(a) John Gay (b) Daniel Defoe
(c) Swift (d) Robert Blair

110. In *Robinson Crusoe*, Man Friday is a
(a) hero (b) whiteman
(c) cannibal (d) sailor

111. *Roxana* is a fiction by
(a) Steele (b) Johnson (c) Defoe (d) Sterne

112. Who has been hailed as "the master of illusionist"?
(a) Richardson (b) Sterne
(c) Defoe (d) None

113. "The shortest way with the Dissenters", is a remarkable pamphlet written by
(a) Richardson (b) Defoe
(c) Fielding (d) Smollett

114. Defoe was tried, found guilty of seditious libel and was imprisoned. He was released from prison in
(a) 1704 (b) 1705 (c) 1706 (d) 1707

115. Which book of Defoe made him famous all over Europe?
(a) *Moll Flanders* (b) *Robinson Crusoe*
(c) *Captain Singleton* (d) *Roxana*

116. "Robinson Crusoe is a study of the human will—of patience fortitude and the indomitable saxon spirit overcoming all obstacles. It was this element which made—recommend Robinson Crusoe as a better treatise on education than anything which Aristotle or the moderns had ever written." Who said this?
(a) Edmund Burke (b) Gibbon
(c) Rousseau (d) Boswell

117. In which work of Defoe the horrors of a frightful plague are minutely recorded?
(a) *Memoirs of a Cavalier* (b) *Journal of the Plague Year*
(c) *Captain Singleton* (d) None of the above

118. Defoe was arrested for writing an ironical satire on High Church extremism. Name the satire?
(a) *A Journal of the Plague year* (b) *The Shortest way with Dissenters*
(c) *The Complete English Gentleman* (d) *The Complete English Tradesman*

## UNIT E: JOSEPH ADDISON

119. *The Vision of Mirza* is a political allegory by
(a) Addision (b) Swift (c) Steele (d) Defoe

120. *Account of the Greatest English Poets* was written by
(a) Swift (b) Lamb (c) Bacon (d) Addison

121. Addison's *The Drummer* is
(a) an opera (b) a masque
(c) a tragedy (d) a prose-comedy

122. *The West Indian* and *The Fashionable Lover* are two plays by
(a) Pope (b) Addison (c) Steele (d) None

123. Who said this?
"Whoever wishes to attain an English style, famili'ar but not coarse, and elegant but not ostentatious, must give his days and nights to the volumes of Addison."
(a) Dr. Johnson (b) William Hazlitt
(c) Richard Steele (d) Jonatnon swift

124. Which work of Addison offers an excellent example of the rhetoric and fine sentiment, which are essentials of good writing?
(a) *Tatler* (b) *Spectator*
(c) *Cato* (d *Account of the Greatest English Poets*

125. "I shall endeavour to enlighten morality with wit, and to temper wit with morality." Here 'I' stands for
(a) Cowley (b) Addison (c) Steele (d) Defoe

## UNIT F: RICHARD STEELE

126. Who among the following, wrote prose comedies?
(a) Addison (b) Steele
(c) Dr. Johnson (d) None

127. Who started the journal, *The Tatler*?
(a) Addison (b) Steele
(c) Dr. Johnson (d) Defoe

128. The first number of *The Tatler* came out in
(a) 1707 (b) 1708 (c) 1709 (d) 1710

129. Which author was awarded the position of official gazetteer on account of his talent in writing political pamphlets?
(a) Addison (b) Swift (c) Steele (d) Goldsmith

130. Steele at first signed his essays with the name of
(a) Isaac Bickerstaff (b) Isaac Walton
(c) Isaac Mount (d) Isaac Newton

131. *The Spectator* was a joint enterprise of
(a) Steele and Addison (b) Steele and Sterne
(c) Addison and Sterne (d) Defoe and Steele

## ANSWERS

### Unit A

| | | | | | | | |
|---|---|---|---|---|---|---|---|
| 1. | (c) | 2. | (b) | 3. | (b) | 4. | (c) |
| 5. | (a) | 6. | (a) | 7. | (d) | 8. | (c) |
| 9. | (d) | 10. | (b) | 11. | (b) | 12. | (a) |
| 13. | (a) | 14. | (b) | 15. | (a) | 16. | (c) |
| 17. | (b) | 18. | (c) | 19. | (d) | 20. | (a) |
| 21. | (a) | 22. | (c) | 23. | (c) | 24. | (b) |
| 25. | (a) | | | | | | |

### Unit B

| | | | | | | | |
|---|---|---|---|---|---|---|---|
| 26. | (a) | 27. | (c) | 28. | (a) | 29. | (c) |
| 30. | (d) | 31. | (c) | 32. | (b) | 33. | (d) |
| 34. | (a) | 35. | (c) | 36. | (d) | 37. | (d) |
| 38. | (b) | 39. | (d) | 40. | (a) | 41. | (b) |
| 42. | (c) | 43. | (d) | 44. | (b) | 45. | (b) |
| 46. | (c) | 47. | (c) | 48. | (a) | 49. | (c) |
| 50. | (a) | 51. | (b) | 52. | (a) | 53. | (c) |
| 54. | (c) | 55. | (a) | 56. | (b) | 57. | (a) |
| 58. | (d) | 59. | (a) | 60. | (b) | 61. | (b) |
| 62. | (a) | 63. | (a) | 64. | (a) | 65. | (d) |
| 66. | (a) | 67. | (a) | | | | |

### Unit C

| | | | | | | | |
|---|---|---|---|---|---|---|---|
| 68. | (d) | 69. | (d) | 70. | (c) | 71. | (b) |
| 72. | (a) | 73. | (a) | 74. | (d) | 75. | (a) |
| 76. | (a) | 77. | (a) | 78. | (d) | 79. | (a) |
| 80. | (a) | 81. | (d) | 82. | (a) | 83. | (b) |
| 84. | (d) | 85. | (b) | 86. | (b) | 87. | (b) |
| 88. | (b) | 89. | (a) | 90. | (b) | 91. | (c) |
| 92. | (d) | 93. | (b) | 94. | (a) | 95. | (b) |
| 96. | (b) | 97. | (d) | 98. | (b) | 99. | (c) |
| 100. | (a) | 101. | (a) | 102. | (c) | 103. | (b) |

| | | | |
|---|---|---|---|
| 104. (d) | 105. (b) | 106. (c) | 107. (d) |
| 108. (b) | | | |

**Unit D**

| | | | |
|---|---|---|---|
| 109. (b) | 110. (c) | 111. (c) | 112. (c) |
| 113. (b) | 114. (a) | 115. (b) | 116. (c) |
| 117. (b) | 118. (b) | | |

**Unit E**

| | | | |
|---|---|---|---|
| 119. (a) | 120. (d) | 121. (c) | 122. (b) |
| 123. (a) | 124. (c) | 125. (b) | |

**Unit F**

| | | | |
|---|---|---|---|
| 126. (b) | 127. (b) | 128. (c) | 129. (c) |
| 130. (a) | 131. (a) | | |

# The Age of Reason (1740–1770)

# 5

## UNIT A: HISTORICAL PERSPECTIVE AND BACKGROUND

1. The war of Austrian succession took place in
   (a) 1740 (b) 1745 (c) 1750 (d) 1755
2. The cynical and corrupt practices of Walpole, the premier of the first Tory cabinet were replaced by the more enlightened policies of Pitt in
   (a) 1755 (b) 1757 (c) 1759 (d) 1761
3. The conquest of India begins under General Clive in
   (a) 1757 (b) 1767 (c) 1762 (d) 1772
4. George III succeeds the throne in
   (a) 1750 (b) 1755 (c) 1760 (d) 1765
5. The period of French Revolution was
   (a) 1779 – 1789 (b) 1784 – 1794
   (c) 1789 – 1799 (d) 1794 – 1804
6. American Declaration of Independence took place in
   (a) 1775 (b) 1776 (c) 1777 (d) 1778
7. Slave trade was abolished in England in
   (a) 1785 (b) 1786 (c) 1787 (d) 1788
8. *The Town and Country Mouse* has been written by
   (a) Goldsmith (b) Matthew Prior
   (c) John Gay (d) Richardson
9. The trial of Warren Hastings took place in
   (a) 1785 (b) 1787 (c) 1789 (d) 1786

10. The treaty of Paris was signed in the year
    (a) 1781 (b) 1782 (c) 1783 (d) 1784

## UNIT B: DR. SAMUEL JOHNSON

11. Which of the following works has been authored by Dr. Johnson?
    (a) *The Vanity of Human Wishes* (b) *Tristram Shandy*
    (c) *Tom Jones* (d) *The Vicar of Wakefield*
12. Which of the following works has not been authored by Dr. Johnson?
    (a) *Lives of the Poets* (b) *London*
    (c) *A Dictionary of the English Language* (d) *Candida*
13. Which of the following is distinguished as the writer of a dictionary?
    (a) Dr. Johnson (b) Ben Jonson
    (c) John Dryden (d) Alexander Pope
14. The age of Dr. Johnson is also known as
    (a) the Age of Romanticism (b) the Age of transition
    (c) the Age of Victorianism (d) Modern age
15. Which of the following statements may be true in the context of the age of Dr. Johnson?
    (a) it was purely classical in its attitude
    (b) there was a romantic reaction against the old classical order
    (c) it had no sympathy for the poor and the oppressed
    (d) it was an age which followed the conventional literary techniques
16. Which of the following works has been authored by Dryden?
    (a) "Annus Mirabilis" (b) "Essay on Criticism"
    (c) "The Temple of Fame" (d) "Windsor Forest"
17. Which of the following works has been authored by Dryden?
    (a) "Essay on Dramatic Poesy" (b) "Essay on Man"
    (c) "Essay on Criticism" (d) "The Dunciad"

18. Which of the following works has not been authored by Dryden?
    (a) "Annus Mirabilis"
    (b) "Essay on Dramatic Poesy"
    (c) "Wild Gallant"
    (d) "Satire against Wit"
19. The poet who succeeded Dryden as Laureate was
    (a) Pope
    (b) Shadwell
    (c) Dr. Johnson
    (d) Fletcher
20. The libel in which Blackmore traduced Dryden was
    (a) "Fables"
    (b) "Satire against Wit"
    (c) "Dunciad"
    (d) "The School of Abuse"
21. "Dryden may be properly considered as the father of English criticism."
    Who stated this?
    (a) Alexander Pope
    (b) Dr. Johnson
    (c) Bolingbroke
    (d) Jonson
22. "What was said of Rome, adorned by Augustus, may be applied by an easy metaphor to English poetry embellished by Dryden." This is a praise of Dryden from
    (a) Alexander Pope
    (b) Dr. Johnson
    (c) Jonathan Swift
    (d) Melbourne
23. "The voice of which of the following authors, when young, was so pleasing that he was called in fondness the little Nightingale." Dr. Johnson said this about whom?
    (a) Dryden (b) Milton (c) Pope (d) Swift
24. "Ode on Solitude" is one of the earliest productions of which of the following great names?
    (a) Dryden (b) Milton (c) Pope (d) Swift
25. In "The Dunciad" Pope has put which of the following great personalities at the head of the dunces
    (a) Theobald
    (b) Swift
    (c) Addison
    (d) Steele
26. The Scribbler's Club was formed by
    (a) Pope alone
    (b) Pope and Swift
    (c) Pope, Swift and Dr. Arbuthnot
    (d) Pope, Swift and Bolingbroke

27. "Pope is a velvet lawn, shaven by the scythe and levelled by the roller"
This quotation is from
(a) Dr. Johnson (b) Bolingbroke
(c) Milton (d) Cowley

28. Dr. Johnson in his *Lives of the English Poets* has made an elaborate comparison between which of the following two authors?
(a) Pope and Swift (b) Pope and Milton
(c) Pope and Dryden (d) Pope and Cowley

29. The following quotation about Pope is from which of the following?
"One of his greatest, though of his earliest works, is the Essay on Criticism, which if he had written nothing else, would have placed him among the first critics and the first poets"
(a) Dr. Johnson (b) Boileau
(c) Bolingbroke (d) None of these

30. "Music is inarticulate poetry" Who has said this?
(a) Pope (b) Dryden (c) Milton (d) Cowley

31. Alexander Pope is known for his 'Epitaphs'. Epitaph means
(a) inscription on a Tomb (b) a short love poem
(c) a mournful poem (d) a short satire

32. 'To this sad shrine, who'er thou art, draw near;
Here lies the friend most loved, the son most dear;
The lines are from one of Pope's
(a) epitaphs (b) satires
(c) translations (d) pastorals

33. History of the four last years of Queen Anne has been written by which of the following?
(a) Swift (b) Pope (c) Dryden (d) Milton

34. Which of the following was privately married to Mrs. Johnson in 1716?
(a) Dr. Johnson (b) Swift
(c) Dryden (d) Pope

35. Which of the following authors had the appellation of The Dean?
    (a) Dr. Johnson (b) Swift
    (c) Dryden (d) Pope
36. Which of the following poets was blind?
    (a) Dr. Johnson (b) Milton
    (c) Dryden (d) Pope
37. Which of the following books was authored by Milton?
    (a) "Lycidas" (b) "Prometheus"
    (c) "Alcestis" (d) "The Dunciad"
38. Which of the following books was not authored by Milton?
    (a) "Paradise Lost" (b) "Lycidas"
    (c) "Metamorphosis" (d) "Accidence Commenced Grammar"
39. Which of the following books was authored by Milton?
    (a) *Samson Agonistes* (b) *The Faerie Queene*
    (c) *The Pilgrim's Progress* (d) None
40. Which of the following works of Milton is an elegy on the death of Mr. King, the son of Sir John King?
    (a) *Paradise Lost* (b) *Lycidas*
    (c) *Paradise Regained* (d) *Samson Agonistes*
41. Which of the following authors, in his youth, was so beautiful as to have been called 'The Lady of the College'?
    (a) Milton (b) Swift (c) Dryden (d) Pope
42. Which of the following works of Milton has been written in pastoral form?
    (a) *Paradise Lost* (b) *Paradise Regained*
    (c) *Lycidas* (d) *Comus*
43. Which of the following works of Milton is an epic poem?
    (a) *Paradise Lost* (b) *Lycidas*
    (c) *Comus* (d) None

44. Which of the following is not an important feature of an epic poem?
    (a) the occasional interposition of supernatural power
    (b) the subject of an epic poem is naturally an event of great importance
    (c) an epic must be written in a language which is so far removed from common use that an unlearned reader, when he first opens the book, finds himself surprised by a new language
    (d) the characters should be very realistic, close to life
45. Which of the following was not a work of Dr. Johnson?
    (a) *Rasselas* (b) *Prince of Abyssinia*
    (c) *The Rambler* (d) *The Citizen of the World*
46. Dr. Johnson left out one important poet in his *Lives of the Poets*. Who was that poet?
    (a) Gray (b) Collins
    (c) Goldsmith (d) Thomson
47. Dr. Johnson formed the Literary Club with the help of
    (a) Goldsmith (b) Addison
    (c) Steele (d) Pitt
48. Who said, "A book should help us either to enjoy life or to endure it"?
    (a) Pope (b) Bacon
    (c) Dr. Johnson (d) Wordsworth
49. *Irene* is a rhetorical tragedy by
    (a) Dryden (b) Jonson
    (c) Johnson (d) None
50. In the life of which poet did Dr. Johnson apply the term 'Metaphysical School of Poets'?
    (a) Milton (b) Cowley (c) Gray (d) Donne
51. Who said, "Tediousness is the most fatal of all faults"?
    (a) Pope (b) Johnson (c) Eliot (d) None
52. "London" is a poem by
    (a) Pope (b) Addison (c) Johnson (d) Steele

53. Dr. Johnson's *Dictionary* came out in
(a) 1755 (b) 1776 (c) 1800 (d) none
54. The epithet 'Augustan' was first applied to Dryden by
(a) Pope (b) Arnold
(c) Dr. Johnson (d) Coleridge
55. "Dryden found English poetry brick and left it marble." Who made this remark?
(a) Dr. Johnson (b) Arnold
(c) Coleridge (d) Pope
56. "The Vanity of Human Wishes" is a poem by
(a) Samuel Johnson (b) Thomson
(c) Cowper (d) Crabbe
57. "Season" is
(a) an elegy (b) a nature poem
(c) a love poem (d) a sonnet
58. Dr. Johnson founded the Literary Club in
(a) 1755 (b) 1764 (c) 1778 (d) 1785
59. Who said, "Nothing add will do long;/Tristram Shandy did not last"?
(a) Arnold (b) Leavis (b) Eliot (d) Johnson
60. The 'Coffee House Culture' flourished in
(a) the age of Ben Jonson (b) the age of Dr. Johnson
(c) the age of Wordsworth (d) the age of Dryden
61. Who said, 'What is fit for everything can fit nothing well'?
(a) Pope (b) Bacon (c) Johnson (d) George
62. Johnson's *Lives of the Poets* appeared in the year
(a) 1755 (b) 1779 (c) 1788 (d) 1781

## UNIT C: THE POETRY OF SENTIMENT

### 1. William Collins

63. *Persian Eclogues* is the first work of
(a) Thomas Gray (b) William Collins
(c) George Crabbe (d) James Thomson

64. Which of the following has been written by Collins?
(a) "Ode to Evening" (b) "Ode to Simplicity"
(c) "Ode to the West" (d) None

65. Which of the following odes is an interesting event in the romantic revival for it introduced a new world of witches, pygmies, fairies and medieval kings, for the imagination to play in?
(a) "Ode to Simplicity" (b) "Ode to Fear"
(c) "Ode to the Passions" (d) "Ode on the Popular Superstitions of the Highlands"

66. *Oriental Eclogues* though romantic in feeling, is written in the prevailing mechanical
(a) triplets (b) couplets
(c) quatrains (d) sestets

67. Which poet was lamented by William Collins in his poem "In Yonder Grave a Druid Lies"?
(a) Pope (b) James Thomson
(c) Crabbe (d) None

**2. Thomas Gray**

68. Which poem begins with the line: "The curfew tolls the knell of parting day"?
(a) Collins' "Ode to Evening"
(b) Collins' "Ode on the Passions"
(c) Gray's "Elegy Written in a Country Churchyard"
(d) Gray's "On the Death of a Favourit Cat"

69. 'Nor second He, that rode sublime Upon the seraph-wings of Ecstasy'.
These lines quoted from Gray's "The Progress of Poesy" alludes to
(a) Shakespeare (b) Milton
(c) Spenser (d) Donne

70. The theme of Gray's "The Bard" is the curse inflicted upon king Edward I and his progeny by
(a) some gods desecrated by him (b) some poets killed by him

(c) some patriots killed by him (d) none

71. "The Gray's Bard" and "The Progress of Poesy" are
(a) long lyrics (b) verse tales
(c) pindaric odes (d) narrative poems

72. Gray's "Elegy written in a Country Churchyard", the most perfect poem of the age was written in the year
(a) 1749 (b) 1750 (c) 1751 (d) 1752

73. Gray's poetic career has been divided into how many periods?
(a) two (b) three (c) four (d) five

74. In which period of his poetic career Gray turns momentarily from his Welsh and material and reveals a new field of romantic interest in Norse poems?
(a) First (b) Second (c) Third (d) None

75. In which of the following poems Gray translated his material from the Latin and which is remarkable for the use of Northern mythology?
(a) "The Progress of Poesy" (b) "The Fatal Sisters"
(c) "The Bard" (d) "Elegy"

## UNIT D: THE NOVEL OF SENTIMENT

### 1. Samuel Richardson

76. Which of the following novels is written by Richardson?
(a) *Humphry Clinker* (b) *Roderick Random*
(c) *Clarissa Harlowe* (d) *Joseph Andrews*

77. Fielding, Smollett, Sterne and .......... formed the four wheels of the van of the English novel.
(a) Richardson (b) Goldsmith
(c) Defoe (d) Swift

78. Richardson's *Pamela* came out in
(a) 1742 (b) 1749 (c) 1740 (d) 1719

79. *Virtue Rewarded* is the subtitle of which novel?
(a) *Joseph Andrews* (b) *Pamela*
(c) *Vanity Fair* (d) None of these

80. Which of the following is/are the epistolary novel(s) of Samuel Richardson?
    (a) *Sir Charles Grandison* (b) *Clarissa Harlowe*
    (c) *Pamela* (d) all of these

81. Who is known as not only "the first novelist of character but also the first novelist of feminine character"?
    (a) Richardson (b) James Joyce
    (c) Fielding (d) George Eliot

82. The credit of writing the first modern novel goes to
    (a) Fielding (b) Sterne
    (c) Richardson (d) Defoe

83. Richardson's novel *Pamela* was published .......... volumes.
    (a) three (b) four (c) five (d) six

84. In which novel of Richardson, the hero was presented as model of aristocratic manners and virtues for the middle class people?
    (a) *Clarissa Harlowe* (b) *Pamela*
    (c) *Sir Charles Grandison* (d) None of the above

85. Lovelace, the mechanical hero is the creation of
    (a) Defoe (b) Fielding
    (c) Smollett (d) Richardson

**2. Laurence Sterne**

86. Which novelist has been compared to a "little bronze satyr of antiquity in whose hollow exquisite odors were stored."?
    (a) Smollet (b) Richardson
    (c) Sterne (d) Fielding

87. In which novel, many of the passages have ben adapted or taken bodily from Burton,Rabelais and a score of other writers?
    (a) Richardson's *Pamela* (b) Smollett's *Humphrey Clinker*
    (c) Sterne's *A Sentimental Journey* (d) Fielding's *Joseph Andrews*

88. Sterne's *A Sentimental Journey* through France and Italy was written in the year
    (a) 1760 (b) 1765 (c) 1790 (d) 1768
89. Corporal Trim is a character in
    (a) *Pamela* (b) *Joseph Andrews*
    (c) *Tristram Shandy* (d) None of these
90. The last volume of *Tristram Shandy* came out in
    (a) 1760 (b) 1767 (c) 1757 (d) 1765
91. The seventh and eighth volumes of *Tristram Shandy* came out in
    (a) 1759 (b) 1758 (c) 1765 (d) 1770

## UNIT E: REALISM

### 1. Henry Fielding

92. Which of the following novels was written by Henry Fielding?
    (a) *Robinson Crusoe* (b) *Tom Jones*
    (c) *Ulysses* (d) *Moll Flanders*
93. Which of the following novels was not written by Henry Fielding?
    (a) *Robinson Crusoe* (b) *Joseph Andrews*
    (c) *Tom Jones* (d) *Shamela*
94. Which of the following novelists is a contemporary of Fielding?
    (a) Daniel Defoe (b) Joseph Conrad
    (c) Charles Dickens (d) Thomas Hardy
95. Which of the following novelists is not a contemporary of Fielding?
    (a) Daniel Defoe (b) Samuel Richardson
    (c) Tobias Smollett (d) James Joyce
96. Which of the following novels has been written by Samuel Richardson?
    (a) *The Castle* (b) *Moll Flanders*
    (c) *Pamela* (d) *Shamela*

97. Which of the novels has been written by Richardson?
    (a) *Jane Eyre* (b) *A Farewell to Arms*
    (c) *Gone with the Wind* (d) *Clarissa*

98. Which of the novels has not been written by Richardson?
    (a) *Pamela* (b) *Clarissa*
    (c) None (d) *Gone with the Wind*

99. Epistolary novel is a novel
    (a) which is written in the form of letters
    (b) which is based on a letter written by a great man
    (c) which is based on fanciful stories of ghosts and witches
    (d) which is a science fiction

100. Fielding's *Shamela* seems to be a parody of
    (a) *Pamela* (b) *Clarissa*
    (c) *Robinson Crusoe* (d) *Moll Flanders*

101. Which of these novels has been written in Epistolary style?
    (a) *Joseph Andrews* (b) *Tom Jones*
    (c) *Shamela* (d) *Pamela*

102. Sophia is the leading female character in which of the novels of Fielding?
    (a) *Shamela* (b) *Joseph Andrews*
    (c) *Tom Jones* (d) *Jonathan Wild*

103. Henry Fielding can be put in which of the following categories?
    (a) A prose-romance writer of 16th century (b) early 18th century novelist
    (c) gothic novelist (d) modern novelist

104. E.M. Forster has divided characters in a novel into two categories—round and flat. In which category would you keep the majority of characters in *Tom Jones*?
    (a) round characters (b) flat characters
    (c) flat and round both (d) neither flat nor round

105. Which of the following statements may be true about the protagonists of Fielding's *Tom Jones*?
    (a) Tom and Sophia are rebels, revolting against the respectable accepted domestic standards of eighteenth century society
    (b) Tom and Sophia are anti-social elements of 18th century society
    (c) Tom and Sophia have revolted against the King of England
    (d) Tom and Sophia suffer meekly and teach us the moral lesson of patience and stoicism

106. In the context of Fielding's *Tom Jones* which of the following statements may be true?
    (a) Blifil has a friendly relationship with Tom
    (b) Blifil thinks Tom is an illegitimate upstart who ought to be put firmly in his place
    (c) Blifil is the godfather of Tom
    (d) Tom is the godfather of Blifil

107. In *Tom Jones* conventional society may be said to be embodied in
    (a) the character of Tom (b) the character of Sophia
    (c) the character of Blifil (d) the character of Lady Bellaston

108. Which of the following statements gives a very accurate picture of Blifil in Fielding's *Tom Jones?*
    (a) Blifil is treacherous, lecherous, hypocritical and entirely self-seeking
    (b) Blifil is naïve and he is deceived by all in the novel
    (c) Blifil is very kind and generous towards the poor people in his neighbourhood so he was very popular among them
    (d) Blifil is a comic figure and a miser

109. The following lines from the novel give a beautiful description of one of the leading characters in *Tom Jones*
    "He cast himself on his bed, where he lay abandoning himself to despair, and drowned in tears; not in such tears as flow from contrition and wash away guilt from

minds —— these tears were such as the frightened thief sheds in his cart, and are indeed the effect of that concern which the most savage natures are seldom deficient in feeling for themselves"

Which character of *Tom Jones* has been referred to in the above lines?

(a) Tom (b) Blifil
(c) Allworthy (d) Squire Western

110. Heartfree is a leading character in which of the following novels of Fielding?

(a) *Jonathan Wild* (b) *Tom Jones*
(c) *Joseph Andrews* (d) *Shamela*

111. Which of the following statements about Tom and Sophia in *Tom Jones* may be true?

(a) Tom and Sophia are lover and beloved
(b) Tom and Sophia are brother and sister
(c) Sophia and Tom are mother and son
(d) None of these

112. In Fielding's *Tom Jones* Mr. Western, the father of Sophia, wants her to marry

(a) Tom Jones (b) Mr. Blifil
(c) Allworthy (d) Black George

113. In Fielding's *Tom Jones* 'Nightingale' is the name of

(a) a bird (b) an Inn
(c) a male character (d) a female character

114. In *Tom Jones* by Henry Fielding, who saved the life of Mrs. Waters from the villain Northerton?

(a) Tom (b) An oldman
(c) Allworthy (d) Blifil

115. After reading Fielding's *Tom Jones* which of the following inferences will you derive?

(a) reputation, which is the yardstick by which society measures its citizens, may have little to do with humanity, or compassion or simple goodness of heart
(b) eat drink and be merry who knows the world may end to-night

(c) sexual immorality and goodness of heart cannot go together. An incestful person is bound to be store house of all the vices
(d) none of these

116. Which of the observations about the characters in *Tom Jones* may be correct?
(a) Tom has no prudence at all, and his moral judgements are not in the least conventional, or even rational in their approach
(b) Mr. Allworthy is always right in his observations about other characters in the novel. He can even 'smell the soul' of the characters
(c) Mr. Blifil is a man of principle, he never deceived anyone rather he is deceived by many other characters in the novel
(d) Sophia had love for Tom but she wanted to marry Mr. Blifil, as Tom was a thorough rake

117. "Whoever is too hungry for sexual pleasure will end up being fed from his own flesh." This can be applied to which character in Fielding's *Tom Jones?*
(a) Tom Jones as he has a misapprehension of having committed incest with his mother
(b) Blifil, as he has a great hunger for sex
(c) Lady Belaston who is sexually hungry for Tom Jones
(d) Sophia who has a great passion for Tom Jones

118. In Fielding's *Tom Jones*, Tom has a misapprehension of having committed incest with his mother, Mrs. Waters, This situation may be called
(a) Quixotic (b) Homeric
(c) Oedipus-like (d) Herculean

119. "In *Tom Jones* there is too much plot." Who said this?
(a) Arnold Kettle (b) F.R. Leavis
(c) Coleridge (d) Ian Watt

120. The novels of which novelist have been termed 'comic epic in prose'?
(a) Henry Fielding (b) Henry James
(c) Jane Austen (d) James Joyce

121. A reading of Fielding's *Tom Jones* may lead a reader to infer
   (a) goodness of heart with sins of the flesh is better than sexual morality with sins against generosity of feeling
   (b) the ways of God to man is unjustified
   (c) public reputation and private virtue are concomitant
   (d) you must have sexual morality, other evils are venial

122. Tom in Fielding's *Tom Jones* is found as a new-born infant in the bed of a benevolent person. Who is this character?
   (a) Squire Allworthy (b) Blifil
   (c) Black George (d) Thwackum

123. In the context of Fielding's *Jonathan Wild* which of the statements may be true?
   (a) Jonathan Wild was a philanthropist
   (b) Jonathan Wild was a priest
   (c) Jonathan Wild was an organiser of thieves
   (d) None of these

124. Blueskin is a character in which of the following novels of Fielding?
   (a) *Joseph Andrews* (b) *Jonathan Wild*
   (c) *Amelia* (d) *Tom Jones*

125. Whom does Jonathan Wild marry in Fielding's novel *Jonathan Wild*?
   (a) *Pamela* (b) *Fanny*
   (c) *Shamela* (d) *Laetitia Snap*

126. At the end of the novel *Jonathan Wild*
   (a) Jonathan Wild marries Mrs. Heartfree
   (b) Jonathan Wild is hanged
   (c) Jonathan Wild renounces the world and becomes a priest
   (d) None of these

127. In Fielding's *Joseph Andrews* Joseph Andrews is
   (a) a footman in the house of Lady Brooby
   (b) priest
   (c) the husband of Pamela
   (d) the brother of Parson Adams

128. In Fielding's *Joseph Andrews*, Joseph Andrews was turned out of the house for which of the following reasons?
    (a) Joseph Andrews was very lazy
    (b) Joseph Andrews was dishonest
    (c) Joseph Andrews refused to satisfy the sexual desire of Lady Booby
    (d) None of these

129. In Fielding's *Amelia*, Amelia was married to which of the following characters?
    (a) Booth (b) Mr. Fitzpatrick
    (c) Parson Andrews (d) Blifil

130. Fielding's *Amelia* is written in a tone slightly different from the one we find in *Tom Jones*. What is this difference?
    (a) *Amelia* is a novel of love and *Tom Jones* is a novel of hate and revenge
    (b) compared to *Tom Jones*, in *Amelia* there is less of irony, the prevailing attitude is one of discontent, impatience and indignation, tempered with pity for the victims of selfishness and folly
    (c) *Tom Jones* is a comedy, *Amelia* is a tragedy
    (d) None of these

131. In Fielding's *Amelia*, which of the following statements is true about Dr. Harrison?
    (a) Dr. Harrison was a benefactor for Booths
    (b) Dr. Harrison was a villain always trying to do some harm to Amelia
    (c) Dr. Harrison is the narrator in the novel
    (d) None of these

132. How many books are there in *Tom Jones*?
    (a) 15 (b) 16 (c) 17 (d) 18

133. In *Tom Jones*, Sophia is finally married to
    (a) Blifil (b) Squire Western
    (c) Tom Jones (d) None

134. Comic epic in prose was initiated by
(a) Richardson (b) Fielding
(c) Pope (d) Prior

135. Henery Fielding's *Tom Jones* was dedicated to
(a) Josheph Andrews (b) The Jolly Beggars
(c) Richardson (d) None

**2. Tobias Smollett**

136. Which novelist was associated with medical profession which he used later in his novels?
(a) Tobias Smollett (b Henry Fielding
(c) Samuel Richardson (d) Daniel Defoe

137. Which of the following novels was not written by Smollett?
(a) *Roderick Random* (b) *Clarissa Harlowe*
(c) *Peregrine Pickle* (d) *Humphrey Clinker*

138. Tobias Smollett lived for how many years?
(a) fifty (b) fifty five (c) sixty (d) sixty five

139. Which is Smollett's last work?
(a) *Peregrine Pickle* (b) *Roderick Random*
(c) *Humphrey Clinker* (d) None of the above

140. By portraying such characters as Commodore Trunnion Matthew Bramble and Bowling, he laid the foundation for exaggeration in portraiture of human eccentricities. This quality formed the climax in
(a) Charles Dickens (b) Thackeray
(c) George Meredith (d) George Eliot

141. Smollett models his novels on
(a) Cervantes' *Don Quixote* (b) Defoe's *Robinson Crusoe*
(c) Swift's *Gulliver's Travels* (d) Fielding's *Joseph Andrews*

**UNIT F: THE REVIVAL OF COMEDY**

**1. Oliver Goldsmith**

142. Oliver Goldsmith belonged to which century?
(a) 17th century (b) 18th century
(c) 19th century (d) 20th century

143. Which of the following works has been authored by Goldsmith?
   (a) *The Alchemist* (b) *The Rivals*
   (c) *The Apple Cart* (d) *The Vicar of Wakefield*

144. Which of the following works has not been authored by Goldsmith?
   (a) *The Good Natur'd Man* (b) *She Stoops to Conquer*
   (c) *The Traveller* (d) *The Old Bachelor*

145. Which of the following statements about Goldsmith may be true?
   (a) the comedies of Goldsmith are steeped in sentimentalism
   (b) it was to protest against the flood of sentimentalism which was invading the stage, that Goldsmith put on his comedies
   (c) in all his comedies Goldsmith has satirized a particular political party of his time
   (d) the plays of Goldsmith are problem plays.

146. Goldsmith's *She Stoops to Conquer* was not exactly an original work, it is derived from
   (a) Congreve's *The Way of the World*
   (b) Sheridan's *The Rivals*
   (c) Farquhar's *Beaux Stratagem*
   (d) Richard Steele's *Tender Husband*

147. The complete title of Goldsmith's *She Stoops to Conquer* is
   (a) *She Stoops to Conquer or The Mistakes of a Night*
   (b) *She Stoops to Conquer or The Mistakes of a Morning*
   (c) *She Stoops to Conquer or The Mistakes of an Evening*
   (d) *She Stoops to Conquer or The Mistakes of a Noon*

148. The following lines have been extracted from which of the following works of Goldsmith?

   "All is not gold that glitters/Pleasure seems sweet, but proves a glass of bitters."

   (a) *The Vicar of Wakefield* (b) *She Stoops to Conquer*
   (c) *The Good Natured Man* (d) *The Traveller*

149. In the title of the play *She Stoops to Conquer* 'She' stands for
   (a) Mrs. Hardcastle (b) Miss Kate Hardcastle
   (c) Miss Neville (d) None of these

150. The title of the comedy, *She Stoops to Conquer* is very apt because
   (a) Miss Hardcastle stoops to be a barmaid to conquer Marlowe
   (b) Miss Hardcastle supplied very low quality wine to Marlowe
   (c) Miss Hardcastle debases herself to fight against Marlowe
   (d) Miss Hardcastle is prepared to do anything to possess Marlowe

151. In Goldsmith's *She Stoops to Conquer* Tony Lumpkin is
   (a) the son of Mr. Hardcastle
   (b) the son of Mr. and Mrs. Hardcastle
   (c) the son of Mrs. Hardcastle and her first husband
   (d) the son of Mrs. Hardcastle

152. These lines occur in which work of Goldsmith?
   "Those who have most virtue in their mouths, have least of it in their bosoms".
   (a) *The Vicar of Wakefield* (b) *She Stoops to Conquer*
   (c) *The Good Natured Man* (d) *The Traveller*

153. Marlowe mistakes the house of Mr. Hardcastle for an inn. who played the mischief?
   (a) Mr. Hardcastle himself (b) Tony Lumpkin
   (c) Hastings (d) Diggory

154. Which of the following statements may be true about Oliver Goldsmith?
   (a) Goldsmith promoted sentimental comedy in English literature
   (b) Goldsmith gave a hard blow to sentimental comedy
   (c) the plays of Goldsmith are full of pathos, preaching and meddling sentimentality
   (d) the comedies of Goldsmith are adult comedies as they mainly deal with sex

155. There is a character in *She Stoops to Conquer* who is always playing mischievous and roguish tricks upon others. Who is this character?
(a) Marlowe (b) Tony Lumpkin
(c) Mr. Hardcastle (d) Hastings

156. There is a character in *She Stoops to Conquer* who loves "everything that's old; old friends, old times, old manners, old books, old wine". Who is he?
(a) Marlowe (b) Tony Lumpkin
(c) Mr. Hardcastle (d) Hastings

157. The old friend of Mr. Hardcastle in *She Stoops to Conquer* was
(a) Sir Charles Marlowe (b) Diggory
(c) Hastings (d) Tony Lumpkin

158. In *She Stoops to Conquer* Mrs. Hardcastle wanted Tony Lumpkin to marry
(a) Kate (b) Miss Neville
(c) the barmaid (d) the village girl

159. Sir Charles Marlowe in *She Stoops to Conquer* has proposed a match between young Marlowe and
(a) Miss Neville (b) Kate Hardcastle
(c) Mrs. Hardcastle (d) None of these

160. What is the relationship between Hastings and Marlowe in *She Stoops to Conquer*?
(a) brother (b) friends
(c) father and son (d) uncle and nephew

161. Why did Marlowe mistake Mr. Hardcastle's house for an inn?
(a) it looked like an inn
(b) Tony Lumpkin misguided them into thinking so
(c) the inmates of this house looked like inn keepers
(d) none of these

162. Which of the following statements in the context of *She Stoops to Conquer* is correct?
(a) the old mawkish sentimentality is driven out, and the sense of pathos is supplanted by mirth and delight

(b) like Sheridan's female protagonist Lydia in *The Rivals*, Miss Hardcastle in *She Stoops to Conquer* is a model of sentimentalism
(c) *She Stoops to Conquer* is a typical sentimental comedy
(d) *She Stoops to Conquer* is a bitter satire on the social evils of the time

163. In Goldsmith's *She Stoops to Conquer*, she is to conquer whom?
(a) Tony Lumpkin (b) Mr. Hardcastle
(c) Hastings (d) Marlowe

164. "The Comic Muse long sick is now dying." This line appears in
(a) Prologue to *She Stoops to Conquer*
(b) Preface to *The Good Natured Man*
(c) Act I of *She Stoops to Conquer*
(d) Act II of *The Good Natured Man*

165. "The Mistakes of a Night" is the subtitle of the play
(a) *She Stoops to Conquer* (b) *The Rivals*
(c) *Evelina* (d) None

166. *She Stoops to Conquer* is a comedy by
(a) Goldsmith (b) Butler
(c) Eliot (d) Austen

167. Goldsmith's *The History of Rome* came out in
(a) 1768 (b) 1769 (c) 1800 (d) 1791

168. Whose essays were originally published as "Chinese Letters"?
(a) Addison (b) Steele (c) Goldsmith(d) Johnson

169. "When lovely women stoops to folly" refers to a work by
(a) Goldsmith (b) Sheridan
(c) Shakespeare (d) None

170. Sir William Thomhill (alias Mr. Burchel) figures in
(a) *She Stoops to Conquer* (b) *Amelia*
(c) *The Vicar of Wakefield* (d) None

171. Dr. Primrose is a character in the novel
(a) *Robinson Crusoe* (b) *Pamela*
(c) *Moll Flanders* (d) *The Vicar of Wakefield*

172. Which novel is regarded as a "novel of the family and of the home"?
(a) *Pamela* (b) *Ulysses*
(c) *The Vicar of Wakefield* (d) *Tom Jones*

173. Goldsmith made use of the .......... in his "The Deserted Village".
(a) blank verse (b) sonnet form
(c) heroic couplet (d) none

174. Goldsmith's *The Vicar of Wakefield* is a
(a) play (b) romance (c) essay (d) novel

175. Goldsmith's periodical *Bee* started in
(a) 1762 (b) 1759 (c) 1791 (d) 1756

176. Oliver Goldsmith's *Animated Nature* appeared in
(a) 1771 (b) 1772 (c) 1773 (d) 1774

177. The essay on "The Present State of Polite Learning" against sentimental comedy was written by
(a) Collier (b) Gosson
(c) Addison (d) Goldsmith

178. Goldsmith produced his play *The Good-Natured Man* in
(a) 1762 (b)1763 (c) 1768 (d) 1774

179. *The Vicar of Wakefield*, written in 1762, was published in
(a) 1778 (b) 1764 (c) 1770 (d) 1776

**2. Richard Sheridan**

180. Sheridan belonged to
(a) medieval period (b) late 18th century
(c) early 20th century (d) Elizabethan period

181. The plays of which of the following dramatists can be called anti-sentimental comedy?
(a) G.B. Shaw (b) Shakespeare
(c) Sheridan (d) Congreve

182. Which of the following statements about Sheridan is true?
(a) Sheridan promoted sentimental comedy
(b) Sheridan reacted against the sentimental comedy
(c) the plays of Sheridan carry the reader away in a fanciful world away from reality
(d) the plays of Sheridan are problem plays

183. Sheridan is famous for his
(a) pastorals (b) tragedies (c) comedies (d) allegories

184. Which of the following plays is not written by Sheridan?
(a) *The Rivals* (b) *The School for Scandal*
(c) *The Critics* (d) *She Stoops to Conquer*

185. Which of the following plays is written by Sheridan?
(a) *The Rivals* (b) *The Good Natured Man*
(c) *The Old Bachelor* (d) *Arms and the Man*

186. Which of the following is an opera?
(a) *The Rivals* (b) *The School for Scandal*
(c) *The Critic* (d) *The Duenna*

187. Who was Lady Sneerwell in *The School for Scandal*?
(a) mother of Mr. Snake (b) a poor woman
(c) a religious and kind-hearted woman (d) a rich widow and the chief of the scandal group

188. Who is the agent of Lady Sneerwell in *The School for Scandal*, who spreads the scandals?
(a) Mr. Snake (b) Joseph
(c) Maria (d) None of these

189. Name the character who has been "the cause of six matches being broken off and three sons disinherited, four forced elopements, and as many close confinements, nine separate maintenances and two divorces".
(a) Lady Sneerwell (b) Mrs. Clackit
(c) Mr. Snake (d) None of these

190. Who has acted as a guardian to two young men, Joseph and Charles, after their father's death?
(a) Rawley (b) Sir Oliver
(c) Sir Peter Teazle (d) None of these

191. Why did Joseph want to marry Mary?
   (a) he loved her very much
   (b) she was very beautiful and virtuous
   (c) Mary loved Joseph
   (d) she was the only heiress of a considerable wealth

192. Name the scandal monger who was responsible for the following scandals, Miss Gadabout has eloped with Sir Fligue, Miss Prim has committed an indiscretion and eloped with her dancing master?
   (a) Mrs. Candour (b) Lady Sneerwell
   (c) Lady Teazle (d) None of these

193. Name the character in *The School for Scandal* who was deaf and who asked "Has Miss Piper had Twins"?
   (a) Mrs. Clackit (b) Mrs. Candour
   (c) Lady Dundizzy (d) None of these

194. Who is the character in *The School for Scandal*, whom Sheridan has presented as a poet?
   (a) Benjamin Backbite (b) Charles
   (c) Crabtru (d) None of these

195. In *The School for Scandal*, Sir Peter Teazle married a young girl from countryside.What were the reasons for this?
   (a) he hated the ways of the society of London
   (b) he loved that young woman
   (c) he was neglected by town's women
   (d) he was very old and none wanted to marry him

196. Why did Sir Oliver not inform his nephews, Joseph and Charles about his arrival?
   (a) he wanted to give them a surprise
   (b) he wanted to examine their conduct
   (c) Joseph and Charles did not want to see him
   (d) none of these

197. Who has said this: 'though she was brought up in the countryside she knows that women of fashion in London are accountable to nobody after they are married'?
   (a) Maria (b) Lady Teazle
   (c) Lady Sneerwell (d) None of these

198. Sir Benjamin says that after she has finished painting her face, "She joins it so badly to the neck that she looks like a mended statue, in which the connoisseur sees at once that the head's modern, though the trunk's antique". Who is being described?
(a) Maria (b) Lady Teazle
(c) Lady Sneerwell (d) Mrs. Ochre

199. "Nine out of ten of the malicious inventions are founded on some ridiculous misinterpretation." Who said it in Sheridan's *The School for Scandal*?
(a) Sir Peter Teazle (b) Sir Oliver
(c) Benjamin Backbite (d) None of these

200. Who is the beloved of Charles in Sheridan's *The School for Abuse*?
(a) Lady Teazle (b) Maria
(c) Lady Sneerwell (d) None of these

201. In Sheridan's *The School for Scandal*, a character has said about Charles that he had nothing against him just because he was extravagant. If his nephew did not do anything false or mean, he would make good the money he had lost. Who says this about Charles?
(a) Sir Peter (b) Joseph
(c) Sir Oliver (d) None of these

202. Rowley suggests that he should go to his nephews as Stanley, then he would be able to judge their real nature. In *The School for Scandal*, who is 'he'?
(a) Joseph (b) Sir Benjamin
(c) Sir Peter (d) Sir Oliver

203. In *The School for Scandal*, who goes to Charles' house posing as Mr. Premium?
(a) Sir Oliver (b) Joseph
(c) Rowley (d) None of these

204. To whom does Charles ask to be the auctioneer in the sale of the paintings of his ancestors?
(a) Sir Harry Bumber (b) Joseph
(c) Careless (d) None of these

205. Which scene is known as the 'screen scene' in *The School for Scandal*?
   (a) Act I, Scene III (b) Act II, Scene III
   (c) Act IV, Scene III (d) Act III, Scene III

206. Why was Joseph so worried in Act IV, Scene III of *The School for Scandal*?
   (a) he was seriously ill (b) he had lost everything
   (c) Maria refused him to marry (d) lady Teazle had not come

207. Who disguised himself as Mr. Stanley?
   (a) Rowley (b) Sir Oliver
   (c) Joseph (d) None of these

208. "When an old bachelor marries a young wife, he deserves, no, the crime carries its punishment along with it." In this quotation who is this 'old bachelor'?
   (a) Sir Peter Teazle (b) Joseph
   (c) Charles (d) Benjamin Backbite

209. What is the name of Charles' Uncle who had fought in all the wars fought by the Duke of Marlborough?
   (a) Sir Oliver (b) Richard Raveline
   (c) Sir Harry Bumper (d) None of these

210. The rivalry in Sheridan's *The Rivals* is related to
   (a) love (b) wealth
   (c) pride (d) inheritance

211. Which of the following statements in Sheridan's *The Rivals* may be true?
   (a) Lydia herself is poor but she wants to marry a rich man
   (b) Lydia herself is rich but she wants to marry a poor man
   (c) Lydia is prepared to marry the boy chosen for her by her aunt
   (d) None of these

212. Which of the following characters in Sheridan's *The Rivals* is fond of reading sentimental novels?
   (a) Captain Absolute (b) Lydia
   (c) Julia (d) Faulkland

213. The rivals in Sheridan's *The Rivals* are
(a) Captain Absolute and Ensign Beverley
(b) Captain Absolute and Faulkland
(c) Julia and Lydia
(d) Bob Acres and Faulkland

214. In Sheridan's *The Rivals* Mrs. Malaprop is in love with which of the following characters?
(a) Faulkland (b) Captain Absolute
(c) Sir Lucius O'Trigger (d) Bob Acres

215. In Sheridans's *The Rivals* who is the aunt of Lydia?
(a) Julia (b) Lucy
(c) Millamant (d) Mrs. Malaprop

216. Which of the following statements may be true in the context of Sheridan's *The Rivals*?
(a) Captain was the nephew of Sir Anthony Absolute
(b) Captain Absolute and Faulkland are rivals in love
(c) Captain Absolute and Ensign Beverley are one and the same person
(d) None of these

217. Mrs. Malaprop in Sheridan's *The Rivals* is a comic character, as
(a) she has excessive greed for wealth
(b) she is too fashionable
(c) she is old yet the flame of love is burning in her heart
(d) none of these

218. In Sheridan's *The Rivals* Sir Anthony Absolute wants his son Captain Absolute to marry which of the following characters?
(a) Julia (b) Lucy
(c) Lydia (d) None of these

219. In Sheridan's *The Rivals*, when Lydia comes to know that her lover was the son of a rich man,
(a) she felt very happy (b) she was very disappointed
(c) she was neutral (d) she did not believe it

220. Sheridan published his play *The Duenna* in the year
(a) 1770 (b) 1774 (c) 1775 (d) none

221. *Count Basil* appeard in the year
(a) 1781 (b) 1782 (c) 1798 (d) 1799

222. Which is not a play by Sheridan?
(a) *The Rivals* (b) *The Duenna*
(c) *Tragedy Rehearsed* (d) *Irene*

223. Who has been called 'a dramatic star of the first magnitude'?
(a) G.B. Shaw (b) Shakespeare
(c) Ibsen (d) Sheridan

224. Sheridan's play *The School for Scandal* came out in
(a) 1783 (b) 1780 (c) 1777 (d) 1775

225. "Malapropism" is coined after a character in
(a) *The Way of the World* (b) *Love of Love*
(d) *The Rivals* (d) None

226. The character, Mrs. Malaprop was created by
(a) Samuel Johnson (b) William Wycherey
(c) Richard Sheridan (d) None of these

227. Sheridan's play *The Rivals* came out in
(a) 1770 (b) 1775 (c) 1781 (d) 1784

228. Who has written *The School for Scandal*?
(a) Sheridan (b) Swift
(c) Smollett (d) Richardson

229. In Sheridan's play *The School for Scandal*, Charles Surface is in love with
(a) Sady Teazle (b) Maria
(c) Mrs. Candour (d) None

230. Sheridan's farce-play *St. Patrick's Day* appeared in
(a) 1770 (b) 1775 (c) 1780 (d) 1785

## ANSWERS

### Unit A

| | | | | | | | |
|---|---|---|---|---|---|---|---|
| 1. | (a) | 2. | (b) | 3. | (a) | 4. | (c) |
| 5. | (c) | 6. | (b) | 7. | (c) | 8. | (b) |
| 9. | (d) | 10. | (c) | | | | |

## Unit B

| | | | | | | | |
|---|---|---|---|---|---|---|---|
| 11. | (a) | 12. | (d) | 13. | (a) | 14. | (b) |
| 15. | (b) | 16. | (a) | 17. | (a) | 18. | (d) |
| 19. | (b) | 20. | (b) | 21. | (b) | 22. | (b) |
| 23. | (c) | 24. | (c) | 25. | (a) | 26. | (c) |
| 27. | (a) | 28. | (c) | 29. | (a) | 30. | (b) |
| 31. | (a) | 32. | (a) | 33. | (a) | 34. | (b) |
| 35. | (b) | 36. | (b) | 37. | (a) | 38. | (c) |
| 39. | (a) | 40. | (b) | 41. | (a) | 42. | (c) |
| 43. | (a) | 44. | (d) | 45. | (d) | 46. | (c) |
| 47. | (d) | 48. | (c) | 49. | (c) | 50. | (b) |
| 51. | (b) | 52. | (c) | 53. | (a) | 54. | (c) |
| 55. | (a) | 56. | (a) | 57. | (b) | 58. | (b) |
| 59. | (d) | 60. | (b) | 61. | (c) | 62. | (d) |

## Unit C

| | | | | | | | |
|---|---|---|---|---|---|---|---|
| 63. | (b) | 64. | (a) | 65. | (d) | 66. | (b) |
| 67. | (b) | 68. | (c) | 69. | (b) | 70. | (b) |
| 71. | (c) | 72. | (b) | 73. | (b) | 74. | (c) |
| 75. | (b) | | | | | | |

## Unit D

| | | | | | | | |
|---|---|---|---|---|---|---|---|
| 76. | (c) | 77. | (a) | 78. | (c) | 79. | (b) |
| 80. | (d) | 81. | (a) | 82. | (c) | 83. | (b) |
| 84. | (c) | 85. | (d) | 86. | (c) | 87. | (c) |
| 88. | (d) | 89. | (c) | 90. | (b) | 91. | (c) |

## Unit E

| | | | | | | | |
|---|---|---|---|---|---|---|---|
| 92. | (b) | 93. | (c) | 94. | (a) | 95. | (d) |
| 96. | (c) | 97. | (d) | 98. | (d) | 99. | (a) |
| 100. | (a) | 101. | (d) | 102. | (c) | 103. | (b) |
| 104. | (b) | 105. | (a) | 106. | (b) | 107. | (c) |
| 108. | (a) | 109. | (b) | 110. | (a) | 111. | (a) |
| 112. | (b) | 113. | (c) | 114. | (a) | 115. | (a) |

116. (a) 117. (a) 118. (c) 119. (a)
120. (a) 121. (a) 122. (a) 123. (c)
124. (b) 125. (d) 126. (b) 127. (a)
128. (c) 129. (a) 130. (a) 131. (a)
132. (d) 133. (c) 134. (b) 135. (a)
136. (a) 137. (b) 138. (a) 139. (c)
140. (a) 141. (a)

## Unit F

142. (b) 143. (d) 144. (d) 145. (b)
146. (c) 147. (a) 148. (b) 149. (b)
150. (a) 151. (c) 152. (b) 153. (b)
154. (b) 155. (b) 156. (c) 157. (a)
158. (b) 159. (b) 160. (b) 161. (b)
162. (a) 163. (d) 164. (a) 165. (a)
166. (a) 167. (b) 168. (c) 169. (a)
170. (c) 171. (d) 172. (c) 173. (c)
174. (d) 175. (b) 176. (d) 177. (d)
178. (c) 179. (d) 180. (b) 181. (c)
182. (b) 183. (c) 184. (d) 185. (a)
186. (d) 187. (d) 188. (a) 189. (b)
190. (c) 191. (d) 192. (a) 193. (b)
194. (a) 195. (a) 196. (b) 197. (b)
198. (d) 199. (a) 200. (b) 201. (c)
202. (d) 203. (a) 204. (c) 205. (c)
206. (d) 207. (b) 208. (a) 209. (b)
210. (a) 211. (b) 212. (b) 213. (a)
214. (c) 215. (d) 216. (c) 217. (c)
218. (c) 219. (b) 220. (c) 221. (c)
222. (d) 223. (d) 224. (c) 225. (d)
226. (c) 227. (b) 228. (a) 229. (b)
230. (b)

# Precursors of Romanticism (1770–1798)

# 6

## UNIT A: HISTORICAL PERSPECTIVE AND BACKGROUND

1. *The Wealth of Nations* is a prose work on economics, written by
   (a) Addison (b) Gibbon
   (c) Burke (d) Adam Smith
2. *Doughlas* is a tragedy by
   (a) Collins (b) Dr. Johnson
   (c) John Home (d) None
3. Who is considered to be the first of the women novelists?
   (a) Jane Austen (b) Virginia Woolf
   (c) George Eliot (d) F. Burney
4. "Timon" is a poem by
   (a) Pope (b) Goldsmith
   (c) Rochester (d) Smart
5. Who said: "Man is born free but everywhere he is in chains"?
   (a) J.J. Rousseau (b) Francis Bacon
   (c) Socrates (d) E. Burke
6. The concept of 'Royal divine right' was supported by
   (a) Tory party (b) Whig party
   (c) Dryden (d) None
7. The eighteenth century in English literature is also called
   (a) the age of excessive passion (b) the age of sentimentalism
   (c) the age of puritanism (d) the age of reason

8. "Song to David" is a poem by
   (a) Pope (b) Gay
   (c) Matthew Prior (d) C. Smart
9. "The Spleen" is a
   (a) short story (b) essay
   (c) play (d) pindaric ode
10. Which age is considered to be the golden age of political pamphleteering?
    (a) Augustan (b) Victorian
    (c) Restoration (d) None
11. *Evelina* is a novel by
    (a) Fielding (b) Burney (c) Austen (d) G. Eliot
12. Which one of the following is a characteristic of the Augustan Age?
    (a) moderation (b) tolerance
    (c) common sense (d) all of these
13. Ulysses, the hero of Homer's *Odyssey*, was the king of
    (a) Ithaca (b) Rome (c) Athens (d) Sparta
14. The Scribbler's Club was an association of
    (a) Whig wits (b) Tory wits
    (c) Pope and Swift (d) None
15. *The Biography of Johnson* was written by
    (a) James Boswell (b) Goldsmith
    (c) Sheridan (d) George Eliot
16. Which poem is known as a 'rhymed gazette'?
    (a) "The Campaign" (b) "The Wasteland"
    (c) "London" (d) None
17. *The Critic, a Tragedy Rehearsed* is a
    (a) sentimental comedy (b) restoration tragedy
    (c) tragedy (d) farce
18. Matthew Prior's *Alma* is an imitation of
    (a) *Paradise Lost* (b) *Emma*
    (c) *Hudibras* (d) None

19. Who wrote *The Moss House*, a book for children?
    (a) Agnes Strickland (b) Swift
    (c) Blake (d) Lamb
20. *The Sick Lady Cure* is a comedy by
    (a) Cibber (b) Sheridan
    (c) Steele (d) None
21. Thomas used ... in his *The Castle of Indolence.*
    (a) spenserian stanza (b) terza rima
    (c) heroic couplets (d) Chaucerian stanza
22. *The Invisible Man* is a picaresque novel by
    (a) Ralph Ellison (b) Thomas Mann
    (c) Thackeray (d) Fielding
23. *Jack of Newbury* is a novel about
    (a) washerman (b) a farmer
    (c) the shoemaker's trade (d) the weaver's craft
24. *The Gentle Craft* is about
    (a) washerman (b) the shoemaker's trade
    (c) the weaver's craft (d) the art of farming
25. John Gay's "Black-eyed Susan" is a
    (a) play (b) novel
    (c) short-story (d) ballad
26. The hero of the poem "The Campaign" is
    (a) Steele (b) Neander
    (c) Marlborough (d) None
27. *Love's Last Shift* is a Sentimental comedy by
    (a) Cibber (b) Collins (c) Steele (d) Goldsmith
28. *The Vindication of the Rights of Women* is a milestone in the history of
    (a) Neo-Classicism (b) Feminism
    (c) Logism (d) Romanticism
29. J.J. Rousseau died in
    (a) 1778 (b) 1775 (c)1766 (d)1763
30. *The Natural History of Selborne* was written by
    (a) Adam Smith (b) William Paley
    (c) Gilbert White (d) None

31. *The Poetical Sketches* came out in
    (a) 1785 (b) 1786 (c) 1783 (d) none
32. Which one of the following is a parody of the style and ideas of Bolingbroke?
    (a) *The Life of Samuel Johnson* (b) *A Vindication of Natural Society*
    (c) *Cecilia* (d) None
33. *Fingal and Temora* were written by
    (a) Macpherson (b) Pope
    (c) Crabbe (d) None
34. Who poisoned himself with arsenic when he was only eighteen?
    (a) Thomas Chatterson (b) Macpherson
    (c) Burns (d) None
35. The freedom of the press was restored in the year
    (a) 1682 (b) 1701 (c) 1712 (d) 1721
36. *The Times* acquired this name in 1788. What was its name earlier?
    (a) *The Telegraph* (b) *Tatler*
    (c) *Sunday Mirror* (d) *Daily Universal Register*
37. The Pre-Romantics were influenced by the Middle Ages.
    (a) yes (b) no (c) may be (d) none
38. The Neo-classical Age in English Literature follows the models of
    (a) Anglo-Saxon Literature (b) Greek Literature
    (c) The Elizabethan Literature (d) Roman Literature
39. The Circulating Libraries were popular during
    (a) the 19th century (b) the 18th century
    (c) the 17th century (d) none
40. Whig party was in favour of
    (a) purposelessness (b) love at first sight
    (c) dictatorship (d) pre-eminence of personal freedom

41. The year 1776 was associated with
    (a) American independence (b) the War of the Roses
    (c) invention of steam engine (d) none
42. James II ascended the throne after
    (a) James I (b) Charles I
    (c) Charles II (d) Cromwell
43. The Sentimental comedy was a reaction against the
    (a) renaissance (b) romantic comedies
    (c) comedy of manners (d) none
44. *The Married Philosopher* is a sentimental comedy by
    (a) Dryden (b) Johnson
    (c) Sheridan (d) John Kelly
45. *Vathak* is a fiction by
    (a) Smollett (b) Fielding
    (c) William Beckford (d) M. G. Lewis
46. Who pictured Boswell as being a knavish buffoon?
    (a) Arnold (b) Ruskin
    (c)Macaulay (d) Rossetti
47. Which one of the following was not written by Matthew Prior?
    (a) *The Chameleon* (b) *The Thief and the Cordelier*
    (c) *To Chloe* (d) *Alma*
48. *Don Quixote* is a work by
    (a) Boccaccio (b) Cervantes
    (c) Dante (d) Rossetti
49. *The Mysteries of Udalpho* is a
    (a) historical novel (b) Picaresque novel
    (c) Gothic novel (d) domestic novel
50. *The Rights of Man* was written by
    (a) Coleridge (b) Dr. Johnson
    (c) Thomas Paine (d) Robert Clive
51. *The Agony and The Esctasy* is a biography of
    (a) Michelangelo (b) Galsworthy
    (c) Poe (d) Emerson

52. *The Castle of Indolence* was written by
    (a) William Collins (b) Oliver Goldsmith
    (c) James Thomson (d) None

## UNIT B: POETRY

### 1. William Cowper

53. "The Definition of Love" is a poem by
    (a) Shakespeare (b) Donne
    (c) William Cowper (d) Vaughan
54. "The Task" is a poem by
    (a) Gray (b) Cowper
    (c) Goldsmith (d) Crabbe
55. "The Liberty" appeared in
    (a) 1781 (b) 1768 (c) 1771 (d) 1784
56. "The Castaway" was written by
    (a) William Cowper (b) Crabbe
    (c) Blake (d) None
57. Who is the writer of "God made the country and man made the town"?
    (a) George Crabbe (b) Gray
    (c) William Cowper (d) James Thomson
58. William Cowper "John Gilpin" is a burlesque by
    (a) Collins (b) Gray (c) Cowper (d) Goldsmith
59. William Cowper's last poem is
    (a) "God Made the Country" (b) "The Castaway"
    (c) "The Task" (d) "John Gilpin"

## UNIT C: PRE-ROMANTIC NOVEL

### 1. Henry Mackenzie

60. Who was known as "the man of feeling"?
    (a) Henry Mackenzie (b) Walpole
    (c) Sterne (d) None

61. *The Man of Feeling* is a work by
    (a) Sterne (b) Walpole
    (c) Mackenzie (d) None
62. Henry Mackenzie died in the year
    (a) 1831 (b) 1832 (c) 1835 (d) 1840

**2. Horace Walpole**

63. Who is regarded as the father of the Gothic novels?
    (a) Walpole (b) Burke (c) Boswell (d) None
64. Who is the author of *Castle of Otranto*?
    (a) Horace Walpole (b) Clara Reeve
    (c) Radcliffe (d) M. G. Lewis
65. Horace Walpole is credited with the starting of a new tradition named
    (a) Gothic (b) Science Fiction
    (c) Both (d) None

**3. Mrs. Ann Radcliffe**

66. Mrs. Radcliffe's *Mysteries of Udolpho* came out in the year
    (a) 1794 (b) 1790 (c)1787 (d) 1770
67. Which of the following books was written by Mrs. Anne Radcliffe?
    (a) *A Sicilian Romance* (b) *The Romance of the Forest*
    (c) *The Mysteries of Udolpho* (d) All of these

## UNIT D: EDWARD GIBBON

68. In the *Memories* we find an interesting reflection of whose personality?
    (a) Edward Gibbon (b) Edmund Burke
    (c) Dr. Johnson (d) Robert Burns
69. Who said this? "I sighed as a lover but I obeyed as a son".
    (a) William Blake (b) Edward Gibbon
    (c) Robert Burns (d) None of the above

70. *The Decline and Fall of the Roman Empire* was published in
    (a) 1775 (b) 1776 (c) 1777 (d) 1778
71. Gibbon's history begins with the reign of Trozan in A.D. 98 and ends with the fall of the Byzantine empire in
    (a) 1451 (b) 1452 (c) 1453 (d) 1454
72. Which writer has given us the first history in English?
    (a) Edward Gibbon (b) Dr Johnson
    (c) William Blake (d) Edmund Burke
73. Gibbon's *Memories* appeared in the year
    (a) 1770 (b) 1776 (c) 1788 (d) 1796
74. Gibbon's first book *A History of Switzerland* appeared in
    (a) 1779 (b) 1760 (c) 1770 (d) 1780

## UNIT E: JANE AUSTEN

75. How many novels did Jane Austen write?
    (a) 6 (b) 7 (c) 8 (d) 9
76. *Pride and Prejudice* was published in
    (a) 1813 (b) 1810 (c) 1806 (d) 1801
77. *Mansfield Park* is a novel written by
    (a) Austen (b) Edgeworth
    (c) J. Galt (d) Scott
78. Jane Austen's subject matter for her novels is
    (a) human nature (b) frustration
    (c) revenge (d) none
79. "It is a truth universally acknowledged that a single man's possession of a good fortune must be in want of a wife." In which novel of Austen does this sentence occur?
    (a) *Pride and Prejudice* (b) *Sense and Sensibility*
    (c) *Emma* (d) *Persuasion*
80. Harriet Smith is a character in the novel
    (a) *Mansfield Park* (b) *Hard Times*
    (c) *Emma* (d) *Pamela*

81. Austen's *Northanger Abbey* was published in
(a) 1812 (b) 1818 (c) 1823 (d) 1832

82. Frank Churcill is a character in the novel
(a) *Emma* (b) *Adam Bede*
(c) *Mansfield Park* (d) *Pamela*

## UNIT F: REALISTIC POETRY

### 1. George Crabbe

83. George Crabbe was born in the year
(a) 1751 (b) 1752 (c) 1753 (d) 1754

84. Which poet is a fine combination of realism and romanticism?
(a) George Crabbe (b) James Thomson
(c) William Collins (d) Thomas Percy

85. Which poem of George Crabbe echoes Fielding's coarse vigour and Dryden's precision?
(a) "The Village" (b) "The Parish Register"
(c) "The Borough" (d) "Tales in Verse"

86. Crabbe's poems are written in
(a) triplets (b) quatrains
(c) couplets (d) sextets

87. "The Village" is a poem composed by
(a) George Crabbe (b) James Thoma
(c) Goldsmith (d) William Collins

## UNIT G: PRE-ROMANTIC POETRY

### 1. Robert Burns

88. *The Jolly Beggars* is a sequence of ballads by
(a) Burns (b) Byron (c) Buxton (d) Gay

89. Robert Burns was born in 1759 and he died in
(a) 1795 (b) 1861 (c) 1814 (d) 1796

90. "Tom O'Shanter" was written by
(a) Crabbe (b) Fielding (c) Burns (d) None

91. Who wrote, "My Love is like a Red Red Rose"?
    (a) Robert Burns (b) William Shakespeare
    (c) William Wordsworth (d) None

92. "To a Mountain Daisy" is a poem composed by
    (a) Robert Burns (b) Blake
    (c) Gray (d) Collins

**2. William Blake**

93. Which of the following is not a poetical work of William Blake?
    (a) *Songs of Experience* (b) *Songs of Innocence*
    (c) *Poetical Sketches* (d) *The Parish Register*

94. Blake's *Songs of Innocence* is about?
    (a) the pastoral world (b) the joys of childhood
    (c) both (d) none

95. "Pity would be no more, if we did not make somebody poor...."
    Who wrote this line?
    (a) Wordsworth (b) Coleridge
    (c) Shelley (d) Blake

96. In which of his works, Blake denounced the subordination of women?
    (a) *Songs of Innocence* (b) *The Book of Urizen*
    (c) *Songs of Experience* (d) *Visions of the Daughters of Abion*

97. Blake printed his own works by a method devised by himself
    (a) true (b) false
    (c) perhaps (d) wooden blocks

98. "The French Revolution" is a poem by
    (a) Blake (b) Gray (c) Johnson (d) None

99. "The Task" appeared in
    (a) 1781 (b) 1774 (c) 1768 (d) 1785

100. Blake's *The Book of Urizen* is about
    (a) human liberation (b) the origin of evil
    (c) the art of writing (d) none

101. Blake's *Songs of Experience* deals with
   (a) sorrow and suffering
   (b) social and religious oppression
   (c) experience of the hard realities of sorrow and suffering
   (d) life of labour

102. "Holy Thursday" is a poem by
   (a) Blake (b) Cowper (c) Arnold (d) Pope

103. Who does not belong to "Satanic school of criticism"?
   (a) Yeats (b) Auden (c) Eliot (d) Blake

104. Who made the cryptic remark that "Milton was of the Devil's Party without knowing it"?
   (a) Cowper
   (b) Blake
   (c) Arnold
   (d) Dr. Johnson

105. Who was of the view: "Without contraries there is no progression"?
   (a) Arnold (b) Addison (c) Blake (d) Swift

## ANSWERS

### Unit A

| | | | | | | | |
|---|---|---|---|---|---|---|---|
| 1. | (d) | 2. | (c) | 3. | (d) | 4. | (c) |
| 5. | (a) | 6. | (a) | 7. | (d) | 8. | (d) |
| 9. | (d) | 10. | (a) | 11. | (b) | 12. | (d) |
| 13. | (a) | 14. | (b) | 15. | (a) | 16. | (a) |
| 17. | (d) | 18. | (c) | 19. | (a) | 20. | (a) |
| 21. | (a) | 22. | (a) | 23. | (d) | 24. | (b) |
| 25. | (d) | 26. | (c) | 27. | (a) | 28. | (b) |
| 29. | (a) | 30. | (c) | 31. | (c) | 32. | (b) |
| 33. | (a) | 34. | (a) | 35. | (a) | 36. | (d) |
| 37. | (a) | 38. | (d) | 39. | (b) | 40. | (d) |
| 41. | (a) | 42. | (c) | 43. | (c) | 44. | (d) |
| 45. | (c) | 46. | (c) | 47. | (d) | 48. | (b) |
| 49. | (c) | 50. | (c) | 51. | (a) | 52. | (c) |

### Unit B

| | | | |
|---|---|---|---|
| 53. (c) | 54. (b) | 55. (a) | 56. (a) |
| 57. (c) | 58. (c) | 59. (b) | |

### Unit C

| | | | |
|---|---|---|---|
| 60. (a) | 61. (c) | 62. (a) | 63. (a) |
| 64. (a) | 65. (a) | 66. (a) | 67. (d) |

### Unit D

| | | | |
|---|---|---|---|
| 68. (a) | 69. (b) | 70. (b) | 71. (c) |
| 72. (a) | 73. (d) | 74. (c) | |

### Unit E

| | | | |
|---|---|---|---|
| 75. (a) | 76. (a) | 77. (a) | 78. (a) |
| 79. (c) | 80. (c) | 81. (b) | 82. (a) |

### Unit F

| | | | |
|---|---|---|---|
| 83. (d) | 84. (a) | 85. (a) | 86. (c) |
| 87. (a) | | | |

### Unit G

| | | | |
|---|---|---|---|
| 88. (a) | 89. (d) | 90. (c) | 91. (a) |
| 92. (a) | 93. (d) | 94. (c) | 95. (d) |
| 96. (d) | 97. (a) | 98. (a) | 99. (a) |
| 100. (b) | 101. (c) | 102. (a) | 103. (d) |
| 104. (b) | 105. (c) | | |

# The Romantic Period (1798–1832)

# 7

## UNIT A: HISTORICAL PERSPECTIVE AND BACKGROUND

1. The *Borderers* is a
   (a) comedy (b) novel
   (c) epic (d) blank verse tragedy
2. Peterloo massacre took place in
   (a) 1891 (b) 1890 (c) 1819 (d) 1765
3. Theodore Watts Duntan gives the title "The Renaissance of Wonder" to the
   (a) Elizabethan Age (b) Restoration Age
   (c) Romantic Age (d) None
4. *The Battle of Marathon* was written by
   (a) Arnold (b) Anne Bronte
   (c) Elizabeth Barret (d) Tennyson
5. Who gave the slogan "back to nature"?
   (a) Rousseau (b) Cowper
   (c) Wordsworth (d) Pope
6. Cobbett's *Political Register* appeared in
   (a) 1800 (b) 1802 (c) 1793 (d) 1811
7. The old French word, 'Romans,' from which the word "Romantic" was derived, means
   (a) a vernacular language descended (b) a group of tribes from Latin
   (c) both (a) and (b) (d) none of these

8. The Romantics' view of religion is that
   (a) they looked towards the church for answers
   (b) Christianity failed to be satisfactory
   (c) they searched personally for the spiritual truth outside religion
   (d) both b and c
9. The French Revolution took place in
   (a) 1778 (b) 1789 (c) 1776 (d) 1767
10. Nature for the Romantics is
    (a) independence of man (b) nature is the setting of man
    (c) something that is needed for his fulfilment (d) all these three
11. Peninsular War began in
    (a) 1798 (b) 1808 (c) 1882 (d) 1782
12. *Life of Walter Scott* was written by
    (a) John Lockhart (b) Wordsworth
    (c) Southey (d) Mary Lamb
13. *The Absentee* is the best novel by
    (a) Edgeworth (b) Ferrier
    (c) Austen (d) F. Burney
14. *The Westminster Review* came out in the year
    (a) 1830 (b) 1834 (c) 1824 (d) 1817
15. Corneille is the name of a
    (a) French dramatist (b) Italian essayist
    (c) Greek historian (d) Spanish poet
16. Who wrote *The Four Ages of Poetry*?
    (a) Shelley (b) Peacock (c) Eliot (d) Collins
17. Walter Landor's *Count Julian* is a
    (a) poem (b) essay (c) drama (d) memoir
18. *The Four Ages of Poetry* was an attack on
    (a) romanticism (b) neo-classicism
    (c) Elizabethan poetry (d) Victorian age
19. *The Old English Baron* is a novel by
    (a) Lewis (b) Walpole
    (c) Clara Reeve (d) Mrs. Shelley

20. Who is the author of *Heroic Idylls?*
    (a) W.S. Landor (b) L. Hunt
    (c) W. Scott (d) W. Cobbett
21. *Edinburgh Review* was founded in
    (a) 1809 (b) 1802 (c) 1817 (d) 1819
22. *Punch* was produced by
    (a) Thomas Hood (b) Leigh Hunt
    (c) Robert Southey (d) John Keats
23. *John Woodwil* came out in the year
    (a) 1801 (b) 1807 (c) 1817 (d) 1822
24. Sidney Smith's *Wit and Wisdom* came out in
    (a) 1850 (b) 1857 (c) 1860 (d) 1863
25. Thomas Moore's *Lalla Rookh* is a/an
    (a) play (b) essay
    (c) short story (d) oriental romance
26. Which among the following was not written by John Clare?
    (a) *The Village Minstrel* (b) *The Rural Muse*
    (c) *Punch* (d) *The Shepherd's Calender*
27. *Tales from Shakespeare* came out in the year
    (a) 1801 (b) 1802 (c) 1804 (d) 1807
28. *The Road to Ruin* is a sentimental comedy by
    (a) Thomas Holcraft (b) Sheridan
    (c) Goldsmith (d) Cumberland
29. *Ancient Spanish Ballads* was produced by
    (a) L. Hunt (b) De Quincey
    (c) Southey (d) Lokhant
30. *Recess* was written by
    (a) Sophia Lee (b) Walpole
    (c) Dickens (d) Scott
31. Mason wrote an elegy "In a Churchyard in South Wales" in
    (a) 1778 (b) 1777 (c) 1724 (d) 1787

32. Thomas Holcraft died in
    (a) 1819 (b) 1810 (c) 1818 (d) 1809
33. The quality of self-effacement is called
    (a) hedonism (b) neologism
    (c) baroque (d) negative capability
34. Who postulated the concept of 'noble savage'?
    (a) Southey (b) Blake
    (c) Hazlitt (d) Rousseau
35. *Rejected Addresses* was written by
    (a) J. Smith (b) Horace Smith
    (c) both a & b (d) none of the above
36. Who remarked "Literature is the humanisation of the whole world"?
    (a) A.C. Ward (b) Goethe
    (c) Aristotle (d) Arnold
37. When was the Reform Bill passed?
    (a) 1837 (b) 1845 (c) 1849 (d) 1832
38. Who regarded Waverly as one of the best things that has been written?
    (a) Gaskell (b) Goethe
    (c) Godwin (d) Thackeray
39. Who wrote "Magnificence"?
    (a) Shelley (b) Skelton (c) Keats (d) Dryden
40. *Cloudesley* is a weak novel by
    (a) Anne Radcliffe (b) Clara Reeve
    (c) Jane Austen (d) Godwin
41. Epistle I of *An Essay on Man* deals with
    (a) importance (b) religion
    (c) emotional crime (d) sincere man
42. "Say not, the Struggle nought Availeth" is a poem by
    (a) L. Hunt (b) A.H. Clough
    (c) Browning (d) Shakespeare
43. Blackwood's Magazine came out in
    (a) 1800 (b) 1802 (c) 1811 (d) 1817

44. Who says, "The romantic movement was the expression of individual genius rather than the established rules"?
(a) W.J. Long (b) Charles Lamb
(c) Walter Pater (d) John Keats

45. *Valerius* is a novel by
(a) Galt (b) Austen
(c) Peacock (d) J.G. Lockhart

46. Thomas Love Peacock died in the year
(a) 1886 (b) 1866 (c) 1824 (d) 1830

47. *Rural Rides* came out in the year
(a) 1832 (b) 1831 (c) 1830 (d) 1801

48. "The Rural Muse" (1835) is a poem by
(a) Thomas Hood (b) John Clare
(c) Shelley (d) Keats

## UNIT B: THE FIRST GENERATION OF ROMANTIC POETS

### 1. William Wordsworth

49. Who said, "Nature never did betray/The heart that loved her"?
(a) Byron (b) Coleridge
(c) Wordsworth (d) None of these

50. *The Prelude* has been divided into .......... books.
(a) 14 (b) 16 (c) 18 (d) 20

51. *The Lyrical Ballads* was written by
(a) Wordsworth (b) Coleridge
(c) both (d) None

52. Wordsworth died in
(a) 1840 (b) 1815 (c) 1850 (d) 1860

53. Who is the composer of Lucy poems?
(a) Shelley (b) Wordsworth
(c) Shakespeare (d) None of these

54. How many poems of Wordsworth are included in the *Lyrical Ballads*?
(a) 4 (b) 12 (c) 17 (d) 19

55. Wordsworth was made the "Poet Laureate" in
(a) 1850 (b) 1843 (c) 1831 (d) 1837

56. *The Prelude* completed in 1805 but was published in
(a) 1850 (b) 1840 (c) 1830 (d) 1810

57. "The Waggoner" is a poem by
(a) Wordsworth (b) Shelley
(c) Keats (d) Byron

58. Who said:"The Child is the father of the Man"?
(a) Pope (b) Arnold
(c) Shakespeare (d) Wordsworth

59. In which poem do these lines appear, "We have given our hearts away" and "we are out of tune"?
(a) "Tintern Abbey" (b) "Dover Beach"
(c) "Daffodils" (d) "The World is Too Much With Us"

60. Wordsworth's *The Prelude* is a/an
(a) Philosophical poem (b) Metaphysical poem
(c) Autobiographical poem (d) Biographical poem

61. "Resolution and Independence" is a poem by
(a) Byron (b) Keats
(c) Leigh Hunt (d) Wordsworth

62. "Daffodils" is a poem by
(a) D.G. Rossetti (b) Yeats
(c) Coleridge (d) Wordsworth

63. Who called Wordsworth a 'moral eunuch'?
(a) Arnold (b) Coleridge
(c) Shelley (d) Browning

64. Who is of the view: "All things that love the sun are out of doors"?
(a) Wordsworth (b) Shelley
(c) Keats (d) Coleridge

**2. Samuel Taylor Coleridge**

65. S.T. Coleridge produced a play *Remorse* in the year
(a) 1800 (b) 1808 (c) 1813 (d) 1824

66. The phrase "the high road of life" was used by
(a) Eliot (b) Kipling
(c) Wordsworth (d) Coleridge

67. Who is the lost leader in Browning's poem "The Lost Leader"?
(a) Shelley (b) Milton
(c) Shakespeare (d) Wordsworth

68. "Table Talk" is an essay on Shakespeare by
(a) Coleridge (b) Pope
(c) Bradley (d) Johnson

69. The great ode "Dejection" was written by
(a) Keats (b) Byron
(c) Coleridge (d) Wordsworth

70. Coleridge met Wordsworth in
(a) 1797 (b) 1790 (c) 1798 (d) 1802

71. Coleridge and Lamb died in the same year. The year is
(a) 1830 (b) 1834 (c) 1850 (d) 1828

72. "Christabel" is an unfinished poem by
(a) Byron (b) Keats (c) Shelley (d) Coleridge

73. Which one of the following tragedies was written by Coleridge?
(a) *The Borderers* (b) *The Cenci*
(c) *Otho, the great* (d) *Remorse*

74. To which of the following poets does the phrase "willing suspension of disbelief" apply?
(a) Wordsworth (b) Coleridge
(c) Shelley (d) Keats

75. The author of *Biographia Literaria* is
(a) Coleridge (b) Hazlitt
(c) Arnold (d) Ruskin

76. Who was opium addicted?
(a) Wordsworth (b) Keats
(c) Southey (d) Coleridge

77. Which one of Coleridge's poems was included in *Lyrical Ballads?*
    (a) "The Rime of Ancient Mariner" (b) "Christabel"
    (c) "Kubla Khan" (d) All of these
78. Coleridge's *Biographia Literaria* appeared in the year
    (a) 1817 (b) 1821 (c) 1823 (d) 1829
79. Who wrote: "O Lady We receive but what we give, /And in our life alone does Nature live"?
    (a) Keats (b) Coleridge
    (c) Wordsworth (d) Rousseau
80. "Motiveless, malignity" is a phrase from
    (a) Eliot (b) Donne
    (c) Coleridge (d) Keats
81. Who talked of the 'divinity of Shakespeare'?
    (a) Johnson (b) Arnold
    (c) Coleridge (d) Eliot
82. "He Prayeth best, who loveth best, /All things, great and small". In which of the following poems do these lines occur?
    (a) "Kubla Khan" (b) "The Rime of the Ancient Mariner"
    (c) "Christabel" (d) "Dejection: An Ode"

**3. Robert Southey**

83. Southey's *The Life of Nelson* is a prose work which came out in
    (a) 1801 (b) 1805 (c) 1813 (d) 1817
84. Which one is not a poetic work by Robert Southey?
    (a) "Joan of Arc" (b) "Thalaba the Destroyer"
    (c) "The Curse of Kehoma" (d) *The Life of Nelson*
85. *The Life of Nelson* is a prose piece by
    (a) Shelley (b) Keats (c) Coleridge (d) Southey
86. Robert Southey's *A Vision of Judgement* is a ludicrous eulogy of:
    (a) George II (b) Charles II
    (c) George III (d) Queen Mary

87. After whom did Wordsworth become the poet Laureate of England?
(a) Coleridge (b) Scott (c) Southey (d) Dryden

### 4. Sir Walter Scott

88. Walter Scott's novel *Rob Roy* came out in
(a) 1817 (b) 1819 (c) 1821 (d) 1822

89. *The House of Aspen* is the only play by
(a) Scott (b) Byron (c) Keats (d) Dryden

90. Walter Scott was born in
(a) 1800 (b) 1785 (c) 1771 (d) 1790

91. "Proud Maisie" is a ballad by
(a) Scott (b) Keats (c) Byron (d) Coleridge

92. "The Lady of the Lake" is a poem by
(a) Scott (b) Byron (c) Keats (d) Shelley

93. In *Ivanhoe* what is the name of the disguised Robin Hood?
(a) Scott (b) Tennyson
(c) George Eliot (d) Swinburne

94. *Waverley* is a historical novel by
(a) Tennyson (b) George Eliot
(c) Scott (d) Dickens

95. Who gave birth to historical novel?
(a) Shakespeare (b) Austen
(c) Smollett (d) Scott

96. "The Lay of the Last Minstrel" is a poem by
(a) Tennyson (b) Rossetti (c) Coleridge (d) Scott

97. Mike Lambourne is a character from
(a) Scott (b) Austen (c) Eliot (d) Shelley

98. Sir Walter Scott has been best remembered for his book
(a) *Old Mortality* (b) *Ivanhoe*
(c) *The Talisman* (d) None

99. *The Heart of Midlothian* and *Castle Dangerous* are novels by
(a) Walter Scott (b) Emily Bronte
(c) George Eliot (d) Middleton Murry

100. Walter Scott's *The Talisman* is about
(a) Arabic islands (b) the Crusades
(c) bloodless revolution (d) English folk stories

101. *Old Mortality* is a novel by
(a) Charlotte Bronte (b) George Eliot
(c) Walter Scott (d) W. Godwin

102. Who is considered to be the founder of historical novel?
(a) Richardson (b) Walter Scott
(c) Virginia Woolf (d) James Joyce

103. In which novel did Scott raise the Scottish esteem?
(a) *Waverley* (b) *Ivanhoe*
(c) *Old Mortality* (d) *The Antiquary*

104. *Life of Napoleon* is a prose piece by
(a) Cobbett (b) Southey
(c) Scott (d) W.S. Lander

105. After whose refusal the poet Laureateship was conferred on Robert Southey?
(a) Scott (b) Coleridge (c) Pope (d) Dryden

106. *The Talisman* is a novel by
(a) Scott (b) Austen (c) Coleridge (d) Dickens

## UNIT C: THE SECOND GENERATION OF ROMANTIC POETS

### 1. Percy Bysshe Shelley

107. Shelley's "O World! O Life! O Time!" is a
(a) play (b) memoir (c) lyric (d) masque

108. Who married Marry Wallstone Craft?
(a) Shelley (b) Godwin
(c) Horace Walpole (d) None of these

109. Shelley was influenced by
(a) "The Medal" (b) "Political Justice"
(c) "The Season" (d) "Songs of Innocence"

110. Shelley was interested in the teachings of
(a) Thomas Hobbes (b) William Godwin
(c) Both (d) None

111. Who composed "Ode to Skylark"?
(a) Shelley (b) Keats
(c) Wordsworth (d) Pope

112. Shelley's "To a Skylark" came out with
(a) Epipsychidion (b) Adonis
(c) Cenci (d) Prometheus Unbound

113. Shelley's *Prometheus Unbound* written in 1818-19 was published in
(a) 1820 (b) 1824 (c) 1832 (d) 1828

114. Who died by drowning?
(a) Shakespeare (b) Pope
(c) Lamb (d) Shelley

115. The prophetic words: "If winter comes, can spring be far behind" have been uttered by
(a) Arthur Clough (b) Keats
(c) Browning (d) Shelley

116. *Prometheus Unbound* was written by
(a) Shelley (b) Keats (c) Scott (d) Peacock

117. Shelley's "Adonais" is
(a) a satire (b) a defence (c) an elegy (d) a lyric

118. "Queen Mab" is an aesthetic poem of
(a) Keats (b) Shelley (c) Coleridge (d) Eliot

119. Shelley's *Defence of Poetry* written in 1821, was published in
(a) 1822 (b) 1830 (c) 1835 (d) 1840

120. On which work was Shelley working when he died?
(a) "Queen Mab" (b) "Alaster"
(c) "The Cenci" (d) "The Triumph of Life"

121. *Intellectual Beauty* is a composition by
(a) Keats (b) Yeats
(c) Shelley (d) Coleridge

122. "Hell is a city much like London." Whose view is this?
(a) Wordsworth (b) Scott
(c) Shelley (d) Byron

123. Shelley was expelled from the Oxford University for the publication of
(a) "The Mask of Anarchy" (b) "The Revolt of Islam"
(c) "On the Necessity of Atheism" (d) "Hellas"

124. Shelley's "Julian and Maddalo" written in 1818 was published in
(a) 1819 (b) 1824 (c) 1829 (d) 1817

125. "The Cloud" is a poem by
(a) Wordsworth (b) Keats
(c) Shelley (d) Coleridge

126. Which is Shelley's autobiographical poem?
(a) "Alastor" (b) "Queen Mab"
(c) "Adonais" (d) "The Cenci"

127. Shelley was expelled from Oxford in
(a) 1817 (b) 1818 (c) 1811 (d) 1825

128. Whose first wife committed suicide?
(a) Keats (b) Shelley
(c) Coleridge (d) Wordsworth

129. Shelley's "The Revolt of Islam" appeared in
(a) 1802 (b) 1814 (c) 1817 (d) 1822

130. Which work of Shelley was written in irregular unrhymed metre?
(a) "Queen Mab" (b) "Laon and Cythna"
(c) "The Revolt of Islam" (d) None

131. Shelley's "The Witch of Atlas", which was written in 1820, was published in
(a) 1821 (b) 1824 (c) 1828 (d) 1835

**2. John Keats**

132. "To Autumn" is a poem composed by
(a) Keats (b) Yeats (c) Horace (d) Pope

133. Who is not a Lake Poet?
(a) Coleridge (b) Keats
(c) Wordsworth (d) Southey

134. Keats died in 1821 and Shelley died in
(a) 1829 (b) 1821 (c) 1819 (d) 1822

135. Who made the statement? "A thing of beauty is a joy forever".
(a) Keats (b) Pope
(c) Coleridge (d) Shakespeare

136. Which work of Keats deals with the murder of a lady's lover by her two wicked brothers?
(a) "Endymion" (b) "Hyperion"
(c) "Lamia" (d) "Isabella"

137. Who died at the age of 25?
(a) Shelley (b) Keats (c) L. Hunt (d) Southey

138. John Keats came in contact with Leigh Hunt in the year
(a) 1811 (b) 1807 (c) 1816 (d) 1818

139. Keats took the Endymion story from
(a) Greek mythology (b) Italian folk tales
(c) Irish legends (d) Roman myths

140. *Adonais* is an elegy on
(a) Shakespeare (b) Dryden
(c) Keats (d) Wordsworth

141. Who died of tuberculosis?
(a) Coleridge (b) Keats
(c) Shelley (d) Scott

142. "A thing of beauty is a joy forever." A verse-tale of Keats begins with this line. Identify the poem.
(a) "Hyperion" (b) "Endymion"
(c) "The Eve of St. Agnes" (d) "Eve of St. Mark"

143. Which one of Keats' odes ends with this line: "For ever will thou love, and she fair"?
(a) "Ode to a Nightingale" (b) "Ode to Autumn"
(c) "Ode To Psyche" (d) "Ode on a Grecian Urn"

144. Keats' volume of poems was dedicated to
(a) Spenser (b) Fanny Brawne
(c) Leigh Hunt (d) Wordsworth

145. Keats' "La Belle Dame Sans Merci" is a
(a) drama (b) short story
(c) lyrical ballad (d) essay

146. Which is not an ode by Keats?
(a) "Ode to a Nightingale" (b) "Ode on a Grecian Urn"
(c) "Ode on Melancholy" (d) "Ode to the West Wind"

147. Who wrote *Chapman's Homer*?
(a) Keats (b) Arnold (c) Dryden (d) Pater

148. The term 'negative capability' was given by
(a) Coleridge (b) Keats
(c) Eliot (d) Wordsworth

149. Who said: "What the imagination seizes as Beauty must be truth"?
(a) Keats (b) Shelley
(c) Lamb (d) De Quincey

150. Which poem of Keats highly impressed Shelley?
(a) "Ode to a Nightingale" (b) "Hyperion"
(c) "I Had a Dove" (d) "To Autumn"

151. Who said: "If poetry comes not as naturally as the leaves to a tree, it had better not come at all"?
(a) Keats (b) Coleridge
(c) Wordsworth (d) Spenser

152. Which one of Keats' works is based on Drayton's "The Man in the Moon" and Fletcher's "The Faithful Shepherdess"?
(a) "Isabella" (b) "Endymion"
(c) "Hyperion" (d) "The Eve of St. Agnes"

153. "Here lies one whose name was writ in water." This epitaph is written on whose tombstone in Rome?
(a) Sidney (b) Byron (c) Keats (d) Shelley

154. The name of John Keats' first poem is
(a) "To Autumn" (b) "When I have Fears"
(c) "Endymion" (d) "I Had a Dove"

## 3. Lord Byron

155. "Don Juan" was written by
(a) Tennyson (b) Pound (c) Eliot (d) Byron

156. Byron wrote his tragedies in
(a) heroic couplets (b) ottava rhyma
(c) blank verse (d) none

157. Who made this statement?
"Whom the gods love die young".
(a) Shelley (b) Byron (c) Austen (d) Yeats

158. "Child's Harold's Pilgrimage" was written by
(a) Lord Byron (b) Wordsworth
(c) Keats (d) L. Hunt

159. Who died of fever?
(a) Byron (b) Keats (c) Shelley (d) None

160. "She walks in Beauty" and "To Thyrza" are mild lyrics by
(a) Keats (b) Coleridge
(c) Wordsworth (d) Byron

161. Which poem of Byron came out in 1814?
(a) "The Giaour" (b) "The Bride of Abydos"
(c) "Lora" (d) "Pasisina"

162. Byron's first volume "Hours of Idleness" came out in the year
(a) 1800 (b) 1807 (c) 1810 (d) 1815

163. Who wrote: "It is strange but true, for truth is always strange; stranger than fiction"?
(a) Keats (b) Shelley (c) Blake (d) Byron

164. A Byronic hero is he who is
(a) vain and melancholy (b) cynical
(c) finds no good in life or love or anything (d) all of the above

## UNIT D: ESSAYISTS AND CRITICS

### 1. Charles Lamb

165. *Rosamund Gray* is a novel by
(a) Dickens (b) Lamb (c) Johnson (d) Kipling

166. Jane Austen and Charles Lamb were born in the same year, i.e.
(a) 1770 (b) 1772 (c) 1775 (d) 1785

167. Who had an afflicted sister?
(a) Shakespeare (b) Wordsworth
(c) Scott (d) Charles Lamb

168. Lamb produced his *Essays of Elia* in
(a) 1817 (b) 1823 (c) 1797 (d) 1805

169. Charles Lamb is best known for his
(a) *Essays of Elia* (b) *Tales from Shakespeare*
(c) *Lyrics* (d) *Short Stories*

170. Who wrote, "For thy sake, tobacco, I would do anything but die"?
(a) Keats (b) Lamb (c) Coleridge (d) Shelley

171. *The Specimens of English Dramatic Poets* was written by
(a) Lamb (b) Hazlitt (c) Addison (d) Bacon

172. *John Woodvil* is a drama by
(a) Shelley (b) Lamb
(c) Coleridge (d) Wordsworth

### 2. Leigh Hunt

173. Leigh Hunt, a poet associated with Keats was born in 1784 and died in
(a) 1850 (b) 1849 (c) 1859 (d) 1840

174. Leigh Hunt wrote continuously for more than
(a) 15 years (b) 20 years (c) 25 years (d) 30 years

### 3. William Hazlitt

175. Hazlitt's "The Spirit of the Age" came out in the year
(a) 1820 (b) 1822 (c) 1823 (d) 1825

176. Which author treated all reading as a kind of romantic journey into new and pleasant countries?
   (a) Leigh Hunt (b) Charles lamb
   (c) William Hazlitt (d) De Quincey

177. Whose work with that of Lamb strongly influenced Keats last and best volume of poetry?
   (a) William Hazlitt (b) De Quincey
   (c) Leigh Hunt (d) P. B. Shelley

**4. Thomas De Quincey**

178. *Confessions of an English Opium Eater* was written by
   (a) Leigh Hunt (b) Thomas Cooper
   (c) De Quincey (d) Robert Southey

179. Who said: "Not to sympathise is not to understand"?
   (a) Addison (b) Eliot
   (c) De Quincey (d) Arnold

180. Which periodical founded in 1820, encouraged De Quincey?
   (a) *London Magazine* (b) *Blackwood's Magazine*
   (c) *Fraser's Magazine* (d) *Edinburgh Review*

181. Which of these authors was an opium addict?
   (a) Charles Lamb (b) Thomas De Quincey
   (c) Leigh Hunt (d) William Hazlitt

182. In whose works life was seen as nebulous and chaotic?
   (a) Leigh Hunt (b) John Keats
   (c) P.B. Shelley (d) Thomas De Quincey

183. Which work of De Quincey reveals his grotesque humour?
   (a) *Confessions of an English Opium Eater* (b) *The Revolt of the Tartars*
   (c) *Murder Considered* (d) *The English Mail Coach*

184. Thomas De Quincey was born in the year
   (a) 1782 (b) 1783 (c) 1784 (d) 1785

185. Who ran away from the Grammar School at Manchester finding the instruction far below his abilities?
   (a) Thomas De Quincey (b) Leigh Hunt
   (c) Lord Byron (d) Charles Lamb

186. *Literary Reminiscences* is the most illuminating critical work of
   (a) William Hazlitt (b) Thomas De Quincey
   (c) Leight Hunt (d) Lord Byron

187. Which author has been called "the psychologist of style"?
   (a) Thomas De Quincey (b) Leigh Hunt
   (c) Charles Lamb (d) John Keats

188. Of the following works of De Quincey which is a novel?
   (a) *Suspiria de profundis* (b) *Klosterheim*
   (c) *The English Mail Coach* (d) *Joan of Arc*

## ANSWERS

### Unit A

| | | | | | | | |
|---|---|---|---|---|---|---|---|
| 1. | (d) | 2. | (c) | 3. | (c) | 4. | (c) |
| 5. | (a) | 6. | (b) | 7. | (b) | 8. | (d) |
| 9. | (b) | 10. | (d) | 11. | (b) | 12. | (a) |
| 13. | (a) | 14. | (c) | 15. | (a) | 16. | (b) |
| 17. | (c) | 18. | (a) | 19. | (c) | 20. | (a) |
| 21. | (b) | 22. | (a) | 23. | (b) | 24. | (c) |
| 25. | (d) | 26. | (c) | 27. | (d) | 28. | (a) |
| 29. | (d) | 30. | (a) | 31. | (d) | 32. | (d) |
| 33. | (d) | 34. | (d) | 35. | (c) | 36. | (b) |
| 37. | (d) | 38. | (b) | 39. | (b) | 40. | (d) |
| 41. | (a) | 42. | (b) | 43. | (d) | 44. | (a) |
| 45. | (d) | 46. | (b) | 47. | (c) | 48. | (b) |

### Unit B

| | | | | | | | |
|---|---|---|---|---|---|---|---|
| 49. | (c) | 50. | (a) | 51. | (c) | 52. | (c) |
| 53. | (b) | 54. | (d) | 55. | (b) | 56. | (a) |
| 57. | (a) | 58. | (d) | 59. | (d) | 60. | (c) |
| 61. | (d) | 62. | (d) | 63. | (c) | 64. | (a) |
| 65. | (c) | 66. | (d) | 67. | (d) | 68. | (a) |
| 69. | (c) | 70. | (a) | 71. | (b) | 72. | (d) |

| | | | | | | | |
|---|---|---|---|---|---|---|---|
| 73. | (d) | 74. | (b) | 75. | (a) | 76. | (d) |
| 77. | (a) | 78. | (a) | 79. | (b) | 80. | (c) |
| 81. | (c) | 82. | (b) | 83. | (c) | 84. | (d) |
| 85. | (d) | 86. | (c) | 87. | (c) | 88. | (a) |
| 89. | (a) | 90. | (c) | 91. | (a) | 92. | (a) |
| 93. | (a) | 94. | (c) | 95. | (d) | 96. | (d) |
| 97. | (a) | 98. | (b) | 99. | (a) | 100. | (b) |
| 101. | (c) | 102. | (b) | 103. | (b) | 104. | (c) |
| 105. | (a) | 106. | (a) | | | | |

## Unit C

| | | | | | | | |
|---|---|---|---|---|---|---|---|
| 107. | (c) | 108. | (a) | 109. | (b) | 110. | (b) |
| 111. | (a) | 112. | (d) | 113. | (a) | 114. | (d) |
| 115. | (d) | 116. | (a) | 117. | (c) | 118. | (b) |
| 119. | (d) | 120. | (d) | 121. | (c) | 122. | (c) |
| 123. | (d) | 124. | (b) | 125. | (c) | 126. | (a) |
| 127. | (c) | 128. | (b) | 129. | (c) | 130. | (a) |
| 131. | (b) | 132. | (a) | 133. | (b) | 134. | (d) |
| 135. | (a) | 136. | (d) | 137. | (b) | 138. | (c) |
| 139. | (a) | 140. | (c) | 141. | (b) | 142. | (b) |
| 143. | (d) | 144. | (c) | 145. | (c) | 146. | (d) |
| 147. | (a) | 148. | (b) | 149. | (a) | 150. | (b) |
| 151. | (a) | 152. | (b) | 153. | (c) | 154. | (c) |
| 155. | (d) | 156. | (c) | 157. | (b) | 158. | (a) |
| 159. | (a) | 160. | (d) | 161. | (c) | 162. | (b) |
| 163. | (d) | 164. | (d) | | | | |

## Unit D

| | | | | | | | |
|---|---|---|---|---|---|---|---|
| 165. | (b) | 166. | (c) | 167. | (d) | 168. | (b) |
| 169. | (b) | 170. | (b) | 171. | (a) | 172. | (b) |
| 173. | (c) | 174. | (d) | 175. | (d) | 176. | (c) |
| 177. | (a) | 178. | (c) | 179. | (c) | 180. | (a) |
| 181. | (b) | 182. | (d) | 183. | (a) | 184. | (d) |
| 185. | (a) | 186. | (b) | 187. | (a) | 188. | (b) |

# Mid-Nineteenth Century (1832–1875)

# 8

## UNIT A: HISTORICAL PERSPECTIVE AND BACKGROUND

1. Which literary period has been called a homogeneous period?
   (a) Romantic (b) Puritan
   (c) Victorian (d) Edwardian
2. Who wrote *History of the Revolution*?
   (a) James Mackintosh (b) Max Muller
   (c) Thomas Carlyle (d) Macaulay
3. Macaulay entered the House of Commons in
   (a) 1813 (b) 1820 (c) 1830 (d) 1840
4. In Macaulay's *The History of England,* merits and defects of his "Essays" are
   (a) repeated (b) removed
   (c) exaggerated (d) stressed upon
5. Sir G.C. Lewis' "Remarks on the Use and Abuse of some Political Terms" shows his
   (a) philosophical side (b) practical side
   (c) religious side (d) literary side
6. The philosophical side of Lewis' mind is best represented in
   (a) His letters
   (b) Remarks on the Use and Abuse of some Political Terms
   (c) Inquiry on the Credibility of early Roman History
   (d) On the Influence of Authority in Matters of Opinion

7. With a volume of autobiographic action, *Shadows of the Clouds* ......... James Anthony Froude's literary career.
(a) opened (b) finished (c) boosted (d) endangered

8. James Anthony Froude's *The Nemesis of Faith* was a blow not only to the Tractarians but in general to
(a) religion (b) literary faith
(c) orthodoxy (d) philosophy

9. First important production of Froude after the works of the Oxford period was
(a) *Shadows of the Clouds* (b) *The Nemesis of Faith*
(c) *Short Stories on Great Subjects* (d) *History of England from the Fall of Wolsey to the defeat of the Spanish Armada*

10. Richard Hurrell Froude's characteristics are
(a) A Sense of history (b) A good storyteller
(c) Narrative skills and meticulous research (d) Topical issues

11. Freeman's *History of the Norman Conquest* is a glorification of
(a) religion (b) romance
(c) aristocracy (d) teutonism

12. The essays gathered together by F.W. Maitland in his 'Roman Canon Law in the Church of England' are ......... in number.
(a) four (b) six (c) eight (d) ten

13. Who wrote *The Making of England* under the shadow of death?
(a) Charles Henry Pearson (b) Robert Louis Stevenson
(c) Freeman (d) John Richard Green

14. *Lives of Eminent British Statesmen* was edited and partly written by
(a) John Forster (b) G.H. Lewes
(c) Thomas Carlyle (d) Andrew Lang

15. Samuel Smiles' *Self Help* and *Thrift* are in principle
    (a) historic (b) philosophic
    (c) biographic (d) romantic
16. The deepest interest of Smiles lay in the problems suggested by the organization of
    (a) ancient industry (b) workers
    (c) modern industry (d) employers
17. The French Revolution was for
    (a) France (b) Russia (c) Europe (d) Asia
18. After French Revolution, what was immediately visible was the wreck of the
    (a) ancient regime (b) literary tradition
    (c) moral norms (d) none
19. Which Victorian writer satirised the fantastic romance?
    (a) Carlyle (b) Darwin
    (c) Cervantes (d) Adam Smith
20. Hegels and the Hegelians are called 'the romantic school' by
    (a) Carlyle (b) Hume (c) Kant (d) Hoffding
21. Who said,
    "Every literature unless it be crossed by some other of different breed, tends to superannuation."?
    (a) Hume (b) Carlyle
    (c) De Quincey (d) Jeremy Bentham
22. Who spoke of Goethe as 'the greatest man of Germany-perhaps of Europe?
    (a) Byron (b) Bacon
    (c) Carlyle (d) De Quincey
23. Coleridge's "Wallenstein" was a fine tribute to
    (a) Schiller (b) Goethe (c) Hume (d) Kant
24. Coleridge condemned some scenes of *Faust* as
    (a) unrealistic (b) mere magic lantern picture
    (c) foolish (d) nonsensical
25. *Life of Sterling* appeared in
    (a) 1751 (b) 1851 (c) 1890 (d) 1900

26. Who said,"Sir William Hamilton was among the greatest of the great"?
(a) Carlyle (b) Newman
(c) Freeman (d) J.F. Ferrier

27. Who said, "A God understood would be no God at all"?
(a) Hamilton (b) Freeman
(c) Carlyle (d) J.S. Mill

## UNIT B: PHILOSOPHY/ESSAY

### 1. John Stuart Mill

28. The greatest of the opponents of utilitarianism went back for their inspiration to
(a) Russia (b) Europe (c) Germany (d) France

29. To describe the spiritual fathers of Utilitarianism, the adjective 'Utilitarian' was substituted by the adjective
(a) classical (b) socialistic
(c) philosophical (d) transcendental

30. John Stuart Mill based his theory upon
(a) Kant (b) Hume (c) Goethe (d) Carlyle

31. J.S. Mill from cradle was a
(a) Benthamite (b) Jew
(c) Russian (d) British

32. J.S. Mill became editor of "London Review" in
(a) 1804 (b) 1814 (c) 1824 (d) 1834

33. The first important work of J.S. Mill was
(a) *System of Logic* (b) *Logica*
(c) *Utilitarianism* (d) *Principles of Political Economy*

34. Last work published during J.S. Mill's life was
(a) *Logica* (b) *Utilitarianism*
(c) *Political Economy* (d) *The Subjection of Women*

35. J.S. Mill's *Utilitarianism* is devoted to
(a) ethics (b) religion (c) philosophy (d) art

36. Who shows himself an ardent positivist in *Problems of Life and Mind*?
    (a) J.S. Mill (b) George Henry Lewes
    (c) Thomas Carlyle (d) Newman
37. The translation of the *Dialogues of Plato* was the most important work of
    (a) Freeman (b) Newman (c) Jowett (d) J.S. Mill
38. In *The Descent of Man* Charles Darwin applies the evolutionary laws specifically to the
    (a) poets (b) writers
    (c) philosophers (d) human race
39. J.S. Mill's thought and attitude was characterized by
    (a) Liberalism (b) Scepticism
    (c) Utilitarianism (d) None
40. Who was the founder of the Utilitarianism school?
    (a) James Mill (b) Hamilton
    (c) Newman (d) Carlyle

**2. Thomas Carlyle**

41. Thomas Carlyle, the foremost man of letters of his time, was obliged to earn by
    (a) writing (b) lecturing
    (c) acting (d) poetry writing
42. The complete and perfect Carlyle migrated to London in
    (a) 1834 (b) 1824 (c) 1844 (d) 1864
43. To Carlyle, the tremendous civil war in America was a
    (a) nightmare (b) challenge
    (c) misfortune (d) smoky chimney which had taken fire
44. Carlyle in his essay on "State of German Literature" denied
    (a) English philosophy (b) French philosophy
    (c) Russian philosophy (d) German philosophy
45. *Life of Schiller* was authored by
    (a) Carlyle (b) Goethe
    (c) Wordsworth (d) Kant

46. Goethe is 'the only living model of a great writer' to
    (a) Coleridge (b) Kant (c) Schiller (d) Carlyle
47. Who translated *Wilhelm Master's Apprenticeship*?
    (a) Coleridge (b) Kant (c) Schiller (d) Carlyle
48. Carlyle got married in
    (a) 1816 (b) 1826 (c) 1836 (d) 1840
49. Carlyle's idea of the relation between power and right is similar in meaning to that of
    (a) Aristotle (b) Plato (c) Kant (d) Rousseau
50. Shakespeare's lines—
    "We are such stuff
    As dreams are made on; and our little life
    Is rounded with a sleep".
    —are a favourite of
    (a) Aristotle (b) J.S. Mill (c) Ruskin (d) Carlyle
51. Behind everything in Carlyle lay an unalterable belief in the
    (a) Law of Universe (b) Gravitational Law
    (c) Law of Newton (d) Grimm's Law

### 3. John Ruskin

52. John Ruskin was the son of a
    (a) writer (b) philosopher
    (c) teacher (d) wine merchant
53. Ruskin's mother was a strict
    (a) vegetarian (b) puritan
    (c) disciplinarian (d) evangelical
54. The influence of the English *Bible* gave dignity to the rhetoric and thought of
    (a) John Ruskin (b) Newman
    (c) Thomas Carlyle (d) J.S. Mill
55. John Ruskin tells about his home life in his delightful
    (a) *Proeterita* (b) *The Seven Lamps of Architecture*
    (c) *Modern Painters* (d) None

56. Ruskin's *Proeterita* reminds one of Dickens'
    (a) *Hard Times* (b) *Oliver Twist*
    (c) *David Copperfield* (d) *The Bleak House*
57. On his thirteenth birthday, Ruskin's father Henry Telfourd gave him
    (a) Dickens' *Hard Times* (b) Rogers' *Italy*
    (c) Milton's *Paradise Lost* (d) Keats's *Hyperion*
58. John Ruskin entered as a Gentleman Commoner at Christ Church in January
    (a) 1837 (b) 1857 (c) 1860 (d) 1870
59. The first fruits of Ruskin's tours abroad came in the shape of the
    (a) *Modern Painters* (b) *Proeterita*
    (c) *The Seven Lamps of Architecture* (d) *The Stones of Venice*
60. Ruskin was elected Slade Professor of Art at Oxford in
    (a) 1849 (b) 1858 (c) 1869 (d) 1879
61. From 1843 to 1860, Ruskin concerned himself with
    (a) religion (b) philosophy
    (c) fine arts (d) literature
62. Mr. J.A. Hobson has called John Ruskin a
    (a) teacher (b) puritan
    (c) social reformer (d) philosopher
63. John Ruskin insists on the dominance of
    (a) discipline (b) philosophy
    (c) utilitarianism (d) moral ideas
64. Upon the Gospel of Work, Ruskin is as emphatic as
    (a) J.S. Mill (b) Thomas Carlyle
    (c) Newman (d) Freeman
65. Ruskin's passion for Gothic was due to his temper of
    (a) sensuousness (b) medievalism
    (c) romanticism (d) artistry
66. Who declared that Ruskin was one of the greatest men of the age?
    (a) Thomas Carlyle (b) J.S. Mill
    (c) J.A. Hobson (d) Leo Tolstoy

67. Ruskin's *Fors Clavigera* sums up the trend of his
(a) philosophy (b) teaching
(c) writing (d) religion

68. Who said,
"Religion as a mere sentiment is to me a dream and a mockery"?
(a) Newman (b) John Ruskin
(c) Carlyle (d) Martineau

69. John Ruskin won the Newdigate Prize for his
(a) *Modern Painters* (b) *Salsette and Elephanta*
(c) *The King of the Golden River* (d) *Stones of Venice*

70. Ruskin wrote *The King of the Golden River* for his
(a) wife (b) father (c) son (d) brother

71. Ruskin's works on art *Modern Painters* are in ......... volumes.
(a) four (b) five (c) six (d) eight

72. A connection between literature and the fine arts can be traced as far back as Dryden's essay on
(a) *Poetry and Painting* (b) *Mac Fleckno*
(c) *Essays on Dramatic Poesy* (d) None

73. Gothic architecture is extolled and Renaissance architecture is condemned in Ruskin's
(a) *The Stones of Venice* (b) *Modern Painters*
(c) *The King of the Golden River* (d) *Salsette and Elephanta*

74. *Sesame and Lilies* (1865) is the most popular book of
(a) Cervantes (b) Firdausi
(c) Shakespeare (d) John Ruskin

**4. John Henry Newman**

75. Who calls Newman 'the indicating number'?
(a) Froude (b) J.S. Mill (c) Ruskin (d) Carlyle

76. Newman's *Tracts for the Times* appeared in
(a) 1813 (b) 1823 (c) 1833 (d) 1843

77. *Lectures on Justification* of Newman appeared in
    (a) 1818 (b) 1828 (c) 1838 (d) 1840

78. Which work of Newman drew from Macaulay the remark that 'the times require a Middleton'?
    (a) *The Essay on Miracles* (b) *Apologia*
    (c) *Lectures on Justification* (d) *Loss and Gains*

79. Next to *Apologia*, the most remarkable of Newman's works is
    (a) *Calista* (b) *Loss and Gains*
    (c) *The Essay on Miracles* (d) *Development of Christian Doctrine*

80. Where does Newman say there is 'no medium, in true philosophy between Atheism and Catholicity'?
    (a) *Apologia* (b) *Calista*
    (c) *Loss and Gains* (d) *Lectures on Justification*

81. Newman has been praised for the subtlety of his
    (a) logic (b) philosophy
    (c) style (d) literary art

82. In Newman's case, the use of reason is always
    (a) subordinate (b) primary
    (c) dominant (d) obvious

83. It was observed 'Nothing more characterised Newman than his unconscious'
    (a) logic (b) style
    (c) refinement (d) philosophy

84. 'Out of the strong came forth sweetness'—about whom was it said?
    (a) Newman (b) Carlyle
    (c) Ruskin (d) J.S. Mill

85. Which work of Newman gave the idea that the novel might be used as a vehicle for disseminating Catholic truth?
    (a) *Loss and Gains* (b) *Apologia*
    (c) *Calista* (d) *The Grammar of Ascent*

## UNIT C: THE NOVEL

### 1. Charles Dickens

86. Charles Dickens was the son of a
    (a) writer (b) philosopher (c) clerk (d) priest
87. *The Authoritative Life of Charles Dickens* was written by
    (a) Thackeray (b) Disraeli
    (c) John Forster (d) Anthony Trollope
88. *The Essence of History* was biography to
    (a) Charles Dickens (b) Thackeray
    (c) John Forster (d) None
89. Charles Dickens was sent to school in
    (a) 1804 (b) 1814 (c) 1824 (d) 1830
90. Dickens became a staff reporter for
    (a) *Edinburgh Review* (b) *The True Son*
    (c) *The Quarterly Review* (d) *New Sporting Magazine*
91. Dickens' first article was printed in
    (a) *Life of Dickens* (b) *David Copperfield*
    (c) *Sketches by Boz* (d) *Hard Times*
92. In which magazine was Dickens both a reporter as well as a contributor?
    (a) *Morning Chronicle* (b) *New Sporting Magazine*
    (c) *The Monthly Magazine* (d) None
93. Who is the author of *The Pickwick Papers*?
    (a) Charles Dickens (b) George Eliot
    (c) William Thackeray (d) Anthony Trollope
94. *Oliver Twist* was published in
    (a) 1818 (b) 1827 (c) 1838 (d) 1840
95. After *Pickwick*, the life of Dickens is mainly a record of
    (a) romance (b) satires
    (c) epistles (d) publications

96. Charles Dickens was suspected of, having written *The Four Georges* in order to
    (a) flatter American prejudices (b) please the public
    (c) gain popularity (d) earn money
97. Uriah Heep is a character in
    (a) *Hard Times* (b) *The Pickwick Papers*
    (c) *David Copperfield* (d) *Oliver Twist*
98. The administration of the poor law and the making of criminals is dealt in
    (a) *Hard Times* (b) *The Bleak House*
    (c) *Oliver Twist* (d) *David Copperfield*
99. The obvious purpose of *Nicholas Nickleby* is
    (a) reform of schools (b) reform of society
    (c) reform of jails (d) utilitarianism
100. An attack upon the orthodox political economy is made in
    (a) *Oliver Twist* (b) *Nicholas Nickleby*
    (c) *Hard Times* (d) *The Bleak House*

**2. Benjamin Disraeli**

101. Benjamin Disraeli was born in
    (a) 1800 (b) 1802 (c) 1804 (d) 1810
102. Disraeli entered the House of Commons in
    (a) 1820 (b) 1826 (c) 1837 (d) 1840
103. Disraeli's novel of society is
    (a) *Vivian Grey* (b) *The Young Duke*
    (c) *Venetia* (d) *The Wondrous Tale of Alroy*
104. Disraeli's *Tale of Alroy* was remarkably
    (a) oriental (b) romantic (c) satiric (d) none
105. Disraeli became leader of the opposition in the House of Commons in
    (a) 1830 (b) 1835 (c) 1840 (d) 1848

### 3. Mrs. Gaskell

106. Elizabeth Cleghorn Gaskell was the daughter of a
    (a) poet (b) philosopher
    (c) unitarian minister (d) miner
107. Mrs. Gaskell's life in Manchester gave her the materials of her novel
    (a) *Mary Burton* (b) *Cranford*
    (c) *Our Village* (d) *North and South*
108. Mrs. Gaskell's most precious gift was
    (a) humour (b) romance (c) satire (d) imagery
109. Mrs. Gaskell's *Cranford* was written in
    (a) 1853 (b) 1867 (c) 1870 (d) 1875
110. Captain Brown is a character of Mrs. Gaskell's
    (a) *Our Village* (b) *Mary Burton*
    (c) *Cranford* (d) *Cousin Phillips*
111. Mrs. Gaskell's short stories appeared serially in
    (a) *The Cornhill Magazine* (b) *The Westminster Review*
    (c) *The Christian Observer* (d) *Blackwood's Magazine*

### 4. The Bronte Sisters

112. Charlotte Bronte was born in
    (a) 1806 (b) 1816 (c) 1855 (d) 1860
113. *College Poems* and *Rural Minstrel* were authored by
    (a) Charlotte Bronte (b) Emily Bronte
    (c) Patrick Bronte (d) Anne Bronte
114. The Bronte family had .......... son.
    (a) two (b) three (c) one (d) none
115. The career of Charlotte Bronte was fixed by the success of
    (a) *Jane Eyre* (b) *Shirley*
    (c) *Villete* (d) *The Professor*
116. Charlotte died on 31st March
    (a) 1855 (b) 1845 (c) 1860 (d) 1865
117. Emily died at the age of
    (a) thirty (b) forty (c) thirty-five (d) twenty-five

118. Heathcliff appears in the novel of
   (a) Charlotte Bronte (b) Anne
   (c) Emily Bronte (d) Patrick Bronte

## UNIT D: THE POETRY

### 1. Alfred Tennyson

119. Whose death brought end of an era?
   (a) Tennyson (b) Browning
   (c) Arnold (d) Gray
120. The second volume of Tennyson's verse was published in
   (a) 1813 (b) 1832 (c) 1833 (d) 1836
121. The period between the close of the interregnum and the end of the nineteenth century may be roughly divided into
   (a) 2 parts (b) 3 parts (c) 4 parts (d) 5 parts
122. Alfred Tennyson was born in
   (a) 1800 (b) 1805 (c) 1809 (d) 1815
123. Out of a family of eight sons and four daughters, Tennyson was the
   (a) second (b) fourth (c) sixth (d) tenth
124. The first independent volume of Tennyson's poems, which appeared in 1830, is
   (a) *Poems, Chiefly Lyrical* (b) *The Miller's Daughter*
   (c) *The Princess* (d) *The Lady of Shalott*
125. Tennyson's long silence of nearly ten years was broken by
   (a) "In Memoriam" (b) "Maud"
   (c) "The Lover's Tale" (d) "The Princess"
126. The poet who among Tennyson's immediate predecessors, had the greatest influence on him was
   (a) Byron (b) Shakespeare
   (c) John Keats (d) P.B. Shelley
127. In 1833, a heavy blow fell on Alfred Tennyson in the death of
   (a) his father (b) his wife
   (c) his brother (d) his friend Arthur Hallam

128. Tennyson's *The True Voices* was originally entitled
(a) *The Miller's Daughter* (b) *The May Queen*
(c) *The Gardener's Daughter* (d) *Thoughts of a Suicide*

129. Who declared Tennyson's mind to be 'saturated with astronomy'?
(a) Emily Sellwood (b) Coventry Patmore
(c) Norman Lockyer (d) None

130. Who pronounced Tennyson to be 'the first poet since Lucretius who understood the drift of science'?
(a) Mill (b) Huxley (c) Arnold (d) Fitzgerald

131. Tennyson's "Ulysses" was written soon after the death of
(a) Browning (b) Arnold
(c) Hallam (d) A.C. Clough

132. Tennyson's "Ulysses", "The Two Voices" and the early fragments of "In Memoriam" were directly associated with his memory of
(a) Milton (b) Shakespeare
(c) Bacon (d) Hallam

133. The best proof of the great advance which Tennyson had made in the art of construction is to be found in
(a) "In Memoriam" (b) "The Two Voices"
(c) "The Vision of Sin" (d) "The Lotos Eaters"

134. "The Lotos Eaters" was a perfect picture of life of
(a) dreamful ease (b) splendour
(c) harmonious nature (d) none

135. Alfred Tennyson matriculated from Trinity College in
(a) 1826 (b) 1828 (c) 1830 (d) 1832

136. The quality of Keats which impressed Tennyson most was his
(a) sensuousness (b) medievalism
(c) imagery (d) romanticism

137. Tennyson left Cambridge and his father died in
(a) 1820 (b) 1823 (c) 1830 (d) 1831

138. The most perfect and thoughtful of his songs hitherto published is
    (a) "Maud" (b) "In Memoriam"
    (c) "Lotos Eaters" (d) "Break, Break, Break"
139. In 1835, "Morte d' Arthur" was read to
    (a) Swinburne (b) Rossetti
    (c) Morris (d) Edward Fitz Gerald
140. Which Tennyson's poem is a picture of 'dreamful ease'?
    (a) "The Lotos Eaters" (b) "Maud"
    (c) "The Princess" (d) "In Memoriam"
141. "In Memoriam" appeared in
    (a) 1820 (b) 1825 (c) 1845 (d) 1850
142. Which Tennyson's poem was published anonymously?
    (a) "In Memoriam" (b) "Maud"
    (c) "Morte d'Arthur" (d) None
143. Which poet's scepticism was anticipated in the quality of Tennyson's faith?
    (a) W.B. Yeats (b) W.H. Auden
    (c) T.S. Eliot (d) None
144. Scientific leaders like Herschel, Owen, Sidgwick and Tyndall regard Tennyson as a champion of
    (a) Victorian faith (b) Science
    (c) Scepticism (d) Religious faith

**2. Robert Browning**

145. Robert Browning was born in
    (a) 1810 (b) 1812 (c) 1820 (d) 1825
146. Browning got married to Elizabeth in
    (a) 1826 (b) 1836 (c) 1840 (d) 1846
147. In 1824, Browning privately printed a collection of his son's verses under the title of
    (a) "Incondita" (b) "Pauline"
    (c) "Men and Women" (d) "Sordello"
148. Rossetti compares Browning's scholarship with that of
    (a) Bacon (b) Dickens (c) Ruskin (d) None

149. Browning's first publication was
(a) "Sordello" (b) "Ring and the Book"
(c) "Pauline" (d) None

150. Browning's Ottima and Sebald in "Pippa Passes" are equivalent to
(a) *Othello and Desdemona* (b) *Ferdinand and Miranda*
(c) *Romeo and Juliet* (d) *Macbeth and Lady Macbeth*

151. The two numbers of Browning which were not filled with dramas were
(a) "Dramatic Lyrics" and "Dramatic Romance"
(b) "In a Gondola" and "Porphyria's Lover"
(c) "The Lost Leader" and "Pauline"
(d) "Men and Women" and "The Pied Piper of Hamelin"

152. Browning's expression of surprise and regret at the sudden disappearance of a precious friend is
(a) "Waring" (b) "Pauline"
(c) "Men and Women" (d) "The Portrait"

153. Browning chose ......... to attack the two extreme forms of faith which divide his countrymen.
(a) "Christmas Eve" (b) "Pauline"
(c) "Dramatic Lyrics" (d) None

154. Browning's home, till Mrs. Browning's death was at
(a) London (b) New York
(c) Florence (d) Italy

155. The poem addressed to Browning's wife is
(a) "One Word More" (b) "Pauline"
(c) "Parleyings" (d) None

156. Which work of Browning gives one phase of jealousy?
(a) "James Lee's Wife" (b) "Pauline"
(c) "Caliban" (d) "The Worst of it"

157. A perfect picture of cold blooded heartlessness is Browning's
(a) "The Grammarian's Funeral" (b) "Holy Cross Day"
(c) "Youth and Art" (d) "My Last Duchess"

158. Who said,
"Robert Browning is unerring in every sentence he writes of the Middle Ages"?
(a) Tennyson (b) Ruskin (c) Eliot (d) Yeats

159. A group of dramatic monologues penned by Browning is
(a) "The Ring and the Book" (b) "The Pope"
(c) "Dramatis Personoe" (d) None

160. The greatest of all Browning's works is
(a) "The Pope" (b) "Rabbi Ben Ezra"
(c) "The Ring and the Book" (d) "Pomilia"

161. Which of these is Browning's female character?
(a) Pompilia (b) Miranda
(c) Desdemona (d) Olivia

162. An undisguised dissertation on immortality is Browning's
(a) "La Saisiaz" (b) "Saul"
(c) "The Flight of the Duchess" (d) "Childe Roland"

163. "Prince Hohenstiel – Schwangan" by Browning is a poem founded upon the history of
(a) Napoleon I (b) Napoleon II
(c) Napoleon III (d) Edward II

164. Don Juan and his wife Elvire are the characters of Browning's
(a) "Fifine at the Fair" (b) "Ferishta's Fancies"
(c) "Parleyings" (d) "Fra Lippo Lippi"

165. Browning's "Ferishta's Fancies" is a collection of
(a) poems (b) parable
(c) short stories (d) dramatic monologues

166. Who said,
'God's in His Heaven and all's right with the world.'?
(a) Tennyson (b) Browning
(c) Arnold (d) Macaulay

167. Which Browning's poem deplores Wordsworth's political apostasy?
(a) "Fra Lippo Lippi" (b) "Men and Women"
(c) "My Last Duchess" (d) "The Lost Leader"

## 3. Matthew Arnold

168. Queen Victoria ascended the throne in
(a) 1827 (b) 1837 (c) 1845 (d) 1850

169. In Victorian period, criticism developed very distinctly through
(a) two phases (b) three phases
(c) four phases (d) five phases

170. Queen Victoria passed away in
(a) 1901 (b) 1905 (c) 1910 (d) 1915

171. Matthew Arnold blended Hebraism with
(a) Romanticism (b) Classicism
(c) Hellenism (d) Medievalism

172. Prof. Saintsbury wrote his famous *History of Criticism* in/at
(a) 1850 (b) 1864
(c) 1879 (d) the close of the 19th century

173. Who has described Matthew Arnold as the great modern critic?
(a) David Daiches (b) I.A. Richards
(c) F.R. Leavis (d) T.S. Eliot

174. Arnold's views on poetry and criticism are discussed in
(a) "Preface to the Poems" (b) "On Translating Homer"
(c) "Scholar Gypsy" (d) "Culture and Anarchy"

175. Arnold expounds his classical creed and disapproves romantic style in a clear and forceful manner in
(a) "Essays in Criticism" (b) "Culture and Anarchy"
(c) "Preface to the Poems" (d) "Scholar Gypsy"

176. Which work of Arnold was published posthumously in first, second and third series?
(a) "Essays in Criticism" (b) "Culture and Anarchy"
(c) "Dover Beach" (d) "On Translating Homer"

177. Matthew Arnold's conception of poetry is
(a) romantic (b) classical
(c) Keatsian (d) Aristotelian

178. In his famous expression, Arnold has called poetry
(a) the song of life (b) the criticism of life
(c) way of life (d) none of the above

179. Both Arnold and Aristotle appeared to be
(a) enamoured of poetry (b) fed up of poetry
(c) impressed by poetry (d) oblivious of lyrical poetry

180. The basic idea of the term 'grand style' was elaborated and illustrated in Arnold's
(a) "On Study of Poetry" (b) "On Translating Homer"
(c) "Scholar Gypsy" (d) "Essays in Criticism"

181. Whom has Arnold acknowledged as his master in criticism?
(a) J.S. Mill (b) Keats
(c) Milton (d) Sainte-Beuve

182. Arnold as a critic was heavily run down by
(a) F.R. Leavis (b) T.S. Eliot
(c) W.B. Yeats (d) Ezra Pound

183. Arnold's "Thyrsis" came out in
(a) 1826 (b) 1836 (c) 1845 (d) 1866

184. Arnold's "Westminster Abbey" is occasioned by the death of
(a) A.H. Clough (b) Arthur Hallam
(c) Stanley (d) None

185. Arnold's volume of poems which contained *Sohrab and Rustum* also included
(a) "Scholar Gypsy" (b) "Balder Dead"
(c) "Switzerland" (d) "Faded Leaves"

186. Who said,
'Standing between two worlds, one dead,
The other powerless to be born'?
(a) Arnold (b) Tennyson
(c) Browning (d) Hopkins

187. In "Dover Beach", Arnold hears the melancholy, long, withdrawing roar of the sea of
(a) emotion (b) doubt (c) faith (d) grief

188. Matthew Arnold's "Switzerland" comprises ......... poems.
(a) six (b) seven (c) eight (d) nine

189. In "Rugby Chapel", Arnold pays a noble tribute to the memory of his
(a) father (b) brother (c) sister (d) friend

190. In his sonnet "Shakespeare", Arnold praises above all other qualities, Shakespeare's
(a) romanticism (b) imagination
(c) philosophy (d) objectivity

191. Arnold's "Sohrab and Rustum" is a mini-epic in blank verse drawing on the *Shah-Nama* of
(a) Homer (b) Dante (c) Firdausi (d) None

192. Arnold's "The Scholar Gypsy" a pastoral poem is based upon an old legend related by
(a) Alfred Tennyson (b) Robert Browning
(c) Mrs. Browning (d) Joseph Glanvil

193. Arthur Hugh Clough, Arnold's friend died in
(a) 1861 (b) 1875 (c) 1880 (d) 1890

## UNIT E: THE PRE-RAPHAELITES

### 1. D.G. Rossetti

194. The works of Pre-Raphaelite group is characterized by
(a) scepticism (b) religious faith
(c) emotional indulgence (d) preponderance of art

195. Arthur Hugh Clough visited France in 1850 and began his most ambitious poem
(a) "Dipsy Chus" (b) "Bothie"
(c) "The Marble Faun" (d) "Amours de Voyage"

196. 'Sit if ye will, sit down upon the ground
Yet not to weep, and wait, but calmly look around.
.......... cries.
(a) D.G. Rossetti (b) Tennyson
(c) A.H. Clough (d) Browning

197. The leading spirit in the Pre-Raphaelite group was
(a) William Morris (b) D.G. Rossetti
(c) W.M. Rossetti (d) Christina Rossetti

198. D.G. Rossetti's devoted friend Thomas Gordon Hake was also a
(a) poet (b) teacher
(c) physician (d) philosopher

199. Best pieces of D.G. Rossetti are contained in
(a) *New Symbols* (b) *Vates*
(c) *The Blessed Damozel* (d) *The Philosophy of Madness*

200. D.G. Rossetti was a true descendant of
(a) Shelley (b) Keats
(c) Charles Lamb (d) De Quincey

201. The sonnet-sequence in which D.G. Rossetti expresses his love for his wife is
(a) "The Blessed Damozel" (b) "The House of Life"
(c) "Ballads and Sonnets" (d) "Love's Nocturn"

202. The story of the murder of King James I is told in D.G. Rossetti's
(a) "The King's Tragedy" (b) "The Blessed Damozel"
(c) "Ballads and Sonnets" (d) None

**2. Christina Rossetti**

203. Christina Rossetti was D.G. Rossetti's
(a) wife (b) mother (c) niece (d) sister

204. Christina Rossetti's *New Poems* was edited after her death by
(a) D.G. Rossetti (b) W.M. Rossetti
(c) William Morris (d) William Thackeray

205. Christina Rossetti sings renunciation in
(a) "Goblin Market" (b) "The Prince's Progress"
(c) "Despised and Rejected" (d) "Monna Innomimata"

206. "Goblin Market" of Christina Rossetti is a charming excursion into
(a) fairyland (b) dreamland
(c) wasteland (d) real world

207. Coventry Patmore's first volume of poems was published in
(a) 1804 (b) 1814 (c) 1834 (d) 1844

208. The adjective 'Spasmodic' was given to the poets by
(a) D.G. Rossetti (b) W.E. Aytoun
(c) Tennyson (d) T. Young Simpson

209. Sydney Dobell's *Balder* has been compared by many critics to
(a) Ibsen's *Brand* (b) Byron's *Don Juan*
(c) Ibsen's *Peer Gynt* (d) Shaw's *St. Joan*

### 3. William Morris

210. "Well, if this is poetry, it is very easy to write"—said
(a) Carlyle (b) Ruskin
(c) Maurice (d) William Morris

211. Carlyle's *Past and Present* was one of the holy books of
(a) D.G. Rossetti (b) Christina Rossetti
(c) William Morris (d) Tennyson

212. William Morris saw modern industrialism divorced from
(a) art (b) faith (c) religion (d) emotion

213. William Morris' *The Walter of the Wondrous Isles* and *The Story of the Sundering Flood* were
(a) romantic (b) classical
(c) religious (d) posthumous

214. A.C. Swinburne was introduced to William Morris and Burne Jone in
(a) 1830 (b) 1857 (c) 1860 (d) 1870

215. Who was named along with Mazzini and Hugo as one of the three gods of the poet's worship?
(a) D.G. Rossetti (b) William Morris
(c) A.C. Swinburne (d) None

216. The most successful of Swinburne's poems is
(a) "Atlanta" (b) "Poems and Ballads"
(c) "The Queen Mother and Rosamond" (d) "Laus Veneris"

217. The most powerful expression of physical passion is found in Swinburne's
   (a) "Atlanta"
   (b) "Hymn to Prospero"
   (c) "Laus Veneris"
   (d) "In Memory of Walter Savage Landor"
218. "Do noble deeds, not dream them all day long"—said
   (a) Kingsley
   (b) Newman
   (c) D.G. Rossetti
   (d) William Morris
219. Which William Morris' work bears on Chaucer for a model?
   (a) "Jason"
   (b) "The Defence"
   (c) "The Earthly Paradise"
   (d) "The Lovers of Gudrun"
220. The story "The Man who never Laughed Again" of William Morris' *The Earthly Paradise* is drawn from
   (a) Chaucer's *The Knight's Tale*
   (b) *Arabian Nights*
   (c) Chaucer's *The Miller's Tale*
   (d) None
221. The forgotten form of the medieval drama is reviewed by William Morris in
   (a) "Love is Enough"
   (b) "The Lovers of Gudrun"
   (c) "Balder is Dead"
   (d) None
222. *The Oxford and Cambridge Magazine* (1856) was founded and conducted for a year by
   (a) D.G. Rossetti
   (b) Christina Rossetti
   (c) A.C. Swinburne
   (d) William Morris
223. William Morris drew his poems from purely
   (a) Latin sources
   (b) Greek sources
   (c) German sources
   (d) English or Scandinavian sources
224. Who published the free version of Omar Khayyam's *The Rubaiyat of Omar Khayyam?*
   (a) Tennyson
   (b) Robert Browning
   (c) D.G. Rossetti
   (d) Edward Fitzgerald

225. A.C. Swinburne startled London in 1866 with
(a) "Poems and Ballads" (b) "Erecthus"
(c) "Songs after Sunrise" (d) "Atalanta in Calydon"

226. William Morris's *The Defence of Guinevere* shows him following Rossetti into a
(a) medieval world (b) romantic world
(c) dream world (d) none

227. In which poem, William Morris goes back to Chaucer's way of using verse for story-telling?
(a) "The Earthly Paradise" (b) "A Dream of John Bull"
(c) "News from Nowhere" (d) "The Well at the World's End"

228. *A Dream of John Bull* is a prose written by
(a) William Morris (b) D.G. Rossetti
(c) A.C. Swinburne (d) Edward Fitzgerald

229. Coventry Patmore's *The Angel in the House* is a
(a) poem (b) play
(c) narrative poem (d) novel in verse

## UNIT F: REALISM

### 1. William M. Thackeray

230. In 1829, W.M. Thackeray went to Cambridge and was one year junior to
(a) Tennyson (b) Arnold
(c) Dickens (d) Trollope

231. Whose intercourse with Goethe is recollected in Lewes's *Life of Goethe*?
(a) Dickens (b) D.G. Rossetti
(c) W.M. Thackeray (d) Anthony Trollope

232. From 1842 to 1854, Thackeray was a regular contributor to
(a) "Punch" (b) "The New Monthly Magazine"
(c) "Fraser's Magazine" (d) None

233. Thackeray's *Pendennis* corresponds to Dickens'
   (a) "David Copperfield" (b) "The Pickwick Papers"
   (c) "The Bleak House" (d) "Hard Times"

234. Thackeray's *Rebecca and Rowena* is the best ever penned
   (a) romance (b) burlesque (c) satire (d) comedy

235. Thackeray's criticism in *The Four Georges* was
   (a) literary (b) moral (c) religious (d) heartless

236. The influence of Scott is felt in Thackeray's
   (a) *Esmond* (b) *Pendennis*
   (c) *The Newcomes* (d) *The Four Georges*

237. William Thackeray was born in
   (a) London (b) America (c) Russia (d) Calcutta

238. Becky Sharp is a character in Thackeray's
   (a) *Vanity Fair* (b) *Pendennis*
   (c) *Esmond* (d) None

**2. Anthony Trollope**

239. Anthony Trollope was born in
   (a) 1810 (b) 1815 (c) 1820 (d) 1825

240. Anthony Trollope's *Chronicles of Barset shire* consists of .......... novels.
   (a) six (b) nine (c) ten (d) fifteen

241. The plot of *Doctor Thorne* was drawn for Anthony Trollope by his
   (a) wife (b) brother (c) sister (d) father

242. Trollope's *Framley Parsonage* forms a good criticism of
   (a) society (b) religion
   (c) his own work (d) the literary contemporaries

243. Mrs. Proudie is a character in the work of
   (a) Dickens (b) George Eliot
   (c) Thackeray (d) Anthony Trollope

244. In which work, Anthony Trollope discussed the simplicity of novel writing?
   (a) *Autobiography* (b) *The Warden*
   (c) *The Three Clerks* (d) *Rachael Ray*

245. Who is called by I for Evans, a male Jane Austen?
(a) George Eliot (b) Emily Bronte
(c) Anthony Trollope (d) Charlotte Bronte

246. That Rudyard Kipling has remained deservedly popular can be seen in *A Choice of Kipling's Verse* of
(a) T.S. Eliot (b) D.G. Rossetti
(c) William Morris (d) Walt Whitman

247. Katherine Mansfield was the wife of
(a) Middleton Murry (b) Charles Dickens
(c) Anthony Trollope (d) W.M. Thackeray

### 3. George Eliot

248. George Eliot was originally named
(a) Mary Ann Evans (b) Florence
(c) Mary Smith (d) Anna Hathaway

249. George Eliot was first sent to School at
(a) Attleborough (b) London
(c) Paris (d) Ottawa

250. The name George Eliot was adopted while ......... was appearing.
(a) *The Mill on the Floss* (b) *Silas Marner*
(c) *Adam Bede* (d) *Scenes of Clerical Life*

251. *Romola* is a turning point in the career of
(a) Charlotte Bronte (b) Mrs. Gaskell
(c) George Eliot (d) Emily Bronte

252. George Eliot's *The Mill on the Floss* appeared in
(a) 1860 (b) 1870 (c) 1890 (d) 1900

253. The last novel of George Eliot written in 1876 was
(a) *Silas Marner* (b) *Daniel Deronda*
(c) *Romola* (d) *Adam Bede*

254. The volume of literary essays which closed George Eliot's literary career was
(a) *Impressions of Theophrastus* (b) *The Legend of Jubal Such*
(c) *Felix Holt* (d) *Romola*

255. George Eliot's *Adam Bede* is a tale of
   (a) humour (b) seduction
   (c) exploitation (d) child abuse

256. A foreign land and a distant age is presented in George Eliot's
   (a) *Romola* (b) *Daniel Deronda*
   (c) *Silas Marner* (d) *Felix Holt*

257. Which work of George Eliot marks a decline in her powers?
   (a) *Daniel Deronda* (b) *Middlemarch*
   (c) *Adam Bede* (d) *The Mill on the Floss*

258. Which Victorian novelist acted as assistant editor of *The Westminster's Review*?
   (a) Charles Dickens (b) George Eliot
   (c) Charlotte Bronte (d) Emily Bronte

259. Who was the great stimulant of George Eliot's genius?
   (a) Herbert Spencer (b) G.H. Lewes
   (c) Charles Dickens (d) Anthony Trollope

260. Which work of George Eliot was a Wordsworth story told in prose as well as a novel?
   (a) *Adam Bede* (b) *Silas Marner*
   (c) *The Mill on the Floss* (d) *Middlemarch*

## ANSWERS

### Unit A

| | | | | | | | |
|---|---|---|---|---|---|---|---|
| 1. | (c) | 2. | (a) | 3. | (c) | 4. | (a) |
| 5. | (b) | 6. | (d) | 7. | (a) | 8. | (c) |
| 9. | (d) | 10. | (c) | 11. | (d) | 12. | (b) |
| 13. | (d) | 14. | (a) | 15. | (c) | 16. | (c) |
| 17. | (c) | 18. | (a) | 19. | (c) | 20. | (d) |
| 21. | (c) | 22. | (a) | 23. | (a) | 24. | (b) |
| 25. | (b) | 26. | (d) | 27. | (a) | | |

## Unit B

| | | | | | | | |
|---|---|---|---|---|---|---|---|
| 28. | (c) | 29. | (d) | 30. | (b) | 31. | (a) |
| 32. | (d) | 33. | (a) | 34. | (d) | 35. | (a) |
| 36. | (b) | 37. | (c) | 38. | (d) | 39. | (a) |
| 40. | (a) | 41. | (b) | 42. | (a) | 43. | (d) |
| 44. | (a) | 45. | (a) | 46. | (d) | 47. | (d) |
| 48. | (b) | 49. | (a) | 50. | (d) | 51. | (a) |
| 52. | (d) | 53. | (d) | 54. | (a) | 55. | (a) |
| 56. | (c) | 57. | (b) | 58. | (a) | 59. | (a) |
| 60. | (c) | 61. | (c) | 62. | (c) | 63. | (d) |
| 64. | (b) | 65. | (b) | 66. | (d) | 67. | (d) |
| 68. | (a) | 69. | (b) | 70. | (a) | 71. | (b) |
| 72. | (a) | 73. | (b) | 74. | (d) | 75. | (a) |
| 76. | (c) | 77. | (c) | 78. | (a) | 79. | (d) |
| 80. | (a) | 81. | (a) | 82. | (a) | 83. | (c) |
| 84. | (a) | 85. | (a) | | | | |

## Unit C

| | | | | | | | |
|---|---|---|---|---|---|---|---|
| 86. | (c) | 87. | (c) | 88. | (c) | 89. | (c) |
| 90. | (b) | 91. | (c) | 92. | (a) | 93. | (a) |
| 94. | (c) | 95. | (d) | 96. | (a) | 97. | (c) |
| 98. | (c) | 99. | (a) | 100. | (c) | 101. | (c) |
| 102. | (c) | 103. | (a) | 104. | (a) | 105. | (d) |
| 106. | (c) | 107. | (a) | 108. | (a) | 109. | (a) |
| 110. | (c) | 111. | (a) | 112. | (b) | 113. | (c) |
| 114. | (c) | 115. | (a) | 116. | (a) | 117. | (a) |
| 118. | (c) | | | | | | |

## Unit D

| | | | | | | | |
|---|---|---|---|---|---|---|---|
| 119. | (b) | 120. | (c) | 121. | (b) | 122. | (c) |
| 123. | (b) | 124. | (a) | 125. | (c) | 126. | (c) |
| 127. | (d) | 128. | (d) | 129. | (c) | 130. | (b) |
| 131. | (c) | 132. | (d) | 133. | (d) | 134. | (a) |

| | | | | | | | |
|---|---|---|---|---|---|---|---|
| 135. | (b) | 136. | (a) | 137. | (d) | 138. | (d) |
| 139. | (d) | 140. | (a) | 141. | (d) | 142. | (a) |
| 143. | (c) | 144. | (b) | 145. | (b) | 146. | (d) |
| 147. | (a) | 148. | (c) | 149. | (c) | 150. | (d) |
| 151. | (a) | 152. | (a) | 153. | (a) | 154. | (c) |
| 155. | (a) | 156. | (a) | 157. | (d) | 158. | (b) |
| 159. | (a) | 160. | (a) | 161. | (a) | 162. | (a) |
| 163. | (c) | 164. | (a) | 165. | (d) | 166. | (b) |
| 167. | (d) | 168. | (b) | 169. | (b) | 170. | (a) |
| 171. | (c) | 172. | (d) | 173. | (a) | 174. | (d) |
| 175. | (c) | 176. | (a) | 177. | (b) | 178. | (b) |
| 179. | (d) | 180. | (b) | 181. | (d) | 182. | (b) |
| 183. | (d) | 184. | (c) | 185. | (a) | 186. | (a) |
| 187. | (c) | 188. | (b) | 189. | (a) | 190. | (d) |
| 191. | (c) | 192. | (d) | 193. | (a) | | |

**Unit E**

| | | | | | | | |
|---|---|---|---|---|---|---|---|
| 194. | (d) | 195. | (a) | 196. | (c) | 197. | (b) |
| 198. | (c) | 199. | (a) | 200. | (b) | 201. | (b) |
| 202. | (a) | 203. | (d) | 204. | (c) | 205. | (d) |
| 206. | (a) | 207. | (d) | 208. | (b) | 209. | (a) |
| 210. | (d) | 211. | (c) | 212. | (a) | 213. | (d) |
| 214. | (b) | 215. | (c) | 216. | (a) | 217. | (c) |
| 218. | (a) | 219. | (a) | 220. | (b) | 221. | (a) |
| 222. | (d) | 223. | (d) | 224. | (d) | 225. | (a) |
| 226. | (a) | 227. | (a) | 228. | (a) | 229. | (d) |

**Unit F**

| | | | | | | | |
|---|---|---|---|---|---|---|---|
| 230. | (a) | 231. | (c) | 232. | (a) | 233. | (a) |
| 234. | (b) | 235. | (b) | 236. | (a) | 237. | (d) |
| 238. | (a) | 239. | (b) | 240. | (a) | 241. | (b) |
| 242. | (c) | 243. | (d) | 244. | (a) | 245. | (c) |
| 246. | (a) | 247. | (a) | 248. | (a) | 249. | (a) |

| | | | | | | | |
|---|---|---|---|---|---|---|---|
| 250. | (d) | 251. | (c) | 252. | (a) | 253. | (b) |
| 254. | (b) | 255. | (b) | 256. | (a) | 257. | (a) |
| 258. | (b) | 259. | (b) | 260. | (c) | | |

# Later Nineteenth Century (1875–1914)

# 9

## UNIT A: HISTORICAL PERSPECTIVE AND BACKGROUND

1. Edward VII came to the throne in
   (a) 1900 (b) 1901 (c) 1902 (d) 1903
2. The accession of George V took place in
   (a) 1908 (b) 1909 (c) 1910 (d) 1911
3. Queen Victoria succeeded to the throne of England after
   (a) George III (b) George IV
   (c) William IV (d) Edward VII
4. Queen Victoria became the Empress of India in
   (a) 1857 (b) 1837 (c) 1876 (d) 1887
5. The Golden Jubilee of Queen Victoria's reign was celebrated in
   (a) 1837 (b) 1887 (c) 1865 (d) 1901
6. Who is not a member of the Bloomsbury Group?
   (a) E.M. Forster (b) Leonard Woolf
   (c) Lytton Strachey (d) G.B. Shaw
7. The Irish National Theatre was constructed in
   (a) America (b) London (c) Dublin (d) Scotland
8. Who formed the Rhymer's Club?
   (a) the Expressionists (b) the Impressionists
   (c) the Surrealists (d) the Naturalists
9. Who is the pioneer of the Aesthetic Movement?
   (a) Walter Pater (b) Butler
   (c) Stevenson (d) Oscar Wilde

10. Who was the promoter of the slogan – 'Art for Art's Sake'?
    (a) Chesterton (b) Bennett
    (c) Conrad (d) Oscar Wilde

11. The revolt of the nineties against Victorianism
    (a) reiterates the old formula of Liberty, Equality and Eternity in a new setting
    (b) worships power rather then beauty
    (c) challenges the older values of art and life
    (d) All

12. Benedetto Croce was the main exponent of the
    (a) Surrealism (b) Expressionism
    (c) Dadaism (d) Impressionism

13. Pre-Raphaelite Brotherhood was formed in England in
    (a) 1846 (b) 1848 (c) 1850 (d) 1852

14. Which poetry is strongly pictorial?
    (a) Metaphysical Poetry (b) Romantic Poetry
    (c) Pre-Raphaelite Poetry (d) Victorian Poetry

15. The Oxford Movement was fundamentally a movement for
    (a) religious reform (b) political reform
    (c) social reform (d) economic reform

16. The chief exponent of the Oxford Movement was
    (a) Ruskin (b) John Henry Newman
    (c) Carlyle (d) John Stuart Mill

17. Who is considered to be the founder of the Oxford Movement?
    (a) John Kable (b) Mill
    (c) Newman (d) E.B. Pusey

18. Expressionism, a European artistic movement, started in 1900 in
    (a) England (b) America (c) Germany (d) France

19. Expressionism was a revolt against
    (a) naturalism (b) realism
    (c) impressionism (d) surrealism

20. Strindberg, the Swedish dramatist is an exponent of
    (a) Dadaism (b) Expressionism
    (c) Naturalism (d) Impressionism
21. *Dream Play* is a famous work of
    (a) Strindberg (b) Zola
    (c) Baudelaire (d) Dante
22. *The Cabinet of Dr. Caligari*, a film in the Expressionist manner, has been directed by Robert Wiene in
    (a) 1915 (b) 1920 (c) 1922 (d) 1925
23. Imagism was a self conscious movement in
    (a) drama (b) fiction (c) poetry (d) painting
24. Imagism was initiated by Ezra Pound and T.E. Hulme in about
    (a) 1911 (b) 1912 (c) 1913 (d) 1914
25. *A Retrospect* is an essay written in 1918 by
    (a) Ezra Pound (b) Amy Lowell
    (c) T.E. Hulme (d) T.S. Eliot
26. 'Bloomsbury Group' is the name given to those writers who were associated with the Bloomsbury area of London from about
    (a) 1907-1939 (b) 1909-1939
    (c) 1908-1938 (d) 1907-1937
27. All the members of the Bloomsbury Group were influenced by the philosopher
    (a) John Stuart Mill (b) Jacques Derrida
    (c) G.E. Moore (d) Aristotle
28. The main exponents of Aestheticism as a self conscious movement were
    (a) the American (b) the British
    (c) the Greek (d) the French
29. Who has propounded the theory of 'the poem for the poem's sake'?
    (a) Walter Pater (b) Oscar Wilde
    (c) Edgar Allan Poe (d) Arthur Symons

30. *The Poetic Principle* is a well-known book written by
    (a) Edgar Allan Poe (b) Baudelaire
    (c) Walter Pater (d) A.C. Swinburne
31. Flaubert, one of the main exponents of Aestheticism, was a/an
    (a) German (b) French (c) Indian (d) American
32. The poem *Less Fleurs du mal* has been written by
    (a) Baudelaire (b) Flaubert
    (c) Gautier (d) Mallarme
33. *A Rebours* (Against the Grain) is a novel written in 1884 by
    (a) Mallarme (b) Lionel Johnson
    (c) Huysman (d) Dowson
34. *The Yellow Book* is the name of a
    (a) novel (b) magazine (c) drama (d) biography
35. The editor of the first four volumes of *The Yellow Book* is
    (a) Aubery Beardsley (b) Lionel Johnson
    (c) Max Beerbohm (d) Frederick Rolfe
36. *The Yellow Book* is a magazine which appeared between
    (a) 1891-94 (b) 1892-95 (c) 1894-97 (d) 1893-96
37. Ford Madoc Ford is a famous novelist of
    (a) the Victorian Period (b) the Edwardian Period
    (c) the Post I World War Period (d) the Post II World War Period

## UNIT B: THE REVOLT AGAINST MECHANISM

### 1. Samuel Butler

38. Samuel Butler was born in
    (a) 1830 (b) 1832 (c) 1835 (d) 1837
39. Butler's *Erewhon* which is a series of episodes and dissertations, is worthy of being compared with
    (a) *Gulliver's Travels* (b) "Mac Flecknoe"
    (c) "The Rape of the Lock" (d) None of the above

40. *Erewhon* is a well-known novel written by
    (a) Samuel Butler (b) George Gissing
    (c) Arnold Bennett (d) None of the above
41. Butler's *Erewhon* stands for the country
    (a) America (b) England
    (c) New Zealand (d) India
42. The title of Butler's *Hudibras* has been taken from
    (a) *The Faerie Queene* (b) *Paradise Lost*
    (c) *The Pilgrim's Progress* (d) *The Shoemaker's Holiday*
43. Theobald Pontifex is a character portrayed by
    (a) Kipling (b) Butler (c) Stevenson (d) H.G. Wells
44. 'Family life is a prison where parents are the tyrannical keepers... school education is a humbug...'
    This is the main theme in Butler's
    (a) *Hudibras* (b) *The Way of All Flesh*
    (c) *Erewhon* (d) None of the above
45. Which work of Butler was published posthumously in 1903?
    (a) *Erewhon* (b) *The Way of All Flesh*
    (c) *Hudibras* (d) None of the above

**2. George Meredith**

46. Samuel Butler's *The Way of All Flesh*
    (a) puritanical (b) semi-autobiographical novel
    (c) drama (d) none
47. Butler's ideas influenced by
    (a) Dr. Johnson (b) George Bernard Shaw
    (c) Oldham (d) Swift
48. George Meredith is a great .......... novelist of the Victorian Age.
    (a) historical (b) social
    (c) psychological (d) political
49. Meredith's novels express his .......... attitude towards life.
    (a) pessimistic (b) optimistic
    (c) nihilistic (d) opportunistic

50. Meredith's characters are drawn from
    (a) upper middle class society (b) lower class society
    (c) middle class society (d) upper class society
51. Meredith concentrates on the .......... life of his characters.
    (a) outer (b) inner
    (c) outward (d) typical trail of the period
52. 'Under Yonder beech-treesingle on the grenn sward,
    Couched with her arms behind her golden head.
    Knees and tresses folded to slip and ripple idly.
    Lies my young love sleeping in the shade.'
    These lines have been written by
    (a) Swinburne (b) Morris
    (c) C.G. Rossetti (d) Meredith
53. Which of the following works by Meredith is a prose piece?
    (a) *The Shaving of Shagpat* (b) *The Ordeal of Richard Feveral*
    (c) *Evan Harrington* (d) *The Egoist*
54. For Meredith, the novel was far more than mere
    (a) melodrama (b) social reflection
    (c) story writing (d) none
55. Who is known as the 19th century Richardson?
    (a) Emily Bronte (b) George Meredith
    (c) Thomas Hardy (d) Conrad
56. Mrs. Berry, the old nurse is a character in Meredith's
    (a) *Evan Harrington* (b) *The Ordeal of Richard Feverel*
    (c) *The Tragic Comedians* (d) None of the above
57. Meredith explored the utmost panorama of the interpretation of life through the rudiments of
    (a) religion (b) philosophy
    (c) satire (d) divinity

58. Lucy, Clara, Diana—these heroines appear in the novels of
    (a) Meredith (b) Hardy
    (c) Dickens (d) Oscar Wilde
59. *The Egoist* is one of the popular novels of
    (a) Kipling (b) Meredith (c) Conrad (d) Stevenson
60. *Diana of the Crossways* was one of the works of
    (a) Hardy (b) Meredith (c) Conrad (d) Bennett
61. Which is the easiest of Meredith's novels?
    (a) *The Adventures of Henry Richmond* (b) *The Egoist*
    (c) *The Ordeal of Richard Feverel* (d) None of the above
62. Meredith's *Beauchamp's Career* was written in
    (a) 1874 (b) 1872 (c) 1876 (d) 1878
63. George Meredith was born in
    (a) 1828 (b) 1833 (c) 1838 (d) 1843
64. Meredith wrote his first novel *The Ordeal of Richard Feverel* in
    (a) 1856 (b) 1858 (c) 1859 (d) 1860
65. *Modern Love*, a series of poems based on the story of Meredith's own marriage was published in
    (a) 1860 (b) 1862 (c) 1864 (d) 1866
66. After whose death Meredith was elected President of the Society of Authors in 1892?
    (a) Tennyson (b) Browning
    (c) Arnold (d) None of the above
67. Meredith died in
    (a) 1906 (b) 1907 (c) 1908 (d) 1909
68. In which work of Meredith we find the portrayal of national struggle?
    (a) *The Egoist* (b) *Vittoria*
    (c) *Diana of the Crossways* (d) *The Amazing Marriage*

69. Sir Willoughby Patterne is a character in Meredith's
    (a) *The Adventures of Harry Richmond* (b) *The Shaving of Shagpat*
    (c) *The Egoist* (d) *Vittoria*
70. Which writer spoke out for full female emancipation?
    (a) Thomas Hardy (b) Meredith
    (c) Anthony Trollope (d) George Eliot

**3. Thomas Hardy**

71. Hardy is a ..... novelist.
    (a) social (b) regional (c) political (d) historical
72. Hardy's characters belong to the
    (a) lower class (b) middle class
    (c) upper class (d) upper middle class
73. Hardy's *Tess of D'Urbervilles* deals with the tragedy of a village
    (a) boy (b) maid (c) man (d) woman
74. Thomas Hardy died in
    (a) 1923 (b) 1928 (c) 1933 (d) 1938
75. Hardy's novels are novels of ...... life.
    (a) rustic (b) urban (c) town (d) country
76. Thomas Hardy was born in
    (a) 1830 (b) 1835 (c) 1840 (d) 1845
77. Thomas Hardy was initially a
    (a) novelist (b) playwright
    (c) poet (d) story writer
78. Hardy's first novel *Desperate Remedies* appeared in
    (a) 1871 (b) 1881 (c) 1876 (d) 1886
79. Hardy's first successful novel was
    (a) *The Woodlanders* (b) *The Mayor of Casterbridge*
    (c) *Far From the Madding Crowd* (d) *Jude, the Obscure*

80. Hardy's last novel was
    (a) *Jude, the Obscure* (b) *The Woodlanders*
    (c) *The Return of the Native* (d) *Far From the Madding Crowd*

81. Arabella Donn, a character of Hardy appears in his novel
    (a) *The Mayor of Casterbridge* (b) *Jude, the Obscure*
    (c) *The Woodlanders* (d) None of the above

82. The first novel of Thomas Hardy is
    (a) *The Return of the Native* (b) *Jude, the Obscure*
    (c) *Desperate Remedies* (d) *The Woodlanders*

83. Thomas Hardy was by profession
    (a) an engineer (b) an architect
    (c) a secretary to the British Authority (d) none of the above

84. Hardy was a/an
    (a) pessimist (b) fatalist (c) optimist (d) methodist

85. Hardy was influenced by the teaching of
    (a) Hobbes (b) Locke
    (c) Darwin (d) Wordsworth

86. Eustacia Vye meets his end by
    (a) suicide (b) accidentally falling from the cliff
    (c) murder (d) accidentally drowning in the lake

87. To which novel Hardy added the sub-title 'a rural painting of the Dutch school'?
    (a) *Under the Greenwood Tree* (b) *The Return of the Native*
    (c) *Far From the Madding Crowd* (d) *The Mayor of Casterbridge*

88. Gabriel Oak is a character in Hardy's
    (a) *Far From the Madding Crowd* (b) *The Woodlanders*
    (c) *Tess of D'Urbervilles* (d) *Jude, the Obscure*

89. Eustacia Vye is a character in Hardy's
   (a) *The Return of the Native* (b) *Tess of D'Urbervilles*
   (c) *The Mayor of Casterbridge* (d) *The Woodlanders*

90. Which of Hardy's novel is regarded as his tragic masterpiece?
   (a) *The Woodlanders* (b) *Jude, the Obscure*
   (c) *Tess of D'Urbervilles* (d) None of the above

91. Which novel of Hardy portrays a girl 'simple, sensuous and passionate' who never comes to terms with the world?
   (a) *The Return of the Native* (b) *Tess of D'Urbervilles*
   (c) *The Mayor of Casterbridge* (d) *The Woodlanders*

92. In Hardy's *Jude, the Obscure* Jude is the name of a
   (a) boy (b) girl (c) man (d) woman

93. What is meant by 'Wessex'?
   (a) The region where Bronte sisters lived
   (b) The name of a country in Scotland
   (c) The region in which Hardy's novels are set
   (d) The home town of George Eliot

94. In which of Hardy's novels the scene of a wife's auction takes place?
   (a) *Jude, the Obscure* (b) *Tess of D'Urbervilles*
   (c) *The Mayor Of Casterbridge* (d) *Return of the Native*

95. Hardy's *The Dynasts* deals with
   (a) the Napoleonic Wars (b) Queen Victoria's reign
   (c) the Industrial Revolution (d) science and religion

96. Which novelist was given the award of 'Order of Merit'?
   (a) Thomas Hardy (b) Charles Dickens
   (c) Emily Bronte (d) Charlotte Bronte

97. 'Happiness is but an occasional episode in the general drama of pain.' This line appears in Hardy's
   (a) *Tess of D'Urbervilles* (b) *The Mayor of Casterbridge*
   (c) *The Return of the Native* (d) *Jude, the Obscure*

98. Hardy believed in the philosophy of
    (a) Free will (b) Character is Destiny
    (c) Man as the master of his own fate (d) Immanent Will

99. Name the novel of Hardy in which he quotes Shakespeare's remark:
    'As flies to the wanton boys are we to the gods
    They kill us for their sport.'
    (a) *Tess of D'Urbervilles* (b) *The Mayor of Casterbridge*
    (c) *The Woodlanders* (d) *Jude, the Obscure*

100. Hardy's *The Dynasts* is a
    (a) drama (b) novel (c) poem (d) essay

### 4. George Gissing

101. George Gissing dealt mainly with the
    (a) upper class people (b) lower class
    (c) middle class (d) upper middle class

102. Which work of Gissing shows his liveliness as an essayist?
    (a) *Demos* (b) *The Nether World*
    (c) *New Grub Street* (d) *The Private Papers of Henry Ryecroft*

103. Which novel of Gissing tells of the rise and moral decline of a politician?
    (a) *The Nether World* (b) *Demos*
    (c) *New Grub Street* (d) None of the above

104. Sidney Kirkwood, a character of Gissing, appears in his novel
    (a) *Born in Exile* (b) *New Grub Street*
    (c) *The Nether World* (d) None of the above

105. *The Old Women* is a well known novel written by
    (a) Hardy (b) Gissing (c) Meredith (d) Thomson

## UNIT C: THE NEW ROMANTICISM

### 1. A.C. Swinburne

106. A.C. Swinburne was born in
    (a) 1835 (b) 1836 (c) 1837 (d) 1838

107. Who was called 'a reed through which all things blew to music'?
(a) Morris (b) Swinburne
(c) D.G. Rossetti (d) None of the above

108. 'If you were April's lady
And I were lord in May
We'd throw with leaves for hours
And draw for days with flowers.'
These lines occur in Swinburne's
(a) "Atalanta in Calydon" (b) "A Match"
(c) "Poems and Ballads" (d) None of the above

109. Swinburne's "Atlanta in Calydon" is a
(a) comedy (b) tragedy
(c) tragi comedy (d) history

110. Swinburne's "Atlanta in Calydon", a beautiful lyric drama is modelled on
(a) Greek tragedy (b) Roman tragedy
(c) English tragedy (d) Spanish tragedy

111. "Songs before Sunrise" is a well-known work of
(a) Morris (b) D.G. Rossetti
(c) A.C. Swinburne (d) Edith Sitwell

**2. R.L. Stevenson**

112. R.L. Stevenson was born in
(a) 1860 (b) 1870 (c) 1850 (d) 1840

113. Stevenson's first masterpiece.....was published in 1883.
(a) *Kidnapped* (b) *Treasure Island*
(c) *Beach of Falesa* (d) *Weir of Hermiston*

114. Which fiction of Stevenson illustrates the doubleness of man's nature?
(a) *Treasure Island* (b) *Kidnapped*
(c) *Weir of Hermiston* (d) *Dr. Jekyll and Mr. Hyde*

115. Besides being a novelist, Stevenson was also a/an
(a) poet (b) historian
(c) essayist (d) philosopher

116. *An Inland Voyage* written in 1878, is a work of
   (a) Kipling (b) Chesterton
   (c) Stevenson (d) Conrad
117. *Travels with a Donkey*, a travel book has been written by
   (a) Stevenson (b) George Gissing
   (c) George Moore (d) Rudyard Kipling
118. Besides *St. Ives*, which novel was left unfinished at Stevenson's death?
   (a) *Kidnapped* (b) *The Master of Ballantrae*
   (c) *Weir of Hermiston* (d) *An Inland Voyage*
119. *Dr. Jekyll and Mr. Hyde* is a
   (a) modern allegory (b) romance
   (c) satire (d) fable
120. *Treasure Island* was published in a
   (a) periodical (b) London daily
   (c) British Journal (d) none of the above
121. Which novel by Stevenson was left unfinished by his early death?
   (a) *Treasure Island* (b) *Kidnapped*
   (c) *St. Ives* (d) None of the above
122. Stevenson's *Underwoods* is a volume of
   (a) stories (b) poems (c) essays (d) hymns
123. Whose novels mark a return to the pure romanticism of Walter Scott?
   (a) Meredith (b) Stevenson
   (c) Hardy (d) Oscar Wilde
124. The novels *The Master of Ballantrae* and *David Balfour* have been written by
   (a) Stevenson (b) Conrad
   (c) H.G. Wells (d) Hardy
125. *New Arabian Nights*, written in 1882 is a work of
   (a) Butler (b) Stevenson
   (c) Kipling (d) H.G. Wells

126. Who is a writer of novel of adventure?
   (a) Kipling (b) Meredith
   (c) Stevenson (d) Hardy
127. The novel *Treasure Island* has been written by
   (a) H.G. Wells (b) Stevenson
   (c) Conrad (d) Oscar Wilde

**3. Walter Pater**

128. *Marius, the Epicurean*, a well-known novel has been written by
   (a) Meredith (b) Wilde
   (c) Walter Pater (d) Hardy
129. *Essay on Style*, a critical work has been composed by
   (a) Walter Pater (b) Matthew Arnold
   (c) John Symonds (d) None of the above
130. Who formulated a philosophy of receptivity to works of art as a means of enriching human experience through the intensest responses of the sensibilities?
   (a) Ruskin (b) Walter Pater
   (c) Morris (d) Swinburne
131. The Core of Pater's thinking can be found in the famous 'Conclusion' to his work
   (a) *Studies in the Hisory of the Renaissance* (b) *Essay on Style*
   (c) *Marius, the Epicurean* (d) *Imaginary Portraits*
132. The expression 'hedonistic aestheticism' is related to
   (a) Swinburne (b) Meredith
   (c) Walter Pater (d) Morris

**4. Oscar Wilde**

133. Oscar Wilde was born in Ireland in
   (a) 1854 (b) 1856 (c) 1858 (d) 1860
134. *The Picture of Dorian Gray* is a ... written by Wilde.
   (a) novel (b) drama (c) poem (d) short story
135. Wilde's play *The Importance of Being Earnest* was published in
   (a) 1890 (b) 1893 (c) 1895 (d) 1898

136. Oscar Wilde died in France in
(a) 1898 (b) 1900 (c) 1902 (d) 1905

137. Which work of Oscar Wilde was written in imprisonment?
(a) *A Woman of No Importance* (b) *The Happy Prince*
(c) *De Profundis* (d) *The Duchess of Padua*

138. Which play of Wilde was first written in French?
(a) *The Duchess of Padua* (b) *Salome*
(c) *A Woman of No Importance* (d) *An Ideal Husband*

139. Which work of Wilde reflects his aestheticism in all its aspects?
(a) *The House of Pomegranates* (b) *The Happy Prince*
(c) *De Profundis* (d) *The Picture of Dorian Gray*

140. Which author, being charged with a breach of morality spent two years in penal servitude?
(a) Walter Pater (b) Oscar Wilde
(c) Swinburne (d) Arthur Symons

141. Who has paid explicit tribute to Keats and Shelley in his poem "The Garden of Eros"?
(a) Oscar Wilde (b) A.E. Housman
(c) Robert Bridges (d) Morris

142. In which work of Wilde, the cruelty of sexual passion has been studied in a realsitic manner?
(a) *Salome* (b) *The Importance of Being Earnest*
(c) *De Profundis* (d) *Windermere's Fan*

## UNIT D: NOVEL

### 1. William Ernest Henley

143. Name the writer who wrote for the stage in collaboration with Stevenson?
(a) Kipling (b) William Henley
(c) Shaw (d) Wells

144. William Ernest Henley, a contemporary of Kipling, has the temperament of
(a) imperialism (b) traditionalism
(c) socialism (d) realism

145. Henley's collection of poems *A Book of Verses* was published in
(a) 1886 (b) 1887 (c) 1888 (d) 1889

146. Which of the following writers led the life of an invalid?
(a) Kipling (b) William Henley
(c) Carlyle (d) Kingsley Amis

147. Henley is chiefly a contemporary of
(a) Kipling (b) Carlyle (c) Ruskin (d) Chesterton

**2. Rudyard Kipling**

148. Rudyard Kipling was born in
(a) 1860 (b) 1865 (c) 1870 (d) 1875

149. Rudyard Kipling was born in
(a) England (b) America (c) India (d) Scotland

150. Kipling is a writer of
(a) *Wandering Willie's Tale* (b) *The White Stocking*
(c) *The Case Book of Sherlock Holmes* (d) *Willie Winkie*

151. *The Brushwood Boy* is a novelette written by
(a) Kipling (b) Chesterton
(c) Conrad (d) Oscar Wilde

152. Kipling was essentially the poet of
(a) soldiers (b) sailors
(c) fighters (d) both a and b

153. "The Barrack Room Ballads", "The Seven Seas", "The Five Nations" – these poems have been written by
(a) Hopkins (b) Kipling
(c) Francis Thompson (d) None of the above

154. Kipling's first published volume, which had been in verse was
(a) *Departmental Ditties* (b) *Barrack-Room Ballads*
(c) *Ballad of East and West* (d) None of the above

155. *Life's Handicap* and *Many Inventions*—these volumes of short stories were written by
(a) Stevenson (b) Kipling (c) Meredith (d) Hardy

156. Besides being a novelist, Kipling was also a/an
(a) dramatist (b) essayist (c) poet (d) journalist

157. Kipling, in his mastery of rhythm, comes close to
(a) Morris (b) Rossetti
(c) Swinburne (d) None of the above

158. 'But there is neither East nor West, ——
When two strongmen stand face to face,
Though they came from the end of the earth'.
These lines occur in the poem of
(a) Morris (b) Swinburne
(c) Arnold (d) Kipling

159. *The Jungle Book* has been written by
(a) Rudyard Kipling (b) George Moore
(c) Stevenson (d) Gissing

160. Which work of Kipling contains the stories of the British in India?
(a) *Puck of Pook's Hill* (b) *Plain Tales from the Hills*
(c) *The Jungle Book* (d) None of the above

161. *Kim* is a well-known novel in English written by
(a) Stevenson (b) Anthony Trollope
(c) Kipling (d) Samuel Butler

162. Which poem was written by Kipling to celebrate Queen Victoria's Diamond Jubilee in 1897?
(a) "Fuzzy Wuzzy" (b) "Recessional"
(c) "Gunga Din" (d) "The Mary Gloster"

163. Which of the following writers has been a considerable traveller?
(a) Rudyard Kipling (b) H.G. Wells
(c) G.K. Chesterton (d) Arnold Bennett

164. The Imperialistic note is prominent in the works of
(a) G.B. Shaw (b) Galsworthy
(c) Rudyard Kipling (d) None of the above

165. The only romance Kipling wrote is
(a) *The Friend*
(b) *The Naulakha*
(c) *The Devil and the Deep Sea*
(d) *Captains Courageous*

166. Rudyard Kipling received the Nobel Prize for Literature in the year
(a) 1905 (b) 1906 (c) 1907 (d) 1908

167. Kipling tried his hand on a Gothic tale of mystery and horror in
(a) *Captains Courageous*
(b) *The Mark of the Beast*
(c) *The Tomb of His Ancestors*
(d) *The Man Who Was Thursday*

### 3. G.K. Chesterton

168. *The Napoleon of Notting Hill* is a novel written by
(a) G.K. Chesterton
(b) William Henley
(c) Kipling
(d) George Moore

169. Chesterton's *The Father Brown Stories* is a collection of
(a) love stories
(b) detective stories
(c) historical stories
(d) religious stories

170. The novel *The Man Who Was Thursday* has been written by
(a) Joseph Conrad
(b) G.K. Chesterton
(c) Rudyard Kipling
(d) H.G. Wells

171. *Heretics*, *Orthodoxy* and *What's Wrong with the World?*- these are Chesterton's
(a) essays
(b) poems
(c) philosophical works
(d) criticisms

172. Chesterton's full name is
(a) Gilbert Keith Chesterton
(b) George Keith Chesterton
(c) George Kingsley Chesterton
(d) Gilbert Kent Chesterton

### 4. H.G. Wells

173. In his novels of character, H.G. Wells portrays
(a) lower middle class
(b) lower class
(c) upper class
(d) middle class

174. In which novel of H.G. Wells there is a reference of a young woman who rebels against the social evils?
(a) *Tono Bungay* (b) *The World of William Clissold*
(c) *Ann Veronica* (d) *Kipps*

175. *The Invisible Man* is a well known work of
(a) Arnold Bennett (b) H.G. Wells
(c) Butler (d) Gissing

176. *The Time Machine* is a well-known novel written by
(a) H.G. Wells (b) Meredith
(c) Stevenson (d) Hardy

177. The novels like *Kipps* and *The History of Mr. Polly* have been written by
(a) H.G. Wells (b) Joseph Conrad
(c) Kipling (d) Arnold Bennett

178. The book *An Experiment in Autobiography* has been written by
(a) Bennett (b) Hardy
(c) H.G. Wells (d) Shaw

179. H.G. Wells formed a novel technique of
(a) technical exploration (b) scientific romance
(c) historical inclination (d) all

180. H.G. Wells was born in
(a) 1864 (b) 1866 (c) 1868 (d) 1870

181. H.G. Wells' *First and Last Things* is a work of
(a) philosophy (b) history
(c) polity (d) sociology

182. Wells' *The New Machiavelli* portrays the struggle between
(a) life and death (b) love and hatred
(c) political ambition and love (d) politics and philosophy

183. *My Days and Dreams* is an autobiography of
(a) H.G. Wells (b) Edward Carpenter
(c) Mary Arnold (d) E.F. Benson

184. Wells' well-known novel *The Time Machine* was published in
(a) 1890 (b) 1895 (c) 1898 (d) 1900

185. Mr. Hoopdriver is a character in Wells' novel
(a) *Mr. Lewisham* (b) *Kipps*
(c) *The Wheels of Chance* (d) *The Time Machine*

186. *Tono Bungay* is a famous novel of
(a) H.G. Wells (b) Stevenson
(c) Kipling (d) Oscar Wilde

187. The voluminous book *Outline of History* has been written by
(a) Rudyard Kipling (b) Samuel Butler
(c) H.G. Wells (d) James M. Barrie

188. Which work of H.G. Wells presents a realistic portrayal of English society in the dark days of the First World War?
(a) *The Time Machine* (b) *The Wheels of Chance*
(c) *Tono Bungay* (d) *Mr. Britling sees it Through*

189. In H.G. Wells' *Tono Bungay*, 'Tono Bungay' is the name of a
(a) medicine (b) person (c) village (d) town

190. In Wells' *The History of Mr. Polly*, Polly is a
(a) teacher (b) doctor
(c) shopkeeper (d) banker

191. Which work of H.G. Wells reminds us of Swift's *Gulliver's Travels*?
(a) *The Food of the Gods* (b) *The Sea Lady*
(c) *The Day of the Comet* (d) *The Island of Dr. Moreau*

192. Which work of Wells centres round certain developments of modern journalism?
(a) *The Wonderful Visit* (b) *The Day of the Comet*
(c) *The First Man in the Moon* (d) *The Invisible Man*

**5. Joseph Conrad**

193. Conrad's main concern was with
(a) plot (b) characters
(c) effect of events on the persons involved (d) story

194. Conrad's novels deal with the adventure and romance of
(a) mountain life (b) sea life
(c) jungle life (d) social life

195. Which writer was strongly influenced by the literature of France?
(a) Conrad (b) Wells
(c) Kipling (d) Oscar Wilde

196. Mr. Kurtz is a character in Conrad's
(a) *Lord Jim* (b) *Heart of Darkness*
(c) *Nostromo* (d) *Under Western Eyes*

197. Which novel of Conrad has its setting in Tsarist Russia?
(a) *Under Western Eyes* (b) *Typhoon*
(c) *Heart of Darkness* (d) *Lord Jim*

198. Which writer was born of Polish parents in the Ukraine?
(a) Kipling (b) Conrad (c) Stevenson (d) Bennett

199. *Under Western Eyes,* a novel dealing with life in the Ukraine under the Tsar's domination, has been written by
(a) Bennett (b) Kipling (c) Conrad (d) Barrie

200. Conrad's first novel *Almayer's Folly* was published in
(a) 1890 (b) 1892 (c) 1894 (d) 1896

201. In which work of Conrad, the extravagant loyalty of man to man has been shown?
(a) *Lord Jim* (b) *Typhoon*
(c) *Youth* (d) *The Nigger of the Narcissus*

202. *Lord Jim*, a well-known novel has been written by
(a) Conrad (b) Bennett
(c) H.G. Wells (d) Stevenson

203. In which novel of Conrad, there appears a French officer?
(a) *Almayer's Folly* (b) *The Nigger of the Narcissus*
(c) *Lord Jim* (d) *The Secret Agent*

204. Which of the following novelists was born in the year of Sepoy Mutiny?
(a) Joseph Conrad (b) H.G. Wells
(c) Bennett (d) Galsworthy

205. Which writer was known for his passion for the sea?
(a) Galsworthy (b) Kipling
(c) H.G. Wells (d) Conrad

206. In which novel of Conrad, there is a scene of a ship, laden with pilgrims, sinking?
(a) *Lord Jim* (b) *An Outcast of the Islands*
(c) *Almayer's Folly* (d) *The Nigger of the Narcissus*

207. In which of Conrad's novel, the sea plays no part?
(a) *Typhoon* (b) *An Outcast of the Islands*
(c) *Under Western Eyes* (d) *Lord Jim*

208. Which novel of Conrad is a vast study of a South American country 'Costaguana'?
(a) *Under Western Eyes* (b) *Nostromo*
(c) *The Nigger of the Narcissus* (d) *Almayer's Folly*

209. Which novel of Conrad has a Malayan background?
(a) *An Outcast of the Islands* (b) *Lord Jim*
(c) *The Nigger of the Narcissus* (d) *Heart of Darkness*

210. Which novelist was a seafarer for twenty years?
(a) Rudyard Kipling (b) H.G. Wells
(c) G.B. Shaw (d) Joseph Conrad

211. 'Korzeniowski' is the surname of
(a) Conrad (b) Kipling
(c) Galsworthy (d) Wells

212. 'French is the only modern language fit for literature.' Who said this?
(a) Shaw (b) Galsworthy
(c) Kipling (d) Conrad

213. Alone, alone, all, all alone,
Alone on a wide, wide sea.
These lines echo the philosophy of which writer?
(a) J.M. Barrie (b) H.G. Wells
(c) Conrad (d) Chesterton

214. Which work of Conrad verges on melodrama?
(a) *Typhoon* (b) *Victory*
(c) *Under Western Eyes* (d) *The Nigger of the Narcissus*

215. Which of Conrad's novels is considered to be the best?
(a) *The Nigger of the Narcissus* (b) *Almayer's Folly*
(c) *Under Western Eyes* (d) *Victory*

216. *The Mirror of the Sea* is Conrad's
(a) novel (b) short story
(c) essay (d) autobiography

217. *The Secret Agent* is a famous novel by
(a) Joseph Conrad (b) Samuel Butler
(c) Arnold Bennett (d) H.G. Wells

**6. Arnold Bennett**

218. *The Old Wives' Tale* is a work of
(a) Lawrence (b) Samuel Butler
(c) Arnold Bennett (d) Thomas Hardy

219. Bennett has a fascination towards reading the French models particularly
(a) Zola (b) Bergson
(c) Maupassant (d) None of the above

220. *Truth about an Author* is an autobiography of
(a) Stevenson (b) Bennett
(c) Butler (d) Conrad

221. *Clayhanger*, a well known novel of Bennett, has been written in
(a) 1908 (b) 1909 (c) 1910 (d) 1911

222. Arnold Bennett was born in the year
(a) 1861 (b) 1863 (c) 1865 (d) 1867

223. Bennett's first popular book *Anna of the Five Towns* was published in
(a) 1895 (b) 1900 (c) 1905 (d) 1910

224. Mrs. Baines, a character of Bennett appears in
(a) *Anna of the Five Towns* (b) *Clayhanger*
(c) *Old Wives' Tale* (d) None of the above

225. Which is Arnold Bennett's first novel?
(a) *Clayhanger* (b) *The Pretty Lady*
(c) *A Man from the North* (d) *Anna of the Five Towns*

226. Bennett is known mainly for his
(a) novels (b) short stories
(c) criticisms (d) a and b

227. Which author was greatly influenced by French culture?
(a) Joseph Conrad (b) John Galsworthy
(c) Arnold Bennett (d) J.M. Barrie

## UNIT E: POETRY

### 1. J.M. Barrie

228. *The Little Minister* and *Sentimental Tommy* have been written by
(a) Stevenson (b) J.M. Barrie
(c) Kipling (d) Oscar Wilde

229. 'His softness was really a kind of toughness, and the most deplorable fault of his work is not sensibility run to seed, but obduracy'—This remark to Edwin Muir applies to
(a) Beckett (b) Shaw
(c) James Matthew Barrie (d) Galsworthy

230. *Dear Brutus* and *Mary Rose* are the plays written by
(a) J.M. Barrie (b) Beckett
(c) Granville Barker (d) Galsworthy

231. J.M. Barrie was born in
(a) 1850 (b) 1855 (c) 1860 (d) 1865

232. *The Window in Thrums* is a well known prose fiction written by
(a) G.B. Shaw (b) J.M. Barrie
(c) Stevenson (d) Kipling

233. The gipsy girl is a character in Barrie's
(a) *The Little Minister* (b) *A Window in Thrums*
(c) *Sentimental Tommy* (d) *Tommy and Grizel*

234. J.M. Barrie produced a light comedy
(a) *Walker, London* (b) *Sentimental Tommy*
(c) *The Little Minister* (d) None of the above

235. Name a satire in one act written by J.M. Barrie
(a) *The Little Minister* (b) *The Twelve Pound Look*
(c) *The Window in Thrums* (d) *The Admirable Crichton*

236. Which play of Barrie is considered to be his finest dramatic work?
(a) *The Admirable Crichton* (b) *The Little Minister*
(c) *Walker, London* (d) *The Boy, David*

237. "Farewell, Miss Julie Logan" is a long short story written by
(a) J.M. Barrie (b) Galsworthy
(c) G.B. Shaw (d) Stevenson

### 2. Walter de la Mare

238. Which poem of Walter de la Mare portrays dreadful figures of the criminal in the dock, the drug addict the suicide?
(a) "The Fleeting" (b) "Martha"
(c) "The Veil" (d) None of the above

239. Martha is a character in the work of
(a) Walter de la Mare (b) W.B. Yeats
(c) T.S. Eliot (d) Kipling

240. Walter de la Mare is a poet of
(a) the Georgian Period (b) the Romantic Period
(c) the Victorian Period (d) the Edwardian Period

241. "Her voice and her narrow chin
Her grave small lovely head

Seemed half the meaning
Of the words she said."
These lines have been composed by

(a) W.H. Davies (b) Sir Henry Newbolt
(c) Walter de la Mare (d) Edward Thomas

242. Which poet is considerd to be a master in the art of creating atmosphere alive with mystery and strangeness?

(a) W.H. Davies (b) John Masefield
(c) A.E. Housman (d) Walter de la Mare

### 3. John Masefield

243. Masefield's poem "The Everlasting Mercy" has a ......... theme.

(a) religious (b) political (c) social (d) moral

244. Masefield's later plays show an appreciable evidence of the

(a) American influence (b) French influence
(c) Japanese influence (d) Latin influence

245. Which work of Masefield brought out fully his genius as a poet?

(a) "Salt Water Ballads" (b) "The Everlasting Mercy"
(c) "The Widow in the Bye Street" (d) "The Daffodil Fields"

246. "It has not been done, the sea, not yet been done.
From the inside, by one who really knows."
These lines have been written by

(a) A.E. Housman (b) Swinburne
(c) John Masefield (d) Alfred Noyes

247. "Beauty", "Her Heart" and "Being Her Friend" are the poems written by

(a) John Masefield (b) Robert Bridges
(c) A.C. Swinburne (d) Walter de la Mare

### 4. A.E. Housman

248. *A Shropshire Lad* is a volume of poems written by

(a) Walter de la Mare (b) A.E. Housman
(c) Rudyard Kipling (d) Robert Bridges

249. A.E. Houseman was a Professor of
(a) Latin (b) French (c) Greek (d) Religion

250. Housman is prominently compared with
(a) Yeats (b) Gray (c) Eliot (d) Browning

251. Which collection of poems of Housman was published posthumously?
(a) *More Poems* (b) *Last Poems*
(c) *Shropshire Lad* (d) None

252. They say my verse is sad: no wonder;
Its narrow measure spans
Tears of eternity, and sorrow,
Not mine, but man's.
These are the lines of
(a) John Masefield (b) A.E. Housman
(c) Alfred Noyes (d) Walter de la Mare

## UNIT F: DRAMA

### 1. John Galsworthy

253. Which novel of Galsworthy portrays a miserly London bookseller and is a masterly study of human eccentricity?
(a) *Lord Raingo* (b) *Riceyman Steps*
(c) *Clayhanger* (d) *Anna of the Five Towns*

254. *A Modern Comedy* and *The End of the Chapter* have been written by
(a) John Galsworthy (b) H.G. Wells
(c) Bennett (d) Conrad

255. The characters of Galsworthy are never drawn from
(a) lower class (b) middle class
(c) aristocratic class (d) upper class

256. John Galsworthy was a better
(a) dramatist (b) poet (c) critic (d) novelist

257. In *The Man of Property* Galsworthy paints the life of
(a) upper class (b) middle class
(c) lower middle class (d) upper middle class

258. The plays *Justice* and *Loyalties*, which are known for their technical competence and humane feelings have been written by
   (a) Galsworthy (b) Shaw
   (c) Beckett (d) None of the above

259. Lady Adla is a character in Galsworthy's
   (a) *Justice* (b) *Loyalties*
   (c) *The Pigeon* (d) *The Man of Property*

260. 'I didn't come because I feel Christian;
   I am a Jew. I'll take no money...
   Give it to a charity....'
   These lines occur in
   (a) *St. Joan* (b) *Justice*
   (c) *Loyalties* (d) None of the above

261. John Galsworthy was born in the year
   (a) 1865 (b) 1867 (c) 1869 (d) 1871

262. Galsworthy became reputed in 1906 after the publication of
   (a) *The Silver Box* (b) *Indian Summer of a Forsyte*
   (c) *The Man of Property* (d) None of the above

263. Jolyon is a character who appears in Galsworthy's
   (a) *Indian Summer of a Forsyte* (b) *The Silver Box*
   (c) *The Man of Property* (d) *Justice*

264. Who wrote *The Forsyte Saga*?
   (a) Bennett (b) Galsworthy
   (c) Shaw (d) H.G. Wells

265. Which novel of Galsworthy depicts a younger generation, disillusioned by the First World War?
   (a) *Flowering Wilderness* (b) *Indian Summer of a Forsyte*
   (c) *The Man of Property* (d) None of the above

266. *The Pigeon* is a well known play written by
(a) J.M. Barrie (b) Oscar Wilde
(c) Shaw (d) Galsworthy

267. Galsworthy had close friendship with
(a) Bennett (b) Conrad
(c) Chesterton (d) Butler

268. Which was Galsworthy's first publication?
(a) *The Silver Box* (b) *The Island Pharisees*
(c) *From the Four Winds* (d) *The Man of Property*

269. Which play of Galsworthy was immediately accepted by Shaw and H.G. Barker and was produced at the Court Theatre in 1906?
(a) *The Silver Box* (b) *Justice*
(c) *The Skin Game* (d) *Loyalties*

270. Which play of Galsworthy was first staged?
(a) *The Skin Game* (b) *Loyalties*
(c) *Justice* (d) *The Fugitive*

271. Galsworthy was awarded the Nobel Prize for Literature in
(a) 1930 (b) 1932 (c) 1931 (d) 1933

272. Galsworthy became the first President of P.E.N. Club in
(a) 1921 (b) 1922 (c) 1923 (d) 1924

**2. G.B. Shaw**

273. G.B. Shaw was born in Dublin in
(a) 1854 (b) 1856 (c) 1858 (d) 1860

274. 'He has improved philosophic discussions by making them more popular. But he has also improved popular amusements by making them more philosophic.'
This remark of Chesterton applies to
(a) Shaw (b) Galsworthy
(c) Beckett (d) Barrie

275. In which of Shaw's plays, there is a reference of three men discussing a historical problem?
(a) *Arms and the Man* (b) *Candida*
(c) *Saint Joan* (d) *Pygmalion*

276. Which dramatist has given the philosophy of Life Force?
(a) Oscar Wilde (b) G.B. Shaw
(c) John Galsworthy (d) None of the above

277. Eugene Marchbanks, a Shavian character, appears in the play
(a) *Man and Superman* (b) *Arms and the Man*
(c) *Candida* (d) *Major Barbara*

278. Which work of G.B. Shaw opened the religious phase in his career?
(a) *The Doctor's Dilemma* (b) *Back to Methuselah*
(c) *Major Barbara* (d) *Arms and the Man*

279. Which play of Shaw is considered to be the most Ibsen-like play?
(a) *Pygmalion* (b) *St. Joan*
(c) *Candida* (d) *Widower's House*

280. "I am a typical Irishman. My family came from Yorkshire."
Who has said this?
(a) Galsworthy (b) Shaw
(c) Bennett (d) Beckett

281. Shaw's first comedy was
(a) *Pygmalion* (b) *Widower's House*
(c) *Arms and the Man* (d) *Candida*

282. The dramatic career of Shaw began with
(a) *Man and Superman* (b) *St. Joan*
(c) *Widower's House* (d) *Pygmalion*

283. The Concept of 'Life Force' displayed in *Man and Superman* is indicative of Shaw's
(a) theism (b) atheism (c) realism (d) idealism

284. Problem plays deal with
(a) social problems (b) ethical problems
(c) moral problems (d) problems of humanism

285. King Magnus appears in Shaw's play
(a) *Pygmalion* (b) *The Apple Cart*
(c) *Candida* (d) *Man and Superman*

286. There is an Interlude in
(a) *Candida* (b) *St. Joan*
(c) *The Apple Cart* (d) *Pygmalion*

287. In which play of Shaw, a Professor changes the life of a flower girl?
(a) *Pygmalion* (b) *Candida*
(c) *Widower's House* (d) None of the above

288. Which play of Shaw has a soldier as its central character?
(a) *Man and Superman* (b) *St. Joan*
(c) *Major Barbara* (d) *Arms and the Man*

289. 'I write plays with the deliberate purpose to convert the nation to my opinions.'
This is a statement of
(a) G.B. Shaw (b) Samuel Butler
(c) Arnold Bennett (d) Joseph Conrad

290. Which play of Shaw was staged only in America?
(a) *The Doctor's Dilemma* (b) *Back to Methuselah*
(c) *The Devil's Disciple* (d) *Caesar and Cleopatra*

291. In which play Shaw dramatizes the Greek myth of a sculptor who fell in love with an ivory statue, which at his prayer was changed into a living woman?
(a) *St. Joan* (b) *Major Barbara*
(c) *Candida* (d) *Pygmalion*

292. Which play of Shaw has the sub-title 'A Comedy and a Philosophy'?
(a) *The Apple Cart* (b) *Man and Superman*
(c) *Arms and the Man* (d) *St. Joan*

293. 'Life levels all men; death reveals the eminent.'
Who has said this?
(a) G.B. Shaw (b) John Masefield
(c) Rudyard Kipling (d) Joseph Conrad

294. Jack Tanner is a character in Shaw's
(a) *Major Barbara* (b) *Arms and the Man*
(c) *Man and Superman* (d) *Pygmalion*

295. Octavius is a famous character of
   (a) Shaw (b) James M. Barrie
   (c) Joseph Conrad (d) John Galsworthy
296. Which of the following writers has the longest span of life?
   (a) John Galsworthy (b) H.G. Wells
   (c) G.B. Shaw (d) Rudyard Kipling
297. Which play of Shaw was transformed into a movie?
   (a) *Candida* (b) *Pygmalion*
   (c) *St. Joan* (d) *Man and Superman*
298. 'No man is a match for a woman except with a poker and a pair of hobnailed boots...'
   These lines occur in Shaw's play
   (a) *Arms and the Man* (b) *Major Barbara*
   (c) *Candida* (d) *Man and Superman*
299. Which play of Shaw deals with the theme of prostitution?
   (a) *Mrs. Warren's Profession* (b) *Candida*
   (c) *Caesar and Cleopatra* (d) *Pygmalion*
300. In which play of Shaw there is fusion of social economic theory with human interest?
   (a) *The Doctor's Dilemma* (b) *Arms and the Man*
   (c) *Major Barbara* (d) *You Never Can Tell*
301. The theme of which play of Shaw has been taken from Smollett's *Peregrine Pickle*?
   (a) *Widower's House* (b) *Pygmalion*
   (c) *Candida* (d) *Mrs. Warren's Profession*
302. In which play Shaw presents social crisis and has used his study of Chekhov's *The Cherry Orchard*?
   (a) *Man and Superman* (b) *Androcles and the Lion*
   (c) *Heartbreak House* (d) *Back to Methuselah*
303. Shaw has depicted Joan of Arc in his play
   (a) *Major Barbara* (b) *Pygmalion*
   (c) *The Apple Cart* (d) None of the above
304. Which play of Shaw dramatizes an abstract theme?
   (a) *St. Joan* (b) *Man and Superman*
   (c) *Caesar and Cleopatra* (d) *Arms and the Man*

305. In *St. Joan*, Joan tried to free the land of France from the English armies in the
(a) 14th century (b) 15th century
(C) 16th century (d) 17th century

306. Which character in *St. Joan* has been called the 'most effective piece of character creation'?
(a) *The Earl of Warwick* (b) *Dauphin*
(c) *Captain Robert* (d) *Cauchon, the Bishop of Beauvais*

307. In *St. Joan*, Joan is the daughter of a
(a) farmer (b) doctor
(c) teacher (d) businessman

## ANSWERS

### Unit A

| | | | |
|---|---|---|---|
| 1. (b) | 2. (c) | 3. (c) | 4. (c) |
| 5. (b) | 6. (d) | 7. (c) | 8. (b) |
| 9. (a) | 10. (d) | 11. (d) | 12. (b) |
| 13. (b) | 14. (c) | 15. (a) | 16. (b) |
| 17. (a) | 18. (c) | 19. (b) | 20. (b) |
| 21. (a) | 22. (b) | 23. (c) | 24. (b) |
| 25. (a) | 26. (a) | 27. (c) | 28. (d) |
| 29. (c) | 30. (a) | 31. (b) | 32. (a) |
| 33. (c) | 34. (b) | 35. (a) | 36. (c) |
| 37. (a) | | | |

### Unit B

| | | | |
|---|---|---|---|
| 38. (c) | 39. (a) | 40. (a) | 41. (c) |
| 42. (a) | 43. (b) | 44. (b) | 45. (b) |
| 46. (b) | 47. (b) | 48. (c) | 49. (b) |
| 50. (a) | 51. (d) | 52. (d) | 53. (d) |
| 54. (c) | 55. (b) | 56. (b) | 57. (b) |
| 58. (a) | 59. (b) | 60. (b) | 61. (a) |
| 62. (c) | 63. (a) | 64. (c) | 65. (b) |

| | | | | | | | |
|---|---|---|---|---|---|---|---|
| 66. | (a) | 67. | (d) | 68. | (b) | 69. | (c) |
| 70. | (b) | 71. | (b) | 72. | (a) | 73. | (b) |
| 74. | (b) | 75. | (a) | 76. | (c) | 77. | (c) |
| 78. | (a) | 79. | (c) | 80. | (a) | 81. | (b) |
| 82. | (c) | 83. | (b) | 84. | (b) | 85. | (c) |
| 86. | (d) | 87. | (a) | 88. | (a) | 89. | (a) |
| 90. | (c) | 91. | (b) | 92. | (a) | 93. | (c) |
| 94. | (c) | 95. | (a) | 96. | (a) | 97. | (b) |
| 98. | (d) | 99. | (a) | 100. | (a) | 101. | (b) |
| 102. | (d) | 103. | (b) | 104. | (c) | 105. | (b) |

## Unit C

| | | | | | | | |
|---|---|---|---|---|---|---|---|
| 106. | (c) | 107. | (b) | 108. | (b) | 109. | (b) |
| 110. | (a) | 111. | (c) | 112. | (c) | 113. | (b) |
| 114. | (d) | 115. | (c) | 116. | (c) | 117. | (a) |
| 118. | (c) | 119. | (a) | 120. | (b) | 121. | (c) |
| 122. | (b) | 123. | (b) | 124. | (a) | 125. | (b) |
| 126. | (c) | 127. | (b) | 128. | (c) | 129. | (a) |
| 130. | (b) | 131. | (a) | 132. | (c) | 133. | (a) |
| 134. | (a) | 135. | (c) | 136. | (b) | 137. | (c) |
| 138. | (b) | 139. | (d) | 140. | (b) | 141. | (a) |
| 142. | (a) | | | | | | |

## Unit D

| | | | | | | | |
|---|---|---|---|---|---|---|---|
| 143. | (b) | 144. | (a) | 145. | (c) | 146. | (b) |
| 147. | (a) | 148. | (b) | 149. | (c) | 150. | (d) |
| 151. | (a) | 152. | (d) | 153. | (b) | 154. | (a) |
| 155. | (b) | 156. | (c) | 157. | (c) | 158. | (d) |
| 159. | (a) | 160. | (b) | 161. | (c) | 162. | (b) |
| 163. | (a) | 164. | (c) | 165. | (b) | 166. | (c) |
| 167. | (b) | 168. | (a) | 169. | (b) | 170. | (b) |
| 171. | (c) | 172. | (a) | 173. | (a) | 174. | (c) |
| 175. | (b) | 176. | (a) | 177. | (a) | 178. | (c) |

| | | | | | | | |
|---|---|---|---|---|---|---|---|
| 179. | (b) | 180. | (b) | 181. | (a) | 182. | (c) |
| 183. | (a) | 184. | (b) | 185. | (c) | 186. | (a) |
| 187. | (c) | 188. | (d) | 189. | (a) | 190. | (c) |
| 191. | (a) | 192. | (b) | 193. | (c) | 194. | (b) |
| 195. | (a) | 196. | (b) | 197. | (a) | 198. | (b) |
| 199. | (c) | 200. | (c) | 201. | (d) | 202. | (a) |
| 203. | (c) | 204. | (a) | 205. | (d) | 206. | (a) |
| 207. | (c) | 208. | (b) | 209. | (a) | 210. | (d) |
| 211. | (a) | 212. | (d) | 213. | (c) | 214. | (b) |
| 215. | (a) | 216. | (d) | 217. | (a) | 218. | (c) |
| 219. | (c) | 220. | (b) | 221. | (c) | 222. | (d) |
| 223. | (b) | 224. | (c) | 225. | (c) | 226. | (d) |
| 227. | (c) | | | | | | |

## Unit E

| | | | | | | | |
|---|---|---|---|---|---|---|---|
| 228. | (b) | 229. | (c) | 230. | (a) | 231. | (c) |
| 232. | (b) | 233. | (a) | 234. | (a) | 235. | (b) |
| 236. | (d) | 237. | (a) | 238. | (c) | 239. | (a) |
| 240. | (a) | 241. | (c) | 242. | (d) | 243. | (a) |
| 244. | (c) | 245. | (a) | 246. | (c) | 247. | (a) |
| 248. | (b) | 249. | (a) | 250. | (b) | 251. | (a) |
| 252. | (b) | | | | | | |

## Unit F

| | | | | | | | |
|---|---|---|---|---|---|---|---|
| 253. | (b) | 254. | (a) | 255. | (c) | 256. | (d) |
| 257. | (d) | 258. | (a) | 259. | (b) | 260. | (c) |
| 261. | (b) | 262. | (c) | 263. | (a) | 264. | (b) |
| 265. | (a) | 266. | (d) | 267. | (b) | 268. | (c) |
| 269. | (a) | 270. | (a) | 271. | (b) | 272. | (a) |
| 273. | (b) | 274. | (a) | 275. | (c) | 276. | (b) |
| 277. | (c) | 278. | (b) | 279. | (c) | 280. | (b) |
| 281. | (b) | 282. | (c) | 283. | (a) | 284. | (a) |
| 285. | (b) | 286. | (c) | 287. | (a) | 288. | (d) |

| | | | | | | | |
|---|---|---|---|---|---|---|---|
| 289. | (a) | 290. | (c) | 291. | (d) | 292. | (b) |
| 293. | (a) | 294. | (c) | 295. | (a) | 296. | (c) |
| 297. | (b) | 298. | (d) | 299. | (a) | 300. | (c) |
| 301. | (b) | 302. | (c) | 303. | (d) | 304. | (b) |
| 305. | (b) | 306. | (b) | 307. | (a) | | |

# The Twentieth Century (1917–1963)

# 10

## UNIT A: HISTORICAL PERSPECTIVE AND BACKGROUND

1. Who was the King of England in the second decade of England?
   (a) George II (b) George III
   (c) George IV (d) George V
2. When did George V die?
   (a) 1914 (b) 1936 (c) 1940 (d) 1935
3. After George V who sat on the throne of England?
   (a) Edward VIII (b) George VI
   (c) Elizabeth II (d) Elizabeth
4. Which of the following is the period of World War I?
   (a) 1939-1944 (b) 1914-1919
   (c) 1917-1920 (d) 1920-1924
5. Which of the following is the period of World War II?
   (a) 1939-1944 (b) 1914-1919
   (c) 1917-1920 (d) 1920-1924
6. By the beginning of 20th century
   (a) there was a complete breakdown of the agrarian way of life and economy
   (b) England still had an agrarian economy
   (c) life moved as gaily as the sparkling Thames
   (d) none of these
7. Which of the following is not a characteristic of 20th century English society?
   (a) there was loosening in sex taboos and an increase in sexual promiscuity

(b) there had been problems like the problem of over-crowding, housing storage, a significant increase in vice and crime
(c) the impact of the psychologists like Freud, Jung & Bergson was seen in English Literature
(d) Ennui and boredom were not the part of city life

8. Which one of the following is not a characteristic of 20th century English society?
(a) there was a rise of scientific spirit which led to the questioning of accepted social beliefs, conventions and traditions
(b) there was an atmosphere of perplexity, confusion and anxiety
(c) sexual renunciation ceased to be a theme of literature, interest in sex-perversion grew, and there is a free and frank discussion of sex
(d) people enjoyed a very happy and peaceful life

9. Which of the following group of writers can be associated with 20th century literature?
(a) Milton, Donne & Herbert (b) Fielding, Richardson & Smollett
(c) Hardy, Dickens & Jane Austen (d) Shaw, Wells & Galsworthy

10. The term 'Imagism' is associated with which of the following?
(a) T.S. Eliot (b) F.R. Leavis
(c) Ezra Pound (d) D.H. Lawrence

## UNIT B: THE NOVEL AND THE SHORT STORIES

### 1. George Orwell

11. Eric Blair is the original name of which of the following writers?
(a) Henry James (b) James Joyce
(c) George Orwell (d) D.H. Lawrence

12. Which of the following authors was born in India?
(a) James Joyce (b) Henry James
(c) T.S. Eliot (d) George Orwell

13. To which period will you associate George Orwell with?
    (a) 17th Century (b) 18th Century
    (c) 19th Century (d) 20th Century
14. Which of the following novels has been written by George Orwell?
    (a) *Ulysses* (b) *A Portrait of a Lady*
    (c) *Burmese Days* (d) *Of Human Bondage*
15. Which of the following novels has not been written by George Orwell?
    (a) *A Clergyman's Daughter* (b) *Animal Farm*
    (c) *Nineteen Eighty Four* (d) *The Heart of the Matter*
16. *Animal Farm* is George Orwell's indictment of which of the following?
    (a) socialism (b) democracy
    (c) monarchy (d) communism
17. George Orwell firmly believed 'absolute power corrupts absolutely'.
    The quotation is from
    (a) George Orwell (b) Lord Acton
    (c) Abraham Lincoln (d) None of these
18. Which of the following statements is true about George Orwell's *Animal Farm*?
    (a) it is a satire on French Revolution
    (b) it is a satire on Russian Revolution
    (c) it is an allegory on the American War of Independence
    (d) none of these
19. "All animals are equal but some animals are more equal than others." This quotation is from which of the following works of George Orwell?
    (a) *Nineteen Eighty Four* (b) *Animal Farm*
    (c) *A Clergyman's Daughter* (d) *Burmese Days*
20. In Orwell's *Animal Farm* which of the following characters raises the animals to a rebellion?
    (a) Old Major (b) Farmer Jones
    (c) Snowball (d) Napoleon

21. In Orwell's *Animal Farm* the animals rebelled against
    (a) Old Major (b) Farmer Jones
    (c) Snowball (d) Napoleon
22. Orwell's *Animal Farm* is an allegory. Characters are symbolic. Which of the following characters stands for Marx and the principles of Marxism?
    (a) Old Major (b) Fredrick
    (c) Farmer Jones (d) Snowball
23. In the satire of Orwell's *Animal Farm* ' humans' represent Marx's capitalists and 'animals' represent
    (a) upper class of society (b) the common mass of people
    (c) the rulers (d) none of these
24. In the satire of Orwell's *Animal Farm* Stalin is represented by which of the following characters?
    (a) Napoleon (b) Snowball
    (c) Farmer Jones (d) Old Major
25. Orwell's *Animal Farm* symbolically presents the Russian Communist History. Leon Trotsky who worked with Lenin in preparing the way for the Russian Revolution is represented by which of the following characters?
    (a) Napoleon (b) Squealor
    (c) Snowball (d) Old Major
26. In Orwell's *Animal Farm*, after Snowball is banished who takes over the control of the Animal Farm?
    (a) Squealor (b) Napoleon (c) Boxer (d) Benjamin
27. In Orwell's *Animal Farm* the Tsar of Russia is represented by which of the following characters?
    (a) Snowball (b) Napoleon
    (c) Fredarick (d) Mr. Jones
28. In George Orwell's *Animal Farm*, animals turn on Mr. Jones and his men and drive them off the farm. This incident allegorically refers to
    (a) the French Revolution (b) the Russian Revolution of 1917
    (c) the War of American Independence (d) none of these

29. Animal Farm in Orwell's *Animal Farm* represents which of the following countries?
    (a) France (b) Germany (c) England (d) Russia

30. Which of the following conclusions is seen to be drawn by Orwell in his *Animal Farm*?
    (a) animals are better than human beings
    (b) human beings treat animals very cruelly
    (c) what began as Utopia as heaven on earth, has ended as the opposite
    (d) none of these

31. Which of the following novels of Orwell may be called an autobiographical novel?
    (a) *Animal Farm* (b) *Nineteen Eighty Four*
    (c) *Down & Out in London & Paris* (d) none of these

32. Which of the following novels of Orwell has a grim story of attempted escape from the rat race of striving for material success?
    (a) *Keep the Aspidistra Flying* (b) *Animal Farm*
    (c) *Nineteen Eighty Four* (d) *Down & Out in London & Paris*

33. Which of the following novels of George Orwell is 'an anti-Utopia, picturing in self-torturing detail the destruction of all human values in future society which exists simply to stamp out individuality and to maintain the machinery for stamping it out in devilishly perfect condition'?
    (a) *Animal Farm* (b) *Nineteen Eighty Four*
    (c) *The Road to Wigan Pier* (d) *Homage to Catalonia*

34. Orwell believed that the communists had betrayed a popular revolution that might otherwise have given the working classes true freedom and status. Which of the following novels reveals this belief of Orwell?
    (a) *Homage to Catalonia* (b) *A Clergyman's Daughter*
    (c) *Burmese Days* (d) None of these

35. Like *Animal Farm* which of the following novels of Orwell is cast in the form of an animal satire?
    (a) *Homage to Catalonia* (b) *A Clergyman's Daughter*
    (c) *Burmese Days* (d) *Nineteen Eighty Four*

**2. Henry James**

36. To which period does Henry James belong?
    (a) early Nineteenth Century (b) late Nineteenth Century
    (c) late Twentieth Century (d) eighteenth Century

37. Which of the following works has not been authored by Henry James?
    (a) *The Wings of the Dove* (b) *The Golden Bowl*
    (c) *The Portrait of a Lady* (d) *The End of the Affair*

38. Which of the following works has been authored by Henry James?
    (a) *The Portrait of a Young Man as an Artist*
    (b) *The Heart of the Matter*
    (c) *Of Human Bondage*
    (d) *Daisy Miller*

39. Which of the following may be Henry James' view on art?
    (a) art is for art's sake (b) life is chaotic and art is selective
    (c) art is merely craftsmanship and beauty (d) none of these

40. In James' *The Portrait of a Lady* who is the lady?
    (a) Mrs. Touchett (b) Isabel Archer
    (c) Henrietta Stackpole (d) None of these

41. "The compulsions of history, the encrustations of society, the confines of a close family, etc., don't exist for her—she will assert her liberty." The above lines describe which female character in James's *The Portrait of a Lady*?
    (a) Isabel Archer (b) Madam Merle
    (c) Henrietta Stackpole (d) Pansy Osmond

42. Isabel Archer in James' *The Portrait of a Lady* came from America to England. Which of the following characters had brought her to England?
    (a) Damil Touchett (b) Ralph Touchett
    (c) Mrs. Touchett (d) Lord Warburton

43. Garden court in James' *The Portrait of a Lady* is
    (a) the name of a female character
    (b) the name of a male character loved by Isabel Archer
    (c) the name of the estate owned by Mr. Touchett
    (d) none of these

44. Which of the following characters in James' *The Portrait of a Lady* had proposed to Isabel Archer for marriage, but the proposal was rejected?
    (a) Casper Goodwood (b) Lord Warburton
    (c) Ralph (d) Mr. Touchett

45. Who left a legacy of 10,000 pounds for Isabel Archer in James' *The Portrait of a Lady*?
    (a) Osmond (b) Mr. Touchett
    (c) Casper Goodwood (d) Mr. Warburton

46. Which of the following characters in James' *The Portrait of a Lady* made a proposal of marriage to Isabel Archer and it was accepted?
    (a) Casper Goodwood (b) Mr. Warburton
    (c) Osmond (d) Ralph

47. Which of the following characters in James' *The Portrait of a Lady* is the daughter of Osmond?
    (a) Pansy (b) Henrietta
    (c) Isabel (d) Madam Merle

48. Pansy in James' *The Portrait of a Lady* was in love with which of the following characters?
    (a) Lord Warburton (b) Ralph
    (c) Rosier (d) Casper Goodwood

49. Pansy's father Osmand in James' *The Portrait of a Lady* wants her daughter to marry which of the following characters?
    (a) Ralph (b) Lord Warburton
    (c) Casper Goodwood (d) None of these

50. In James' *The Portrait of a Lady* who is the step mother of Pansy?
    (a) Henrietta (b) Madam Merle
    (c) Mrs. Touchett (d) Isabel

51. Mr. Osmond in James' *The Portrait of a Lady* wanted her daughter Pansy to marry Lord Warburton for which of the following reasons?
    (a) Lord Warburton was temperamentally suited to her
    (b) Lord Warburton was very gentle
    (c) Lord Warburton was wealthy
    (d) None of these

52. In James' *The Portrait of a Lady* Isabel's choice of Osmond as her husband may be compared with which of the following in Hardy's *Far From the Madding Crowd?*
    (a) Bathsheba's choice of Boldwood
    (b) Bathsheba's choice of Sergeant Troy
    (c) Bathsheba's choice of Gabriel Oak
    (d) None of these

53. In James' *The Portrait of a Lady* Osmond had married Isabel for which of the following reasons?
    (a) she was extremely beautiful
    (b) for her wealth
    (c) to bring a mother for his daughter
    (d) none of these

54. In James' *The Portrait of a Lady* Isabel's marriage with Osmond was
    (a) happy marriage
    (b) unhappy marriage
    (c) a marriage only to get a mother for Osmond's daughter
    (d) spiritually satisfying

55. Read the following quotation from James' *The Portrait of a Lady*:
    "It could not be, she was to live only to suffer, she was still young after all and a great many things might happen yet, to live only to suffer—only to feel the injury of life repeated and too capable for that ..."
    In the above quotation 'she' refers to which of the following characters?
    (a) Pansy
    (b) Henrietta
    (c) Isabel
    (d) Mrs. Touchett

56. What is 'Cardinal Jamesian Sin'?
    (a) it is the infidelity of a wife to her husband
    (b) it is the infidelity of a husband to his wife
    (c) it is a total appropriation of another person's life for egotistical ends
    (d) none of these
57. Which of the following characters in James' *The Portrait of a Lady* has committed the 'Cardinal Jamesian Sin'?
    (a) Ralph (b) Mr. Warburton
    (c) Osmond (d) Mr. Goodwood
58. Which of the following statements is true about Henry James' early novel *Daisy Miller*?
    (a) it is a beautiful love story
    (b) it is a story of a man fighting against the hostile forces of life
    (c) it portrays the contact of Americans with European life
    (d) none of these
59. Which of the following statements is true about Henry James' novel *Tragic Muse*?
    (a) it is a story of a man fighting against the hostile forces of life
    (b) it is a beautiful love story
    (c) it portrays the contact of Americans with European life
    (d) it is a study of English life

**3. Rudyard Kipling**

60. Rudyard Kipling was born in which of the following countries?
    (a) England (b) Ireland (c) India (d) America
61. Which of the following statements may be true about Rudyard Kipling?
    (a) Kipling's fame rests principally on his short stories dealing with India, the sea, the jungle and its beast
    (b) Kipling's novels have fantasy stories
    (c) Kipling's novels are criticism of Indian society
    (d) None of these

62. To which period did Kipling belong?
(a) 16th century (b) 17th century
(c) 18th century (d) 20th century

63. Which of the following writers is a contemporary of Rudyard Kipling?
(a) Samuel Richardson (b) Henry Fielding
(c) Tobias Smollett (d) Joseph Conrad

64. Which of the following writers is not a contemporary of Rudyard Kipling?
(a) Arnold Bennett (b) John Galsworthy
(c) H.G. Wells (d) Charles Dickens

65. Which of the following novels is written by Kipling?
(a) *The Golden Bowl* (b) *Of Human Bondage*
(c) *A Passage to India* (d) *The Light that Failed*

66. Which of the following novels is not written by Kipling?
(a) *The Light that Failed* (b) *The Seven Seas*
(c) *Kim* (d) *The Portrait of the Artist as a Youngman*

67. Mowgli is a character in which of the following novels of Rudyard Kipling?
(a) *The Light that Failed* (b) *Kim*
(c) *The Jungle Books* (d) *Puck of Pook's Hill*

68. Which of the following statements is true about Kipling's creation of Mowgli?
(a) Mowgli is a child who was brought up by wolves and taught by them and black panther, the law of the jungle
(b) Mowgli is a little wolf who was brought up by little children
(c) Mowgli is an animal trainer
(d) None of these

69. Which of the following statements is true about Kipling's *The Light that Failed*?
(a) the hero of the novel is Mowgli who was brought up by wolves

(b) the hero of the novel is a young man who goes blind but still manages to lead a strenuous life
(c) the hero presents the experiences of a boy wandered over India in the company of a holy man
(d) none of these

70. Which of the following statements is true about Kipling's *Kim*?
(a) Kim presents the experience of a boy who wandered over India in the company of a holy man
(b) the hero of the novel is Mowgli who was brought up by wolves
(c) the hero of the novel is a young man who goes blind but still manages to lead a strenuous life
(d) none of these

71. What is the theme of the novel *Kim* by Rudyard Kipling?
(a) the blindness of the hero reveals Kipling's own anxiety for hi own wanting eyesight
(b) the work gives a realistic picture of Indian life and the faith of the people in supernaturalism and mysticism
(c) the work emphasises upon man's compassion for animals
(d) none of these

72. What is the theme of Rudyard Kipling's *Captain Courageous*?
(a) *Captain Courageous* is an adventurous story of boys dealing with a boy who fell overboard from a ship
(b) this novel presents the adventures of British soldiers in Simla
(c) it presents the prosaic lot of the civil servants and their sense of duty
(d) none of these

73. In Kipling's *The Plain Tales From the Hills*, the 'Hills' stands for which of the following cities?
(a) Mussoorie (b) Nainital (c) Ooty (d) Simla

74. Which of the following statements is true about Rudyard Kipling?
    (a) Kipling was an anti-imperialist
    (b) Kipling was an imperialist at heart and the note of imperialism is sounded in his works with a touch of jingoism
    (c) Kipling has given pictures of modern London life in his works
    (d) None of these
75. *Just So Stories* is a story collection by
    (a) Kipling (b) Poe
    (c) Mark Twain (d) Tennyson
76. Kipling's novel *Stalky* & *Co*. came out in
    (a) 1891 (b) 1890 (c) 1899 (d) 1892
77. Kipling produced his classic story *Puck of Pook's Hill* in
    (a) 1902 (b) 1906 (c) 1910 (d) 1895
78. Rudyard Kipling's *Barrack-room Ballads* came out in the year
    (a) 1892 (b) 1898 (c) 1899 (c) 1902
79. Rudyard Kipling, born in 1865 in Bombay, died in
    (a) 1917 (b) 1936 (c) 1942 (d) 1927
80. Which of Kipling's poems is an English version of Indian lullaby?
    (a) "Our Lady of the snows" (b) "Shiva and the Grasshopper"
    (c) "Mother O'Mine" (d) "Gungadin"
81. Rudyard Kipling wrote a poem in cockney dialect. The name of the poem is
    (a) "Danny Deever" (b) "Mandalay"
    (c) "Fuzzy Wuzzy" (d) None of the above
82. Which of Kipling's lyrics offended the feelings of another country and destroyed foreign relations?
    (a) "Mandalay" (b) "The Ballad of the Red Earle"
    (c) "Lord Robert" (d) "Danny Deever"

83. Kipling's *Just So Stories* was published in
    (a) 1902 (b) 1919 (c) 1920 (d) 1918
84. 'The River of Arrow' is mentioned in the novel
    (a) *Kim* (b) *Heart of Darkness*
    (c) *Eveline* (d) *Hurry on Down*

**4. E.M. Forster**

85. Which of the following is a contemporary of Forster?
    (a) Daniel Defoe (b) Charles Dickens
    (c) Samuel Richardson (d) D.H. Lawrence
86. Which of the following is not a contemporary of Forster?
    (a) James Joyce (b) Virginia Woolf
    (c) Aldous Huxley (d) Walter Scott
87. Which of the following works has been authored by Forster?
    (a) *Robinson Crusoe* (b) *Hard Times*
    (c) *The Return of the Native* (d) *Where Angels Fear to Tread*
88. Which of the following works has not been authored by Forster?
    (a) *A Passage to India* (b) *The Longest Journey*
    (c) *A Room With a View* (d) *Women in Love*
89. Dr. Aziz is a character in which of the following novels of Forster?
    (a) *Where Angels Fear to Tread* (b) *A Passage to India*
    (c) *The Longest Journey* (d) *A Room with a View*
90. Mrs. Moore in Forster's *A Passage to India* was the mother of which of the following characters?
    (a) Dr. Aziz (b) Ronny Heaslop
    (c) Adela (d) Prof. Godbole
91. Which of the following characters in Forster's *A Passage to India* is the prospective fiancé of Heaslop?
    (a) Adela Quested (b) Mrs. Moore
    (c) Stella (d) None of these

92. Which of the following characters in Forster's *A Passage to India* is the Principal of the Government College?
    (a) Dr. Aziz (b) Prof. Godbole
    (c) Mr. Fielding (d) Ronny Heaslop
93. In Forster's *A Passage to India*, there is reference to some caves. It is which one of the following caves?
    (a) Ajanta and Ellora Caves (b) Elephanta Caves
    (c) Marabar Caves (d) None of these
94. Dr. Aziz in Forster's *A Passage to India* was arrested. What was the charge against him?
    (a) Dr. Aziz had murdered Adela in Marabar Caves.
    (b) Dr. Aziz had attacked Adela in Marabar Caves
    (c) Dr. Aziz had committed a rape upon Mrs. Moore.
    (d) None of these
95. In Forster's *A Passage to India*, what was the conclusion of the Trial going against Dr. Aziz?
    (a) Dr. Aziz was sentenced to death
    (b) Dr. Aziz was sentenced to life imprisonment
    (c) Adela withdrew all charges against him and he was acquitted
    (d) None of these
96. In the context of Forster's *A Passage to India*, Stella was the daughter of which of the following characters?
    (a) Mr. Fielding (b) Ronny Heaslop
    (c) Mrs. Moore (d) Adela
97. In Forster's *A Passage to India*, Mr. Fielding was married to which of the following characters?
    (a) Mrs. Moore (b) Adela
    (c) Stella (d) None of these
98. Forster's *A Passage to India* has been divided into three sections. These three sections are
    (a) Mosque, Caves and Temple (b) Mosque, Church and Temple
    (c) Hindus, Muslims and Christians (d) None of these

99. What do you think is the theme of Forster's *A Passage to India*?
    (a) Forster had come to India as a tourist and he has written *A Passage to India* as a guide book for foreign tourists.
    (b) the book deals with various routes to India from foreign countries.
    (c) *A Passage to India* has two aspects—the political and the mystical. Politically, it deals with tension between the natives and Britons and also with the tension between the Hindus and the Muslims. From the mystical aspect it is concerned with the search after the infinite and the eternal, and with illogical and inexplicable element in human life
    (d) none of these

100. Which of the following is not the theme of Forster's *A Passage to India*?
    (a) *A Passage to India* has presented the racial problem and the problem of human relationship very effectively
    (b) *A Passage to India* deals with its ancient art and culture.
    (c) *A Passage to India* is unrivalled in English fiction in its presentation of the complex problems which were to be found in the relationship between English and the native people in India
    (d) the novel seeks to portray the relations of the British with the Indians round about the year 1924

101. Forster's *A Passage to India* has been divided into three parts—'Mosques', 'Caves' and 'The Temple'. The three fold divisions of the book is symbolic
    (a) they are related to three religions
    (b) they are related respectively to the seasons of spring, summer and the wet monsoon autumn of India and to the man's emotional nature, his intellect and his capacity for love
    (c) they are related to three periods—The Mughals, The English and The Modern Period of India
    (d) none of these

102. The characters of Forster's *A Passage to India* seek to represent three attitudes towards life—emotional nature, intellect and his capacity for love. Which of the following characters stands for emotion?
   (a) Dr. Aziz (b) Fielding
   (c) Adela (d) Mrs. Moore

103. "Forster is a novelist difficult to assess: he can be easily overestimated or underestimated." This quotation about Forster is from which of the following critics?
   (a) Walter Allen (b) Diana Neil
   (c) E. Albert (d) Fredrick Karl

104. Which of the following statements about Forster as a novelist may not be true?
   (a) Forster disregards conventional plot construction and frequently introduces startling, unexpected incidents
   (b) the characters of Forster are types rather than individuals. They are embodiment of certain values of life
   (c) Forster's novels are written against rural background
   (d) Forster is basically a moralist upholding the cause of culture, tolerance and civilization in a world open to the attacks of barbarism, materialism and provincialism

105. Which of the following is the theme of Forster's *Howard's End*?
   (a) *Howard's End* presents the conflict between the rich and the poor
   (b) *Howard's End* presents the conflict between two classes of people, one representing the hard realists and materialists represented by the Wilcoxes and other deeply rooted in moral and aesthetic values represented by Schlegels
   (c) *Howard's End* presents the devastation caused to modern civilization by the advancement in science
   (d) None of these

106. In Forster's *Howard's End*, Howard's End is the name of a
   (a) house (b) town (c) bridge (d) road

107. In Forster's *Howard's End*, Howard's End is the name of a house. What does it symbolise?
   (a) it symbolises the heart of England which mystically holds the secret of true personal relationship
   (b) it stands for the end of the journey of life that is death
   (c) it is a symbol of modern civilization which is at the brink of disintegration
   (d) none of these

108. Margaret Schlegel is a character in which of the following novels of Forster?
   (a) *A Passage to India* (b) *Where Angels Fear to Tread*
   (c) *The Longest Journey* (d) *Howard's End*

109. Margaret Schlegel in Forster's *Howard's End* is married to which of the following characters?
   (a) Dr. Aziz (b) Adela Quested
   (c) Wilcox (d) None of these

110. Which one is not a novelist of 'Stream of Consciousness Techniques'?
   (a) D.H. Lawrence (b) Forster
   (c) James Joyce (d) Virginia Woolf

**5. D.H. Lawrence**

111. 'Religion by the Blood' is a phrase which is associated with
   (a) James Joyce (b) Conrad
   (c) Virginia Woolf (d) D.H. Lawrence

112. In which of the following centuries D.H. Lawrence was born?
   (a) 17th century (b) 18th century
   (c) 19th century (d) 20th century

113. Which of the following statements is true about D.H. Lawrence?
   (a) the father of D.H. Lawrence was a well-read, refined, aristocratic person

(b) the mother of D.H. Lawrence had no influence over him in his novels
(c) the father of D.H. Lawrence was an uneducated coal-miner
(d) the married life of Lawrence's parents was quite happy

114. Which of the following statements is false about D.H. Lawrence?
(a) the strongest influence in the life of D.H. Lawrence was that of his mother
(b) the father of D.H. Lawrence was a coal-miner
(c) the married life of Lawrence's parents was quite happy
(d) D.H. Lawrence seemed to suffer from Oedipus Complex

115. In Lawrence's *Sons and Lovers* the protagonist reflects Oedipus Complex.
Which of the following can be associated with Oedipus Complex?
(a) abnormal attachment of a son for his mother
(b) abnormal attachment of a son for his father
(c) abnormal attachment of a daughter for her father
(d) abnormal attachment of a daughter for her mother

116. Which of the following novels was written by D.H. Lawrence?
(a) *The White Peacock* (b) *The Golden Gate*
(c) *The Scientific Man* (d) *The Brave New World*

117. Which of the following novels is not written by D.H. Lawrence?
(a) *Sons and Lovers* (b) *The Trespasser*
(c) *The Rainbow* (d) *Lolita*

118. Which of the following women was instrumental in launching Lawrence as a writer?
(a) Jessica Chambers (b) His mother, Lydia
(c) Frieda Weekly (d) None of these

119. Which of the following statements is true about Lawrence's *Sons and Lovers*?
   (a) *Sons and Lovers* is the most autobiographical of Lawrence's novels and it faithfully records his mental torture as he struggled between his mother and Jessica Chambers
   (b) *Sons and Lovers* is a novel depicting the immorality of the contemporary society
   (c) *Sons and Lovers* is a political novel supporting the communistic ideology
   (d) None of these
120. Which of the following statements may be true about modern novels?
   (a) modern novels carry the readers away from reality
   (b) modern fiction is pre-occupied with the problem of objective reality
   (c) modern fiction is basically pornographic
   (d) none of these
121. Which of the following statements is true about modern fiction?
   (a) modern novelists asserted their belief in the inner reality and expressed their dissatisfaction with the earlier depiction of character.
   (b) right from Defoe to Bennett and Galsworthy, the novelists concentrated on the depiction of external reality. Modern novelists, too, followed the same trend
   (c) modern novelists were inhibited to present the reality of sex in their novels
   (d) none of these
122. Which of the following statements may be true about the novels of D.H. Lawrence?
   (a) D.H. Lawrence regarded sex as a sin and through his novels exhorted the people to keep away from it.
   (b) D.H. Lawrence felt that sexual harmony was an essential condition for the attainment of happiness in life

(c) D.H. Lawrence did not have the courage to deal frankly with the sex involvements in his novels.
(d) None of these

123. Which of the following statements may be true about modern novels?
(a) modern novels contain interesting stories
(b) modern novelist never aims at telling a story. His purpose is to portray the reality of life in the most authentic manner, and if he discovers a well-defined plot to be a hindrance, he does not hesitate to dispense with it
(c) In modern novels the incidents in the plot are arranged in a chronological order
(d) none of these

124. In which of D.H. Lawrence's novel the story has been narrated by Cyril Beardsall?
(a) *The White Peacock* (b) *The Rainbow*
(c) *Sons and Lovers* (d) *Women in Love*

125. Which of the following statements may be true about Lawrence's *The White Peacock?*
(a) the novel deals with the happy relationship existing between the two sexes
(b) Cyril Beardsall, in the novel, is a pen-portrait of the novelist himself
(c) the novel is about love for birds specially white peacock
(d) none of these

126. Which of the following statements may be true about Lawrence's *The Trespasser?*
(a) the novel describes the frustrated love affair of a thirty-eight years old violinist Siegmund and Helena, a school teacher
(b) the novel describes the relationship between Paul Morel and Mrs. Morel
(c) the novel deals with the love-affair of George Saxton and Lettie
(d) none of these

127. Which of the following is the theme of Lawrence's *The Rainbow*?
    (a) *The Rainbow* traces the history of three generations of the Brangwens living on the marsh farm
    (b) the novel deals with the love affair of George Saxton and Lettie
    (c) the novel deals with the love affair of Siegmund and Helen
    (d) none of these

128. Which of the following novels of D.H. Lawrence is a sequel to his novel *The Rainbow*?
    (a) *Women in Love* (b) *Sons and Lovers*
    (c) *Lady Chatterley's Lover* (d) *The White Peacock*

129. In Lawrence's *Lady Chatterley's Lover* which of the following characters is Lady Chatterley's lover?
    (a) Clifford Chatterley (b) Mellors
    (c) Paul (d) Siegmund

130. In Lawrence's *Sons and Lovers*, who is the mother of Paul?
    (a) Annie (b) Gertrude
    (c) Clara (d) Miriam

131. Which of the following statements may be true about Gertrude in the context of Lawrence's *Sons and Lovers*?
    (a) Gertrude had a very unhappy marital life and her only solace lay in her children
    (b) Walter Morel was a responsible bread winner for the family
    (c) Gertrude neglected her children for the love she had for her husband
    (d) none of these

132. Miriam Leivers was in love with which of the following characters in Lawrence's *Sons and Lovers*?
    (a) Arthur (b) William
    (c) Paul (d) Baxter Dawes

133. Which of the following statements may be true about Paul in the context of Lawrence's *Sons and Lovers*?
   (a) Paul was prepared to separate himself from his mother and other members of the family for the sake of his love for Miriam
   (b) Paul's mother was the only woman to whom he could turn for complete understanding and love
   (c) Paul kept himself from Miriam when he came to know that the latter was a girl of little means
   (d) None of these

134. In *Sons and Lovers*, by the time Miriam and Paul had grown into their twenties, Paul realized that Miriam loved him deeply and that he, too, loved her. But for some reason he could not bring himself to touch her. What was that reason?
   (a) Paul was a misogynist
   (b) Paul was sexually impotent
   (c) Paul was very shy
   (d) the Oedipus Complex in Paul prevented him

135. Which of the following statements may be true in the context of Lawrence's *Sons and Lovers*?
   (a) Paul could not continue his love-relationship with Miriam because she had tried to possess him and Clara maintained a barrier against him
   (b) Paul could not continue his love with Miriam because he found Clara more attractive than Miriam
   (c) Paul's mother wanted Paul to marry Clara instead of Miriam
   (d) None of these

136. *Sons and Lovers* may be taken as
   (a) an autobiographical novel
   (b) expression of the political convictions of the author
   (c) a criticism of the contemporary society
   (d) none of these

137. In which of the following manner Lawrence's *Sons and Lovers* ends?
   (a) Paul is married to Miriam
   (b) Paul is married to Clara

(c) Mrs. Morel dies of cancer and Paul's life sinks into shadowiness and insubstantiality
(d) None of these

138. Which of the following characters in Lawrence's *Sons and Lovers* is drawn after Lawrence's mother?
(a) Gertrude Morel (b) Clara
(c) Miriam (d) Annie

139. Which of the following characters in Lawrence's *Sons and Lovers* reflects the novelist himself?
(a) William (b) Arthur
(c) Paul (d) Baxter Dawes

140. Which of the following statements may be true about Lawrence's philosophy of life?
(a) Lawrence believes the modern age to be essentially tragic and traces the roots of this tragedy to the over-intellectualisation of human beings
(b) Lawrence believes the modern age to be essentially tragic, it is because impulse thrives at the cost of scientific thinking
(c) Lawrence was against those who said "My own religion is a belief in the blood, the flesh, as being wiser than intellect"
(d) None of these

141. In Lawrence's *Sons and Lovers*, are sons themselves lovers or are there sons and lovers?
(a) in the novel there are three sons and they have lovers
(b) the novel does not have different people as sons and lovers. It presents the story of a woman, who disillusioned with her husband, accepts two of her sons as lovers
(c) the mother has nothing to do in sons-lovers affair
(d) none of these

142. Who said, "All I want is to answer my blood direct"?
(a) W.H. Davis (b) D.H. Lawrence
(c) W.H. Hudson (d) W.H. Auden

143. Which novel did D.H. Lawrence call 'thought adventure'?
(a) *The White Peacock* (b) *The Trespasser*
(c) *The Rainbow* (d) *Kangaroo*

144. D.H. Lawrence's novel *The Rainbow* which was banned for obscenity appeared in
(a) 1910 (b) 1915 (c) 1921 (d) 1929

145. Which of the following begins with: 'Ours is essentially a tragic age'?
(a) *Sons and Lovers* (b) *Lady Chatterley's Lover*
(c) *The Rainbow* (d) *Women in Love*

**6. Aldous Huxley**

146. Which of the following authors is a contemporary of Aldous Huxley?
(a) Thomas Carlyle (b) George Meredith
(c) Charles Dickens (d) W.S. Maugham

147. Which of the following authors is not a contemporary of Aldous Huxley?
(a) E.M. Forster (b) James Joyce
(c) Virginia Woolf (d) W.M. Thackeray

148. Which of the following works has been written by Huxley?
(a) *Howard's End* (b) *Tristram Shandy*
(c) *Ulysses* (d) *Crome Yellow*

149. Which of the following works has not been authored by Huxley?
(a) *Crome Yellow* (b) *Antic Hay*
(c) *Those Barren Leaves* (d) *Mrs. Dalloway*

150. Which of the following novels of Huxley is concerned with Wimbush family and its young hero Denis?
(a) *Antic Hay* (b) *Crome Yellow*
(c) *Point Counter Point* (d) *Those Barren Leaves*

151. Which novel of Huxley is a critical study of post war disillusionment and immortality presented through the character of Gumbril bringing out the ugliness and

futility of the intellectual society of London after the First World War?

(a) *Antic Hay* (b) *Crome Yellow*
(c) *Point Counter Point* (d) *Those Barren Leaves*

152. With which novel of Huxley will you associate the following statement: "It is set in Italy and studies the acquisitive nature of women through the character of Mrs. Aldwinkle"?

(a) *Point Counter Point* (b) *Those Barren Leaves*
(c) *Crome Yellow* (d) *Antic Hay*

153. What is the theme of Huxley's *Point Counter Point*?

(a) it is a critical study of post war disillusionment and immorality
(b) it studies the acquisitive nature of women through the character of Mrs. Aldwinkle
(c) it presents the conflict between passion and reason and the foolishness of sticking to only one point of view with dogged tenacity without ever caring to look at the other side of the medal. Rampion provides the solution by pointing out to different protagonists of sense, intellect and reason that 'civilization is harmony and completeness—reason, feeling and instinct'
(d) none of these

154. In one of his novels, Huxley satirises a scientific utopia in which everything is controlled by science and even mind, body, poetry, art and literature are all conditioned by the steam roller of scientific uniformity. The severe critic of this controlled world is the savage John who pleads for greater freedom of the individual and spiritual life. With which novel of Huxley will you associate this?

(a) *Point Counter Point* (b) *Those Barren Leaves*
(c) *The Brave New World* (d) *Crome Yellow*

155. In which novel of Huxley, a work of mysticism and spirituality, the hero of the novel is Anthony Beavis?

(a) *After Many a Summer* (b) *Eyeless in Gaza*
(c) *The Brave New World* (d) *The Perennial Philosophy*

156. Which of the following statements correctly describes Anthony Beavis in Huxley's *Eyeless in Gaza*?
   (a) through the character of Antony Beavis, the novelist brings out the ugliness and futility of the intellectual society of London
   (b) Anthony Beavis is another Hamlet in whom reflection mars his capacity for action
   (c) in the early years of his life Anthony Beavis is intelligent, witty, pagan and flippant. But gradually as time passes on, he drifts more and more towards spiritual life
   (d) none of these

157. In which novel Huxley mocks at the corrupting influence of wealth in the new world?
   (a) *Time must have a Stop* (b) *Crome Yellow*
   (c) *Antic Hay* (d) *The Brave New World*

158. Which of the following novels of Huxley is inspired by the message of *Bhagwat Geeta*.
   (a) *The Brave New World* (b) *Time must have a Stop*
   (c) *The Perennial Philosophy* (d) *Crome Yellow*

159. Which of the following statements about Huxley as a novelist may be correct?
   (a) the novels of Huxley have been written against a rural background
   (b) Huxley mirrors the misery of the poor and downtrodden in society
   (c) Huxley mirrors the empty lives of the people, mostly of the high cultured classes, chasing illusions and marked pretensions
   (d) none of these

160. The term 'musicalization of fiction' is associated with which of the following novelists?
   (a) James Joyce (b) Virginia Woolf
   (c) Aldous Huxley (d) E.M. Forster

161. Which novel of Huxley is a light-hearted satire on contemporary society?
   (a) *Crome Yellow* (b) *Antic Hay*
   (c) *Those Barren Leaves* (d) *Point Counter Point*

162. In which of his novels, Aldous Huxley imagines a world without disease, without pain, without emotion and without spiritual life?
(a) *Brave New World* (b) *After Many a Summer*
(c) *Time must have a Stop* (d) *Point Counter Point*

163. In which of his novel, Aldous Huxley attempts 'musicalization fiction'?
(a) *Crome Yellow* (b) *Antic Hay*
(c) *Those Barren Leaves* (d) *Point Counter Point*

**7. Graham Greene**

164. To which period Graham Greene belongs?
(a) 17th century (b) 18th century
(c) 19th century (d) 20th century

165. Which of the following is the autobiography of Graham Greene?
(a) *A Sort of Life* (b) *The Revolver in the Cupboard*
(c) *Babbling April* (d) *The Man Within*

166. Which of the following writers is a contemporary of Graham Greene?
(a) Jane Austen (b) Thomas Hardy
(c) Joseph Conrad (d) George Orwell

167. Which of the following novels has been written by Graham Greene?
(a) *The End of the Affair* (b) *The Portrait of a Lady*
(c) *The Portrait of a Youngman as an Artist* (d) *Animal Farm*

168. Which of the following novels has not been written by Graham Greene?
(a) *The Man Within* (b) *The End of the Affair*
(c) *The Quiet American* (d) *Lord Jim*

169. Which of the following statements is true in the context of Greene's *The End of the Affair*?
(a) *The End of the Affair* is heavy with hatred. Bendrix is frustrated in love, so he expresses his hatred for his old love Sarah and her husband Henry

(b) this novel has the Vietnamese war as its background
(c) this novel depicts the dilemma of Querry who is the hero
(d) none of these

170. Bendrix is the main character in which one of the following novels of Graham Greene?
(a) *The Heart of the Matter* (b) *The Man Within*
(c) *The End of the Affair* (d) *The Quiet American*

171. In Greene's *The End of the Affair* which of the following characters was the old love of Bendrix?
(a) Isabel (b) Dorothy (c) Sarah (d) Jones

172. In Greene's *The End of the Affair* which of the following characters was the husband of Sarah?
(a) Henry (b) Bendrix (c) Ralph (d) Warburton

173. Who is the detective in Greene's *The End of the Affair*?
(a) Henry (b) Bendrix (c) Parkis (d) Sarah

174. Which of the following statements may be true about Bendrix's character in *The End of the Affair*?
(a) he is a person with a considerable store of natural unpleasantness which has been aggravated and stimulated by circumstances
(b) he is a truly religious, God fearing man
(c) he is a simpleton whom everybody deceives
(d) none of these

175. Which of the following statements may be true in context of Greene's *The End of the Affair*?
(a) Sarah is dead and is forgiven by Bendrix
(b) Sarah leaves her husband and comes back to her lover Bendrix
(c) Sarah is dead, the hatred has lost its object, and so it is transferred to God. Bendrix hates God for He has taken away Sarah.
(d) None of these

176. Which of the following statements may be true about Graham Greene as a novelist?
(a) Graham Greene is a social novelist
(b) Graham Greene is a satirist

(c) Greene is predominantly a religious writer
(d) None of these

177. Which of the following statements is true in the context of Greene's *Brighton Rock*?
(a) Pinkie is the leader of the adolescent criminals who are engaged in crimes like murder
(b) Pinkie is the leader of a trade union
(c) Pinkie is a social reformer working for the upliftment of the downtrodden in society
(d) None of these

178. Major Scobie is a character in which of the following novels of Graham Greene?
(a) *The End of the Affair* (b) *The Quiet American*
(c) *The Man Within* (d) *The Heart of the Matter*

179. Which of the following statements is true about the character of Major Scobie in Greene's *The Heart of the Matter*?
(a) Major Scobie is an officer devoted and dedicated to the service of the nation
(b) Major Scobie is surrounded by corruption, the illicit diamond trade, cut-throat rivalry between traders like Fusuf and Tallit
(c) Major Scobie is a corrupt politician
(d) None of these

180. In the following lines Greene throws light on the grim conditions in which human beings are compelled to live an ignoble existence: "Women lived in two of the huts, the pigs in another; in the last unruined hut where maize was stored, an old man and a boy and a tribe of rats.... Living on the edge of subsistence nothing much could ever change him". From which novel of Graham Greene these lines have been taken?
(a) *The Power and the Glory* (b) *The Man Within*
(c) *The End of the Affair* (d) *The Heart of the Matter*

181. Ida is a character in which of the following novels of Graham Greene?
(a) *The Heart of the Matter* (b) *Brighton Rock*
(c) *The End of the Affair* (d) *The Power and the Glory*

182. Helen is a character in which of the following novels of Graham Greene?
   (a) *The Heart of the Matter* (b) *Brighton Rock*
   (c) *The End of the Affair* (d) *The Power and the Glory*

183. In the context of Green's *The Heart of the Matter* who is the wife of Scobie?
   (a) Helen (b) Louise (c) Isabel (d) Dorothy

184. Which of the following statements may be true about Greene's *The Man Within*?
   (a) the theme is the struggle between the Church and the State
   (b) this novel has the theme of the hunting down of the young gangster Pinkie by Ida
   (c) the novel shows the psychological insight into the character of Andrews who realizes the mystery of self
   (d) none of these

185. Which of the following will you associate with Greene's *A Burnt-Out Case*?
   (a) the novel depicts the dilemma of Querry. Burnt out by his success as an architect and as a womanizer in Europe, he arrives at a leper village in the Belgian Congo
   (b) the novel has a Vietnamese War as its background
   (c) Bendrix is the main character through whom Greene expresses his ideas
   (d) none of these

186. With which novel of Greene will you associate the following statement: 'This novel has the background of the Spanish Civil War'?
   (a) *The Power and the Glory* (b) *The Confidential Agent*
   (c) *The Heart of the Matter* (d) *The End of the Affair*

187. With which novel of Greene will you associate the following statement: 'The hero of the novel, Dr. Fischer, is a millionaire who finds to his dismay that his wife still seeks the company of a poor clerk who shares her love of music for which Dr. Fischer has no taste.'?
   (a) *The Power and the Glory* (b) *The Confidential Agent*
   (c) *The Bomb Party* (d) *The Heart of the Matter*

188. Which of the following is not a theme in the novels of Graham Greene?
    (a) Greene was not blind to the rampant evil in the society. This consciousness of evil finds expression in his major novels
    (b) closely related to sinfulness is the theme of salvation and damnation
    (c) Greene believes in the original sin of man. As a Catholic he is of the opinion that man has a natural tendency to fall to the path of evil
    (d) there is something divine in everyman
189. Graham Greene's *May We Borrow Your Husband* is a collection of
    (a) essays (b) poems
    (c) short stories (d) novella
190. Which book of Graham Greene is a satire on contemporary spy novels?
    (a) *Shades of Greene* (b) *A Gun for Sale*
    (c) *The Third Man* (d) *Our Man in Havana*

**8. Joseph Conrad**

191. To which period did Joseph Conrad belong?
    (a) Elizabethan period (b) Restoration period
    (c) late 19th and early 20th century (d) Jacobean period
192. Which of the following was the native country of Conrad?
    (a) England (b) Poland (c) Germany (d) France
193. Conrad later adopted the citizenship of which of the following countries?
    (a) England (b) Poland (c) Germany (d) France
194. When Conrad was born
    (a) Poland was occupied by Russia (b) Poland was a free country
    (c) Poland was a superpower (d) the Second World War was going on

195. By profession, Conrad was a
(a) doctor (b) sailor (c) teacher (d) priest

196. Which of the following works has not been authored by Conrad?
(a) *The Pacific Regions of Captain Cook* (b) *The Heart of Darkness*
(c) *The Secret Agent* (d) *Almayer's Folly*

197. Which of the following works has been authored by Conrad?
(a) *Lord Jim* (b) *The Lord of Flies*
(c) *The Portrait of a Lady* (d) *The Golden Gate*

198. Which of the following works has not been authored by Conrad?
(a) *The Nigger of the Narcissus* (b) *Nostromo*
(c) *The Shadow Line* (d) *The Great Tradition*

199. Which of the following statements about Conrad is true?
(a) Conrad was a modernist novelist (b) Conrad was a victorian novelist
(c) Conrad was a modernist dramatist (d) Conrad was a war novelist

200. Conrad collaborated with which of the following novelists to write *The Inheritors* and *Romance*?
(a) Rudyard Kipling (b) Ford Madox Hueffer
(c) James Joyce (d) Henry James

201. Which of the following statements is true about Conrad's *The Secret Agent*?
(a) the story of the novel centres round the absurd cruelty of the Greenwich Park explosion
(b) the story of the novel deals with Marlowe's voyage to the Congo Basin in Africa
(c) the novel has been written against the background of Latin-American atmosphere
(d) the story of the novel deals with Conrad's love affair

202. Mr. Verlock is a character in which of the following novels of Conrad?
(a) *The Heart of Darkness* (b) *The Secret Agent*
(c) *Nostroma* (d) *Lord Jim*

203. In Conrad's *The Secret Agent*, Verloc has a brother-in-law, what is his name?
(a) Stevie (b) Heat (c) Ossipon (d) Vladimir

204. Which of the following statements about Conrad's *The Secret Agent* may be true?
(a) Mr. Verlock was ostensibly engaged in his shop-business. His real work was in a way political
(b) Mr. Verlock was passionately attached to his shop-business
(c) Mr. Verlock wanted to expand his business, he was working very hard for it
(d) Mr. Verlock squandered away his money in business

205. "But as errand boy, he did not turn out a great success. He forgot his message; he was easily diverted from the straight path of duty by the attractions of stray cats and dogs." In these lines he refers to which of the following characters?
(a) Stevie (b) Mr. Verlock
(c) Mr. Vladimir (d) Michaelis

206. Verlock in Conrad's *The Secret Agent* is
(a) an Englishman (b) a Russian
(c) a French (d) a German

207. Which of the following characters in Conrad's *The Secret Agent* is the first secretary in an Embassy?
(a) Verlock (b) Vladimir
(c) Michaelis (d) Ossipon

208. Read the following lines from Conrad's *The Secret Agent* "Do you know how I would call the nature of the present economic conditions? I would call it cannibalistic. That's what it is! They are nourishing their greed on the quivering flesh and the warm blood of the people-nothing else." In these line to whom does 'I' refer?
(a) Ossipon (b) Vladimir
(c) Winnie (d) Stevie

209. Mr. Verlock in *The Secret Agent* was
(a) an anarchist (b) a capitalist
(c) a democrat (d) none of them

210. The husband of Winnie was

(a) Verlock (b) Ossipon
(c) Michaelis (d) Karl Yundt

211. Mrs. Verlock in Conrad's *The Secret Agent* murdered her husband for which of the following reasons?

(a) Mrs. Verlock murdered her husband in a fit of madness
(b) Mrs. Verlock was in love with Ossipon who instigated her to murder
(c) Mr. Verlock had been the cause of her brother's death
(d) None of these

212. How did Stevie in Conrad's *The Secret Agent* die?

(a) Stevie was half-witted, he committed suicide
(b) Stevie was poisoned
(c) Mr. Verlock instigated him to blow up the Greenwich Observatory but he stubles and blows himself to pieces
(d) None of these

213. Which of the following statements may be true about Conrad's *Almayer's Folly*?

(a) Almayer lived an isolated life in the forests of the Congo in Africa
(b) Almayer is a solitary European in one of the remote Dutch possessions in the East
(c) Almayer had the hope of returning some day to his far-off home in Belgium
(d) None of these

214. In Conrad's *The Nigger of the Narcissus*, Narcissus is

(a) the name of a place (b) the name of a ship
(c) the name of a character (d) the name of a forest

215. In Conrad's *The Nigger of the Narcissus*, 'nigger' refers to a negro. Who is the negro?

(a) the nigger refers to one of the ship's crew named James Wait
(b) the Negro is an inhabitant of the forest Narcissus

(c) the Negro is an inhabitant of the island of Narcissus
(d) none of these

216. In Conrad's *Lord Jim*, what is the profession of Lord Jim?
(a) Lord Jim is an courtier in the court of the King of England
(b) Lord Jim is an Army General
(c) Lord Jim is the chief mate of a ship called Patna
(d) None of these

217. Lord Jim in Conrad's *Lord Jim* suffers from a strong sense of guilt. What was the reason behind this guilt consciousness?
(a) Lord Jim had committed a murder
(b) Lord Jim had neglected his wife and children
(c) Lord Jim had deserted the sinking ship with other officers, leaving the eight hundred sleeping pilgrim-passengers to their fate
(d) None of these

218. Which of the following works of Joseph Conrad is a tale of Russian revolutionaries?
(a) *Heart of Darkness* (b) *Typhoon*
(c) *Youth* (d) *Under Western Eyes*

219. *A Simple Tale* is a subtitle of a detective work by Joseph Conrad, the name of which is
(a) *Nostroma* (b) *The Mirror of the Sea*
(c) *The Secret Agent* (d) *A Set of Six*

220. Who called Henry James the 'Victorian of fine consciousness'?
(a) Joseph Conrad (b) James Joyce
(c) G.M. Hopkins (d) E.M. Forster

221. In which work of Joseph Conrad, Kurtz appears?
(a) *The Heart of Darkness* (b) *The Nigger of the Narcissus*
(c) *Nostromo* (d) *The Secret Agent*

### 9. William Somerset Maugham

222. To which period did Somerset Maugham belong?
(a) 16th century (b) 17th century
(c) 18th century (d) 20th century

223. Which of the following is a contemporary of Maugham?
(a) Charles Dickens (b) Benjamin Disraeli
(c) Henry Fielding (d) D.H. Lawrence

224. Which of the following is not a contemporary of Maugham?
(a) Joseph Conrad (b) J.B. Priestley
(c) Aldous Huxley (d) W.M. Thackeray

225. William Somerset Maugham was born in which of the following countries?
(a) India (b) England (c) France (d) Ireland

226. Which of the following works has been authored by Maugham?
(a) *Of Human Bondage* (b) *Middlemarch*
(c) *The Brave New World* (d) *Howard's End*

227. Which of the following works has not been authored by Maugham?
(a) *Christmas Holiday* (b) *Up at the Villa*
(c) *The Razor's Edge* (d) *The Rainbow*

228. Which of the following statements may be associated with Maugham's *Lady Fredrick*?
(a) *Lady Fredrick* is the story of a woman deserted by her husband
(b) *Lady Fredrick* is one of Maugham's satirical comedies exposing the evils running rampant in the upper class of society
(c) *Lady Fredrick* is concerned with the miracles of Christian saints during the middle ages
(d) None of these

229. Which of the following statements will you associate with Maugham's *Mrs. Craddock*?
(a) *Mrs. Craddock* is the story of a woman deserted by her husband in the wrinkled phase of her life
(b) In this novel magic operates fully and the dead are called back to life

(c) *Mrs. Craddock* is a Chinese tale representing the amorous intrigues of a doctor's wife with a colonial officer
(d) None of these

230. Which of the following statements will you associate with Maugham's *The Magician*?
(a) *The Magician* is the story of a woman deserted by her husband in the wrinkled phase of her life
(b) *The Magician* is a novel in which magic operates fully and the dead are called back to life
(c) *The Magician* is a Chinese tale representing the amorous intrigues of a doctor's wife with a colonial officer
(d) None of these

231. Which of the following statements will you associate with Maugham's *Catalina*?
(a) *Catalina* is concerned with the miracles of Christian saints during the Middle ages and the scenes of this rambling tale is medieval Spain
(b) *Catalina* is a Chinese tale representing the amorous intrigues of a doctor's wife with a colonial officer
(c) *Catalina* is the story of a woman deserted by her husband in the wrinkled phase of her life
(d) None of these

232. In one of his works Maugham expresses his view that "the best way to serve God is not fasting and penance nor fighting for the holy cause in foreign lands, but to do one's duty in one's humble sphere of life". Which is the novel expressing this view?
(a) *Lady Fredrick* (b) *Mrs. Craddock*
(c) *Catalina* (d) *Of Human Bondage*

233. Which of the following statements may be true about Maugham's *The Painted Veil*?
(a) *The Painted Veil* is a story of a woman deserted by her husband
(b) *The Painted Veil* is concerned with the miracles of Christian Saints during the Middle Ages

(c) *The Painted Veil* is a Chinese tale representing the amorous intrigues of a doctor's wife with a Colonial Officer

(d) None of these

234. *The Narrow Corner* is a novel by Maugham. Among the given statements which one seems to be correct?

(a) *The Narrow Corner* is a story of a woman deserted by her husband

(b) *The Narrow Corner* is a Chinese tale representing the amorous intrigues of a doctor's wife with a colonial officer

(c) *The Narrow Corner* is a study of the southern seas and exotic scenes where people are governed by wild passions and fierce emotions

(d) None of these

235. What is the theme of Maugham's *Theatre*?

(a) *Theatre* represents the life of an actress who keeps up the fire of youth even in her senile decay

(b) *Theatre* is the story of a Parisian prostitute Lydia who renounces all her pleasures and wealth in order to save the life of her husband undergoing life sentence for the charge of murder

(c) *Theatre* is the life story of Gaugin, a French painter who runs away from human society and civilization to find relief and refuge in a tropical island

(d) None of these

236. What is the theme of Maugham's *The Moon and the Six Pence*?

(a) *The Moon and the Six Pence* is the life story of Gaugin, a French painter, who runs away from human society and civilization to find relief and refuge in a tropical island

(b) *The Moon and the Six Pence* is a philosophic novel representing Maugham's attitude towards life and his faith in renunciation. Larry is the hero of this novel

(c) *The Moon and the Six Pence* is the story of a Parisian prostitute Lydia who renounces all her life pleasures

and wealth in order to save the life of her husband undergoing life sentence for the charge of murder
(d) None of these

237. What is the theme of Maugham's *Christmas Holiday*?
(a) *Christmas Holiday* is the story of a Parisian prostitute Lydia who renounces all her life pleasures and wealth in order to save the life of her husband undergoing life sentence for the charge of murder
(b) *Christmas Holiday* is a philosophic novel representing Maugham's attitude towards life and his faith in renunciation. Larry is the hero of this novel
(c) *Christmas Holiday* is the life story of Gaugin, a French painter, who runs away from human society and civilization to find relief and refuge in a tropical island
(d) None of these

238. What is the theme of Maugham's *The Razor's Edge*?
(a) *The Razor's Edge* is a satirical novel representing the life of Mr. Driffield, the novelist and his bohemian and luxurious wife Rosie who is a full-blooded woman intent upon making the most of life
(b) *The Razor's Edge* is a philosophic novel representing Maugham's attitude towards life and his faith in renunciation. Larry is the hero of the novel
(c) *The Razor's Edge* is the life story of Gaugin, a French painter, who runs away from human society and civilization to find relief and refuge in a tropical island
(d) None of these

239. Larry is the main character in which of the following novels of Maugham?
(a) *Christmas Holiday* (b) *Of Human Bondage*
(c) *The Razor's Edge* (d) *The Moon and the Six Pence*

240. What is true about Larry in the context of Maugham's *The Razor's Edge*?
(a) Larry is a French painter, who runs away from human society and civilization

(b) Larry comes to India and meets Indian sadhus and philosophers from whom he imbibes the lesson of renunciation
(c) Larry is a prostitute who renounces all her pleasures and wealth to save the life of her husband
(d) None of these

241. Philip Carey is the main character in which of the following novels of Maugham?
(a) *Christmas Holiday* (b) *Of Human Bondage*
(c) *The Razor's Edge* (d) *The Moon and the Six Pence*

242. From which of the novels of Maugham, the following lines have been quoted?
"Life had no meaning. It was immaterial whether he was born or not born, whether he lived or ceased to live. Life was insignificant and death without consequences."
(a) *Christmas holiday* (b) *Of Human Bondage*
(c) *The Razor's Edge* (d) *The Moon and the Six Pence*

243. Which of Maugham's novel gives a full account of Philip Carey's childhood, upbringing, education and love. The loneliness of his life is hinted from the start when Phililp Carey's mother dies?
(a) *Christmas Holiday* (b) *Of Human Bondage*
(c) *The Razor's Edge* (d) *The Moon and the Six Pence*

244. About Maugham's *Of Human Bondage* which statements may be true?
(a) *Of Human Bondage* suggests people to live with love and peace
(b) *Of Human Bondage* is an appreciation of Indian social scene
(c) *Of Human Bondage* is Maugham's final judgement on the meaninglessness and loneliness of human life
(d) None of these

245. Which of the following novels of Maugham can be called autobiographical?
(a) *Liza of Lambeth* (b) *Of Human Bondage*
(c) *The Trembling of a Leaf* (d) *The Painted Veil*

246. Which of the following statements about W.S. Maugham may be correct?
(a) Maugham continued the tradition of picaresque novel
(b) Maugham can be ranked with Dickens and other Victorian novelists
(c) Maugham's scenes of life in the Pacific mark him as a follower of Stevenson and Conrad
(d) None of these

247. Which one is a true comedy of manners and one of the best plays of Somerset Maugham?
(a) *Mrs. Dot* (b) *Jack Straw*
(c) *The Circle* (d) *The Constant Wife*

248. Maugham's *A Man of Honour* is a
(a) bitter comedy (b) Restoration comedy
(c) realistic comedy (d) realistic tragedy

**10. James Joyce**

249. Stream of consciousness novel is a product of
(a) 18th century (b) 16th century
(c) 17th century (d) 20th century

250. Which of the following statements may be true about the technique of the Stream of consciousness novel?
(a) it has a well-organized plot structure
(b) it has an interesting story in which incidents are arranged in a chronological order
(c) it is directly or indirectly an interior monologue
(d) none of these

251. *A Portrait of the Artist as a Young Man* may be called
(a) a political novel (b) a historical novel
(c) an autobiographical novel (d) a picaresque novel

252. In Joyce's *A Portrait of the Artist as a Young Man*, the novelist himself is represented by which of the following characters?
(a) Parnell (b) Father Dolan
(c) Stephen Dedalus (d) Father Arnall

253. Which of the following was the first to use the phrase 'Stream of Consciousness'?
(a) James Joyce (b) Walter Allen
(c) W.Y. Tindall (d) William James

254. In which of the following types will you keep the novels of James Joyce?
(a) gothic novel (b) picaresque novel
(c) victorian novel (d) stream of consciousness novel

255. Which of the following is a contemporary of James Joyce?
(a) Daniel Defoe (b) Thomas Hardy
(c) Henry Fielding (d) Virginia Woolf

256. Which of the following is not a contemporary of James Joyce?
(a) Mrs. Dorothy (b) Marcel Proust
(c) Charles Dickens (d) Virginia Woolf

257. Who is the character in Joyce's *A Portrait of the Artist as a Young Man* that recalls his experiences of his childhood days?
(a) Aunt Dante (b) Stephen Dedalus
(c) Charles (d) Eileen Vance

258. In Joyce's *A Portrait of the Artist as a Young Man*, Stephen Dedalus wants to marry which of the following characters?
(a) May Dedalus (b) Mrs. Riordan
(c) Eileen Vance (d) Dante

259. In Joyce's *A Portrait of the Artist as a Young Man*, when Stephen Dedalus was in a boarding school, he was pushed into a ditch of dirty water and he caught cold because of this. Who was his classmate who pushed him?
(a) Eileen Vance (b) Athy
(c) Wells (d) Michael

260. In Joyce's *A Portrait of the Artist as a Young Man*, who was the Latin teacher that punished Stephen?
(a) Father Dolan (b) Parnell
(c) Wells (d) Michael

261. Which of the following characters is the father of Stephen in Joyce's *A Portrait of the Artist as a Young Man*?
(a) Simon (b) Charles (c) Michael (d) Parnell

262. In Joyce's *A Portrait of the Artist as a Young Man*, beauty has been defined—"We can regard a thing as beautiful if its perception pleases." This definition of beauty is by which of the following?
(a) Aristotle (b) Thomas Aquinas
(c) Stephen (d) Plato

263. Stephen in Joyce's *A Portrait of the Artist as a Young Man* divides art into a development of three forms. These three forms are
(a) comedy, tragedy and tragi-comedy (b) lyrical, epic and dramatic
(c) lyrical, epic and ballad (d) none of these

264. In Joyce's *A Portrait of the Artist as a Young Man*, the title of the novel refers to which of the following characters?
(a) Cranly (b) Davin (c) Lynch (d) Stephen

265. In Joyce's *A Portrait of the Artist as a Young Man*, art has been defined—"Art is the human disposition of sensible or intelligible matter for an aesthetic end." This definition of art is from which of the following?
(a) Stephen (b) Aristotle
(c) Thomas Aquinas (d) Lynch

266. Which of the following statements may be true about the ending of Joyce's *A Portrait of the Artist as a Young Man*?
(a) the novel ends with the marriage of Stephen
(b) the novel ends with the death of Stephen

(c) the novel ends with some entries from the diary of Stephen
(d) none of these

267. In Joyce's *A Portrait of the Artist as a Young Man*, is there any symbolic significance of Dedalus in the name of Stephen Dedalus?
(a) it has no significance, it is simply a title of a name
(b) Dedalus was a great artist and Stephen too was an artist
(c) Dedalus is a mythological figure, Dedalus and his son Icarus were imprisoned by the king. Like Dedalus, Stephen also feels imprisoned in Dublin as the mythic hero was in Creto. Both of them escaped from their jails. Stephen and Dedalus both had rebelled
(d) none of these

268. What is the theme of the novel *A Portrait of the Artist as a Young Man*?
(a) the theme of the novel is the love affair of young artist
(b) the theme of the novel is the portrait of the contemporary society
(c) the theme of this novel is the development of the artist from his early childhood to the last days of his youth
(d) none of these

269. Which of the following novels of Joyce was banned for obscenity?
(a) *Finnegans Wake* (b) *Dubliners*
(c) *Ulysses* (d) *A Portrait of the Artist as a Young Man*

270. Leopold Bloom is the protagonist in which of the following novels of Joyce?
(a) *Finnegans Wake* (b) *Dubliners*
(c) *Ulysses* (d) *A Portrait of the Artist as a Young Man*

271. Which of the following statements is true about Stephen Dedalus, a character created by James Joyce?
   (a) Stephen Dedalus is character in Joyce's novels—*Ulysses* and *A Portrait of the Artist as a Young Man*
   (b) Stephen Dedalus is a priest in *A Portrait of the Artist as a Young Man*
   (c) Stephen Dedalus only appears in Joyce's *A Portrait of the Artist as a Young Man* and nowhere else.
   (d) None of these

272. In Joyce's *Ulysses* each episode coincides with which of the following classical books?
   (a) Virgils's *Aenid* (b) Dante's *Divine Comedy*
   (c) Homer's *Odyssey* (d) None of these

273. Which of the following characters in Joyce's *Ulysses* represents *Odysseus* in Homer's Epic?
   (a) Stephen (b) Bloom
   (c) Molly (d) None of these

274. Humphrey Chimpden Earwicker is a character in which of the following novels of Joyce?
   (a) *Ulysses* (b) *Finnegans Wake*
   (c) *Dubliners* (d) *A Portrait of the Artist as a Young Man*

275. Which of the following novels of James Joyce presents the dreams and nightmares of Humphrey Chimpden Earwicker and his family?
   (a) *Ulysses* (b) *Finnegans Wake*
   (c) *Dubliners* (d) *A Portrait of the Artist as a Young Man*

276. Which of the following statements is true of James Joyce's *Dubliners*?
   (a) *Dubliners* is a travelogue (b) *Dubliners* is a drama
   (c) *Dubliners* is a novel (d) *Dubliners* is a volume of short stories

277. The title of Joyce's *Dubliners* refers to
   (a) the people of Dublin
   (b) Joyce has presented Dublin in four of its aspects—Childhood, adolescence, maturity and public life

(c) the visitors of Dublin
(d) none of these

278. What is the significance of the title of Joyce's *Finnegans Wake*?
(a) Finnegans Wake is the protagonist of the novel
(b) Finnegans Wake is the name of a city
(c) the title is a compound of Finn Macool, the Irish folk hero who is supposed to return to life at some future date to become the saviour of Ireland
(d) none of these

279. James Joyce's novel *Dubliners*, which began in 1900, was published in
(a) 1906 (b) 1910 (c) 1919 (d) 1914

280. James Joyce's work *Exiles* is a
(a) novel (b) play (c) essay (d) poem

281. Which one of the following novels is based on Homer's *Odyssey*?
(a) *The Wasteland* (b) *Mrs. Dalloway*
(c) *Ulysses* (d) *Brave New World*

282. Which novel of James Joyce is set in a single day?
(a) *Dubliners* (b) *Stephen Hero*
(c) *Finnegans Wake* (d) *Ulysses*

### 11. Virginia Woolf

283. Virginia Woolf was the daughter of an eminent Victorian critic and scholar. Who was he?
(a) Matthew Arnold (b) Carlyle
(c) John Ruskin (d) Leslie Stephen

284. To which period Virginia Woolf belonged?
(a) 17th century (b) 16th century
(c) 18th century (d) 20th century

285. Which of the following is a contemporary of Virginia Woolf?
(a) Jane Austen (b) George Eliot
(c) Charlotte Bronte (d) Aldous Huxley

286. Which of the following is not a contemporary of Virginia Woolf?
   (a) E.M. Forster (b) Dorothy Richardson
   (c) Elizabeth Bower (d) Jane Austen

287. Which of the following novels has been written by Virginia Woolf?
   (a) *Pride and Prejudice* (b) *Mrs. Dalloway*
   (c) *Wuthering Heights* (d) *Ulysses*

288. Which of the following novels has not been written by Virginia Woolf?
   (a) *To the Light House* (b) *Mrs. Dalloway*
   (c) *Night and Day* (d) *Adam Bede*

289. The novels of Virginia Woolf may be kept in which of the following categories?
   (a) picaresque novel (b) epistolary novel
   (c) historical novel (d) stream of consciousness novel

290. Which was the first novel of Virginia Woolf?
   (a) *The Voyage Out* (b) *Night and Day*
   (c) *Jacob's Room* (d) *Mrs. Dalloway*

291. Jacob is the main character in Woolf's *Jacob's Room*. Which of the following statements may be true about Jacob?
   (a) the novel describes Jacob as a donquixotic character, always lost in his books but having no practical wisdom about life
   (b) Jacob is a passionate lover who has confined himself to his room after his failure in love
   (c) the novel describes the impression of Jacob Flanders about his own life as a student of Cambridge, as a young man in love and as a soldier in war
   (d) none of these

292. Which of the following statements may be true about Virginia Woolf's plot structure?
   (a) there is no attempt at organized story telling in the novel
   (b) the incidents are arranged in a chronological sequence

(c) the novel has a well-knit organised plot
(d) none of these

293. The experiences of Professor Ramsay and his wife have been described in which novel of Woolf?
(a) *Mrs. Dalloway* (b) *To the Light House*
(c) *Orlando* (d) *The Waves*

294. Read the following lines quoted from David Daiches' *A Critical History of English Literature*: "the novel opens with the heroine planning to give a party; parties bring people to-gether—but do they really bring people to-gether or is one lonelier still in a crowd".
These lines refer to which novel of Virginia Woolf?
(a) *To the Light House* (b) *Mrs. Dalloway*
(c) *Night and Day* (d) *The Voyage Out*

295. Mr. and Mrs. Warren Smith are characters in which of the novels of Woolf?
(a) *The Voyage Out* (b) *To the Light House*
(c) *Mrs. Dalloway* (d) *Night and Day*

296. In which of the following novels Virginia Woolf takes a group of characters on holiday on an island in the Hebrides?
(a) *The Voyage Out* (b) *To the Light House*
(c) *Mrs. Dalloway* (d) *Night and Day*

297. Which one of the following novels of Virginia Woolf is known as a prose poem?
(a) *The Voyage Out* (b) *Night and Day*
(c) *Mrs. Dalloway* (d) *The Waves*

298. Which work of Woolf traces the life from Elizabethan to Modern times?
(a) *To the Light House* (b) *Orlando: A Biography*
(c) *Flush* (d) *The Years*

299. Who said: "I believe that all novels deal with character and that it is to express character not to preach doctrines, sing songs, or celebrate the glories of the British Empire."?
(a) James Joyce (b) Virginia Woolf
(c) D.H. Lawrence (d) Osborne

## UNIT C: THE DRAMA

### 1. John Osborne

300. Who has been called the leader of Angry Young Men?
   (a) Alan Sillitoe (b) John Wain
   (c) Colin Wilson (d) John Osborne
301. A group of writers of the late 1950's described by Kenneth Allsop as full of — "irreverence, stridency, vulgarity ... resentment against the cultivated" were called
   (a) New drama (b) the Theatre of Revolt
   (c) the Theatre of Cruelty (d) Angry Young men
302. The Angry Young Men presented
   (a) betrayal and futility (b) post war reforms
   (c) a sense of alienation (d) frustration and deprivation
303. Angry Young Men presented
   (a) jaded aristocracy (b) rich business class
   (c) war machinery (d) lower middle class and working class
304. Which is the most famous play of this movement?
   (a) *Room at the Top* (b) *Lucky Jim*
   (c) *The Outsider* (d) *Look Back in Anger*
305. When was *Look Back in Anger* published?
   (a) 1955 (b) 1954 (d) 1959 (d) 1956
306. Today *Look Back in Anger* is considered
   (a) manifestation of post second world war phenomenon
   (b) a social critique
   (c) a comment of non-redressal of working class grievances
   (d) a voice of dissent
307. In *Look Back in Anger* Jimmy Porter is
   (a) the hero (b) the anti-hero
   (c) the playwright's mouthpiece (d) unrealistic protagonist

308. *Look Back in Anger* is
   (a) a significant drama (b) a great theatre experience
   (c) a good book (d) a harbinger of a revolution in English drama

309. *Look Back in Anger* is a classic because
   (a) it was an attack on British complacency
   (b) it shook the foundation of pro-aristocracy governance
   (c) it was taken as a revolt
   (d) it awakened the policy makers from their slumber

310. *The Entertainer and Luther* lacked
   (a) force and vigour (b) smouldering anger
   (c) commitment (d) the anger of his first play

311. Osborne's later plays show
   (a) anger (b) anger as a matter of the past
   (c) acceptance of the world order (d) more disgruntled than angry

**2. Samuel Beckett**

312. The post Second World War drama presents
   (a) crisis of human predicament (b) war related problems
   (c) economic questions (d) fate of nations

313. The 'Theatre of Absurd' is linked with
   (a) Sartre (b) Samuel Beckett
   (c) Osborne (d) Wesker

314. The 'Theatre of Absurd' is marked by
   (a) funny situations (b) surprise and shock
   (c) human conflicts (d) divinity

315. 'The Kitchen-sink drama' is marked by
   (a) neo-realism (b) pseudo-realism
   (c) kitchen scenes (d) domestic life

316. The comedy of menace and dark comedy were written in
   (a) 18th century
   (b) 19th century
   (c) early twentieth century during First World War
   (d) mid-twentieth century and after

317. The labels of 'Kitchen-sink drama', 'Absurd drama', 'Comedy of menace', 'dark comedy' and 'Drama of cruelty' are used by
(a) journalists (b) playwrights
(c) drama critics (d) men of literature

318. 'The theatre of the Absurd' was first used by
(a) Laurence Kitchin (b) John Russell Taylor
(c) Martin Esslin (d) Hugh Kenner

319. Which drama is "a kind of intellectual shorthand for a complex pattern of similarities in approach, method and convention, of shared philosophical and artistic premises, whether conscious or subconscious ..."?
(a) drama of cruelty (b) absurd drama
(c) dark comedy (d) kitchen-sink drama

320. Which post-Second World War drama is best described by the statement?
The play presents 'a disillusioned, harsh, and stark picture of the world'
(a) the drama of menace (b) the drama of cruelty
(c) the theatre of the Absurd (d) Kitchen-sink drama

321. Who edited a selection of modern drama which includes Eugene Ionesco's *Amedee Arthur* Adamov's *Professor Traranne*, Fernando Arrabal's *The Two Executioners*, and Edward Albee's *The Zoo Story*?
(a) Martin Esslin's The *Theatre of the Absurd*
(b) Bambce Gascoigne's *Twentieth Century Drama*
(c) Laurence Kitchin's *Mid-Century Drama*
(d) Martin Esslin's *Absurd Drama*

322. Who wrote:
"A world that can be explained by reasoning, however faulty, is a familiar world. But in a universe that is suddenly deprived of illusions and of light, man feels a stranger. His is an irremediable exile, because he is deprived of memories of a lost homeland as much as he lacks the hope of a promised land to come. This divorce

between man and his life, the actor and his setting, truly constitutes the feeling of Absurdity."?

(a) Samuel Beckett (b) Eugene lonesco
(b) Martin Esslin (d) Albert Camus

323. Who has written *The Myth of Sisyphus*?

(a) Jean Paul Sartre (b) Albert Camus
(c) Samuel Beckett (d) James Joyce

324. *The Myth of Sisyphus* presents

(a) a sense of futility (b) man as a stranger on the planet earth
(c) an ancient myth (d) re-writing a Greck myth

325. Who described Absurd as "devoid of purpose ....... senseless, absurd, useless."?

(a) Franz Kafka (b) Albert Camus
(c) Samuel Beckett (d) Eugene Ionesco

326. A thinker argues about the absurdity but the playwright

(a) writes about it
(b) presents concrete images of experience of Absurdity
(c) gives form to abstract thought
(d) answers existential questions

327. Name the label which is associated with Samuel Beckett, Eugene Ionesco, Arthur Adamov and Jean Genet.

(a) the Theatre of Revolt (b) the Theatre of Paradox
(c) the Theatre of Cruelty (d) the Theatre of the Absurd

328. When was *Waiting for Godot* first published?

(a) 1950 (b) 1951 (c) 1956 (d) 1952

329. When was *Waiting for Godot* first performed in a theatre?

(a) Janurary 5, 1953 (b) April 13, 1955
(c) January 5, 1952 (d) April 13, 1953

330. Where was *Waiting for Godot* first performed in U.S.A.?

(a) New York theatre (b) San Quenten
(c) Boston (d) Washington D.C.

331. When Alan Schneider asked Beckett, 'who was Godot'? what reply did the playwright give?

(a) 'Godot is a local landlord?' (b) 'Godot is diminuitive God'

(c) 'Godot is a famous cyclist?' (d) 'If knew, I would have said so in the play'

332. Who are waiting for Godot?
(a) Vladimir and Estragon (b) Pozzo and Lucky
(c) the little boy (d) the people in the audience

333. Why are Vladimir and Estragon waiting for Godot?
(a) for food and shelter (b) for money and power
(c) for a prayer and salvation (d) for Godot had promised to come tomorrow, but they don't know why

334. How long have they been waiting?
(a) for two years (b) for two evenings
(c) for a life time (d) for sometime

335. Valdimir and Estragon are waiting for whom?
(a) for Godot
(b) for a resolution of their predicament by a just judge
(c) for salvation giving agent, a sage
(d) for the little boy

336. Godot does not come but why do the two tramps continue waiting?
(a) because the little boy comes late in the evening with a message that tomorrow Godot will certainly come
(b) because the messenger asks them to wait
(c) because they are simply keeping a promise
(d) because they have nothing better to do

337. Vladimir and Estragon represent
(a) North Europe (b) Russia
(c) down-trodden mankind (d) themselves

338. The tramps are
(a) youngmen (b) old and sick
(c) ageless (d) fools

339. Who is Pozzo?
(a) a rich man
(b) a good for nothing aristocrat

(c) a despotic man, like a war lord
(d) a despotic man reminding one of Hitler, and all he stood for

340. Who is Lucky?
(a) a serf
(b) a poor old man
(c) an intelligent man in servitude
(d) a friend of Pozzo

341. Lucky stands for
(a) good intelligent people mentally and physically controlled by men in power
(b) a slave
(c) a moral destitute
(d) an economic disaster

342. Lucky represents
(a) citizens of the world who make this world and life worthwhile yet are not free
(b) he is no good now for he is old
(c) good for nothing, worthless fellow
(d) an enslaved soul struggling for freedom

343. What does the playwright show by lucky on a rope?
(a) knowledge without freedom
(b) hope is inherent even in slavery
(c) attempt of despotic power to stifle the free spirit
(d) the person knows everything even his own key to salvation but is denied access

344. Vladimir - Estragon show that
(a) they are together in their mission
(b) they are mind and body, inseparable
(c) they are waiting for something or someone
(d) they are drowned in a situation with no hope

345. Vladimir - Estragon represent
(a) twins
(b) tied together
(c) friends in failure
(d) symbiotic twins

346. Why don't Vladimir and Estragon not give up waiting and leave?
(a) they cannot leave, physically too weak
(b) they are keeping a promise

(c) they are honouring a life-long commitment (d) waiting is all they know and done

347. What do these lines show?
"Estragon: Let's go
Vladimir: We can't
Estragon: Why not?
Vladimir: We're waiting for Godot."
(a) reference to the theme
(b) a relentless vigil
(c) a purpose, a desire to reveal the mysterious meaning of human existence
(d) a moral commitment

348. What is the refrain in *Waiting for Godot*?
(a) 'I felt lonely' (b) 'I was asleep'
(c) 'Dreadful deprivation' (d) 'We're waiting for Godot'

349. While waiting what do they do to pass the time?
(a) talk, mime, and try to entertain (b) sleep and complain
(c) make plans for the future (d) discuss the philosophy of life

350. What is most conspicuous aspect missing in this play?
(a) nobody comes, nobody goes; inaction
(b) absence of plot
(c) properly dressed characters
(d) dialogues

351. What is the characteristic feature of people in the opinion of the tramps?
(a) moral wreck for they easily believe everything
(b) no good for they are spineless
(c) sloth, in action
(d) bloody ignorant apes

352. Lucky's speech shows
(a) human knowledge (b) human knowledge and action not in harmony
(c) power of speech (d) strength of thought

353. What represents failure of thought process and logic in life?
(a) Pozzo's description of twilight
(b) Vladimir and Estragon's cross-talk
(c) Messenger boy's dialogue
(d) Lucky's long speech

354. Pozzo's speech — "That's how it is on this bitch of an earth" — demonstrates
(a) human effort to be poetic
(b) a desire for being expansive
(c) how to impress lesser fortunate people with a dose of their act of speech
(d) a total collapse of rhetoric and art of speech

355. What do the tramps do with the hat to stop Lucky from continuing with his remorseless speech?
(a) put it on
(b) throw it out of the stage
(c) spit in it
(d) throw it on the ground and trample it

356. At one stage Vladimir compares himself to a divinity. Who is that?
(a) M.K. Gandhi
(b) St. Francis of Assisi
(c) Florence Nightingale
(d) Jesus Christ

357. Who said, 'But at this place, at this moment of time, all mankind is us ...'?
(a) Lucky (b) Pozzo (c) Estragon (d) Vladimir

358. Who said, 'Was I sleeping, while the others suffered'?
(a) Lucky (b) Pozzo (c) Vladimir (d) Estragon

359. What do the tramps do to the fallen Pozzo and Lucky?
(a) they ignore them
(b) they kick them and move away
(c) they steal their food and money
(d) they raise them up

360. What change takes place in the tramp?
(a) the tramps run away
(b) Godot finally arrives and makes them rich

(c) Pozzo gives them shelter
(d) they realize that by helping Pozzo and Lucky they had become men with dignity

### 3. Arthur Adamov

361. Which playwright depicted a senseless and brutal world?
(a) Eugene Ionesco (b) Harold Pinter
(c) Jean Genet (d) Arthur Adamov

362. *The Confessions* presents
(a) spiritual and psychological crisis of Adamov
(b) the lifestyle of a rich Russian aristocracy
(c) Adamov's escape from Russia and settlement in Switzerland
(d) Adamov's French experience

363. *The Confessions* presents
(a) anguish
(b) a ruthless self-revelation
(c) a Dostoyevskian statement of metaphysical anguish
(d) a deep sense of alienation

364. Adamov's war-period experiences are
(a) the endless humiliation
(b) based on escape in dreams
(c) sordid reality of dehumanization of the civilized life
(d) neurotic-leading to endless humiliation

365. Adamov has recorded how a blind beggar was passed by two pretty girls singing a popular refrain—'I had closed my eyes, it was wonderful'. How did he use this idea?
(a) by internal reflection presented through action
(b) action without words
(c) neither action, nor words, only a situation
(d) by realizing loneliness of man, the absence of communication

366. Adamov's *L'Invasion* is a play
(a) about hopelsss search for meaning
(b) showing disintegration of language
(c) about futility of search
(d) about futility—'I'll wait in silence, motionless

367. Adamov's *Le Professeur* Taranne is based on
(a) real experience (b) a dream
(c) a friend (d) a fusion

368. In *Le Professeur Taranne* the hero is
(a) innocent (b) aggressive
(c) mastermind and an exhibitionist (d) a scholar and a friend, a respectable citizen

**4. Eugene Ionesco**

369. Who said that human sadness cannot be abolished?
(a) Arthur Adamov (b) Jean Genet
(c) Harold Pinter (d) Eugene Ionesco

370. Who wrote in context of Ionesco that, a work of art is the expression of an incommunicable reality?
(a) Arthur Adamov (b) Philip Toynbee
(c) Jacques Lemarchand (d) Kenneth Tynan

371. *The Chairs* is a unique play because
(a) it presents an impressive scenic spectacle
(b) it is funny and unusual
(c) it is a multi-dimensional poetic image
(d) it simulates a crowd of invisible characters and is 'tour de force'

372. The theme of *The Chairs* is
(a) futility
(b) failure of human experience
(c) a delusion of the man and admiration of a doting uncritical wife
(d) emptiness of polite conversation

373. *The Chairs* presents
(a) rows of empty chairs
(b) a large number of invisible guests
(c) the old man and his wife facing a total failure
(d) empty chairs, invisible guests and the silent speaker

374. What is the message in *The Chairs?*
(a) human struggle in the face of failure (b) failure of speech
(c) absence of guests (d) meaninglessness of life

375. In which play Jean Anorillh found 'black humour'?
   (a) Ionesco's *The Chairs*
   (b) Osborne's *Look Back in Anger*
   (c) Beckett's *Endgame*
   (d) Genet's *The Confessions*

376. In *Amedee* Amedee and Madeliene are husband and wife who have
   (a) lived together
   (b) not left the apartment for fifteen years
   (c) amicable relationship
   (d) not left the apartment and brought their supplies through the window in a basket

377. What is unique in *Amedee*?
   (a) Madeliene is nagging all the time
   (b) The couple have confined themselves in the apartment for fifteen years
   (c) They make their living by working on a switchboard connecting telephones
   (d) In the next room lies the corpse of young man who visited them some fifteen years ago and who was killed by Amedee in jail or in jealousy

378. What great surprise the playwright presents in *Amedee*?
   (a) corpse does not stink
   (b) corpse grows beard and nails
   (c) the dead body also grows
   (d) the corpse is suffering from incurable disease of the dead – geometrical progression. The body bursts open in the door in the front room and mushrooms proliferate

379. What happens to the growing corpse in *Amedee*?
   (a) it bursts out of the window in the street
   (b) it carries the whole house with its growth
   (c) it draws attention of people
   (d) it grows into a balloon and Amedee floats in the air with it

380. What happens in the end of *Amedee*?
   (a) the corpse – balloon bursts and Amedee returns
   (b) Madeliene is reconciled with Amedee

(c) Amedee does not return and Madeliene remains lamenting
(d) Madeliene wants him back and mushrooms are in bloom but Amedee floats away in the sky

381. What does proliferation of mushroom depict?
(a) regeneration (b) dampness
(c) manifestation of nature (d) symbol of death and decay

382. Berenger's transformation in *Rhinoceros* shows
(a) regeneration
(b) interchange in nature
(c) the whole town has been transformed into rhinoceros
(d) insensitivity of man

383. What happens to Daisy before Berenger also discovers his own skin turning green and thick and growth of horns?
(a) she leaves the town to escape her change into rhino
(b) she also shows signs of transformation and joins the herd
(c) she is unaffected by this mysterious transformation
(d) nothing happens to Daisy

384. What human trait Ionesco wished to show in *Rhinoceros*?
(a) before leaving Rumania in 1938 he had seen his friends accepting Fascicism—herd instinct
(b) human beings have very superficial belief
(c) human trait is to save their own skin.
(d) personal comfort is more important than belief and values

385. What experience Ionesco wishes to depict in *Rhinoceros*?
(a) people are pliable
(b) mankind is really spineless
(c) once human beings put on blinkers—disgusting situation appears good and acceptable
(d) Those people who succumb to accepting change into rhinoceros really become rhinoceros

386. Why it is easier for Daisy to become a rhinoceros than for Berenger?
(a) Daisy resists transformation

(b) Daisy is a strong character yet force of universality is stronger
(c) Berenger resists transformation for he values individuality
(d) Daisy like millions cannot resist being different from the majority

**5. Jean Genet**

387. What happens in *The Maids*?
(a) conflict between a haughty lady and a servile maid
(b) play acting by two maids—one acts the lady Claire and the other his sister, the maid
(c) maids wish to become a lady
(d) a fantasy game cannot last, the mask slips and true identity is revealed—the lady is no lady but a maid like the other one

388. What happens in the end of *The Maids*?
(a) the play acting goes far and playing the role of the lady she has to drink the poisoned tea and dies
(b) the maids are too much involved in their fantasy game and pay the price for it
(c) the maids realize that they are no lady but mere maids
(d) the real lady returns and order is restored

389. The autobiography of Jean Genet is called
(a) *The Thief's Journal* (b) *A Hall of Mirrors*
(c) *Saint Genet* (d) *The Lesson*

390. What is essence of Genet's theatre?
(a) man is trapped like an animal and cannot run
(b) helplessness of man caught in a situation like fascist Germany
(c) man is trapped in a cage of his own creation and choice
(d) man is caught in a maze of mirrors, trapped by his own distorted reflections, no contact with others is possible because of the glass barrier, leading to despair and loneliness

391. What is a perpetual image of man Genet presents in his plays?
(a) man in a hall of mirrors, distorted perception
(b) caged man
(c) man in solitude
(d) man is vulnerable

## 6. Harold Pinter

392. Harold Pinter turned a commonplace situation into
(a) one invested with menace, dread and mystery
(b) an experience of hell
(c) a claustrophobic experience
(d) one with existential dimension

393. *The Room* presents
(a) a situation with two people in a room
(b) the world outside full of apprehensions
(c) the two people in the room who are afraid of overbearing outside world
(d) the idea that the room is a refuge

394. The house may have many rooms, but the room in which Rose is provides her with
(a) security and warmth (b) limitations
(c) bondage (d) her domain however bad it may be

395. What is the focal point of *The Room*?
(a) the fire place
(b) the window
(c) the characters huddled together awaiting disaster
(d) the door which may open ushering in someone with lurking danger

396. Bert, Rose's husband returns from the dark night outside, finds a Negro in the room and beats him savagely. What happens to Rose?
(a) Rose links the menace of the dark night outside, the dark man inside the room and goes blind. Total darkness
(b) Rose assures Bert that darkness is not all that frightening

(c) she tries to protect her friend, the Negro assuring that he is good
(d) Rose is frightened by the dreadful situation and is paralysed

397. In *The Birthday Party* Pinter presents
(a) a situation of horror
(b) horror and mystery
(c) a house which is a safe heaven
(d) a seaside resort kept by Meg and Petey, full of apprehensions

398. What is the relationship of Stanby with Meg?
(a) motherly
(b) full of motherliness, almost incestuous
(c) man—woman love despite age difference
(d) caretaker and guest

399. Goldberg and Mc Cann are sinister visitors who intimidate Stanley by
(a) blocking his exit
(b) forcing him to play blind man's buff
(c) beating him
(d) taking away his glasses leaving him almost blind

400. *The Birthday Party* presents
(a) Stanley's birthday party
(b) a party in which Stanley is intimidated
(c) an allegory of life
(d) an allegory of the pressures of conformity, Stanley is the artist and Goldberg and Mc Cann are the emissaries of the bourgeois world to which the former must conform

401. *The Birthday Party* presents
(a) an allegory of death—man is snatched away from the house he has built for himself with warmth of motherly love and sexuality by the dark angels of nothingness
(b) the human predicament

(c) the power of the unknown is more effective than the strength of the known
(d) unverifiable predicament of man

## UNIT D: POETRY

### 1. T.S. Eliot

402. T.S. Eliot was born in
(a) 1586 (b) 1688 (c) 1768 (d) 1888

403. T.S. Eliot, an American of a New England family adopted British citizenship in
(a) 1900 (b) 1910 (c) 1915 (d) 1922

404. Eliot became a director of the publishing firm of
(a) Oxford University Press (b) Penguin Press
(c) Orient Longman (d) Faber and Faber

405. Eliot was invested with the Order of Merit in the year
(a) 1900 (b) 1930 (c) 1940 (d) 1948

406. Eliot received the Nobel Prize for literature in
(a) 1890 (b) 1899 (c) 1920 (d) 1948

407. Which Indian religious book influenced Eliot most?
(a) *The Mahabharata* (b) *The Puranas*
(c) *The Vedas* (d) *The Bhagvad Gita*

408. "Gerontion" is a poem included in Eliot's
(a) *Poems* (b) *Hollow men*
(c) *Ash Wednesday* (d) *The Wasteland*

409. The most famous as well as the obscurest of Eliot's poem in English language is
(a) *The Wasteland* (b) *Hollow men*
(c) *Ash Wednesday* (d) *Four Quartets*

410. In which Eliot poem is the theme of *Ash Wednesday* repeated, continued and expanded?
(a) *Ariel Poems* (b) *Four Quartets*
(c) *Hollow Men* (d) *Choruses from Rock*

411. When was T.S. Eliot's *The Waste Land* published?
(a) 1900 (b) 1910 (c) 1920 (d) 1922

412. Eliot's *Journey of the Magi* occurs in his
(a) *Ariel Poems* (b) *Poems (1920)*
(c) *The Wasteland* (d) *Four Quartets*

413. Magi of *Journey of the Magi* are
(a) magicians (b) travellers
(c) pilgrims (d) wisemen of the East

414. *Animula* of Eliot was inspired by
(a) Dante (b) *Gita* (c) Arjuna (d) Krishna

**2. W.H. Auden**

415. W.H. Auden was the leader of the
(a) Oxford poets (b) Romantic poets
(c) Pre-Raphaelite poets (d) None

416. Auden found the solution of all social and political ills in
(a) left ideologies (b) humanism
(c) religion (d) pantheism

417. Auden was influenced by
(a) Plato (b) Dante
(c) Socrates (d) Marx and Freud

418. The second phase of Auden's poetry began in 1939 when he emigrated to
(a) Russia (b) U.S.A. (c) London (d) Italy

419. Auden's faith in communism was shaken by
(a) German-Soviet pact (b) Euro-Soviet pact
(c) Anglo-Soviet pact (d) Asia-Europe pact

420. Who called Auden, the most accomplished technician now writing poetry in English?
(a) Louis MacNeice (b) Stephen Spender
(c) T.S. Eliot (d) W.B. Yeats

421. Auden learnt the symbolic method and the use of modern imagery from
(a) W.B. Yeats (b) T.S. Eliot
(c) Stephen Spender (d) Louis MacNeice

422. Auden's use of assonance and internal rhyme is an attribute of
   (a) Hopkins (b) Yeats (c) Eliot (d) Auden
423. A collected edition of Auden's shorter poems appeared in
   (a) 1940 (b) 1945 (c) 1950 (d) 1955
424. W.H. Auden's major critical work is
   (a) *Enchanted Wood* (b) *Prater Violet*
   (c) *Mr. Norris Changes Trains* (d) None

**3. W.B. Yeats**

425. The world of W.B. Yeats is that of
   (a) magic (b) rebellion (c) terror (d) horror
426. Which work of Yeats was written to honour his beloved Maud Gonne?
   (a) *Cathleen in Houlihan* (b) *Deirdre*
   (c) *The Countless Cathleen* (d) *The Green Helmet*
427. The story of which work of Yeats occupies in Irish literature much the same place as that of King Arthur in English?
   (a) *Deirdre* (b) *Cathleen in Houlihan*
   (c) *The Hourglass* (d) *The Green Helmet*
428. In which play of Yeats, a wise-man keeps school and teaches there is no God, no Soul, no Heaven, no Hell?
   (a) *The Green Helmet* (b) *The Hourglass Moon*
   (c) *Deirdre* (d) *A Full Moon in March*
429. W.B. Yeats was awarded Nobel Prize for literature in
   (a) 1903 (b) 1910 (c) 1917 (d) 1923
430. One of the best known of Yeats' early lyrics is
   (a) "Wandering of Oisin" (b) "Poems"
   (c) "The Lake Isle of Innisfree" (d) "The Shadowy Water"
431. Yeats' *The Green Helmet and Other Poems* and *Responsibilities* are
   (a) romantic (b) classical (c) realistic (d) tragic

432. In *The Tower* and *The Winding Stair and Other Poems*, Yeats wrote on
(a) lofty themes (b) philosophical themes
(c) love themes (d) religious themes

433. In old age Yeats came in contact with a great Indian
(a) magician (b) painter
(c) philosopher (d) mystic

434. Who remarked about W.B. Yeats?
'He absorbed all his age had to offer him.'
(a) I.A. Richards (b) David Daiches
(c) F.R. Leavis (d) T.S. Eliot

**4. Stephen Spender**

435. Stephen Spender was born in
(a) 1900 (b) 1904 (c) 1905 (d) 1909

436. Stephen Spender was one of the distinguished poets of
(a) America (b) Britain (c) Italy (d) Paris

437. In the beginning of his political career Spender was attracted by
(a) left wing politics (b) socialistic writings
(c) romanticism (d) religion

438. Who said,
'Auden was the attacker of humanity, Spender its defender.'?
(a) Scott James (b) William James
(c) David Daiches (d) I.A. Richards

439. Spender's *Poems of Dedication* was published in the year
(a) 1926 (b) 1930 (c) 1936 (d) 1946

440. Spender's mother was a/an
(a) French (b) Russian (c) German (d) American

441. Which of Spender's work is his autobiography?
(a) *Trial of a Judge* (b) *The Still Centre*
(c) *World within World* (d) *Ruins and Visions*

442. Spender's *Trial of a Judge* appeared in
(a) 1908 (b) 1910 (c) 1920 (d) 1938

443. *The Still Centre* of Stephen Spender appeared in
(a) 1929 (b) 1919 (c) 1938 (d) 1939

**5. Cecil Day Lewis**

444. C. Day Lewis was born in the year
(a) 1890 (b) 1891 (c) 1895 (d) 1904

445. C. Day Lewis translated the works of
(a) Homer (b) Plato (c) Aristotle (d) Virgil

446. The autobiography of C. Day Lewis appears in
(a) *The Poetic Image* (b) *The Buried Day*
(c) *Starting Point* (d) *Word Over*

447. The later poetry of C. Day Lewis shows the influence of
(a) Eliot (b) Yeats (c) Auden (d) Hardy

448. Cecil Day Lewis appeared as a brilliant critic in
(a) *A Hope for Poetry* (b) *The Buried Day*
(c) *A Time For Dance* (d) *Pegasus*

449. "The Magnetic Mountain" of Cecil Day Lewis appeared in
(a) 1905 (b) 1915 (c) 1925 (d) 1935

450. "An Italian Visit" of C. Day Lewis appeared in
(a) 1923 (b) 1930 (c) 1940 (d) 1953

451. Who said, 'Modern poetry is every poem whether written last year or five centuries ago, that has meaning for us still.'?
(a) W.B. Yeats (b) W.H. Auden
(c) T.S. Eliot (d) C. Day Lewis

452. Cecil Day Lewis was a Professor of poetry at Oxford during
(a) 1940-45 (b) 1945-50 (c) 1935-40 (d) 1951-56

453. Cecil Day Lewis is at present Professor of poetry at
(a) Oxford University (b) Cambridge University
(c) Harvard University (d) University of Hull

454. Cecil Day Lewis was declared Poet Laureate in
(a) 1960 (b) 1965 (c) 1967 (d) 1970

455. C. Day Lewis' *Transitional Poems* was published in
(a) 1909 (b) 1991 (c) 1929 (d) 1939

### 6. Louis MacNeice

456. Louis MacNeice was born in
(a) 1904 (b) 1905 (c) 1906 (d) 1907

457. Louis MacNeice was the son of
(a) an Irish Bishop (b) a Russian soldier
(c) an American merchant (d) an English merchant

458. MacNeice has been a writer and producer of radio plays for BBC for
(a) five years (b) two years
(c) one year (d) two decades

459. MacNeice's *The Earth Compels* appeared in
(a) 1908 (b) 1917 (c) 1921 (d) 1938

460. *Autumn Journal* of Louis MacNeice was published in
(a) 1909 (b) 1919 (c) 1918 (d) 1939

461. Which year saw the publication of Louis MacNeice's *Spring Board*?
(a) 1914 (b) 1924 (c) 1932 (d) 1944

462. When did Louis MacNeice get his *The Dark Tower* published?
(a) 1926 (b) 1946 (c) 1955 (d) 1960

### 7. Dylan Thomas

463. Dylan Thomas was born in
(a) 1904 (b) 1910 (c) 1914 (d) 1920

464. Dylan Thomas is the pioneer of neo-romantic poetry in the
(a) twenties (b) thirties (c) forties (d) fifties

465. Dylan Thomas' early poetry is deeply
(a) romantic (b) passionate
(c) satirical (d) rhetorical

466. "Thomas' verse has an exuberant poetic fervour and an abundant responsiveness to natural beauty."
Who said this?
(a) A.C. Ward (b) David Daiches
(c) T.S. Eliot (d) None of the above

467. Which of the following is not Dylan Thomas' work?
(a) *Fifteen Poems* (b) *Twenty five Poems*
(c) *Pegasus* (d) *Deaths and Entrances*

468. Dylan Thomas' mature work is more
(a) romantic (b) satirical
(c) rhetoric (d) controlled

**8. Robert Bridges**

469. Robert Bridges was born in
(a) 1814 (b) 1818 (c) 1820 (d) 1844

470. Robert Bridges was appointed Poet Laureate in
(a) 1900 (b) 1910 (c) 1913 (d) 1930

471. In 1873 appeared Robert Bridges'
(a) *Shorter Poems* (b) *Eros and Poyche*
(c) *Prometheus, The Fire giver* (d) *The Poetical Works of Robert Bridges*

472. Robert Bridges' masterpiece which appeared in 1929 is
(a) *The Testament of Beauty* (b) *Shorter Poems*
(c) *The Poetical Works of Robert Bridges* (d) *The Growth of Love*

473. Robert Bridges' poetry was influenced by his love for
(a) romanticism (b) classicism
(c) realism (d) none

474. As a poet of nature, he describes the landscape of the
(a) South America (b) South Country
(c) Australia (d) New Zealand

475. 'Thy work with beauty crown, thy life with love,
Thy mind with truth uplift to God above.'
Where does Bridges write these lines?
(a) *The Testament of Beauty* (b) *Shorter Poems*
(c) *The Growth of Love* (d) *Gird on thy Sword*

476. Who said,
'What led me to poetry was the inexhaustible satisfaction of form.'?
(a) W.B. Yeats (b) W.H. Auden
(c) Robert Bridges (d) Dylan Thomas

477. Robert Bridges' outstanding contribution to poetry lies in
(a) sensuous images (b) metaphors
(c) rhyme scheme (d) metrical innovations

478. Robert Bridges died in the year
(a) 1920 (b) 1925 (c) 1915 (d) 1930

## 9. Gerald Manley Hopkins

479. The first full edition of G.M. Hopkins' poems in 1918 was edited by
(a) Coventry Patmore (b) Robert Bridges
(c) Alexander Baillie (d) William Addis

480. Wordsworth's "Ode on Intimations of Immortality" gave G.M. Hopkins
(a) inspiration (b) joy
(c) shock (d) grief

481. G.M. Hopkins was born in
(a) 1844 (b) 1860 (c) 1861 (d) 1865

482. Hopkins' sister Katie had a marked grit for
(a) music (b) poetry (c) drawing (d) none

483. Hopkins won an Exhibition to Balliol College, Oxford in
(a) 1850 (b) 1860 (c) 1862 (d) 1863

484. Which Hopkins' poem won him a school prize?
(a) "The Escorial" (b) "A Vision of the Mermaids"
(c) "Winter with the Gulf Stream" (d) "Windhover"

485. Hopkins was nicknamed
(a) Skin (b) Tommy (c) Willy (d) Harry

486. To whom did Hopkins write,
'You know I once wanted to be a painter'?
(a) Robert Bridges (b) Alexander Baillie
(c) Edward Bond (d) Coventry Patmore

487. Translation of which philosopher's work made Hopkins famous?
(a) Aristotle (b) Dante (c) Plato (d) none

488. In 1854, Hopkins lost the election to the Mastership of Balliol largely because of his
(a) arrogance (b) ignorance
(c) authoritarianism (d) unorthodox religious views

489. The basic poetic form which Hopkins used most was
(a) Petrarchan sonnet (b) Free verse
(c) Italian sonnet (d) none

490. Hopkins' strong love of the Virgin Mary owed a lot to
(a) Plato (b) Arnold
(c) Aristotle (d) Duns Scotus

491. G.M. Hopkins died in
(a) 1850 (b) 1859 (c) 1875 (d) 1889

492. Who remembered Hopkins as a querulous sensitive scholar?
(a) W.B.Yeats (b) W.H. Auden
(c) T.S. Eliot (d) Matthew Arnold

493. Who called Hopkins a 'small and childish looking, yet like a child sage, nervous, too and very sensitive, with a small ivory pale face'?
(a) Katherine Tynan (b) Coventary Patmore
(c) Alexander Wood (d) George Giberne

494. Hopkins' last words were 'I am so happy, I am so happy'. Who said this?
(a) Robert Bridges (b) Fr. G.F. Lahey
(c) W.B. Yeats (d) Katherine Tynan

495. Hopkins first used the terms 'inscape' and 'instress' in notes on
(a) Parmenides (b) Plato
(c) Dante (d) Aristotle

496. Keat's sensuousness, especially his fascination with colour is reflected in Hopkins'
(a) "A Vision of the Mermaids" (b) "The Wreck of the Deutschland"
(c) "The Habit of Perfection" (d) "The Windhover"

497. 'Swinburne is a strange phenomenon.' Hopkins wrote to
(a) Bridges (b) Dixon
(c) D.G. Rossetti (d) Patmore

498. Hopkins employed sprung rhythm because
(a) it is melodious (b) it is easier
(c) it is nearest to the rhythm of prose (d) it is more flexible

499. Hopkins' experiments in either language or rhythm was not tolerated by
(a) Victorian critics (b) modern critics
(c) philosophers (d) contemporary poets

500. Hopkins' 'rhythm without count of syllable' in "The Vision of Holy Church" is attributed to
(a) *Piers Plowman* (b) *Nun's Priest's Tale*
(c) *Morte de Arthur* (d) None

501. "The Wreck of the Deutschland" was written by Hopkins during his stay at
(a) St. Wimfred (b) Dixon's
(c) William Barnes' (d) St. Beuno's

502. One of Hopkins' close contemporaries wrote his memoir of Hopkins which although praising 'exquisite beauties' antagonised Hopkins' lovers. Who was he?
(a) R.W. Dixon (b) Robert Bridges
(c) Coventry Patmore (d) Henry Purcell

503. 'To me his poetry has the effect of pure gold embedded in masses of unpracticable quartz'. Who said this about Hopkins?
(a) Edmund Gosse (b) Coventry Patmore
(c) Henry Purcell (d) Edward Bond

504. In Hopkins' "The Wreck of the Deutschland", the wreck described is both occasion and symbol. Who said this?
(a) T.S. Eliot (b) W.B. Yeats
(c) F.R. Leavis (d) W.H. Auden

505. 'The paradox of suffering' is the ultimate subject in
(a) "The Starlight Night" (b) "The Wreck of the Deuschland"
(c) "Henry Purcell" (d) "The Windhover"

506. Out of the ten sonnets Hopkins wrote, the second is
(a) "The Starlight Night" (b) "Carrion Comfort"
(c) "As Kingfishers Catch Fire" (d) "The Windhover"

507. Hopkins' all sonnets celebrate Christ as
(a) the all forgiving God (b) the creator of Nature
(c) the omnipotent entity (d) an epitome of sacrifice

508. Hopkins' use of a 'sprung line' for the opening of "The Starlight Night" communicates
(a) love for stars (b) love for nature
(c) excitement (d) admiration for God's grandeur

509. Hopkins dated his corrected version of "The Windhover" as
(a) 20th May 1867 (b) 30th May 1877
(c) 31st Aug 1880 (d) 29th Sept 1890

510. The subject of both "The Starlight Night and Hurrahing in Harvest" is
(a) love (b) nature (c) Christ (d) agony

511. William Empson and I.A. Richards have explained "The Windhover" as Hopkins' envy for
(a) mortal beauty (b) divine beauty
(c) natural beauty (d) pristine beauty

512. Which is the longest of Hopkins' self-torturing sonnets?
(a) "Inversmaid" (b) "The Starlight Night"
(c) "Felix Randal" (d) "Spelt from Sybil's Leaves"

513. Hopkins' "Spelt from Sybil's Leaves" can be read as a warning of
(a) last judgement (b) earthquakes
(c) whirlwind (d) revolution

514. Hopkins' "Carrion Comfort" is one of the six sonnets of desolation, the so-called
(a) love sonnets (b) nature sonnets
(c) terrible sonnets (d) mystic sonnets

515. As fellow of the Royal University and Professor of Greek University College, Hopkins spent ... in Dublin.
(a) 5 years (b) 8 years (c) 9 years (d) 11 years

516. Twenty-four sonnets published in 1876 are called
(a) "The Growth of Love" (b) "The Spirit of Man"
(c) "The Terrible Sonnets" (d) "Love Sonnets"

517. Hopkins was made Poet Laureate in
(a) 1915 (b) 1913 (c) 1920 (d) 1929

518. Ernest Hartley Coleridge was
(a) son of S.T. Coleridge (b) brother of S.T. Coleridge
(c) grandson of S.T. Coleridge (d) nephew of S.T. Coleridge

519. Hopkins' first use of oblique stroke '/' is in
(a) "Parmenides" (b) "Resurrection"
(c) "Carrion Comfort" (d) "The Starlight Night"

520. P.G. Patmore, the editor of New Monthly Magazine was Coventry Patmore's
(a) father (b) son
(c) grandfather (d) uncle

## ANSWERS

### Unit A

| | | | |
|---|---|---|---|
| 1. (d) | 2. (b) | 3. (a) | 4. (b) |
| 5. (a) | 6. (a) | 7. (d) | 8. (d) |
| 9. (d) | 10. (c) | | |

## Unit B

| | | | | | | | |
|---|---|---|---|---|---|---|---|
| 11. | (c) | 12. | (d) | 13. | (d) | 14. | (c) |
| 15. | (d) | 16. | (d) | 17. | (b) | 18. | (b) |
| 19. | (b) | 20. | (a) | 21. | (b) | 22. | (a) |
| 23. | (b) | 24. | (a) | 25. | (c) | 26. | (d) |
| 27. | (b) | 28. | (b) | 29. | (d) | 30. | (c) |
| 31. | (c) | 32. | (a) | 33. | (b) | 34. | (a) |
| 35. | (d) | 36. | (b) | 37. | (d) | 38. | (d) |
| 39. | (b) | 40. | (b) | 41. | (a) | 42. | (c) |
| 43. | (c) | 44. | (b) | 45. | (b) | 46. | (c) |
| 47. | (a) | 48. | (c) | 49. | (b) | 50. | (d) |
| 51. | (c) | 52. | (b) | 53. | (b) | 54. | (b) |
| 55. | (c) | 56. | (c) | 57. | (c) | 58. | (c) |
| 59. | (d) | 60. | (c) | 61. | (a) | 62. | (d) |
| 63. | (d) | 64. | (d) | 65. | (d) | 66. | (d) |
| 67. | (c) | 68. | (a) | 69. | (b) | 70. | (a) |
| 71. | (b) | 72. | (a) | 73. | (d) | 74. | (b) |
| 75. | (a) | 76. | (c) | 77. | (b) | 78. | (a) |
| 79. | (b) | 80. | (b) | 81. | (c) | 82. | (b) |
| 83. | (a) | 84. | (a) | 85. | (d) | 86. | (d) |
| 87. | (d) | 88. | (d) | 89. | (b) | 90. | (b) |
| 91. | (a) | 92. | (c) | 93. | (c) | 94. | (b) |
| 95. | (c) | 96. | (c) | 97. | (c) | 98. | (a) |
| 99. | (c) | 100. | (b) | 101. | (b) | 102. | (a) |
| 103. | (a) | 104. | (c) | 105. | (b) | 106. | (a) |
| 107. | (a) | 108. | (d) | 109. | (c) | 110. | (b) |
| 111. | (d) | 112. | (c) | 113. | (c) | 114. | (c) |
| 115. | (a) | 116. | (a) | 117. | (d) | 118. | (a) |
| 119. | (a) | 120. | (b) | 121. | (a) | 122. | (b) |
| 123. | (b) | 124. | (a) | 125. | (b) | 126. | (a) |
| 127. | (a) | 128. | (a) | 129. | (b) | 130. | (b) |

| | | | | | | | |
|---|---|---|---|---|---|---|---|
| 131. | (a) | 132. | (c) | 133. | (b) | 134. | (d) |
| 135. | (a) | 136. | (a) | 137. | (c) | 138. | (a) |
| 139. | (c) | 140. | (a) | 141. | (b) | 142. | (b) |
| 143. | (d) | 144. | (b) | 145. | (b) | 146. | (d) |
| 147. | (d) | 148. | (d) | 149. | (d) | 150. | (b) |
| 151. | (a) | 152. | (b) | 153. | (c) | 154. | (c) |
| 155. | (b) | 156. | (c) | 157. | (a) | 158. | (c) |
| 159. | (c) | 160. | (c) | 161. | (a) | 162. | (a) |
| 163. | (d) | 164. | (d) | 165. | (a) | 166. | (d) |
| 167. | (a) | 168. | (d) | 169. | (a) | 170. | (c) |
| 171. | (c) | 172. | (a) | 173. | (c) | 174. | (a) |
| 175. | (c) | 176. | (c) | 177. | (a) | 178. | (d) |
| 179. | (b) | 180. | (a) | 181. | (b) | 182. | (a) |
| 183. | (b) | 184. | (c) | 185. | (a) | 186. | (b) |
| 187. | (c) | 188. | (d) | 189. | (c) | 190. | (d) |
| 191. | (c) | 192. | (b) | 193. | (a) | 194. | (a) |
| 195. | (b) | 196. | (a) | 197. | (a) | 198. | (d) |
| 199. | (a) | 200. | (b) | 201. | (a) | 202. | (b) |
| 203. | (a) | 204. | (a) | 205. | (a) | 206. | (a) |
| 207. | (b) | 208. | (a) | 209. | (a) | 210. | (a) |
| 211. | (c) | 212. | (c) | 213. | (b) | 214. | (b) |
| 215. | (a) | 216. | (c) | 217. | (c) | 218. | (d) |
| 219. | (c) | 220. | (a) | 221. | (a) | 222. | (d) |
| 223. | (d) | 224. | (d) | 225. | (c) | 226. | (a) |
| 227. | (d) | 228. | (b) | 229. | (a) | 230. | (b) |
| 231. | (a) | 232. | (c) | 233. | (c) | 234. | (c) |
| 235. | (a) | 236. | (a) | 237. | (a) | 238. | (b) |
| 239. | (c) | 240. | (b) | 241. | (b) | 242. | (b) |
| 243. | (b) | 244. | (c) | 245. | (b) | 246. | (c) |
| 247. | (c) | 248. | (d) | 249. | (d) | 250. | (c) |
| 251. | (c) | 252. | (c) | 253. | (d) | 254. | (d) |

| | | | | | | | |
|---|---|---|---|---|---|---|---|
| 255. | (d) | 256. | (c) | 257. | (b) | 258. | (c) |
| 259. | (c) | 260. | (a) | 261. | (a) | 262. | (b) |
| 263. | (b) | 264. | (d) | 265. | (a) | 266. | (c) |
| 267. | (c) | 268. | (c) | 269. | (c) | 270. | (c) |
| 271. | (a) | 272. | (c) | 273. | (b) | 274. | (b) |
| 275. | (b) | 276. | (d) | 277. | (b) | 278. | (c) |
| 279. | (a) | 280. | (b) | 281. | (c) | 282. | (d) |
| 283. | (d) | 284. | (d) | 285. | (d) | 286. | (d) |
| 287. | (b) | 288. | (d) | 289. | (d) | 290. | (a) |
| 291. | (c) | 292. | (a) | 293. | (b) | 294. | (b) |
| 295. | (c) | 296. | (b) | 297. | (d) | 298. | (b) |
| 299. | (b) | | | | | | |

## Unit C

| | | | | | | | |
|---|---|---|---|---|---|---|---|
| 300. | (d) | 301. | (d) | 302. | (a) | 303. | (d) |
| 304. | (d) | 305. | (d) | 306. | (d) | 307. | (b) |
| 308. | (d) | 309. | (a) | 310. | (d) | 311. | (d) |
| 312. | (a) | 313. | (b) | 314. | (b) | 315. | (d) |
| 316. | (d) | 317. | (d) | 318. | (b) | 319. | (c) |
| 320. | (c) | 321. | (d) | 322. | (d) | 323. | (b) |
| 324. | (a) | 325. | (d) | 326. | (b) | 327. | (d) |
| 328. | (d) | 329. | (a) | 330. | (b) | 331. | (d) |
| 332. | (a) | 333. | (d) | 334. | (c) | 335. | (a) |
| 336. | (a) | 337. | (c) | 338. | (c) | 339. | (d) |
| 340. | (c) | 341. | (a) | 342. | (a) | 343. | (c) |
| 344. | (d) | 345. | (d) | 346. | (c) | 347. | (a) |
| 348. | (d) | 349. | (a) | 350. | (a) | 351. | (d) |
| 352. | (b) | 353. | (d) | 354. | (d) | 355. | (d) |
| 356. | (d) | 357. | (d) | 358. | (c) | 359. | (d) |
| 360. | (d) | 361. | (d) | 362. | (a) | 363. | (c) |
| 364. | (d) | 365. | (d) | 366. | (d) | 367. | (b) |
| 368. | (c) | 369. | (d) | 370. | (d) | 371. | (d) |

| | | | | | | | |
|---|---|---|---|---|---|---|---|
| 372. | (c) | 373. | (d) | 374. | (d) | 375. | (a) |
| 376. | (d) | 377. | (d) | 378. | (d) | 379. | (d) |
| 380. | (d) | 381. | (d) | 382. | (a) | 383. | (b) |
| 384. | (a) | 385. | (d) | 386. | (d) | 387. | (d) |
| 388. | (a) | 389. | (a) | 390. | (d) | 391. | (a) |
| 392. | (a) | 393. | (c) | 394. | (a) | 395. | (d) |
| 396. | (a) | 397. | (d) | 398. | (b) | 399. | (d) |
| 400. | (d) | 401. | (a) | | | | |

**Unit D**

| | | | | | | | |
|---|---|---|---|---|---|---|---|
| 402. | (d) | 403. | (d) | 404. | (d) | 405. | (d) |
| 406. | (d) | 407. | (d) | 408. | (d) | 409. | (a) |
| 410. | (b) | 411. | (d) | 412. | (a) | 413. | (d) |
| 414. | (a) | 415. | (a) | 416. | (a) | 417. | (d) |
| 418. | (b) | 419. | (a) | 420. | (b) | 421. | (b) |
| 422. | (a) | 423. | (c) | 424. | (a) | 425. | (a) |
| 426. | (c) | 427. | (a) | 428. | (b) | 429. | (d) |
| 430. | (c) | 431. | (c) | 432. | (b) | 433. | (d) |
| 434. | (b) | 435. | (d) | 436. | (b) | 437. | (a) |
| 438. | (a) | 439. | (d) | 440. | (c) | 441. | (c) |
| 442. | (d) | 443. | (d) | 444. | (d) | 445. | (d) |
| 446. | (b) | 447. | (d) | 448. | (a) | 449. | (d) |
| 450. | (d) | 451. | (d) | 452. | (d) | 453. | (d) |
| 454. | (c) | 455. | (c) | 456. | (d) | 457. | (a) |
| 458. | (d) | 459. | (d) | 460. | (d) | 461. | (d) |
| 462. | (b) | 463. | (c) | 464. | (c) | 465. | (b) |
| 466. | (a) | 467. | (c) | 468. | (d) | 469. | (d) |
| 470. | (c) | 471. | (a) | 472. | (a) | 473. | (b) |
| 474. | (b) | 475. | (d) | 476. | (c) | 477. | (d) |
| 478. | (d) | 479. | (b) | 480. | (c) | 481. | (a) |
| 482. | (c) | 483. | (d) | 484. | (a) | 485. | (a) |
| 486. | (b) | 487. | (c) | 488. | (d) | 489. | (a) |

| | | | | | | | |
|---|---|---|---|---|---|---|---|
| 490. | (d) | 491. | (d) | 492. | (a) | 493. | (a) |
| 494. | (b) | 495. | (a) | 496. | (a) | 497. | (b) |
| 498. | (c) | 499. | (a) | 500. | (a) | 501. | (d) |
| 502. | (b) | 503. | (b) | 504. | (c) | 505. | (b) |
| 506. | (a) | 507. | (b) | 508. | (c) | 509. | (b) |
| 510. | (c) | 511. | (a) | 512. | (d) | 513. | (a) |
| 514. | (c) | 515. | (a) | 516. | (a) | 517. | (b) |
| 518. | (c) | 519. | (a) | 520. | (a) | | |

# American Literature

# 11

## UNIT A: HISTORICAL PERSPECTIVE AND BACKGROUND

1. In which year did Christopher Columbus land on the American mainland?
   (a) 1492 (b) 1493 (c) 1496 (d) 1499
2. Christopher Columbus was
   (a) a Spanish explorer
   (b) an Italian explorer
   (c) a Genoa-born Spanish explorer supported by King Ferdinand and Queen Isabel of Spain
   (d) a Spanish adventure in which Columbus joined
3. He landed on American mainland in 1496, it was his
   (a) first attempt (b) third attempt
   (c) second attempt (d) fourth attempt
4. What is American dream?
   (a) it was woven around the idea of a lost paradise, of a golden age characterized by abundance, absence of war and absence of toil
   (b) it was the Christian myth which was adopted by the western
   (c) lost garden of Eden
   (d) the land promised to Moses, where milk and honey was abundantly available
5. The American dream existed before or after discovery of America
   (a) as a state of mind and a dream, America existed long before its discovery
   (b) the dream existed from the earliest times of Christian era

(c) the dream was America
(d) the discovery of America made fulfilment of the dream feasible and possible

6. The puritans migrated to America for
(a) establishing their own church, after being hounded out of England for their uncompromising non-conformity
(b) getting away from their home for religious freedom
(c) zealously religious nature at times became intolerable in their own homeland
(d) seeking salvation in God's own land

7. The puritans believed in
(a) man being bad needed total dedication to God
(b) inherent sinfulness of man
(c) their being elected people who will be redeemed
(d) simplicity of worship, scripture reading and prayer

8. Which statement describes the Puritans best?
(a) Protestants who believed in the teaching of John Calvin
(b) not satisfied with the establishment of Church of England (Anglicans)
(c) Christians who believed that they alone had found the truth as revealed in *The Bible*
(d) the chosen few who had been led to the promised land

9. What is ironical about the American Puritans?
(a) the Puritans became 'puritans'
(b) in the name of reason they rejected the notion of innate depravity of man
(c) during the 19th and 20th centuries they became less intolerant and developed an intense moral earnestness and a heightened sense of duty
(d) puritanism was dissipated

10. What is the contribution of these New Englanders?
(a) provided the American culture with endurance and moral backbone
(b) inhibited normal development
(c) gave Americans self discipline and a sense of duty
(d) made people industrious

11. Which part of America the Puritans made their home?
    (a) east coast
    (b) Massachusetts and Connecticut
    (c) New England
    (d) Virginia
12. How did the Puritans change the American way of life?
    (a) most of the Puritan leaders who came from England were educated men and they educated America in a way, establishing Harvard College in 1636
    (b) taught people to read and write
    (c) education was a key to salvation for each person was expected to read the *Bible*
    (d) established schools and college in every town
13. The Puritans influenced American intellectual and literary life through
    (a) Emerson, Thoreau, Hawthorne, Emily Dickinson and Robert Frost
    (b) institutions
    (c) life in general and their preaching
    (d) the concept of a promised land
14. There are seven great Americans who gave America its identity. They are:
    (i) George Washington, (ii) Abraham Lincoln,
    (iii) Mark Twain, (iv) Theodore Roosevelt, (v) Justice Oliver Wendell Holmes, (vi) Franklin D. Roosevelt, and (vii)
    (a) Christopher Columbus (b) James Monroe
    (c) Walt Whitman (d) Benjamin Franklin
15. Who spoke, "Give me liberty, or give me death!"?
    (a) Abraham Lincoln (b) Patrick Henry
    (c) George Washington (d) John F. Kennedy
16. Who spoke, "And fired the shot heard round the world."?
    (a) Ralph Waldo Emerson (b) Edwin Mackham
    (c) Benjamin Franklin (d) George Washington
17. Who said this: "The meaning of the word America flows

from one pure source within the soul of America is the freedom of mind and spirit in man."?
(a) Theodore Roosevelt (b) James Monroe
(c) Herbert Hoover (d) John Holmes

18. Who said this about America: "How little do my countrymen know what precious blessings they are in possession of, which no other people on earth enjoy."?
(a) Herbert Hoover (b) Thomas Jefferson
(c) Benjamin Franklin (d) James Monroe

19. Who said about American foreign policy: "Speak softly and carry a big stick."?
(a) Theodore Roosevelt (b) Jefferson
(c) George Washington (d) Benjamin Franklin

20. Who wrote an epitaph for Abraham Lincoln's sweetheart?
(a) Henry Wadsworth Longfellow (b) Robert Frost
(c) Walt Whitman (d) Edgar Lee Masters

21. Who wrote these lines of the declaration of Independence "... that all men are created equal that they are endowed by their Creator with certain unalienable rights, that among certain unalienable rights, that among those are life, liberty and the pursuit of happiness."?
(a) Thomas Paine (b) James Monroe
(c) Thomas Jefferson (d) Daniel Webster

22. Americans believe like Ralph Waldo Emerson. "Whosoever would be a man must be a non-conformist." Besides him who are the other 7 well-known dissenters? (i) John Quincy Adams, (ii) Horace Mann, (iii) William Lloyd Garrison, (iv) Oliver Wendell Holmes, (v) John Dewey, (vi) Robert Frost, and (vii)
(a) Henry David Thoreau (b) Walt Whitman
(c) Abraham Lincoln (d) A.N. Whitehead

23. Democracy in America was strengthened by
(a) free conscientious voice (b) voice of dissension

(c) development of individuality
(d) love for the country, people awareness of rights and duties

24. Enlightenment in America was concerned with
(a) the world and life after death
(b) this world and man's natural powers
(c) the supernatural
(d) religious awareness

25. In the 18th century America the most significant writing was concerned with
(a) American society
(b) government and politics
(c) theology
(d) religion and moral teaching

26. What were the ways of Paine, Adams and Jefferson used to shape democracy in America?
(a) battle for victory of people's will
(b) persuasion and debate
(c) advocating natural right of man to rule
(d) divine right of kings to govern with people's representatives

27. Which world events helped most the struggle for Independence in America?
(a) insensitivity of British towards the English migrants settled in America
(b) writers advocating the role of man to shape his own future
(c) emergence of rationalism
(d) French Revolution

28. Rationalism made people optimistic for
(a) God and nature are benevolent seeking harmony
(b) progress is through human effort
(c) happy society is possible and within reach of man
(d) progress is inevitable if pursued rationally

29. Who demanded complete political independence?
(a) Hamilton
(b) Thomas Paine
(c) Jefferson
(d) Adams

30. Who believed that government existed not to control but to serve people?
    (a) Thomas Paine (b) George Washington
    (c) Thomas Jefferson (d) Adams
31. Which aspect of American life was highlighted by Romanticism?
    (a) intellectual life (b) emotional aspirations
    (c) individualism (d) frustration
32. Emerson, Thoreau and Whitman represented which aspects of American Romanticism?
    (a) individualism and optimism, a bright picture
    (b) emotions rather than intellect
    (c) naturalness
    (d) spontaneity
33. Poe, Hawthorne and Melville represented which aspects of American Romanticism?
    (a) morbid emotional forces
    (b) basic contradiction between man's aspiration and actual conditions
    (c) no faith in the possibilities of social reforms and development
    (d) problems of isolation, liabilities of individualism, pessimistic. A dark picture
34. Washington Irving and James Fenimore Cooper were
    (a) among the first great American writers
    (b) champions of American institutions
    (c) federalists in conviction
    (d) 18th century writers infused with new 19th century Romanticism
35. What does "Flowering of New England" mean?
    (a) coming out of the period of stagnation
    (b) fertilization with European ideas the natural Puritan respect for a life of the mind flowered into American Renaissance
    (c) the new creative outburst resulted in writers of radical and conservative outlook
    (d) the eastern Massachusetts flowered into new possibilities

36. Transcendentalism developed in/by
    (a) Boston (b) New England radicals
    (c) Conservatives (d) The Brahmins
37. American transcendentalism stands for
    (a) romantic distrust of the intellect and exaltation of intuition
    (b) reality can be apprehended through spiritual insight
    (c) German philosophers and English interpretors
    (d) Metaphysical justification
38. Some of the important members of Transcendental group are
    (a) Hawthorne (b) Melville
    (c) Ralph Waldo Emerson and Henry David Thoreau (d) Walt Whitman
39. Emerson's major message was
    (a) self-reliance (b) social-reform
    (c) confidence (d) progress and virtue
40. Henry David Thoreau believed in
    (a) non-conformism (b) philosophic anarchism
    (c) self-denial (d) rugged and uncompromising New Englander
41. Thoreau lived the life of a hermit and wrote a classic named
    (a) *Concord* (b) *Walden*
    (c) *The Scarlet Letter* (d) *Autocrat of the Breakfast Table*
42. The conservative New Englanders generally belonged to
    (a) Harvard (b) Cleveland
    (c) Philadelphia (d) Virginia
43. The conservatives among the New Englanders disapproved of the transcendentalists and
    (a) trusted intellectualism (b) believed in a "genteel tradition"
    (c) were generally Unitarians mercantile oligarchy (d) adhered to traditional values of Boston

44. After the Civil war the ideas of conservatives changed into
    (a) democracy (b) genteel tradition
    (c) abolitionism (d) introspection
45. Some of the significant conservatives are
    (a) Emerson (b) Thoreau
    (c) Henry Wadsworth Longfellow and Nathaniel Hawthorne (d) Edgar Allan Poe
46. Some writers of the South, where literary renaissance reached late, are
    (a) Edgar Allan Poe (b) Emerson
    (c) Longfellow (d) Hawthorne
47. Some significant New Yorkers are
    (a) Fernimore Cooper (b) Herman Melville and Walt Whitman
    (c) Longfellow (d) Hawthorne
48. American literature after 1890 shows
    (a) the complexity and changes in the nature of American life
    (b) the world wars
    (c) economic depression leading to introspection
    (d) emergence of a wide reading public
49. The vast land and variety of cultural background gave birth to
    (a) literature of negroes (b) literature of New Englanders
    (c) regionalism (d) literature of West and Mid-West
50. What were the factors in the 20th century, which helped conformity in literature and life
    (a) trans-continental railroad, radio, television and newspapers
    (b) the idea of one nation
    (c) uniformity of purpose—to safeguard freedom
    (d) moral and religious values

51. During 1890–1965 period what other factors aided in a new American culture and life?
    (a) Education, schools and universities (b) Scientific advancements
    (c) Economic prosperity (d) Leisure
52. Naturalism brought to American literature
    (a) man in his natural habitat
    (b) scientific objectivity and man's natural passions and instincts
    (c) romantic nostalgia
    (d) modification of realism
53. The naturalistic writers were inclined towards
    (a) determinism in their viewing of man
    (b) the question of free-will
    (c) expository interpretation
    (d) dominant bias
54. American literature besides fiction achieved significance in
    (a) general prose writing
    (b) history, biography, criticism, social-political writings
    (c) journalism
    (d) argumentative writings, debate etc.
55. Oratory has always been a proud American tradition and a natural habit which has the most significant factor of
    (a) observing all the available means of persuasion (b) rhetoric
    (c) choice of words (d) tonal appeal
56. Oratory concerns chiefly
    (a) people
    (b) public life of society
    (c) the democratic institutions
    (d) something of a private life with public dimensions
57. Abraham Lincoln's Gettysburg address consists of
    (a) much brooding in solitude, laced with profound emotions
    (b) well-thought, balanced
    (c) powerful emotional associations
    (d) total dedication

58. Who were the first American orators?
    (a) preachers (b) priests
    (c) lay leaders (d) politicians
59. The early American orators were trained in
    (a) Aristotelian rhetorical devices
    (b) need of the hour
    (c) sprinkling of slangs and dialects
    (d) compulsion to reach the audience by any means
60. What is the other part of a great orator which makes him successful?
    (a) a willing, anxious informed and attentive listener
    (b) highly educated audience
    (c) situation can make even an indifferent audience a great listener
    (d) inherent capacity to listen attentively
61. "Literacy and learning were not widespread, but the capacity to listen to speakers and to criticize them know no bounds." These lines show
    (a) why America benefitted so much from oratory
    (b) ability to listen
    (c) ability to listen carefully and speak forcefully
    (d) how American society was committed to freedom of speech
62. Who have been called giants of American oratorical tradition?
    (a) Henry Clay, Daniel Webster, Abraham Lincoln
    (b) Stephon A. Douglas
    (c) Salmon P. Chase
    (d) Edward Everett
63. Which literary work helped Abraham Lincoln become American President?
    (a) *Aunt Phillis's Cabin* (b) *Moby Dick*
    (c) *Walden* (d) *Uncle Tom's Cabin*
64. Harriet Beecher Stowe influenced American life as
    (a) story writer (b) intellectual aristocracy
    (c) political realist (d) introspective nature

65. Which novel is known by the name of "propaganda novel"?
    (a) *Dred: A Tale of the Great Dismal Swamp*
    (b) *Uncle Tom's Cabin*
    (c) *Tom Sawyer*
    (d) *Aunt Phillis's Cabin*
66. Anti-slavery was manifested by
    (a) John G, Whittier (b) Abraham Lincoln
    (c) Harriet Beecher Stowe (d) T.W. Higginson
67. After 1870 millions of immigrants arrived each year and many issues became alive, the greatest was
    (a) housing problem (b) native culture and native tongue
    (c) job front (d) language of communications
68. Americans were influenced by native Indian traditions widely. Some of the most significant are
    (a) chant, incantation, the fairy tale and the myth (b) riddles and anecdotes
    (c) oral tradition (d) humour
69. What are the two traditions which have enriched American language and literature?
    (a) Indian folklore and Negro spirituals
    (b) Indian songs and Negro dreams
    (c) Sayings and tales
    (d) Religious traditions and magic
70. The American folklore consists of
    (a) British folklore
    (b) combination of British, French and Spanish
    (c) Indian and Negro folklores in combination with European traditions
    (d) Chinese and Asian
71. American humour can be best described as
    (a) borne out of incongruities-interaction of varied national traditions including native Indian and Negro traditions

(b) result of finding a common denominator in people of innumerable origins
(c) addition of imaginative sympathy to a sense of reality
(d) attempt to give voice to the new connections amidst people of varied origins

72. Later on American humour acquired
(a) sophistication, urbanity (b) a uniqueness of native origin
(c) dark humour (d) a new shape

73. Purchase of Louisiana opened the vast
(a) west and the frontier (b) the unknown land
(c) the area with vast possibilities (d) rough territory

74. The West as seen from the East was
(a) unknown territory (b) wild land to be tamed
(c) a challenge (d) a new experience

75. What were the most important factors which made re-discovery of America possible?
(a) emergence of an axis of development from Boston to New York to Chicago
(b) relationship between southern plantation class and Western Agrarian development was established
(c) Pacific Railways and National Banking Act
(d) technological improvements and Market Management system was used in farming and industries

76. When it is said that Second Discovery of America was made in 1870s, it means
(a) after First discovery by Columbus, in which land was found, in the second discovery after the Civil War and consolidation of the states, Americans found their identity as a nation
(b) second discovery was made by Americans themselves
(c) second discovery was possible when different people merged their own ethnic identity into a larger national one
(d) first land was found, then people of different origins found themselves

77. During and after this period (1870–1890) Americans faced the gigantic task of working for
    (a) articulation of human desires
    (b) national self-discovery and expression
    (c) national customs and culture
    (d) materialism and market economy
78. Who are called the pilgrims?
    (a) Americans of European origin visiting their country in Europe
    (b) Voyages for pleasure and to see things for themselves
    (c) The second generation went to see the land of their forefathers
    (d) Some returned to their land of origin to take part in freedom struggle
79. *A Tramp Abroad* (1880) was written by
    (a) H.W. Longfellow (b) W.D. Howells
    (c) Mark Twain (d) Emerson
80. Who wrote *Venetian Life* (1866) and *Italian Journeys* (1867)?
    (a) Mark Twain (b) Ralph Waldo Emerson
    (c) William Dean Howells (d) Nathaniel Hawthorne
81. Realism was handled deftly by American writers, they are William Dean Howells, Henrey James and
    (a) Melville (b) Hawthorne
    (c) Emerson (d) Mark Twain

## UNIT B: EARLY WRITERS (AFTER INDEPENDENCE)

### 1. Washington Irving

82. Washington Irving was born in
    (a) 1750 (b) 1783 (c) 1780 (d) 1805
83. The life-period of Irving was
    (a) 1783 – 1859 (b) 1750 – 1839
    (c) 1780 – 1865 (d) 1805 – 1875

84. Irving's writings show the qualities of
   (a) graceful and humorous writing
   (b) journalistic writing
   (c) sensational literature
   (d) stylistic carefulness in language
85. In subject and method Irving was
   (a) traditional and picturesque
   (b) ancient
   (c) pedantic
   (d) spirit of freedom
86. Who wrote *The Sketch Book?*
   (a) Peter Irving
   (b) John Irving
   (c) Pierre Irving
   (d) Washington Irving
87. Who wrote the unforgettable story, entitled *Rip Van Winkle*?
   (a) Peter Irving
   (b) James Fenimore Cooper
   (c) Ralph Waldo Emerson
   (d) Washington Irving
88. The story of *Rip Van Winkle* shows
   (a) the life in the early days before Independence
   (b) the life during the Civil War
   (c) the life after the Civil War
   (d) how life changed after the Civil War
89. How long did the dutchman, Rip Van Winkle sleep on hillside?
   (a) two nights
   (b) fortnight
   (c) one year
   (d) twenty years
90. When Rip Van Winkle returned to his village who recognized him?
   (a) his wife
   (b) his family members
   (c) his friends
   (d) his dog Wolf
91. What happened during the twenty years while Rip Van Winkle was in deep slumber? The most significant event was
   (a) all who knew him died
   (b) everything had changed, people had died and no one recognized him
   (c) his shrewish wife died
   (d) the daughter grew up and married and had children

92. What did he do when he found how things had changed during Revolution?
    (a) he went and lived with his married daughter and her family
    (b) lived in a cottage which he built
    (c) found new friends and lived with them
    (d) went back to the hillside where he had spent twenty years in deep sumber.

**2. James Fenimore Cooper**

93. Rip Van Winkle's funny situation made him
    (a) disgruntled (b) sad
    (c) generous and cheerful (d) calm and collected
94. James Fenimore Cooper's life span was
    (a) 1780 – 1830 (b) 1789 – 1851
    (c) 1775 – 1851 (d) 1789 – 1845
95. Cooper had rich experience of
    (a) farming (b) legal profession
    (c) politics (d) sea-faring
96. Who wrote *The Spy and The Pirate*?
    (a) James Fenimore Cooper (b) Washington Irving
    (c) Ralph Waldo Emerson (d) Herman Melville
97. *The Spy* is a/an
    (a) adventure novel (b) romance
    (c) detective novel (d) story
98. In *The Ways of the Hour* Cooper wrote about
    (a) social reform (b) social justice and its perversion
    (c) revolution (d) freedom from British rule
99. The first book of Leather-Stocking series was
    (a) *The Pathfinder* (b) *The Last of the Mohicans*
    (c) *The Deerslayer* (d) *Upside Down*
100. The most famous Leather-Stocking Tales was
    (a) *The Pathfinder* (b) *The Last of the Mohicans*
    (c) *The Deerslayer* (d) *Upside Down*

101. *The Last of the Mohicans* presents the fight of the early settlers with the
    (a) native Indians (b) other settlers
    (c) new settlers (d) French settlers

102. In *The Last of the Mohicans* the native Indian Magua are called
    (a) brave but unfriendly
    (b) brave and fighting for territory
    (c) treacherous for they refused to accept white people as the masters of the land
    (d) strong and strong willed, friendly with the French

103. *The Last of the Mohicans* presents a war between the native tribes such as
    (a) Magra (b) Uncas
    (c) Hurons (d) Magra and Uncas

**3. Edgar Allan Poe**

104. Edgar Allan Poe was born in
    (a) 1805 (b) 1809 (c) 1815 (d) 1812

105. Poe has written
    (a) poems and short stories (b) essays
    (c) plays (d) novels

106. Who called Poe "three-fifths genius and two-fifths sheer fudge"?
    (a) Emerson (b) Yeats (c) Lowell (d) Cooper

107. Poe had an impact on
    (a) Longfellow (b) Walt Whitman
    (c) Baudelaire, Mallarme and Rimbaud (d) Emily Dickinson

108. "The Purloined Letter" was written by
    (a) Poe (b) Cooper (c) Emerson (d) Hawthorne

109. In "The Purloined Letter" Dupin succeeds in returning
    (a) the stolen letter to the authorities (b) the stolen letter to its owner
    (c) the purloined letter is destroyed (d) the purloined letter is given to the Parisian police

110. "The Purloined Letter" reminds the reader of
   (a) mystery novel (b) horror novel
   (c) Sherlock Holmes (d) science fiction

111. One of Poe's well known stories is
   (a) "The Ravens" (b) "The Fall of the House of Usher"
   (c) "The Masque of Red Death" (d) "The Purloined Letter"

112. Besides the miracles of craftsmanship Poe's stories present
   (a) a sense of perfect beauty matched with pure and bizarre style (b) a sense of mystery
   (c) the unexpected (d) naturalness

113. Emerson called him
   (a) a jingle-man (b) a great lyrical poet
   (c) a great American poet (d) none of the above

114. Who called him a great lyric poet?
   (a) W.B.Yeats (b) Emerson
   (c) Longfellow (d) Whitman

115. *The Tales of Grotesque and Arabesque* contains
   (a) 20 tales (b) 40 tales
   (c) 25 tales written up to 1840 (d) 30 tales

116. Poe's *Tales* contains stories written between
   (a) 1830 – 1840 (b) 1835 – 1840
   (c) 1840 – 45 (d) 1835 – 1845

## UNIT C: NEW ENGLANDERS

### 1. Ralph Waldo Emerson

117. Who said; "Mysticism for mysticism's sake"?
   (a) Edgar Allan Poe (b) H. D. Thoreau
   (c) Nathaniel Hawthorne (d) Herman Melville

118. Which of Emerson's works has this entry; "Little things are often filled with great beauty"?
   (a) *Nature* (b) *American Scholar lecture*

(c) *Harvard Divinity School Address* (d) *Journal for March 1852*

119. For Emerson, nature was the great source of
(a) joy (b) pain
(c) inspiration (d) ecstasy

120. Emerson's central doctrine—that of 'submission to emotion' is inadmissible to
(a) I.A. Richards (b) F. R. Leavis
(c) Wilson Knight (d) Yvor Winters

121. The aspect of Emerson which endeared him to Thomas Carlyle was his
(a) philanthropy (b) love for nature
(c) kindness (d) honesty

122. According to John J. Chapman, Emerson represents a protest against the tyranny of
(a) feudalism (b) christianity
(c) monarchy (d) democracy

**2. Henry David Thoreau**

123. Like Emerson, H.D. Thoreau preached the gospel of
(a) joy (b) pantheism
(c) kindness (d) independence

124. Who spoke of Thoreau as picking up windfalls in Emerson's orchards?
(a) Nathaniel Hawthorne (b) J.R. Lowell
(c) Herman Melville (d) Thomas Carlyle

125. Who said of Thoreau's poems that 'the thyme and marjoram are yet not honey'?
(a) R.W. Emerson (b) Nathaniel Hawthorne
(c) H.D. Thoreau (d) Herman Melville

126. H.D. Thoreau's style is
(a) satirical (b) poetical
(c) conversational (d) rhetorical

127. Thoreau's poems are as—Emerson's
(a) poetical (b) satirical
(c) unsatisfactory (d) political

### 3. Nathaniel Hawthorne

128. Emblem, symbol, moral, analogy, type, image are the favourite words of
    (a) Emerson (b) Thoreau
    (c) Melville (d) Hawthorne

129. Hawthorne's observations are usually of man in
    (a) society (b) nature
    (c) variance with nature (d) woods

130. Nathaniel Hawthorne is a writer of
    (a) prose (b) fiction (c) plays (d) drama

131. Who, regarding Hawthorne, posed this question: 'Could he have been more self-assured'?
    (a) Jack London (b) Henry James
    (c) Stephen Foster (d) Mark Twain

132. Who called Nathaniel Hawthorne a 'harmless Hawthorne'?
    (a) R.W. Emerson (b) H.D. Thoreau
    (c) Herman Melville (d) Edgar Allan Poe

### 4. Herman Melville

133. Herman Melville wrote *Typee* and *Omoo* on the basis of his experiences of
    (a) sea (b) city life (c) forest life (d) family life

134. For whom was the sea a rich source of metaphor?
    (a) Herman Melville (b) Henry James
    (c) H.D. Thoreau (d) R.W. Emerson

135. On which work does Melville castigate white civilisation?
    (a) *Omoo* (b) *Typee*
    (c) *Mardi* (d) *Moby Dick*

136. In *Omoo*, Melville takes up the narrative where he left it in
    (a) *Omoo* (b) *Typee*
    (c) *Moby Dick* (d) *Mardi*

137. Melville's which book is interesting to be studied as a preliminary to his '*Moby Dick*'?
    (a) *Typee* (b) *Omoo*
    (c) *Mardi* (d) *White Jacket*

138. There are traces of Dickens in Herman Melville's
(a) *Moby Dick* (b) *Bertleby the scrivener*
(c) *Typee* (d) *Mardi*

139. In which work does Melville leave the sea and far off places to write in the third person?
(a) *Pierre* (b) *Moby Dick*
(c) *Mardi* (d) *Typee*

140. Which book of Melville reflects Shakespearean, soliloquies?
(a) *Omoo* (b) *Typee*
(c) *Moby Dick* (d) *Pierre*

## UNIT D: AMERICAN HUMOUR

### 1. Mark Twain

141. Samuel Clemens was Mark Twain's
(a) father (b) brother
(c) son (d) original name

142. In *Tom Sawyer, The Adventures of Hucklebery Finn* and *Life on the Mississippi,* Twain wrote about
(a) love (b) religion (c) town (d) nature

143. Mark Twain's early books as well as his lectures established, him as a popular
(a) poet (b) dramatist
(c) satirist (d) humorist

144. Which is Mark Twain's romantic novel with political satire?
(a) *A Tramp Abroad* (b) *The Gilded Age*
(c) *Roughing It* (d) *Life on the Mississippi*

145. When did the first section of *Life on the Mississippi* appear serially in a magazine?
(a) 1872 (b) 1883 (c) 1875 (d) 1885

146. Which of Mark Twain's works was written with fervour in defence of the woman wronged?
(a) *A Tramp Abroad* (b) *Roughing It*
(c) *The Innocents Abroad* (d) *Personal Recollection of Joan of Arc*

147. Which one of the given works is a bitter fable masked as a children's story?
(a) *Life on the Mississippi* (b) *The Prince and the Pauper*
(c) *What is Man?* (d) *The Mysterious Stranger*

## UNIT E: POST-INDEPENDENCE AMERICAN POETRY (19TH CENTURY)

### 1. Emily Dickinson

148. Emily Dickinson belonged to
(a) 1830 – 1886 (b) 1815 – 1850
(c) 1850 – 1906 (d) 1830 – 1896

149. Emily Dickinson had literary affinity with
(a) Emerson (b) Thoreau
(c) Melville (d) Whitman

150. In her poetry one finds turn of wit and elliptical metaphors as in
(a) Hopkins (b) the metaphysical poets
(c) Whitman (d) Longfellow

151. Who wrote? "I find ecstasy in living".
(a) Whitman (b) Longfellow
(c) Frost (d) Dickinson

152. Who wrote: "Because I could stop for death,/He kindly stopped for me;/The carriage held just ourselves/And immortality."
(a) Edward Arlingtin Robinson (b) Robert Frost
(c) Emily Dickinson (d) Vachel Lindsay

153. Her poetry represents
(a) political life at Washington (b) seminary at Amherst
(c) interior life (d) social life

154. Her poetry can be best described as
(a) confessional poetry (b) poetry of recluse
(c) celebration of democracy (d) American dream

155. Dickinson was a prolific writer and the number of her known poems are
(a) 1800 (b) 500 (c) 2000 (d) 1775

156. *The Letters of Emily Dickinson* introduces the reader to
(a) contemporary world
(b) the mind of the poet
(c) religious longings
(d) lamenting unreciprocated love

157. A study of Emily Dickinson's works is puzzling because of
(a) undue attention to biographical details
(b) her being a woman
(c) being a politician's daughter
(d) being a prolific poet

158. What is that in her which appeals most to modern readers?
(a) boldness
(b) imagism and half-rhymes
(c) not being a formula poet
(d) a sense of wording

159. Can she be described as?
(a) feminist
(b) a poet expressing her voice of the self honestly
(c) believer in fine trade
(d) familiar with the art of writing

160. Emily Dickinson is a poet of
(a) the 18th century
(b) the 19th century
(c) the 19th century with modern sensibility
(d) none of the above

**2. Edgar Allan Poe**

161. Edgar Allan Poe was born in
(a) New England
(b) Boston
(c) Washington
(d) Virginia

162. Poe's childhood was
(a) comfortable
(b) full of parental care
(c) insecue caused by father's desertion when he was only two years old
(d) full of negligence

163. Why did Poe attempt sucide in 1848?
   (a) for he had become an alcoholic
   (b) as his wife died at 24 of tuberculosis and he had not established himself at the age of 37
   (c) due to economic reasons
   (d) due to psychological depression
164. How did Poe die?
   (a) after marrying the second time he was driven to death
   (b) it was deep depression which pushed him to his death under mysterious circumstances just after 3 years of his wife's death
   (c) he lay in Richmond, unconscious and dying hit fatally
   (d) natural death at the age of 40
165. In "Sonnet – to Science" Poe comes closest to
   (a) science cannot understand the working of a poet's heart
   (b) poetry is based on scientific knowledge
   (c) Diana's mythology
   (d) summer dream juxtaposed by the reality of a tamarind tree
166. Who is Poe's Helen in "To Helen"?
   (a) Helen of Troy
   (b) any beautiful woman
   (c) a young lady of Richmond who had been kind to him
   (d) Psyche, the goddess of the soul
167. Poe's Helen has been idealized by
   (a) use of Greek and Roman myths of Psyche, Helen of Troy and the nymphs
   (b) his imagination transcending time
   (c) physical beauty and charms
   (d) captivating beauty
168. Who wrote, "There is a twofold Silence – sea and shore–/Body and soul. One dwells in lonely places,/ Newly with grass O'ergrown;/some solemn graces".
   (a) Emily Dickinson (b) Robert Frost
   (c) Ralph Waldo Emerson (d) Edgar Allan Poe

169. "The Raven" was written by
   (a) Robert Frost (b) Emily Dickinson
   (c) Edgar Allan Poe (d) Walt Whitman

170. "The Raven" brings out which quality of Poe which made him famous?
   (a) mystery (b) story depicting manifestation of evil
   (c) spirituality (d) tight structure

171. From which poem of Poe these lines have been taken?
   "Take thy beak from out my heart and take thy form from off my door!"
   Quoth the 'Raven Nevermore'."
   (a) "To One in Paradise" (b) "The Raven"
   (c) "To Helen" (d) "Israel"

### 3. Walt Whitman

172. Walt Whitman was born in
   (a) long Island in 1819 (b) west coast in 1819
   (c) Boston in 1829 (d) Washington in 1910

173. Walt Whitman believed in
   (a) beauty and power of nature (b) picture of leaves and grass
   (c) farm and animal life (d) none of the above

174. In which group of poems he writes of love in rebellion against conventional attitudes towards sex and in praise of physiological functions of human body?
   (a) "Calamus" in *Leaves of Grass* (b) "Children of Adam" in *Leaves of Grass*
   (c) "Passage to India" (d) "Democracy"

175. In "Calamus" Whitman writes about
   (a) love for nature (b) celebration of democracy
   (c) desire for asian spirituality (d) "manly love", dealt with sensuality

176. Walt Whitman had certain tendencies which can be best described as
   (a) masculine vigour (b) homosexuality
   (c) erotic (d) natural

177. Whitman's verse represents a turning point in American Poetry because of certain characteristics best reflected by
(a) American experience and American idiom
(b) new syntax
(c) colloquialism
(d) horrors of war

178. What were the revolutionary characteristics of Whitman's *Leaves of Grass?*
(a) both in form and context
(b) structure
(c) idiom
(d) ideas of liberty

179. What techniques are characteristic of Walt Whitman?
(a) sprawling lines and cataloguing technique
(b) straightforwardness
(c) ornamental and elaborate
(d) use of monosyllables

180. What are the different elements which make Whitman's poetry truly American poem?
(a) included the lovely, the profane, the obscene to assert the strength of vast country with its powerful races
(b) different states with their different background
(c) African and European races
(d) many languages and its influences

181. What part of American geography did Whitman include in his representative American poem?
(a) sea coasts
(b) lakes
(c) priaries
(d) great oceans, its mountains and its illimitable prairies

182. How did Whitmans's poetry achieve universal appeal?
(a) by talking of human aspirations
(b) expressing desire for universal brotherhood
(c) moving beyond the specific American subject to deal with universal themes of nature, fertility and mortality
(d) American talking to mankind

183. What are the two most important aspects of Whitman's characteristics of poetry?
(a) cataloguing technique and inclusion of lowly and profane

(b) sprawling lines and colloquialism
(c) powerful races and magnificent mountains
(d) the historic events and American dream

184. *Leaves of Grass* is Whitman's great poem best defined by
(a) truly American poem
(b) poetry of celebration of American achievements
(c) American puritanism
(d) American experiences of being a great cauldron of human civilization

185. These lines are part of which great American poem?
"I celebrate myself, and sing myself/And what I assume.You shall assume/For every atom belonging to me as good belongs to you".
(a) "One's Self I Sing" (b) "I hear America Singing"
(c) "A Passage to India" (d) "Song of Myself"

186. In which poem did Whitman write: "Do I contradict myself? Very well then I contradict myself, (I am large, I contain multitudes)".
(a) "Song of Myself" (b) "One's Self I sing"
(c) "I Sit and look Out" (d) "Poets to Come"

187. In which poem Whitman says?
"The spotted hawk swoops by and accuse me he complains of my gab and loitering/I am not a bit tamed, I too am untranslatable./I sound barbaric over the roofs of the world".
(a) "Passage to India" (b) "I hear America singing"
(c) "Native Momants" (d) "Song of Myself"

188. In "Passage to India" Walt Whitman records the achievements of man like
(a) telephone cable line across the Atlantic, rail line joining America coast to coast and opening of Suez Canal
(b) the great engineering feats of mankind
(c) making of new canals
(d) archaeological achievements

189. In which poem Whitman wrote: "Singing my days/ Singing the great achievements of the present/Singing the strong light works of engineers/Our modern wonders."
(a) "The Last Invocation" (b) "A Passage to India"
(c) "Song of Myself" (d) "Faces"

190. In which poem Whitman wrote:
"Passage to more than India! Are thy wings plumed indeed for such far flights?/ O soul, voyagest thou indeed on voyages like those? Deportest thou on waters such as those?/ Soundest below the Sanscrit and the Vedas?/Then have thy bent unleash'd."
(a) "Song of Myself" (b) "The Last Invocation"
(c) "Passage to India" (d) "Prayer of Columbus"

191. How best Whitman's "Passage to India" can be described?
(a) a transcendental poem, envisioning the spiritual unification and fulfilment of man
(b) a poem to celebrate achievement of mankind
(c) scientific-sociological record of America
(d) glorification of American life

192. How did Forster pay his tribute to this spiritual endeavour of Whitman?
(a) by using the title "Passage to India" for his novel about India under the British exploring the possibilities of meeting of hearts between East and West
(b) by taking a journey to India
(c) writing on East-West relationship
(d) considering spiritual unification between East and West

193. Does Whitman believe in a unification between East and West?
(a) he explores the possibility
(b) he believed Americans could certainly transcend their materialism with the Indian spiritualism
(c) he did believe in such a unification
(d) West was doomed if not rescued by the East

194. In "Passage to India" Whitman wrote: "The races, neighbours, to marry, and be given in marriage/The oceans to be cross'd, the distant brought near,/The lands to be welded together". What was his real intention?
   (a) marriage of continents, races and oceans
   (b) he is prophetic in these and presents a blue print for globalization, unification of mankind
   (c) East-West encounter and sealing of the contract
   (d) unification

195. Who wrote? "I am of old and young, of the foolish as much as the wise,/Regardless of others, ever regardful of others,/Maternal as well as paternal, a child as well as a man"
   (a) Walt Whitman (b) Robert Frost
   (c) Emily Dickinson (d) Carl Sandburg

196. Who wrote? "I am the poet of the Body and I am the poet of the Soul/The pleasures of heaven are with me and the pain of hell are with me."
   (a) Wallace Stevens (b) William Carlos William
   (c) Walt Whitman (d) Edgar Lee Masters

197. Who wrote? "I am the poet of the woman the same as the man,/And I say it is as great to be a woman as to be a man/And I say there is nothing greater than the mother of men"
   (a) Ezra Pound (b) Walt Whitman
   (c) Emily Dickinson (d) E.E. Cummings

198. When did Whitman write the poem, entitled "O Captain! My Captain"?
   (a) dedicated to the memory of a captain of ship
   (b) written on the death (1865) of the 16th President of America, Abraham Lincoln
   (c) on the death of Abraham Lincoln for he believed in human equality and was against slavery
   (d) none of the above

199. Which is the poem read widely but made the poet regretful?
   (a) "Song for Myself" (b) "O Captain! My Captain"
   (c) "A Woman Waits for me" (d) "Birds of Passage"

200. Why did Whitman regret having written the poem?
    (a) the poet disliked the regularity of stanza form, metre and rhyme
    (b) very moving
    (c) untruthful
    (d) politically incorrect
201. In which poem he wrote about American historical experience of victory over feudalism and monarchy?
    (a) "Turn Liberated"
    (b) "Adieu to a Soldier"
    (c) "Spirit Whose Work Is Done"
    (d) "Long, Too Long America"
202. How American Civil War brought epochal change in history of mankind?
    (a) victory of people over monarchy
    (b) laid the foundation of modern democracy
    (c) it established the liberty of individual as supreme
    (d) brought the end of feudalism
203. What is the family background of Walt Whitman?
    (a) English
    (b) Welsh
    (c) Dutch
    (d) of English-Dutch-Welsh stock
204. Which of these expressions depict Walt Whitman best?
    (a) a Manhattan sage
    (b) a vagrant American poet
    (c) people's poet
    (d) a true American poet
205. His reading was wide and he seriously read
    (a) French poets and philosophers
    (b) Greek and ancient Indian literatures
    (c) German and British writers
    (d) scriptures of the Christians
206. He read and was influenced by
    (a) *The Bible* and Dante
    (b) *The Gita* and *the Ramayana*
    (c) Ruskin and Emerson
    (d) Thoreau and Emmanuel Kant
207. He was influenced by
    (a) Virgil
    (b) Koran
    (c) Shakespeare and Homer
    (d) Buddhism

208. Whitman can be best described as poet with
(a) a free spirit and confident of his task
(b) one who loved mankind
(c) being proud of his heritage
(d) desire for brotherhood

209. Whitman is the great American poet who can be best described as
(a) a modern American sage (b) a vision of a prophet
(c) autocratic (d) desiring American superiority over the world

**4. Ralph Waldo Emerson**

210. Ralph Waldo Emerson is a dominant American literary personality who belonged to
(a) 18th century (b) 19th century
(c) late 19th century (d) ealry 20th century

211. What was the philosophy of life Emerson preached?
(a) individualism, self-reliance and simplicity
(b) simple life
(c) conscientious life
(d) a life which combines philosophy and poetry; conscientious and self-reliant

212. In which poem Emerson demonstrates his understanding of *Vishnu Purana* and *Bhagavad Gita*?
(a) "Days" (b) "Brahma"
(c) "Earth Song" (d) "The Problem"

213. In which poem Emerson expreses the idea that men who claim possession pass away leaving it for those who remain. Earth laughs for man lives, toils and passes away leaving place for others?
(a) "Earth Song" (b) "Brahma"
(c) "Song of the Earth" (d) "Recited to Maitreya in Hamatreya"

214. In which poem these lines occur?
"They called me theirs,/ Who so controlled me;/Yet

everyone wished to stay, and is gone,/How am I theirs/If they cannot hold'me, But I hold them."

(a) "Earth song" (b) "Brahma"
(c) "Hamatreya" (d) "Song of the Earth"

215. In which poem these lines occur?
"If the red slayer think he slays, /Or if the slain think he is slain, / They know not well the subtle ways/I keep, and pass, and turn again."
(a) "Brahma" (b) "Hamatreya"
(c) "Days" (d) "Earth Song"

216. Emerson can be described by which one of the following?
(a) transcendentalist (b) spiritualist
(c) sage (d) philosopher

217. What comes in the way of understanding of the divine, the best description is
(a) ambition, pride, ego (b) wealth, lust
(c) greed (d) wickedness

## 5. Henry Wadsworth Longfellow

218. Henry Wadsworth Longfellow is
(a) a typical American poet
(b) one who brought European culture and models to American poetry
(c) a traditional poet
(d) a plagiarist

219. Longfellow's poetry can be best described as
(a) having no depth
(b) showing metrical skill but little passion and high imagination
(c) sweet on the ears
(d) highly decorous

220. Longfellow was born in
(a) 1800 (b) 1807 (c) 1850 (d) 1882

221. Longfellow is a typical poet of
(a) 19th century (b) late 19th century
(c) mid 19th century (d) American Romantic period

222. Longfellow belonged to
   (a) Great Britain
   (b) America with colonial descendance
   (c) Harvard University
   (d) colonial descendance – a period in which American poetry had not evolved its own identity
223. Longfellow's importance became limited
   (a) as he was hailed as a poet for children, it reduced his adult audience
   (b) for American did not find him relevant
   (c) due to diffused impact
   (d) as he was good poet with limited audience
224. In which poem these lines occur?
   "O star of morning and of liberty !
   O bringer of the light whose splendour shines
   Above the darkness of the Apenries,
   Forerunner of the day that is to be !"
   (a) "The Tide Rises, The Tide Falls" (b) "Divina Commedia"
   (c) "Hymn to the Night" (d) "My Lost Youth"
225. In which poem these lines occur?
   "And my youth comes back to me.
   And a verse of a Lapland song
   Is haunting my memory still:
   A boy's will is the wind's will,
   And the thoughts of youth are long, long thoughts?"
   (a) "Hymn To The Night" (b) "My Lost Youth"
   (c) "Divina Commedia" (d) "The Tide Rises, The Tide Falls"
226. In which poem these lines occur?
   "O holy Night ! from thee I learn to bear
   Thou layest thy finger on the lips of Care, What man has borne before!
   And they complain no more."
   (a) "My Lost Youth" (b) "Divina Commedia"
   (c) "Hymn to the Night" (d) "The Tide Rises, The Tide Falls"

227. Longfellow refers to which poet in these lines?
"He is the poet of the dawn, who wrote
The Canterbury Tales, and his old age
Made beautiful with song."
(a) Spenser (b) Chaucer
(c) Milton (d) Shakespeare

## UNIT F: REALISM IN AMERICAN PROSE

### 1. William Dean Howells

228. Which novel of W.D. Howells shows him at the height of his powers?
(a) *The Rise of Silas Lapham* (b) *The Atlantic*
(c) *Dr. Breen's Practice* (d) *A Woman's Reason*

229. The moral decay of competitive society is described in
(a) *Hazard of New Fortunes* (b) *Harper's Magazine*
(c) *The Rise of Silas Lapham* (d) *Atlantic*

230. In 1907, W. D. Howells wrote his Utopian novel
(a) *A Traveller from Altruria* (b) *Harper's Magazine*
(c) *Through the Eye of the Needle* (d) *Hazard of New Fortunes*

231. W.D. Howells advocated socialism in
(a) *A Traveller from Altruria* (b) *Hazard of New Fortunes*
(c) *The Rise of Silas Lapham* (d) *Through the Eye of the Needle*

232. Howells left Boston for New York in
(a) 1850 (b) 1860 (c) 1800 (d) 1880

### 2. Stephen Crane

233. Who called Howells and Garland as his literary fathers?
(a) Stephen Crane (b) Frank Norris
(c) Jack London (d) Theodore Dreiser

234. Who wrote? "A newspaper is a court /where everyone is kindly and unfairly tried /by a squalor of honest men."
(a) W.D. Howells (b) Hamlin Garland
(c) Stephen Crane (d) Frank Norris

235. Who after Crane's death felt that *Maggie* was the best thing he did?
   (a) Henry Fleming (b) Henry James
   (c) Jack London (d) W.D. Howells

236. Which of Crane's works according to him "tries to show that environment is a tremendous thing in the world"?
   (a) *The Red Badge* (b) *Maggie*
   (c) *The Open Boat* (d) None

237. Which of Crane's works is a rewritten account of a shipwreck he himself experienced?
   (a) *The Red Badge* (b) *The Open Boat*
   (c) *Maggie* (d) *Main Travelled Road*

238. Crane's *The Red Badge of Courage* has as its theme
   (a) love (b) war (c) satire (d) envy

**3. Jack London**

239. In whose books do Nietzsche and Karl Marx clash?
   (a) William Dean Howells (b) Stephen Crane
   (c) Jack London (d) Henry James

240. The hero of Jack London's socialist novel *The Iron Heel* is presented as a
   (a) filmstar (b) superman
   (c) sailor (d) priest

241. Whose hero is not so much a victor as a martyr in a protracted class struggle?
   (a) Jack London (b) W.D. Howells
   (c) Stephen Crane (d) Frank Norris

242. Soviet readers have coupled Jack London with
   (a) Upton Sinclair (b) William Dean Howells
   (c) Stephen Crane (d) Frank Norris

243. In his novels, there are signs of a
   (a) satire (b) romance
   (c) poetic flair (d) comedy

## 4. Theodore Dreiser

244. For whom do the moral and social codes of America represent the truths of human nature?
(a) Frank Norris (b) Theodore Dreiser
(c) W.D. Howells (d) Jack London

245. Who called Dreiser's *An American Tragedy* a harrowing novel?
(a) Irving Babbit (b) I.A. Richards
(c) F.R. Leavis (d) Wilson Knight

246. Theodore Dreiser gives the readers a relief from the American rhetoric of
(a) democracy (b) feudalism
(c) monarchy (d) moral law

247. Which was Theodore Dreiser's first novel for a publisher?
(a) *The Financier* (b) *Sister Carrie*
(c) *The Titan* (d) *An American Tragedy*

248. Carrie in Dreiser's *Sister Carrie* is a
(a) pretty country girl (b) French lady
(c) a sophisticated town lady (d) none

## 5. Henry James

249. In how many periods can Henry James's literature be divided?
(a) three (b) five (c) four (d) two

250. To which period do James's three novels – *Roderick Hudson, The American* and *Daisy Miller* belong?
(a) second (b) first (c) third (d) fourth

251. In which novel does James portray a young businessman Christopher Newman face to face with intriguing aristocracy of France?
(a) *Roderick Hudson* (b) *The American*
(c) *Daisy Miller* (d) *The Tragic Muse*

252. James revealed his mastery of realistic fictional technique in
(a) *Portrait of a Lady* (b) *The Bostonians*
(c) *The American* (d) *The Princess Cassamassima*

253. Which of James's novels explores the artist's dilemma in choosing between the conflicting aims of 'life' and 'art'?
(a) *Portrait of a Lady* (b) *Roderick Hudson*
(c) *The Americans* (d) *The Tragic Muse*

254. Who ridiculed James's concern with style?
(a) H. G. Wells (b) Jack London
(c) Stephen Crane (d) Edith Wharton

255. Who said this?
'It is art that makes life, makes it interesting, important.'
(a) H. G. Wells (b) Stephen Crane
(c) Edith Wharton (d) Henry James

256. When was Henry James's *The Wings of the Dove*' published?
(a) 1900 (b) 1902 (c) 1903 (d) 1904

257. In 1904, Henry James got published his
(a) *Roderick Hudson* (b) *The American*
(c) *The Europeans* (d) *The Golden Bowl*

258. Henry James left behind incompleted
(a) *The Ambassadors* (b) *The Golden Bowl*
(c) *The Outcry* (d) *The Ivory Tower*

**6. Edith Wharton**

259. Edith Wharton has a sharp eye for
(a) Social absurdities (b) love
(c) romance (d) town life

260. Edith Wharton's *The House of Mirth The Custom of the Country* and *Hudson River Bracketed* deal with
(a) London (b) Paris
(c) New York (d) Belgium

261. The hero Vance Weston is a character of Edith Wharton's
(a) *The House of Mirth* (b) *Hudson River Bracketed*
(c) *The Custom of Country* (d) *Ethan Frome*

262. Wharton's stories and novels have been widely compared with
(a) Henry James (b) Henry Adams
(c) Gertrude Stein (d) John Steinbeck

263. Lily Brat occurs in E. Wharton's
    (a) *The Custom of the Country*
    (b) *The House of Mirth*
    (c) *Ethan Frome*
    (d) *Hudson River Bracketed*

264. The absence of a fully realised conflict is especially noticeable in Wharton's
    (a) beginning novels
    (b) later novels
    (c) unfinished novel
    (d) posthumous work

## UNIT G: THE NEW AMERICAN POETRY (20TH CENTURY)

### 1. Ezra Pound

265. Where was Ezra Pound born?
    (a) Boston, Massachusettes
    (b) Philadephia, Pennsylvania
    (c) Hailey, Idaho
    (d) Davenport, Iowa

266. Name the friends and literary associates of Ezra Pound
    (a) William Carlos Williams, Marianne Moore and Hilda Doolittle
    (b) Edwardo Arbington Robinson
    (c) Robert Frost
    (d) T.S. Eliot

267. Who influenced Pound in shaping his literary values?
    (a) American poets
    (b) Greek poets and philosophers
    (c) T.E. Hulme
    (d) Walt Whitman

268. Why did Pound cross the Atlantic and settle in Europe?
    (a) he was looking for his ancestory
    (b) he was drawn by his roots and the literary tradition
    (c) the ancient nations with their heritage pulled him
    (d) he felt comfortable in Europe

269. Who championed and helped in publication of the works of Rabindranath Tagore, James Joyce, D.H. Lawrence, T.S. Eliot and W.B.Yeats in America?
    (a) Robert Frost
    (b) Ezra Pound
    (c) William Carlos Williams
    (d) Archibald Macleish

270. Ezra Pound was well versed in

(a) Greek literature
(b) ancient Indian scriptures
(c) Egyptian literature
(d) Anglo–Saxon, Italian and Chinese literatures

271. What factors Ezra Pound very seriously included in his poetry?

(a) learned and ancient
(b) quality of sound and spoken quality of poetry
(c) metaphoric
(d) freshness and vitality

272. Why was he labelled a "coterie poet"?

(a) he was lively, intelligent and a great craftsman but was unexplainable and unaccessible to common readers
(b) he left America and formed a small group of writers and became a coterie leader
(c) in America also he was projected as the most able and internationally acclaimed poet
(d) he attracted both attention and following of Williams, Marianne Moore and H.D.

273. How did T.S. Eliot show his regard for Ezra Pound?

(a) Eliot dedicated "The Waste Land" to "Ezra Pound, il miglior fabbro"—the master worker a term used by Dante for his own master
(b) by writing about him
(c) acknowledging him as a senior poet of great merit
(d) by writing rave reviews and making Pound feel at home in England

274. 10. Pound has translated extensively from—

(a) French (b) Italian (c) Greek (d) Chinese

275. What was the subject matter of Pound's "Cantos"?

(a) the wreckage of human civilization in the ancient, medieval and modern periods because of the infidelity of man and the resulting catastrophe
(b) rise and fall of civilizations
(c) history of mankind
(d) none of the above

276. What elements make Ezra Pounds's "Cantos" complex?
   (a) the allusions
   (b) the far-reaching allusions, and use of the pattern of associations
   (c) a complex matter needs complex style
   (d) complexity in structure

277. Why Pound was called an "imagist"?
   (a) he used imagery
   (b) he subscribed to the need of direct treatment of the thing, to use a word only which has a direct relevance, to compose in the sequence of musical phrase
   (c) new fashion in poetry
   (d) no ornamentation or good ornamentation

278. What did Pound mean by "image"?
   (a) an "Image" is that which presents an intellectual and emotional complex in an instant of time. It provides a sudden sense of liberation and growth
   (b) an image cannot mix an abstraction with the concrete
   (c) an image is one which refers to abundance
   (d) an image is a mental picture

279. Who said, "It is better to present an image in a life time than to produce voluminous works"?
   (a) Archibald Macleish (b) W.B. Yeats
   (c) Ezra Pound (d) H.D. Thoreau

280. In what words did Ezra Pound pay his homage to Walt Whitman?
   (a) "I make a pact with you, Walt Whitman – I have detested you long enough."
   (b) "I am old enough to make friends."
   (c) "I come to you as a grown child."
   (d) "It was you that broke the new wood, Now is the time for carving.
   We have one sap and one root – Let there be commerce between us."

281. Which poem is one of the first to make Ezra Pound famous?
   (a) "A Virginal" (b) "A Pact"
   (c) "Cantos" (d) "Ballad of the Goodly Fere?

282. What is the story of "Ballad of the Goodly Fere?"
   (a) Christ's crucifixion
   (b) the life of Christ, specially the important events — preaching, crucifixion and resurrection
   (c) in the ballad Simon, one of the disciples tells the story
   (d) it is about Christ, the good companion

283. Who is the good companion in this ballad?
   (a) Simon, the disciple of Christ
   (b) the poet
   (c) the Americans
   (d) Jesus Christ

284. In which poem the following lines occur?
   "Ha' we lost the goodliest fere O' all
   For the priests and the gallows tree?
   Aye lover he was of a brawny men?
   O' ships and the open sea."
   (a) "Cantos"
   (b) "Ballad of the Goodly Fere"
   (c) "Ballad for Gloom"
   (d) "A Virginal"

285. "I ha' seen him drive a hundred men
   Wi' a O' Cords swung free.
   That they took the high and holy house
   For the pawn and treasury"
   To which incident is Ezra Pound referring in the above line in "Ballad of the Goodly Fere"
   (a) Angry Christ
   (b) Reformist Christ chastised and cleared the temple from traders, merchants and money lenders
   (c) men are cruel and wicked
   (d) men generally do not differentiate between holy and profane, and they need to be corrected

286. Is the tone of "Ballad for the Goodly Fere"?
   (a) religious
   (b) secular
   (c) artistic

(d) secular in spirit, artistic in treatment based on Biblical references as recorded by Christ's disciples expected to be factual

287. To which event in Christ's life Pound is talking of in these lines: "I ha' seen him eat o' the honey – comb / Sin' they nailed him to the tree".

(a) reference to crucifixion, and resurrection – honey the food of the saints, tree stands for wood of which the cross was made
(b) the reference of Christ's transformation from one in flesh becoming spirit – recurrection
(c) final achievement of Christ rising from the dead and ascending to heaven
(d) crucified Christ arose from the dead.

288. Whose friend was the "goodly Fere"?

(a) of man in desperation (b) mankind
(c) of man, wind and sea (d) the whole world

289. Pound wrote: "If they think they ha' slain our Goodly Fere / They are fools eternally."
What is the poet referring to—

(a) they cannot kill the Goodly Fere
(b) the goodness he stood for cannot be destroyed
(c) the goodly Fere is eternally good, the son of God can change form, move from earth to heaven but cannot be destroyed – all men in their wisdom know this
(d) The fools live in their own paradise?

290. What is Pound's translation of Li po, (701 – 762) poem, *The River Merchant's Wife: A letter* tell the readers

(a) the River Merchant's Wife married to him at the age of 14 is awaiting his return, She in this poetic letter recalls their past relationship, his departure to the distant hands and the passage of time that has changed everything. She awaits to welcome him on his return
(b) a romantic poem
(c) a balanced love poem full of visual imagery
(d) a woman awaiting her lover and husband's return There is a touch of mystery in it

296. Which one of the following explain the quality of Pound's "Hugh Selwyn Mauberley?"
(a) richness of imagery
(b) extensive sources and references
(c) combination of variety of elements into a great poem
(d) variety and profundity, sustained perfection and powerful execution

**2. Edgar Lee Masters**

297. What secures Edgar Lee Master's position in American poetry?
(a) simplicity (b) a new diction
(c) dramatic monologue (d) short poems

298. Edgar Lee Masters became famous because of
(a) *Across Spoon River* (b) *Spoon River Anthology*
(c) *The New Spoon River* (d) *The Tide of Time*

299. *Spoon River Anthology* is a significant work of Masters in which he writes about
(a) lives of the dead
(b) free-verse epitaphs revealing the secret lives of the persons buried in Midwestern cemetry
(c) simplicity is the characteristic value of the poem
(d) direct and revealing

300. How many volumes of verse, novels and prose writings did he publish?
(a) 20 (b) 30 (c) 10 (d) 50

301. Who wrote these lines?
"But through a long sickness/Coughing myself to death/ I read the *Upanishads* and the poetry of Jesus"
(a) E.A. Robinson (b) Robert Frost
(c) Edgar Lee Masters (d) Carl Sandburg

**3. Carl Sandburg**

302. Carl Sandburg was born in
(a) 1878 (b) 1888 (c) 1900 (d) 1915

303. What is the ancestory of Carl Sandburg?
(a) Swedish immigrants (b) German
(c) Polish (c) Holland

304. Carl Sandburg's language is
(a) Swedish
(b) German
(c) Swedish in childhood, learnt English later
(d) Polish

305. Who wrote "Chicago"?
(a) "Carl Sandburg"
(b) "Wallace Stevens"
(c) "Edgar Lee Masters"
(d) "Archibald Macleish"

306. Why did "Chicago" become famous?
(a) an ode in the free verse to celebrate the spirit of the city
(b) an ode to wicked and brutal city with lots of grit
(c) a profane city
(d) the second largest city with its weakness and strength

307. What are the new features in "Chicago"?
(a) new verse pattern
(b) language of the people and rhythm of the Midwest speech
(c) a direct impact because of the theme
(d) close to the mind and heart of the Americans

308. What were the achievements of Carl Sandburg in his poetry, specially "Chicago"?
(a) people's poem
(b) a sense of immediacy, hopes and fears of the people
(c) depict's the life and songs of the people
(d) voice of the people

309. What qualities attracted Americans towards Sandburg's poetry?
(a) poetic insight
(b) phrasing
(c) the new poetic technique
(d) breaking from the tradition and evolving his own technique

310. Which group of poets are called 'Chicago poets'?
(a) Carl Sanburg, Vachel Lindsay, Edgar Lee Masters, Harriet Monroe
(b) Robert Frost, Edgar Allan Poe, Emerson

(c) William Carlos William, E.E. Cummings, Archibald Macleish
(d) Archibald Macleish, Carl Sandburg, Edgar Allan Poe

311. Which one of the following features describes "Chicago poets', best?
(a) free Verse
(b) oral and bardic tradition
(c) hymnal
(d) cadence

312. Which one of the following poetic qualities describe Sandburg's poetry best?
(a) robust like Whitman's poetry
(b) genuine rhythm and Midwest ballad song
(c) a rebel against the conventional poetry
(d) love for the real resilience of the working class people

313. Whose monumental biography Sandburg wrote making him famous?
(a) George Washington
(b) Abraham Lincoln
(c) Andrew Jackson
(d) Thomas Jefferson

314. Which poem Carl Sandburg wrote?
"They tell me you are wicked and I believe them/ for I have seen your painted women under the gas lamps luring the farm boys/ And they tell me you are crooked and I am answer/: yes, it is true I have seen the gunman Kill and go free to kill again.?/ And they tell me you are brutal and my reply is: on the faces of woman and children I have seen the marks of wanton hunger"
(a) "Monatone"
(b) "Limited"
(c) "Gone"
(d) "Chicago"

315. In which poem of Carl Sandburg these lines occur?
"Laughing the stormy, husky, brawling laughter/ Of youth, half-naked, sweating, proud to be/Hog-Butcher, Tool Maker, Stacker of wheat,/Player with Railroads and Freight Handler to the Nation."
(a) "Limited"
(b) "The People, Yes"
(c) "Chicago"
(d) "Who am I"

316. What is the basic content of Sandburg's "Chicago"?
(a) praising the second largest American city and its industrialization

(b) appreciating the industrial spirit of Chicago, the city of hope
(c) proud of the common people and their indomitable spirit which makes them laugh and sing in the face of problems which every city has its share of – poverty, prostitution, murder and hunger
(d) industrial development and decent people

317. About which city Carl Sandburg wrote? "Come and show me another city with lifted head / singing so proud to be alive and coarse and strong and cunning."
(a) "New York" (b) "Boston"
(c) "Washington" (d) "Chicago"

318. Where did Carl Sandburg find happiness?
(a) Niagara Falls
(b) statue of Liberty
(c) on the bank of Desplaines river in the state of Illinouis
(d) southern deserts

319. In which poem Carl Sandburg wrote the following line? "And I saw a crowd of Hungarians under the trees with their women and children and a keg of beer and on accordion."
(a) "Chicago" (b) "Happines"
(c) "Cool Toombs" (d) "Jazz Fantasia"

320. What is the main idea in Sandburg's poem entitled, "The People, Yes?"
(a) life and people are resilient
(b) the spirit of life cannot be defeated, people are indomitable
(c) life is never lost, it renews itself
(d) mankind has survived all odds

321. In which poem Carl Sandburg wrote these lines? "The people is a tragic and comic two-face: / hero and hoodlum: phantom and gorilla/ twisting to moon with gargoyle mouth:/ they buy me and sell me .../ it's a game ... / sometime I'll break loose ..."
(a) "The People, Yes" (b) "Four Preludes on playthings of the Wind"
(c) "Brass" (d) "Who am I"

322. Why did Sandburg write in "The People, Yes" these lines?

The people will live on.

The learning and blundering people will live on. They will be tricked and sold and again sold And go back to the nourishing earth for rootholds,

The people so peculiar in renewal and come back Your can't laugh off their capacity to take it."

(a) he believed in essential spirit of survival and struggle in man

(b) the man is indomitable, as the rise and fall of civilization, persecution, wars and natural calamities show – Even atomic destruction does not wipe out life, they rebuild, adapt and live on

(c) man is rooted and mere chopping off the branches does no harm

(d) intelligence of man, God's blessings and physical stamina give him the strength to survive

323. In which poem Sandburg wrote?

"I am the people – the mob – the crowd – the mass./ Do you that all the great work of the world is done through me.?/ I am the workingman, the inventor, the maker of world's food and clothes./ I am the audience that witnesses history./ The Napoleons come from me and the Lincolns. They die."

(a) "Caboose thoughts" (b) "I am the Ppeople, the Mob"

(c) "Who am I" (d) "Monotone"

324. What is the main thrust in Sandburg's "I am the People, The Mob"?

(a) democracy

(b) people make individuals great

(c) individuals are mortals but mankind or people are a continuity and their end never comes

(d) Napoleons and Hitlers die, mankind lives on

325. How best can these lines from "Fog" be described?

(a) delicate and realistic (b) idealistic

(c) illusory (d) fake

326. Carl Sandburg says that "Fog" arrives stealthily and coveres up the city and harbour, how does it depart?
(a) as quickly as it comes (b) gradually
(c) hastily (d) lingeringly

**4. Robert Frost**

327. Robert Frost was born in
(a) 1874 (b) 1900 (c) 1884 (d) 1871

328. What is Robert Frost's ancestory?
(a) New England (b) England
(c) Wild West of America (d) New Hampshire

329. What is Robert Frost's true background?
(a) shoemaking and farming (b) teaching
(c) lecturing (d) poetry writing

330. He wanted to write poetry which was
(a) heartfelt (b) as simple and honest as an axe or a hoe
(c) close to nature (d) truly representative of American dream

331. He was called the first American poet
(a) who achieved world recognition
(b) who can be labelled a real master-poet
(c) depicted American landscape
(d) who eulogized shoemaking

332. He was a craftsman and farmer who enriched American poetry by
(a) using his experiences of a craftsman and husbandry
(b) metaphor of farming
(c) imagery of seasonal changes
(d) presenting forest and fauna

333. In his poetry he used
(a) metre (b) free verse and colloquialism
(c) American expressions (d) imitation of Greek poetry

334. Frost's poetry is best explained by
(a) synecdoche (b) ballad
(c) mask (d) monologues

335. Which lines have made him known in India?
   (a) "I have been one acquainted with the night
   I have walked out in rain – and back in rain
   I have outwalked the further city life."
   ("Acquainted with the Night")
   (b) "The woods are lovely, dark and deep,
   But I have promises to keep,
   And miles to go before I sleep,
   And miles to go before I sleep."
   ("Stopping by Woods on a Snowy Evening")
   (c) "But yield who will to their separation,
   My object in living is to unite."
   ("Two Tramps in Mud Time")
   (d) "The land was ours before we were the land's
   She was our land more than a hundred years
   Before we were her people."
   ("The Gift Outright")

336. Who made these lines famous?
   "The woods are lovely, dark and deep,
   But I have promises to keep,
   And miles to go before I sleep,
   And miles to go before I sleep."
   (a) Robert Graves (b) John F. Kennedy
   (c) Jawaharlal Nehru (d) Carl Sandburg

337. In which poem Frost wrote: "Good fences make good neighbours."?
   (a) "Reluctance" (b) "Mending Wall"
   (c) "The Pasture" (d) "In Hardwood Groves"

338. Why Frost did not believe in erecting walls to make good neighbours?
   (a) tresspassers can't be kept away
   (b) neighbour's pines and poet's apple trees will never wrangle
   (c) walls merely mark territory
   (d) walls create a possibility of mischief

291. In which poem Ezra Pound write: "Let us express our envy of the man with a steady job and no worry about the future".
(a) "Salutation" (b) "Further Instructions"
(c) "The Rest" (d) "Ballad of the Goodly Fere"

292. Pound's "Hugh Selwyn Mauberley" can be best described as,
(a) document of an epoch (b) document of poetic sensibility
(c) criticism of life (d) genuine tragedy and comedy

293. From which poem of Ezra Pound the following lines have been taken?
"The age demanded an image
Of its accelerated grievance
Something for the modern stage
Not, at any rate, an Attic grace;"
(a) "Further Instructions" (b) "Hugh Selwyn Mauberley"
(c) "Ballad of the Goodly Fere" (d) "A Virginal"

294. In which poem of Ezra Pound the following lines occur?
"There died a myriad/And of the best, among them/For an old bitch gone in the teeth/For a botched civilization/ Charm, smiling at the good mouth/ Quick eyes gone under earth's lid/For two gross of broken statues/For a few thousand battered looks"
(a) "Hugh Selwyn Mauberley" (b) "Salutation"
(c) "The Rivers Merchant's Wife: A letter" (d) "A Pact"

295. Which one of the following explain the theme of Ezra Pound's "Hugh Selwyn Mauberley" best?
(a) collapse of civilization and alienation from his age and withdrawal
(b) collapse of modern world
(c) an awareness of Francois Villon and Mallarme
(d) hollowness of American dream.

339. For Frost no walls are needed between neighbours for he believed in
(a) universal brotherhood based on love and trust
(b) mutual trust
(c) goodness of man
(d) man's ability to walk in light and darkness

340. In which poem Frost wrote?
"He is all pine and I am apple orchard
My apple trees will never get across
And eat the cones under his pines, I tell him
He only says, 'Good fences make good neighbours."
(a) "The Death of the Hired Man"
(b) "Home Burial"
(c) "Fire and Ice"
(d) "Mending Wall"

341. In "The Death of the Hired Man" Robert Frost talks of
(a) pride
(b) human dignity
(c) love for farming
(d) loss of will to work

342. In which poem of Frost these lines occur?
"If he left then, I said, that ended it.
What good is he? Who else will harbour him
At his age for the little he can do?
What help he is there's no depending on
Off he goes always when I need him most."
(a) "Reluctance"
(b) "The Death of the Hired Man"
(c) "Home Burial"
(d) "After Apple-picking"

343. What is that Frost want to say in "After Apple-picking"?
(a) the task of picking apple hanging on a ladder
(b) the hard labour of the task
(c) ordeals of apple farming
(d) picking apple with care and resultant physical fatigue

344. Why is apple-picking so tiring?
(a) apples must be plucked with hand one by one, for every fallen apple becomes unfit for eating
(b) it is an absorbing task
(c) going up a ladder to reach the apples on the higher reaches
(d) apples must be picked up within a short time

345. In which poem Frost wrote?
"Fort I have had too much
Of apple-picking: I am overtired
Of the great harvest I myself desired.
There were ten thousand fruits to touch,
Cherish in hand, lift down, and not let fall."
(a) "In Hardwood Groves" (b) "After Apple-picking"
(c) "Nothing Good Can Stay" (d) "Precaution"

346. What does Frost see in the birches?
(a) suppleness and resilience (b) life
(c) tenacity (d) strength

347. In a number of poems Frost has used his farming experiences, which one of the following is the typical one?
(a) a farmer desires rich harvest
(b) farming is a caring and hardworking labour
(c) all the toil is forgotten when harvest is good
(d) a farmer has human need of sleep and rest after hard farming work

348. In which poem of Frost the following lines occur?
"When I see birches bend to left and right
Across the lines of straighter darker trees
I like think some boy's been swinging them."
(a) "Stopping by woods on a Snowy Evening"
(b) "The Onset"
(c) "Birches"
(d) "Come In"

349. On what occasion did Frost recite the poem entitled, "The Gift Outright"?
(a) televised inauguration of President John F. Kennedy on January 20, 1961
(b) In England in 1913
(c) on his return to America in 1914
(d) at the Pinkerton Academy

350. What did Frost say in "The Gift Outright"?
(a) the historical past of Americans
(b) the task ahead before the nation

(c) the role of Americans in the post Second Warld War era
(d) the ambiguous relationship of Americans with the land and freedom. Giving gift which was already theirs – the hard way

351. What did Frost mean in the following lines of "The Gift Outright"?
"Possessing what we still were possessed by,
Possessed by what we no more possessed."
(a) moving from the colonial past, through difficult war, to establishment of a free democratic state
(b) they possessed land which was claimed by the British king
(c) they were possessed by the idea of freedom as opposed to slavery
(d) finally getting the possession of land and soul both – held earlier by Britain and settlers respectively

**5. E.E. Cummings**

352. E.E.Cummings was born in the year
(a) 1858 (b) 1884 (c) 1899 (d) 1894

353. Cummings died in the year
(a) 1962 (b) 1950 (c) 1972 (d) 1930

354. Cummings was born and brought up in
(a) Boston (b) Cambridge, Massachusettes
(c) California (d) Texas

355. What are the important features of Cummings' poetry?
(a) satire and sentiment, traditional values and contempt for authority and convention—all combined in a unique way
(b) the qualities of his paintings were merged with his poetry
(c) direct in his writing choosing words meticulously
(d) use of slang gave his poetry a spontaniety—candid.

356. What techniques Cummings used which gave a different outlook to his poetry?
   (a) word spacing and arrangement and typographical distortion
   (b) method of designing of his print material
   (c) liberty in use of punctuation
   (d) mixed ways to startle the reader

357. Which of the following statements explain his poetic qualities best?
   (a) love, nature and individual integrity as subject matter
   (b) lyrical beauty, intensity and tenderness gave his subject matter a new life and power
   (c) unconventional thoughts expressed in a formal way
   (d) basically a traditional poet

358. Who said this? "Life, for eternal us, is now"
   (a) Archibald Macleish (b) Hart Crane
   (c) E.E. Cummings (d) Wallace Stevens

359. Who said this? "Always the beautiful answer who ask a more beautiful question"
   (a) Robert Frost (b) E.E. Cummings
   (c) Ezra Pound (d) William Carlos Williams

360. Why was Cummings imprisoned?
   (a) for his bold poetry (b) bohemian way of life
   (c) irresponsible activities (d) conscientious objectons to participation in war

361. What did Cummings write about the Cambridge ladies?
   (a) their superficialities
   (b) their belief in theory of best value
   (c) their 'coy' appearance and a life of 'bandy scandal' are unrelated fragmented
   (d) beauty, comfort, coyness, lavender are unrealistic

362. In which poem of Cummings these lines occur?
   "I sing of Olaf glad and big"
   Whose warmest heart recoiled at war:
   a conscentious objector.
   (a) "The Cambridge Ladies" (b) "I Sing of OLaf Glad And Big"

(c) "No man, If Men are Gods"
(d) "Among Crumbling People"

363. "I Sing of Olaf Glad And Big" can be best explained by
(a) strong statement about World War I
(b) the tendencies and exigencies which make people itch for war
(c) the strong destroy the weak, human nature is curbed to satisfy the ego of the war monger
(d) the bloated ego becomes a cult of hatred—the protective eagle turns destroyer. Human conscience always objects to this monster in Man

364. In which poem of Cummings these lines occur?
"As freedom is a breakfast food
or truth can live with right and wrong
or molehills are from mountains made
—long enough and just so long
will being pay the rent of seem
and genius please the talant gang
and water most encourage flame"
(a) "I Sing of Olaf Glad And Big"
(b) "The Cambridge Ladies"
(c) "As Freedom is A Breakfastfood"
(d) "Among Crumbling People"

365. Who wrote?
"—time is a tree (this life one leaf)
but love is the sky and I am for you
just so long and long enough"
(a) Hart Crane
(b) E.E. Cummings
(c) Wallace Steavens
(d) Robinson Jeffers

366. In which poem E.E. Cummings wrote this?
"eye perceives
(as the ego approaches)
painfully sterilized contours;
within
which
'ladies and gentleman'
under

glass —
are:
asking"

(a) "Among Crumbling People"
(b) "As Freedom Is A Breakfastfood"
(c) "I Sing of Olaf Glad And Big"
(d) "The Cambridge Ladies"

### 6. Hart Crane

367. When was Hart Crane born?
(a) 1899 (b) 1900 (c) 1905 (d) 1889

368. Hart Crane belongs to which part of America?
(a) Boston
(b) New York
(c) Ohio
(d) Philadelphia

369. What is common in Hart Crane and Edgar Allan Poe?
(a) Americans
(b) committed poets in an established tradition
(c) dark and troubled life, emotionally disturbed and disintegrated
(d) great tradition of American poetry

370. What made Crane an outstanding poet of his period?
(a) faith in the American principle of unity
(b) voice of the different peoples into one nationality
(c) combination of varied languages and customs
(d) unity and diversity

371. What are the symbols of integrity in the American poetry according to Hart Crane?
(a) Columbus, Pocahontas, Rip Wan Winkle, Poe, Whitman, the subway and the Brooklyn Bridge, Unifying past and present
(b) colonial past and emergence of a powerful American nation
(c) statue of liberty
(d) the vast land – fertility and industrialization

372. What are the characteristics of Hart Crane's poetry which one of the following best describe?
(a) control over language and content

(b) sonorous rhetoric, concrete imagery, acute mystical perception
(c) highly readable
(d) voice of millions

373. Why did Hart Crane jump from the ship bringing him home?
(a) his life lacked discipline
(b) he believed that creative ability had dissipated
(c) his mind was tortured for actual life conditions and his faith did not match
(d) acutely stressed

374. How "The Bridge" acquired such great significance for Hart Crane?
(a) the greatest suspension Brooklyn bridge was an engineering feat and for Crane it became a symbol of integration between machine and man, past and present
(b) a myth which made Absolute intelligible to Americans
(c) logo of a new dawn
(d) embodiment of an exile's quest

375. For Hart Crane the Brooklyn bridge is a symbol of
(a) unity which joins city, river and sea
(b) connects the people of the city with the world outside
(c) apans the great river
(d) merican identity

376. In which poem of Hart Crane these lines occur?
"O sleepless as the river under thee,
Vaulting the sea, the prairies' dreaming sod,
Unto us lowliest sometimes sweep, descend
And of the curveship land a myth to God."
(a) "Ave Maria" (b) "The Bridge"
(c) "Cape Hatteras" (d) "Voyages"

377. What is the significance of Hart Crane's "Ave Maria"?
(a) Hail Mary
(b) Christian significance in the poems a prayer, hail Mary

(c) praise of Mary, the mother of Christ
(d) prayer for Mary, Christ's mother

378. In which poem Hart Crane wrote?
"I thought of Genoa; and this truth, now proved,
That made no exile in her streets stood me,
More absolute than ever – biding the moon
Till dawn should clear that dim frontier."
(a) "The Bridge" (b) "Ave Marias"
(c) "Voyages" (d) "At Melville's Tomb"

379. What unique element has been incorporated in Hart Crane's "The Voyages"?
(a) organic structure (b) music
(c) image of "adagios of islands" refers to the motion of a boat, the rhythm of motion (d) directive and creative

380. What other poetic features are achievements of Hart Crane?
(a) music (b) metaphor
(c) logical employment of words (d) combination of music and metaphor.

381. In which poem of Hart Crane these lines occur?
"Salute the crocus lustres of the stars-
In these poinsettia meadows of her tides,
Adagios of islands, O my prodigal
Complete the dark confessions of her veins spell."
(a) "At Melville's Tomb" (b) "The Bridge"
(c) "Voyages" (d) "Ave Maria"

### 7. Archibald Macleish

382. In which poem Archibald Macleish presents his ideas about poetry?
(a) "The End of the World" (b) "Ars Poetica"
(c) "Landscape As A Nude" (d) "Empire Builders"

383. In which poem these lines occur?
A poem should be motionless in time
As the moon climbs,...

A poem should be equal to
Not true"

(a) "Wildwest" (b) "Empire Builders"
(c) "Words in Time" (d) "Ars Poetica"

384. In which poem Archibald Macleish declares?
"A poem should not mean
But be."

(a) "Landscape As A Nude" (b) "The End of the World"
(c) "Empire Builders" (d) "Ars Poetica"

385. Why did Macleish call the Landscape nude in the poem "Landscape As a Nude"?

(a) this poem is part of a discussion on the construction of Rockfellor center in which nude in frescoes and painting was used. Its relevance specially the artists and workers were mostly foreigners was a suspect.
(b) nudes in modern art
(c) nudes in sculpture and mural painting for an imposing building was not easily accepted
(d) landscape is called nude, the issue for the poet centred around the vigour of the West and the delicacy of the British girls not matching, as such inappropriate

386. In which poem of Archibald Macleish these lines occur?
"Ah she is beautiful here in the sun where she lies:
She is not like the soft girls naked in the vineyards
Nor the soft naked girls of the English islands
Where the rain comes in with the surf on an east wind:"

(a) "Wildwest" (b) "Landscape As A Nude"
(c) "The End of the World" (d) "Ars Poetica"

**8. William Carlos Williams**

387. William Carlos Williams was born in

(a) 1880 (b) 1883 (c) 1893 (d) 1900

388. Williams' poetry can be best described as

(a) astute workman in language with the rhythm of speech and the quality of sound
(b) metaphoric

(c) objective presentation
(d) imagism

389. Who said, “an image is not a poem”?
(a) Archibald Macleish (b) Robert Frost
(c) Hart Crane (d) William Carlos Williams

390. In which poem these lines occur?
“Broken,/beaten, desolate, reaching from the dead to be taken up/they cry out, failing, failing ! their cries rising/ in waves still as the skillful yachts pass over.”
(a) “Tract” (b) “This is just to say”
(c) “The Yachts” (d) “Voyage”

391. What did Williams say in the poem, “The Yachts”?
(a) the adventure, thrill, speed are associated with yacht
(b) the controlled yacht moves in the ungoverned sea
(c) the human skill and intelligence can conquer the unknown brute forces of nature
(d) human fear and agony can be overcome by control and confidence

392. Williams comes close to an American poet in having confidence in man, he is
(a) Robert Frost (b) Walt Whitman
(c) E.E. Cummings (d) Hart Crane

393. What are the main ideas contained in Williams’ “Tract”?
(a) he advocates simplicity in the funeral procession. weathered house, practical coffin, no silk or gaudiness in the mourner’s dress. After all man comes in the world unceremoniously and he should depart equally inconspicuously but in dignity
(b) the poem is instruction for simple burial
(c) it is a guideline for his fellow towns people
(d) he teaches frugality and dignity

## 9. Wallace Stevens

394. Wallace Stevens was born in
(a) Reading, Pennsylvania (b) Massachusetts
(c) Ohio (d) Kentucky

395. He was born in the year
(a) 1899 (b) 1879 (c) 1891 (d) 1900

396. Who believed that poetry lies in freedom of expression and not being bound by form?
(a) Robert Frost (b) Wallace Stevens
(c) William Carlos Williams (d) Walt Whitman

397. Wallace Stevens in "Sunday Morning" says
(a) Sunday is the sabbath and must be observed piously
(b) complacency is not desirable
(c) Sunday should be enjoyed like the woman
(d) the woman relaxes on a late Sunday morning, contentment and calmness dawns on her

398. In which poem these lines occur?
"At evening, casual flocks of pigeons make/Ambiguous undulations as they sink,/Downward to darkness, on extended wings."
(a) "The Yachts" (b) "Voyages"
(c) "Ave Maria" (d) "Sunday Morning'

**10. Theodore Roethke**

399. Theodore Roethke was born in
(a) Michigan (b) Boston
(c) New York (d) Kentucky

400. Roethke's lyrics express
(a) growth and decay in plants (b) growth and decay become imagery
(c) this imagery pervades his poetry (d) development

401. Roethke is close to W.B. Yeats in
(a) visionary strain (b) vision of life
(c) understanding of life characteristics (d) great sensitivity

402. In which poem these lines occur?
"In moving slow he has no peer./You ask him something in his ear; / He thinks about it for a year"
(a) "The Lost Son" (b) "The Sloth"
(c) "The Partner' (d) "Elegy for Jane"

403. In which poem these lines occur?
"Between such animal and human heat/I find myself perplexed. What is desire?/The impulse to make someone else complete?/That woman would set sodden straw on fire"
(a) "The Lost Son" (b) "The Sloth"
(c) "The Partner" (d) "Elegy for Jane"

## UNIT H: FICTION SINCE WORLD WAR I

### 1. Ernest Hemingway

404. Which is Ernest Hemingway's first important novel?
(a) *In Our Time* (b) *Men Without Women*
(c) *The Sun also Rises* (d) *A Farewell to Arms*

405. Hemingway's collection of short stories, *In our Time*, was written in
(a) 1900 (b) 1925 (c) 1924 (d) 1930

406. Hemingway reached the height of his creativity in *A Farewell to Arms* and *For whom the Bell Tolls* which were
(a) love poems (b) romantic plays
(c) war novels (d) satirical plays

407. Which of Hemingway's work is based directly on his Italian war experiences?
(a) *In Our Time* (b) *Men without Women*
(c) *The Sun Also Rises* (d) *A Farewell to Arms*

408. Which of Hemingway's works is a Spanish Civil War story?
(a) *The Green Hills of Africa* (b) *Death in the Afternoon*
(c) *For whom Bell Tolls* (d) *In Our Time*

409. Santiago is the hero of
(a) *The Old Man and the Sea* (b) *Death in the Afternoon*
(c) *The Green hills of Africa* (d) *In Our Time*

410. A posthumously published account of his early Paris day is found in
(a) *The Old Man and the Sea* (b) *A Movable Feast*
(c) *To Have and Have Not* (d) *Men Without Women*

**2. F. Scott Fitzgerald**

411. To whom did Fitzgerald say, 'The very rich are different from you and me'?
(a) John Dos Passos (b) William Faulkner
(c) Ernest Hemingway (d) John Steinbeck

412. In which work does Fitzgerald write of men coming out of the trenches, watched by the hero?
(a) *Flappers and Philosophers* (b) *Tales of the Jazz Age*
(c) *The Beautiful and Damned* (d) *The Offshore Pirate*

413. Fitzgerald in his works concentrated particularly upon
(a) love (b) satirising society
(c) the aristocracy of wealth (d) none

414. When was Fitzgerald's *Flappers and Philosophers* published?
(a) 1900 (b) 1915 (c) 1920 (d) 1950

415. In which work of Fitzgerald does the hero reflect 'I know myself but that is all'?
(a) *The Great Gatsby* (b) *Tender is the Night*
(c) *This Side of Paradise* (d) *The Beautiful and Damned*

416. On which of Fitzgerald's works were the reviewers too hard?
(a) *Tender is the Night* (b) *The Great Gatsby*
(c) *This Side of Paradise* (d) *Tales of the Jazz Age*

417. Which of Fitzgerald's works was left unfinished?
(a) *The Last Tycoon* (b) *The Crack-up*
(c) *Tender is the Night* (d) *The Great Gatsby*

418. Which is the posthumous volume of Fitzgerald?
(a) *The Last Tycoon* (b) *The Crack-Up*
(c) *Tender is the Night* (d) *The Great Gatsby*

**3. John Dos Passos**

419. Which is John Dos Passos's first novel?
(a) *One Man's Initiation* (b) *Three Soldiers*
(c) *U.S.A.* (d) *Manhattan Transfer*

420. When was Passos's *Three Soldiers* published?
(a) 1910 (b) 1920 (c) 1921 (d) 1930

421. John Andrews is a character in John Dos Passos's
(a) *Three Soldiers* (b) *U.S.A.*
(c) *One Man's Initiation* (d) *Manhattan Transfer*

422. Passos's *U.S.A.* has been described as an example of
(a) superb romance (b) satire
(c) collectivist novel (d) none

423. 42nd Parallel, 1919 and the Big Money occur in John Dos Passos's
(a) *U.S.A.* (b) *Three Soldiers*
(c) *One Man's Initiation* (d) *Manhattan Transfer*

**4. John Steinbeck**

424. John Steinbeck was awarded the Nobel Prize for Literature in
(a) 1960 (b) 1962 (c) 1965 (d) 1970

425. Which work brought John Steinbeck success?
(a) *Long Valley* (b) *Tortilla Flat*
(c) *In Dubious Battle* (d) *Of Mice and Men*

426. Steinbeck's which novel is the most sensationally impressive book in American literature?
(a) *The Grapes of Wrath* (b) *In Dubious Battle*
(c) *Of Mice and Men* (d) *The Pastures of Heaven*

427. Which Steinbeck's work uses the familiar setting and characters?
(a) *In Dubious Battle* (b) *Of Mice and Men*
(c) *The Grapes of Wrath* (d) *The Chrysanthemums*

428. Steinbeck's *The Red Pony* was published in
(a) 1920 (b) 1925 (c) 1930 (d) 1933

429. Steinbeck's *The Pastures of Heaven* was published in
(a) 1932 (b) 1933 (c) 1935 (d) 1940

**5. William Faulkner**

430. William Faulkner received the Nobel Prize in
(a) 1920 (b) 1925 (c) 1950 (d) 1960

431. Faulkner's vision of the South is
(a) incoherent (b) satirical
(c) poetical (d) very clear

432. For Faulkner the key word is
(a) love (b) god (c) poetry (d) doom

433. There is a curious combination of violence and passivity in
(a) Ernest Hemingway (b) F. Scott Fitzgerald
(c) William Faulkner (d) John Steinbeck

434. William Faulkner's *A Fable* was published in
(a) 1950 (b) 1952 (c) 1954 (d) 1960

435. Faulkner died in
(a) 1960 (b) 1962 (c) 1965 (d) 1970

436. Faulkner spent most of his life in
(a) Cambridge (b) Oxford
(c) Harvard (d) None of these

437. Faulkner's *The Sound and the Fury* was published in
(a) 1919 (b) 1921 (c) 1929 (d) 1930

**6. Thomas Wolfe**

438. Thomas Wolfe lived for
(a) 38 Years (b) 25 Years
(c) 35 Years (d) 50 Years

439. Wolfe is a spokesman for a
(a) wife (b) husband
(c) father (d) mother

440. Which of Thomas Wolfe's works is dominated by hunger for experience and lust for property?
(a) *Look Homeward, Angel* (b) *Letters to His Mother*
(c) *The Hills Beyond* (d) *From Death to Morning*

441. Thomas Wolfe's *Letters to His Mother* is a valuable insight in Wolfe's
(a) creative life (b) love life
(c) married life (d) divorced life

442. Who wrote Thomas Wolfe's biography?
(a) Elizabeth Nowell (b) John Dos Passos
(c) Ernest Hemingway (d) F. Scott Fitzgerald

443. Who was the author of *The Story of a Novel*?
(a) Ernest Hemingway (b) F. Scott Fitzgerald
(c) John Crowe Ransom (d) Thomas Wolfe

444. As a writer, Wolfe's most precious asset was
(a) imagination (b) freedom
(c) love (d) foresight

445. Who wrote *Look Homeward Angel*?
(a) Sinclair Lewis (b) John Dos Passos
(c) Thomas Wolfe (d) John Steinbeck

## UNIT I: THE AMERICAN PLAYWRIGHTS

### 1. Eugene O'Neill

446. Eugene O'Neill is an American playwright of
(a) the 19th century (b) the 20th century
(c) post-Second World War (d) None of the above

447. O'Neill died in
(a) 1953 (b) 1945 (c) 1976 (d) 1963

448. Who wrote *Beyond the Horizon?*
(a) Tennesee Williams (b) Eugene O'Neill
(c) Edward Albee (d) Mark Twain

449. Who wrote *Long Day's Journey into Night*?
(a) Edward Albee (b) Tennesee Williams
(c) Samuel Beckett (d) Eugene O'Neill

450. In *The Hairy Ape* O' Neill presents
(a) realism (b) symbolism
(c) realism with symbolic expression (d) none of the above

451. *The Hairy Ape* depicts the life of
(a) early America (b) post-Colonial America
(c) comedy of ancient and modern life (d) recent times

452. Which of the following refers to O'Neill's style best?
(a) colloquial
(b) American English with an accent
(c) mixture of many European languages
(d) none of the above

453. O'Neill wrote: "There is a menace existing in this country today which threatens the vitals of our fair Republic—as foul a menace against the very life-blood of the American Eagle as was the foul conspiracy of Catiline against the eagles of ancient Rome!" These lines occur in which play of his?
(a) *The Hairy Ape*
(b) *The Emperor Jones*
(c) *Beyond the Horizon*
(d) *The Iceman Cometh*

454. Which of O'Neill's plays present the American dream best?
(a) *The Emperor Jones*
(b) *The Hairy Ape*
(c) *Beyond the Horizon*
(d) *Long Day's Journey into Night*

455. *Beyond the Horizon* is a drama about
(a) Robert Mayo
(b) Ruth
(c) Andrew Mayo
(d) None of the above

456. Who says this? "It isn't the end. It's a free beginning ... beyond the horizon!"
(a) Andrew' Mayo
(b) The consumptive dying Robert Mayo
(c) Ruth
(d) None of the above

457. *Long Day's Journey into Night* presents
(a) alcoholism and drug addiction of Mary Tyrone
(b) James
(c) Jamie
(d) None of the above

458. Mary Tyrone's nostalgic dream is to become
(a) a ballerina
(b) a nun or pianist
(c) a bar attendant
(d) a good wife or mother

459. *The Hairy Ape* is a drama which can be labelled as
(a) realistic
(b) expressionist
(c) American transcendentalist
(d) symbolist

460. In *The Hairy Ape* O'Neill presents a world which can be described best as
(a) lovely
(b) brutal, stupid and profane
(c) religious
(d) advanced technological superiority

461. Yank realizes that
(a) he was a man of progress
(b) technology has given him strength
(c) he did not belong to this brutal world
(d) he was rejected in spite of his adapting the brutal expectations of the world

462. Yank found kinship with
(a) Mildred
(b) Paddy
(c) the ape in the zoo
(d) none of the above

463. *Lazarus Laughed* is O'Neill's
(a) symbolic drama
(b) religious chorus
(c) tribute to Christian character
(d) poetic drama with mystic affirmation of life

464. Who said these lines in *Lazarus Laughed*? "Fear not life! You die—but there is no death for man."
(a) Lazarus
(b) Tiberius
(c) Caligula
(d) Miriam

465. In *Lazarus Laughed*, Lazarus is killed the second time by
(a) Miriam
(b) Tiberius
(c) Pompeia
(d) Caligula

466. In which drama of O'Neill these are the parts—"The Homecoming", "The Hunted", and "The Haunted"?
(a) *Mourning Becomes Electra*
(b) *The Emperor Jones*
(c) *Strange Interlude*
(d) *A Touch of the Poet*

467. *Mourning Becomes Electra* is based on the Greek myth of
(a) incestuous love
(b) bravery
(c) futility of love and life
(d) none of the above

468. Who says this? "Love is not permitted to me. The dead are too strong!"
(a) Christine (b) Lavinia
(c) Hazel (d) None of the above

469. Ezra Mannon's family in New England are descendents of
(a) Quackers (b) Puritan
(c) Calvinists (d) None of the above

470. Christine developed an incestuous relationship with
(a) Orin (b) Adam Brant
(c) Peter (d) None of the above

471. Who avenges murder of Ezra Mannon?
(a) Peter (b) Orin (c) Lavinia (d) Hazel

472. Who is freed of puritan repressions and grows in sensuality and orality?
(a) Christine (b) Hazel
(c) Lavinia (d) None of the above

473. What happens after Lavinia makes love to Peter?
(a) Peter leaves repelled by her eagerness and she becomes a recluse
(b) she is egged on to have relationship with others
(c) Peter is repulsed by her and kills her
(d) she is killed by Orin

474. The lovely Christine killed her husband Orin by
(a) forcing a glass of wine laced with poison
(b) administering poison pretending to give him medicine
(c) poisoning him in his sleep
(d) strangling him in his sleep

475. O'Neill was influenced by
(a) Greek tragedies (b) Ibsen and Strindberg
(c) Shakespeare (d) None of the above

476. In O'Neill's plays one sees the American family of
(a) colonial era (b) present day
(c) colonial era to the present time (d) none of the above

**2. Tennessee Williams**

477. Tennessee Williams is play wright of the
(a) First World War period (b) post-Second World War period
(c) recent times (d) none of the above

478. *The Glass Managerie* and *A Streetcar Named Desire* are the plays written by
(a) Eugene O' Neill (b) Arthur Miller
(c) Tennessee Williams (d) None of the above

479. *The Glass Managerie* is a play of
(a) a mother whose children are dead
(b) a successful mother
(c) sentiments and pathos of a frustrated mother
(d) a mother and her children who are social failures

480. *The Glass Managerie* is a play which depicts
(a) fantasies of a young mother (b) realities of life
(c) war-torn sensibilities (d) a swan song

481. Laura in *The Glass Managerie* is
(a) a healthy woman
(b) a sick woman with happy children
(c) crippled from childhood and is hypersensitive
(d) a psychopath

482. Amanda tries to overcome her physical situation by
(a) fantasising for happy times
(b) dreaming of successful marriage for daughter and a good job for the son
(c) hoping for the return of her husband
(d) accepting the deplorable life of a tenement dweller

483. Amanda's future lies in
(a) secretarial job for Laura and her getting a good husband
(b) Laura's forgetting her handicap and overcoming it
(c) Laura's accepting the situation
(d) none of the above

484. Ananda hopes for a way out when her son
(a) Tom finds a better job (b) keeps on supporting the family
(c) leaves the tenement (d) becomes a mariner

485. Tom loves his mother but wishes to
(a) continue with his warehouse job
(b) continue with his warehouse job and advancing in it
(c) escape from the world and progress
(d) do nothing

486. What happens when Tom brings his friend Jim O'Connor for dinner at home?
(a) Mother sees in him a good husband but Laura is withdrawn
(b) Laura welcomes him
(c) Tom is scandalized by the attitude of the two women
(d) Jim is shocked by the interest shown in him

487. Laura is crippled and hyper-sensitive who is at home only in
(a) her private world which is centred around a collection of animal figures in a glass
(b) a dream world
(c) the sordid reality of a tenement with no future
(d) prayers

488. What is the reaction of Jim towards Laura?
(a) he pays no attention
(b) looks at her casually
(c) he wants her to have self-confidence and says that she was pretty and kisses her
(d) none of the above

489. Jim suddenly withdraws and leaves because
(a) he was already engaged (b) he did not like Laura
(c) he is repulsed by the tenement (d) none of the above

490. What happens to Laura after Jim's departure?
(a) she hopes for a second chance
(b) she is withdrawn and retreats further in her world of glass managerie

(c) she decides to wait
(d) she decides to kill herself

491. What happens to Tom after Jim's departure?
(a) he goes out to bring him back
(b) promises to work for someone else
(c) denies that he had invited Jim for laura
(d) Amanda chastises him forcing his leaving home for ever

492. Which play of Tennessee Williams was awarded a Pulitzer Award?
(a) *The Glass Managerie* (b) *A Streetcar Named Desire*
(c) *You Touched Me* (d) *The Eccentricities of a Nightingale*

493. Who is terrified by the contrast between the glorious past and the squalid present?
(a) Stanley (b) Mitch (c) Blanche (d) Stella

494. Who reacts against the crude humour and animal maleness of Stanley Kowalski?
(a) Stella (b) Mitch
(c) The doctor (d) Blanche

495. Who considers the life of Stanley and Stella as aimless as the 'streetcar named desire' shuttling through the narrow streets?
(a) Stella (b) Blanche (c) Mitch (d) Stanley

496. Who calls Blanche a nymphomaniac?
(a) Stanley (b) Mitch
(c) the doctor (d) Stella

497. Who in anger and lust violates Blanche?
(a) Mitch (b) Stanley
(c) the doctor (d) none of the above

498. Why does Stella, returning from the hospital after confinement, not believe the story of incestuous assault on Blanche?
(a) she does not trust Blanche
(b) she believes it to be one of her fantasies
(c) she is happy that Blanche has been assaulted
(d) none of the above

499. What happens to Blanche when she is betrayed by Stanley, Mitch and Stella?
   (a) she kills herself
   (b) she breaks down
   (c) she accepts that she is of unsound mind and leaves with the doctor
   (d) she runs away

500. Who says, "I have always depended on the kindness of strangers"?
   (a) Mitch (b) Stanley (c) Stella (d) Blanche

501. Stanley and Stella are happy with each other because
   (a) Stella accepts the lusty crudeness of her husband
   (b) Stanley and Stella are cast in the same mould and enjoy a life of lust and sensuality
   (c) Stella refuses to reject the advances of her crude husband
   (d) None of the above

502. Why does Stanley react against the refinement and good taste of Blanche? Because
   (a) she is mad
   (b) she is unrealistic
   (c) she is too good
   (d) she lacks the essential feminine attractiveness

503. Why does Blanche and Mitch relationship fail?
   (a) Blanche is lonely and sad
   (b) Stanley tells a lie about Blanche being a nymphomaniac
   (c) Mitch is like Stanley, unreliable
   (d) Blanche has a superiority complex

504. *Cat on a IIot Tin Roof* is drama which deals with
   (a) fight for the favour of a woman
   (b) struggle for control of the family plantation
   (c) a farming family's drama
   (d) none of the above

505. What is the role of Maggie in *The Cat on a Hot Tin Roof*?
   (a) central for she is the passionate, vital cat who wants to grab the plantation

(b) she is like Mac
(c) she does not know what she wants
(d) none of the above

506. Why does Maggie confess about her extra-marital relationship with Skipper?
(a) she wanted to be interesting and bold
(b) to establish her eagerness to give birth to an heir for the plantation after her husband Buck's failure to do this
(c) she throws a challenge to Mae and Big Mana
(d) none of the above

507. What are the failings of Brick?
(a) failure to become a father
(b) being an ex-football hero
(c) loves alcohol
(d) complacent

508. What did Maggie do to rekindle Brick's desire for her?
(a) locks away the liquor
(b) dances and attracts him
(c) tells untruthful stories
(d) none of the above

509. What is the nearest correct description of this drama?
(a) life is a heap of lies
(b) success at any cost
(c) struggle for land
(d) success is like a cat on a hot tin roof, never fully satisfied or happy

510. Williams wanted to show that
(a) life is a tale told by an idiot signifying nothing
(b) life lies in full involvement with it rather than shrinking from it
(c) life is beautiful, admire it
(d) life is idealistic, worship it

**3. Edward Albee**

511. Who among American playwrights is best described as a representative of the theatre of the Absurd?
(a) Tennessee Williams
(b) Eugene O'Neill
(c) Edward Albee
(d) Robert Sherwood

512. What factors are nearest to a description of Edward Albee?
   (a) mingles the realistic with fantasy
   (b) experiments with the idea of American dream
   (c) writes musical opera
   (d) none of the above

513. In Albee's plays one finds
   (a) spiritual sterility leading to exposition of a deep feeling of the tragedy of alienation
   (b) a sense of doom
   (c) failure of family
   (d) none of the above

514. Who wrote the drama of alienation in the U.S.?
   (a) Robert Sherwood
   (b) Tennessee Williams
   (c) Edward Albee
   (d) None of the above

515. In which play of Albee a homosexual youth kills an unsuspecting innocent stranger?
   (a) *The Death of Bessie Smith*
   (b) *The Sandbox*
   (c) *The Zoo Story*
   (d) *Who is Affraid of Virginia Woolf?*

516. Why does the young man kill the innocent stranger?
   (a) for he neither likes the dream life nor the world of reality
   (b) for he is frustrated
   (c) for he wished to perform a fertility rite
   (d) for he got a kick out of the outrageous act

517. The young man kills the innocent stranger in the central park because
   (a) he wished to overcome his own sexual perversion and inadequacy
   (b) he wanted to inflict injury on someone
   (c) he just wished to be funny
   (d) it is thrilling

518. What does *The Zoo Story* aim at presenting?
   (a) a savage fantasy
   (b) alienation
   (c) a satire on modern American life
   (d) hypocrisy of American life

519. *The Death of Bessie Smith* is a short play about
 (a) conflict between White and Negro Americans
 (b) the nonsense of American being one people
 (c) racial discrimination
 (d) savagery in American society

520. The American Dream in its treatment can be described as
 (a) funny (b) pathetic
 (c) grotesque (d) shattered dream

521. The parents kill their adopted son because
 (a) he is sick
 (b) he will never become what they think to be perfect youngman, American dream youngman
 (c) he is not racially upto their expectations
 (d) they refuse to be his Mummy and Daddy

522. Is the American dream a central idea in Edward Albee's plays? Which of these describe his theme best?
 (a) alienation (b) failure of consumer society
 (c) cold-war considerations (d) a vague superiority complex

523. *Who is Afraid of Virginia Woolf?* is Albee's
 (a) one-act play (b) five-act play
 (c) three-act play (d) none of the above

524. What describes the events of *Who is Afraid of Virginia Woolf* best?
 (a) all-night drinking bout of a middle-aged professor and his wife
 (b) all-night dance and party
 (c) a big party at the home of a professor
 (d) a party at a young couple's house in honour of the professor

525. What happens in *Who is Afraid of Virginia Woolf?*
 (a) there is a verbal articulation of their frustration
 (b) the old couple are joined by an instructor to make them give-up their pretensions
 (c) a fantasy
 (d) comic release

526. The verbal torturing of each other in *Who is Afraid of Virginia Woolf?* is
(a) to overcome the grimness of their predicament
(b) a fixation about a non-existent son to sustain them
(c) a fantasy
(d) creating a world-order to please themselves

527. The professor and his wife create a son in their minds to
(a) be happy
(b) playing a game
(c) a fantasy to make them happy, so strong that it appears realistic
(d) be funny

528. Who wrote, *There Shall be No Night?*
(a) Edward Albee (b) Robert Sherwood
(c) Eugene O'Neill (d) Arthur Miller

529. Sherwood in *There Shall be No Night* deals with
(a) Russian attack on Finland (b) American invasion of North Pole
(c) romantic dream (d) economic depression in America

530. Robert Sherwood in *Idiot's Delight* presents
(a) a call for war
(b) a plea for world peace
(c) a need for economic sharing of world's resources
(d) none of the above

**4. Arthur Miller**

531. Arthur Miller in his plays presents
(a) a fusion of realism and symbolism
(b) a realistic account of the mid-20th century America
(c) war-time American social trauma
(d) military life

532. In *Death of a Salesman* the salesman is faced with
(a) a new dawn
(b) conflicting situation caused by his own false values and American value system
(c) social-economic changes
(d) war and economics of the war-time world

533. Willy Loman sells
(a) ormaments (b) packed food
(c) motor car (d) a dream

534. Willy Loman cannot find happiness in his sons, Biff and Happy because
(a) they have no grit in them
(b) he believes in false values and cannot cope with failure of his sons
(c) the war-time America was facing economic collapse
(d) refuses to accept reality

535. The sons leave their father to lick his own frustration which leads to
(a) he kills
(b) he decides to commit suicide to make insurance money available for his sons
(c) cannot make up his mind
(d) steals to provide for his children

536. What is the role of Ben in the drama?
(a) he is Willy's brother
(b) he is Willy's brother and a self-made successful man
(c) Ben is important for sons to make them return to American life of challenge
(d) nothing

537. Willy Loman stands for
(a) success (b) love
(c) failure (d) alcoholism

538. Willy Loman for his family was
(a) burden (b) nobody
(c) a stranger (d) a salesman who had nothing to sell

539. Who said? "Willy was a salesman ... riding on a smile and a shoeshine ... Nobody *dast* blame this man. A salesman is got to dream, boy. It comes with the territory".
(a) Biff (b) Happy
(c) Charley, a friend (d) Howard Wagner

540. What is the reaction of the family on Willy's death?
(a) sorrow (b) feeling of freedom
(c) mixed feeling (d) none of the above

541. *The Crucible* is Arthur Miller's play about
(a) McCarthyism (b) inhuman
(c) madnes (d) war

542. The real and inner theme of *The Crucible* is
(a) religious understanding
(b) the conscience of the people
(c) socio-political issues
(d) right wing politics which dominated America of 1950s.

543. Who said? "Shall the dust praise him? Shall the worms declare his turth? Go to him, take his shame away!"
(a) Danfarth (b) Hale
(c) Parris (d) Elizabeth

544. Who said? "Clzeave to no faith, when faith brings blood".
(a) Proctor (b) Elizabeth
(c) Danforth (d) Hale

545. The Salem trial of which *The Crucible* reminds was based on
(a) Americans' fear of the wilderness and forests as the abode of the devil
(b) religious fervour
(c) religious discipline to which the Salem community adhered to
(d) none of the above

546. *A View from the Bridge* is about
(a) rivers and ravines of the American continent
(b) illegal immigrants
(c) tears of aliens
(d) American landscape

547. Arthur Miller depicts definite aspects of American life which can be best described by
(a) new universal role (b) problems and maladies of a new nation
(c) racial consciouness (d) a sense of freedom

548. Who sings this song and why is he stopped? "I'll tell you boys, its tough to be alone, And its tough to love a doll that's not yours".
   (a) Marco sings this song and is stopped because he has a bad vocal chord
   (b) Rodolpho sings it and is stopped because it is not in keeping with the narrow discipline of the community
   (c) Eddie sings it and is stopped because it is so common
   (d) Rodolpho sings it and is stopped because it is in bad taste

549. Why are two immigrants in trouble in *A View from the Bridge*?
   (a) inherent dislike for the immigrants
   (b) Racial/natural discrimination
   (c) the immigrants are not peasant
   (d) they take away all the available job causing distrust

550. *Death of a Salesman* a called "time bomb expertly placed under the edifice of Americanism" because of
   (a) general sociological and psychological fear of failure
   (b) fear of Russia subverting American freedom
   (c) In Willy Loman people discovered their own collapse of enterprise
   (d) it strikes at the base of capitalist economic system

551. Miller was a celebrity American playwright and was married to
   (a) Miss U.S. (b) Marilyn Monroe
   (c) a Hollywood actress (d) a theatre actress

## UNIT J: FICTION AFTER WORLD WAR II

### 1. Saul Bellow

552. Saul Bellow's stature in post war American letters can be compared to
   (a) Henry James (b) John Steinbeck
   (c) Edith Wharton (d) Ernest Hemingway

553. Saul Bellow was credited with a sense of history by
(a) Henry James (b) I.A. Richards
(c) William Empson (d) Tonny Tanner

554. Who was the psychologist for whom Bellow expressed the inevitable love/hate?
(a) Freud (b) William James
(c) Henri Bergson (d) None

555. In which of Saul Bellow's works, Joseph says 'Alienation is a fool's plea'?
(a) *Dangling Man* (b) *The Victim*
(c) *The Adventures of Augie March* (d) *Herzog*

556. Which book, according to Bellow, is a comic book about death?
(a) *Dangling Man* (b) *Humboldt's Gift*
(c) *The Adventures of Augie March* (d) *Herzog*

557. Which work of Saul Bellow is preoccupied with social problems?
(a) *Dangling Man* (b) *Herzog*
(c) *The Dean's December* (d) *Humboldt's Gift*

558. Which is Saul Bellow's first novel, written in the diary form?
(a) *The Dean's December* (b) *Herzog*
(c) *Dangling Man* (d) *The Adventures of Augie March*

559. Minna Corde, the most independent and high powered woman character of Bellow's novels occurs in
(a) *The Victim* (b) *Dangling Man*
(c) *The Dean's December* (d) *Herzog*

560. Saul Bellow conveys a religious vision in
(a) *Humboldt's Gift* (b) *Dangling Man*
(c) *Herzog* (d) *More Die of Heartbreak*

561. Saul Bellow rejects the notion that history and culture are exclusive determinants of character in
(a) *More Die of Heart break* (b) *The Closing of the American Mind*
(c) *Humboldt's Gift* (d) *Dangling Man*

**2. John Updike**

562. John Updike was born in
(a) Washington (b) New York
(c) Pennsylvania (d) Paris

563. John Updike worked as the staff of the *New Yorker* in
(a) Pennsylvania (b) Massachusetts
(c) New York (d) Washington

564. Updike's first novel *The Poorhouse Fair* appeared in
(a) 1920 (b) 1928 (c) 1937 (d) 1959

565. The critics have objected to
(a) *The Centaur* (b) *The Poorhouse Fair*
(c) *Rabbit, Run* (d) None

566. John Updike's which novel brought to him the comment as 'the most gifted writer of his generation'?
(a) *The Poorhouse Fair* (b) *Rabbit, Run*
(c) *The Centaur* (d) None of the above

## ANSWERS

### Unit A

| | | | | | | | |
|---|---|---|---|---|---|---|---|
| 1. | (c) | 2. | (c) | 3. | (b) | 4. | (a) |
| 5. | (a) | 6. | (a) | 7. | (a) | 8. | (b) |
| 9. | (c) | 10. | (a) | 11. | (b) | 12. | (a) |
| 13. | (a) | 14. | (d) | 15. | (a) | 16. | (a) |
| 17. | (c) | 18. | (b) | 19. | (a) | 20. | (d) |
| 21. | (c) | 22. | (a) | 23. | (d) | 24. | (b) |
| 25. | (b) | 26. | (b) | 27. | (d) | 28. | (d) |
| 29. | (b) | 30. | (c) | 31. | (c) | 32. | (a) |
| 33. | (d) | 34. | (a) | 35. | (b) | 36. | (a) |

| | | | | | | | |
|---|---|---|---|---|---|---|---|
| 37. | (a) | 38. | (c) | 39. | (a) | 40. | (a) |
| 41. | (b) | 42. | (a) | 43. | (c) | 44. | (b) |
| 45. | (c) | 46. | (a) | 47. | (b) | 48. | (a) |
| 49. | (c) | 50. | (a) | 51. | (a) | 52. | (b) |
| 53. | (a) | 54. | (b) | 55. | (a) | 56. | (c) |
| 57. | (a) | 58. | (a) | 59. | (a) | 60. | (a) |
| 61. | (a) | 62. | (a) | 63. | (d) | 64. | (c) |
| 65. | (b) | 66. | (b) | 67. | (b) | 68. | (a) |
| 69. | (a) | 70. | (c) | 71. | (a) | 72. | (a) |
| 73. | (a) | 74. | (a) | 75. | (d) | 76. | (a) |
| 77. | (b) | 78. | (a) | 79. | (c) | 80. | (c) |
| 81. | (b) | | | | | | |

## Unit B

| | | | | | | | |
|---|---|---|---|---|---|---|---|
| 82. | (b) | 83. | (a) | 84. | (a) | 85. | (a) |
| 86. | (d) | 87. | (d) | 88. | (d) | 89. | (d) |
| 90. | (d) | 91. | (b) | 92. | (a) | 93. | (c) |
| 94. | (b) | 95. | (d) | 96. | (a) | 97. | (b) |
| 98. | (b) | 99. | (a) | 100. | (b) | 101. | (a) |
| 102. | (c) | 103. | (d) | 104. | (b) | 105. | (a) |
| 106. | (c) | 107. | (c) | 108. | (a) | 109. | (b) |
| 110. | (c) | 111. | (b) | 112. | (a) | 113. | (a) |
| 114. | (a) | 115. | (c) | 116. | (c) | | |

## Unit C

| | | | | | | | |
|---|---|---|---|---|---|---|---|
| 117. | (a) | 118. | (d) | 119. | (c) | 120. | (d) |
| 121. | (d) | 122. | (d) | 123. | (d) | 124. | (b) |
| 125. | (a) | 126. | (c) | 127. | (c) | 128. | (d) |
| 129. | (a) | 130. | (b) | 131. | (b) | 132. | (c) |
| 133. | (a) | 134. | (a) | 135. | (b) | 136. | (b) |
| 137. | (c) | 138. | (b) | 139. | (a) | 140. | (c) |

### Unit D

| | | | | | | | |
|---|---|---|---|---|---|---|---|
| 141. | (d) | 142. | (c) | 143. | (d) | 144. | (b) |
| 145. | (c) | 146. | (d) | 147. | (a) | | |

### Unit E

| | | | | | | | |
|---|---|---|---|---|---|---|---|
| 148. | (a) | 149. | (a) | 150. | (b) | 151. | (d) |
| 152. | (c) | 153. | (c) | 154. | (a) | 155. | (d) |
| 156. | (b) | 157. | (d) | 158. | (b) | 159. | (b) |
| 160. | (c) | 161. | (b) | 162. | (c) | 163. | (b) |
| 164. | (b) | 165. | (a) | 166. | (c) | 167. | (a) |
| 168. | (d) | 169. | (c) | 170. | (a) | 171. | (d) |
| 172. | (a) | 173. | (a) | 174. | (b) | 175. | (d) |
| 176. | (b) | 177. | (b) | 178. | (a) | 179. | (a) |
| 180. | (a) | 181. | (d) | 182. | (c) | 183. | (a) |
| 184. | (a) | 185. | (d) | 186. | (a) | 187. | (d) |
| 188. | (a) | 189. | (b) | 190. | (c) | 191. | (a) |
| 192. | (a) | 193. | (b) | 194. | (b) | 195. | (a) |
| 196. | (c) | 197. | (b) | 198. | (c) | 199. | (b) |
| 200. | (a) | 201. | (a) | 202. | (c) | 203. | (d) |
| 204. | (b) | 205. | (b) | 206. | (a) | 207. | (d) |
| 208. | (a) | 209. | (a) | 210. | (b) | 211. | (d) |
| 212. | (b) | 213. | (d) | 214. | (c) | 215. | (a) |
| 216. | (a) | 217. | (a) | 218. | (a) | 219. | (b) |
| 220. | (b) | 221. | (a) | 222. | (d) | 223. | (a) |
| 224. | (b) | 225. | (b) | 226. | (c) | 227. | (b) |

### Unit F

| | | | | | | | |
|---|---|---|---|---|---|---|---|
| 228. | (a) | 229. | (a) | 230. | (c) | 231. | (a) |
| 232. | (d) | 233. | (a) | 234. | (c) | 235. | (d) |
| 236. | (b) | 237. | (b) | 238. | (b) | 239. | (c) |
| 240. | (b) | 241. | (a) | 242. | (a) | 243. | (b) |
| 244. | (b) | 245. | (a) | 246. | (d) | 247. | (b) |
| 248. | (a) | 249. | (c) | 250. | (b) | 251. | (b) |

| | | | | | | | |
|---|---|---|---|---|---|---|---|
| 252. | (a) | 253. | (d) | 254. | (a) | 255. | (d) |
| 256. | (b) | 257. | (d) | 258. | (d) | 259. | (a) |
| 260. | (c) | 261. | (b) | 262. | (a) | 263. | (b) |
| 264. | (b) | | | | | | |

## Unit G

| | | | | | | | |
|---|---|---|---|---|---|---|---|
| 265. | (c) | 266. | (a) | 267. | (c) | 268. | (b) |
| 269. | (b) | 270. | (d) | 271. | (b) | 272. | (a) |
| 273. | (a) | 274. | (d) | 275. | (b) | 276. | (b) |
| 277. | (b) | 278. | (a) | 279. | (c) | 280. | (d) |
| 281. | (d) | 282. | (b) | 283. | (d) | 284. | (b) |
| 285. | (b) | 286. | (d) | 287. | (a) | 288. | (c) |
| 289. | (c) | 290. | (a) | 291. | (b) | 292. | (a) |
| 293. | (b) | 294. | (a) | 295. | (d) | 296. | (d) |
| 297. | (c) | 298. | (b) | 299. | (b) | 300. | (b) |
| 301. | (c) | 302. | (a) | 303. | (a) | 304. | (c) |
| 305. | (a) | 306. | (a) | 307. | (b) | 308. | (b) |
| 309. | (d) | 310. | (a) | 311. | (b) | 312. | (b) |
| 313. | (b) | 314. | (d) | 315. | (c) | 316. | (c) |
| 317. | (d) | 318. | (c) | 319. | (b) | 320. | (b) |
| 321. | (a) | 322. | (b) | 323. | (b) | 324. | (c) |
| 325. | (a) | 326. | (d) | 327. | (a) | 328. | (a) |
| 329. | (a) | 330. | (b) | 331. | (b) | 332. | (a) |
| 333. | (b) | 334. | (a) | 335. | (b) | 336. | (c) |
| 337. | (b) | 338. | (b) | 339. | (a) | 340. | (d) |
| 341. | (b) | 342. | (b) | 343. | (d) | 344. | (a) |
| 345. | (b) | 346. | (a) | 347. | (d) | 348. | (c) |
| 349. | (a) | 350. | (d) | 351. | (a) | 352. | (d) |
| 353. | (a) | 354. | (b) | 355. | (a) | 356. | (a) |
| 357. | (b) | 358. | (c) | 359. | (b) | 360. | (d) |
| 361. | (c) | 362. | (b) | 363. | (d) | 364. | (c) |
| 365. | (b) | 366. | (a) | 367. | (a) | 368. | (c) |

| | | | | | | | |
|---|---|---|---|---|---|---|---|
| 369. | (c) | 370. | (b) | 371. | (a) | 372. | (b) |
| 373. | (b) | 374. | (a) | 375. | (a) | 376. | (b) |
| 377. | (b) | 378. | (b) | 379. | (c) | 380. | (d) |
| 381. | (c) | 382. | (b) | 383. | (d) | 384. | (d) |
| 385. | (d) | 386. | (b) | 387. | (b) | 388. | (a) |
| 389. | (d) | 390. | (c) | 391. | (c) | 392. | (b) |
| 393. | (a) | 394. | (a) | 395. | (b) | 396. | (b) |
| 397. | (d) | 398. | (d) | 399. | (a) | 400. | (b) |
| 401. | (a) | 402. | (b) | 403. | (c) | | |

## Unit H

| | | | | | | | |
|---|---|---|---|---|---|---|---|
| 404. | (c) | 405. | (b) | 406. | (c) | 407. | (d) |
| 408. | (c) | 409. | (a) | 410. | (b) | 411. | (c) |
| 412. | (d) | 413. | (c) | 414. | (c) | 415. | (c) |
| 416. | (a) | 417. | (a) | 418. | (b) | 419. | (a) |
| 420. | (c) | 421. | (a) | 422. | (c) | 423. | (a) |
| 424. | (b) | 425. | (b) | 426. | (a) | 427. | (d) |
| 428. | (d) | 429. | (a) | 430. | (c) | 431. | (a) |
| 432. | (d) | 433. | (c) | 434. | (c) | 435. | (b) |
| 436. | (b) | 437. | (c) | 438. | (a) | 439. | (c) |
| 440. | (a) | 441. | (a) | 442. | (a) | 443. | (d) |
| 444. | (b) | 445. | (c) | | | | |

## Unit I

| | | | | | | | |
|---|---|---|---|---|---|---|---|
| 446. | (b) | 447. | (a) | 448. | (b) | 449. | (d) |
| 450. | (c) | 451. | (c) | 452. | (a) | 453. | (a) |
| 454. | (c) | 455. | (a) | 456. | (b) | 457. | (a) |
| 458. | (d) | 459. | (b) | 460. | (b) | 461. | (c) |
| 462. | (c) | 463. | (d) | 464. | (a) | 465. | (d) |
| 466. | (a) | 467. | (a) | 468. | (b) | 469. | (a) |
| 470. | (b) | 471. | (b) | 472. | (c) | 473. | (a) |
| 474. | (b) | 475. | (a) | 476. | (c) | 477. | (b) |
| 478. | (c) | 479. | (c) | 480. | (a) | 481. | (c) |

| | | | | | | | |
|---|---|---|---|---|---|---|---|
| 482. | (b) | 483. | (a) | 484. | (a) | 485. | (c) |
| 486. | (a) | 487. | (a) | 488. | (c) | 489. | (a) |
| 490. | (b) | 491. | (d) | 492. | (b) | 493. | (c) |
| 494. | (d) | 495. | (b) | 496. | (a) | 497. | (b) |
| 498. | (b) | 499. | (c) | 500. | (d) | 501. | (b) |
| 502. | (b) | 503. | (b) | 504. | (b) | 505. | (a) |
| 506. | (b) | 507. | (a) | 508. | (a) | 509. | (d) |
| 510. | (b) | 511. | (c) | 512. | (a) | 513. | (a) |
| 514. | (c) | 515. | (d) | 516. | (a) | 517. | (a) |
| 518. | (a) | 519. | (a) | 520. | (c) | 521. | (b) |
| 522. | (a) | 523. | (c) | 524. | (a) | 525. | (a) |
| 526. | (b) | 527. | (c) | 528. | (b) | 529. | (a) |
| 530. | (b) | 531. | (a) | 532. | (b) | 533. | (d) |
| 534. | (b) | 535. | (b) | 536. | (b) | 537. | (c) |
| 538. | (a) | 539. | (c) | 540. | (b) | 541. | (a) |
| 542. | (b) | 543. | (b) | 544. | (d) | 545. | (a) |
| 546. | (b) | 547. | (b) | 548. | (b) | 549. | (d) |
| 550. | (a) | 551. | (d) | | | | |

## Unit J

| | | | | | | | |
|---|---|---|---|---|---|---|---|
| 552. | (d) | 553. | (d) | 554. | (a) | 555. | (a) |
| 556. | (b) | 557. | (c) | 558. | (c) | 559. | (c) |
| 560. | (d) | 561. | (b) | 562. | (c) | 563. | (c) |
| 564. | (d) | 565. | (a) | 566. | (b) | | |

# Commonwealth Literature

# 12

## UNIT A: HISTORICAL PERSPECTIVE AND BACKGROUND

1. What comprises Commonwealth literature? Literature written by the writers from Commonwealth countries
   (a) in English language
   (b) in English language with native flavour
   (c) in their native language
   (d) presenting a common agenda
2. Who have contributed significantly to Commonwealth literature?
   (a) third world emigrants
   (b) the native writers with exposure to English language and literature
   (c) the writers in exile
   (d) none of the above
3. Which countries have contributed to Commonwealth literature?
   (a) those who believe in the common heritage of mankind
   (b) those who were former colonies of England and learnt English
   (c) those who acquired English language for their writings
   (d) those who believe that English literature is the richest and try to emulate it
4. When did Commonwealth literature got its official status?
   (a) in 1950 in London
   (b) in 1964 in a Conference at Leeds
   (c) in 1965 in the first Conference of International Association of Commonwealth Literature

(d) in vogue since 1950 to refer to literature written in English produced in the Commonwealth countries

5. Commonwealth literature today stands for literatures written in English
   (a) in the Commonwealth countries
   (b) in the Commonwealth countries outside the Anglo-American tradition
   (c) anywhere
   (d) in India and South Africa only
6. What is the common factor in literature written by Commonwealth writers?
   (a) colonial experience and English language
   (b) Christianity
   (c) British influence in governance and trade
   (d) superiority of English language
7. These Commonwealth writers consciously choose English language because
   (a) it is rich
   (b) it is global in nature
   (c) it is the language they know best and are comfortable with
   (d) they are still under the colonial influence
8. In Commonwealth literature besides the English language what is the common factor?
   (a) their own native culture and tradition and its manifestation
   (b) their respect for British literature
   (c) simple adulation of British writers like Shakespeare and Milton
   (d) none
9. What is that which gives the literature of these Commonwealth writers their identity?
   (a) their own personality
   (b) their own native articulate voice
   (c) names of the characters and places
   (d) the structure of the chosen genre

10. What makes Commonwealth literature so rich?
    (a) variety and traditions
    (b) varied flavour
    (c) different social problems of the country of the writers origin
    (d) mixed experiences
11. The Calcutta Madarsa was established by Warren Hastings in
    (a) 1781 (b) 1783 (c) 1785 (d) 1787
12. Who organized the Royal Asiatic Society of Bengal in 1784?
    (a) Warren Hastings (b) Sir William Jones
    (c) Sir Thomas Munro (d) None of the above
13. India's first newspaper "Hicky's Bengal Gazette" came out in
    (a) 1776 (b) 1778 (c) 1780 (d) 1782
14. The Hindu College at Calcutta was established in
    (a) 1815 (b) 1816 (c) 1817 (d) 1818
15. The Renaissance in modern Indian literature begins with
    (a) Raja Rammohan Roy (b) H.L.V. Derozio
    (c) Rabindranath Tagore (d) Madhusudan Dutt
16. Raja Rammohan Roy started the Atmiya Sabha in
    (a) 1814 (b) 1815 (c) 1816 (d) 1817
17. "Sambad Kaumudi" was the name of a
    (a) magazine (b) paper (c) book (d) journal
18. Who became a teacher of English literature in the Hindu College at the age of 18 only?
    (a) Madhusudan Dutt (b) Raja Rammohan Roy
    (c) Kashiprosad Ghose (d) H.L.V. Derozio
19. 'My country, in thy days of glory past.
    A beauteous halo circled round thy brow.'
    These lines appear in the poem of
    (a) Sarojini Naidu (b) Toru Dutt
    (c) H.L.V. Derozio (d) Madhusudan Dutt

20. The first Railway was opened in India in
    (a) 1853 (b) 1854 (c) 1855 (d) 1856
21. The first telegraph line and a postal system were started in
    (a) 1851 (b) 1853 (c) 1854 (d) 1855
22. 'Poetry' is a sonnet, which explicates the concept of poetic creation of the poet
    (a) H.L.V. Derozio (b) Toru Dutt
    (c) Sarojini Naidu (d) Manmohan Ghose
23. Which poet died at the early age of 21?
    (a) Rabindranath Tagore (b) Sri Aurobindo
    (c) H.L.V. Derozio (d) Kamala Das
24. "The Fakir of Jungheera" is a well-known work written by
    (a) Kashiprosad Ghose (b) H.L.V. Derozio
    (c) Toru Dutt (d) None of the above
25. Who edited the English weekly "The Hindu Intelligence"?
    (a) Madhusudan Dutt (b) Raja Rammohan Roy
    (c) Kashiprosad Ghose (d) H.L.V. Derozio
26. Who has called himself the 'first Hindu' who has ventured to publish a volume of English poem?
    (a) Madhusudan Dutt (b) R.C. Dutt
    (c) K.P. Ghose (d) Sri Aurobindo
27. Which poet has been compared to Keats regarding unbounded sympathy with nature?
    (a) H.L.V. Derozio (b) Toru Dutt
    (c) Sarojini Naidu (d) Madhusudan Dutt
28. Who has composed the great Bengali epic *Meghanad Badha*?
    (a) Raja Rammohan Roy (b) Madhusudan Dutt
    (c) Kashiprosad Ghose (d) None of the above
29. Brahmo Samaj was founded in
    (a) 1824 (b) 1826 (c) 1828 (d) 1830
30. "Let India learn from England practical righteousness. / Let England learn from India devotion, faith and prayer." These words have been spoken by
    (a) Raja Rammohan Roy (b) Kesub Chunder Sen
    (c) Ishwar Chandra Vidyasagar (d) Debendranath Tagore

31. "He is an orator born, not made ... has excellent quality of organization ...lightening like swiftness of thought and expression combined with a most iron self-control." Here 'he' stands for
    (a) Keshub Chunder Sen (b) Rabindranath Tagore
    (c) Dayanand Saraswati (d) Raja Rammohan Roy
32. Who was the founder of the Arya Samaj?
    (a) Raja Rammohan Roy (b) Dayanand Saraswati
    (c) Keshub Chunder Sen (d) Debendranath Tagore
33. Arya Samaj was founded in
    (a) 1870 (b) 1872 (c) 1874 (d) 1875
34. Who translated *The Bhagavad Gita* for *The Sacred Books of the East* series?
    (a) Kashinath Telang (b) M.G. Ranade
    (c) K.P. Ghose (d) None of the above
35. Who amongst the following taught at the Elphinstone College?
    (a) Raja Ram Mohan Roy (b) Dadabhai Naoroji
    (c) Sir Narayan Chandavarkar (d) M.G.Ranade
36. About whom Aurobindo said this? "he was a self illumined ecstatic and mystic without a single trace or touch of the alien thought or education upon him".
    (a) Ramakrishna Paramhamsa (b) Swami Vivekananda
    (c) Dayanand Saraswathi (d) Raja Ram Mohan Roy
37. The book *Gandhi: A Life* has been written by
    (a) Krishna Kripalani (b) N.C. Kelkar
    (c) V.S. Srinivasa Sastri (d) C. Rajagopalachari
38. The well-known novel *Inquilab* has been written by
    (a) K.S. Venkataramani (b) Khwaja Ahmad Abbas
    (c) K. Nagarajan (d) Mahatma Gandhi
39. The eight volume biography *Mahatma* is a work of
    (a) Hiren Mukerjee (b) E.M.S. Namboodripad
    (c) D.G. Tendulkar (d) J.B. Kripalani

40. The classic *Rise of the Maratha Power* was written by
(a) Mahadev Govind Ranade (b) Gopal Krishna Gokhale
(c) Dayanand Saraswati (d) Kashinath Telang

41. Prarthana Samaj was founded in
(a) 1865 (b) 1867 (c) 1869 (d) 1871

42. Who has been called 'the Father of Indian Economics'?
(a) A.O. Hume (b) M.G. Ranade
(c) Kashinath Telang (d) Sir Narayan Chandavarkar

43. Who has written the book *Poverty and Un-British Rule in India*?
(a) Dadabhai Naoroji (b) C. Rangacharlu
(c) M.G. Ranade (d) Phirozeshah Mehta

44. Paramahamsa Sabha was founded in
(a) 1847 (b) 1848 (c)1849 (d) 1850

45. Madame Blavatsky founded .......... at New York in 1875.
(a) Prarthana Samaj (b) Theosophical Society
(c) Paramahamsa Sabha (d) Arya Samaj

46. Who established the Ramakrishna Mission?
(a) Swami Vivekananda (b) Ramakrishna Paramhamsa
(c) Dayanand Saraswati (d) Subramania Bharati

47. *Kamalambal*, one of the great novels in Tamil has been written by
(a) Subramania Bharati (b) B.R. Rajan Iyer
(c) William Q. Judge (d) Vivekananda

## UNIT B: INDIAN WRITING IN ENGLISH: POETRY

### 1. Toru Dutt

48. *The Young Spanish Maiden*, a well known novel has been written by
(a) Toru Dutt (b) Phirozeshah Mehta
(c) Rabindranath Tagore (d) G.K. Gokhale

49. The French novel *Le Journal de Mademoisalled Arvers* has been written by
    (a) Sarojini Naidu (b) Toru Dutt
    (c) Subramania Bharati (d) None of the above
50. 'Love came to Flora asking for a flower / (That would of flowers be undisputed queen.')
    These lines have been written by
    (a) Sarojini Naidu (b) Sri Aurobindo
    (c) Toru Dutt (d) Rabindranath Tagore
51. Whose father was Govin Chunder, a good linguist and a cultured man with literary leanings and generous impulses?
    (a) Sarojini Naidu (b) Rabindranath Tagore
    (c) Toru Dutt (d) Manmohan Ghose
52. Who has written these lines?
    "In memory till the hot tears blind mine eyes!/What is that dirge-like murmur that. I hear/Like the sea breaking on a shingle beach?"
    (a) Toru Dutt (b) Sri Aurobindo
    (c) H.L.V. Derozio (d) Manmohan Ghose
53. Who has written the poem "The Lotus"?
    (a) Rabindranath Tagore (b) Toru Dutt
    (c) Sarojini Naidu (d) None of the above
54. Drunken with beauty then./One night swoon or gaze and gaze/On a primeval Eden, in amaze." These lines appear in which poem of Toru Dutt?
    (a) "Baugmaree" (b) "The Lotus"
    (c) "Our Casuarina Tree" (d) "The Tree of Life"
55. In which poem Toru Dutt has tried to recapture the past and to immortalize the moments of time so recaptured?
    (a) "Our Casuarina Tree" (b) "Baugmaree"
    (c) "The Lotus" (d) "Sita"
56. Who has written the following lines?
    "In those far-off primeval times/Far India's daughters were not pent/In closed zenanas."
    (a) Toru Dutt (b) Sarojini Naidu
    (c) Tagore (d) Sri Aurobindo

## 2. Romesh Chunder Dutt

57. Romesh Chunder Dutt became President of the Indian National Congress in
(a) 1898 (b) 1899 (c) 1900 (d) 1901

58. Who has written the famous book, *The Economic History of British India?*
(a) Romesh Chunder Dutt (b) Bankim Chandra
(c) Madhusudan Dutt (d) K.P. Ghose

59. Which book of Romesh Chunder Dutt gives a picture of Bengali life in the 19th century?
(a) *The Slave Girl*
(b) *The Lake of Palms*
(c) *A Brief History of Ancient and Modern Bengal*
(d) *Lays of Ancient India*

60. Which poet adopted Locksley Hall metre?
(a) Toru Dutt (b) Manmohan Ghose
(c) Romesh Chunder Dutt (d) Sri Aurobindo

61. "Didst thou, mother, bear the hero fathomless like ocean dread,/Whose unfailing glistening arrows like its countless billows sped." These lines have been taken from which poem of Romesh Chunder Dutt?
(a) "The Mahabharata" (b) "The Ramayana"
(c) "Lays of Ancient India" (d) None of the above

62. Which novel of Romesh Chunder Dutt portrays 17th century Agra?
(a) *The Slave Girl* (b) *Todar Mull*
(c) *The Lake of Palms* (d) *Sivaji*

## 3. Manmohan Ghose

63. Manmohan Ghose was the elder brother of
(a) Sri Aurobindo (b) Romesh Chunder Dutt
(c) K.P. Ghose (d) Lotika Ghose

64. "O what a heaven, what land unknown/To Julian's happy sight is shown ! /

To all his agonies, all his sights/What opening, sudden Paradise !" These lines have been written by

(a) Madhusudan Dutt (b) Toru Dutt
(c) Manmohan Ghose (d) Sarojini Naidu

65. *Primavera* is a collection of poems written by

(a) Rabindranath Tagore (b) Manmohan Ghose
(c) Toru Dutt (d) Sri Aurobindo

66. Which was the only collection of poems published during the life time of Manmohan Ghose?

(a) *Primavera* (b) *Songs of Life and Death*
(c) *Love Songs and Elegies* (d) *Immortal Love*

67. Who said this? "I shall bury myself in poetry, simply and solely".

(a) Manmohan Ghose (b) Romesh Chunder Dutt
(c) Aurobindo Ghose (d) Rabindranath Tagore

68. Which work of Manmohan Ghose was published posthumously?

(a) *Love Songs and Elegies* (b) *Songs of Life and Death*
(c) *Perseus, the Gorgon Slayer* (d) *Nala and Damayanti*

### 4. Rabindranath Tagore

69. Who has written *Reminiscences?*

(a) Sri Aurobindo (b) Sarojini Naidu
(c) Rabindranath Tagore (d) Manmohan Ghose

70. Rabindranath Tagore was awarded the Nobel Prize for literature for his masterpiece

(a) *Gora* (b) *Gitanjali*
(c) *The Wreck* (d) *The Home and the World*

71. Which poem of Tagore was first written in English and later translated into Bengali?

(a) "The Child" (b) "Urvashi"
(c) "The Gardener" (d) "Superior"

72. Tagore wrote primarily in

(a) English (b) Hindi (c) Bengali (d) French

73. "Not a man only but an age had made its way at last into history ... He has summed up in himself a whole age

in which India had moved into the modern world." In the above sentence, 'a man' refers to

(a) Aurobindo (b) Tagore
(c) Raja Ram Mohan Roy (d) Ramanujan

74. "The current of daily life moves slowly between the village near the hill and the one by the river bank." These lines appear in which poem of Tagore?
(a) "Heaven of Freedom" (b) "The Gardener"
(c) "Breezy April" (d) "The Child"

75. The poem "Silent Steps" has been composed by
(a) Rabindranath Tagore (b) Sri Aurobindo
(c) Toru Dutt (d) Sarojini Naidu

76. "No body knows the real cause of my tears./All of them seek their cause elsewhere." These lines appear in Tagore's poem
(a) "Dui Nari" (b) "Vadhu"
(c) "Silent Steps" (d) "Heaven of Freedom"

77. Name the first Indian poet who received the Nobel Prize for Literature?
(a) Sri Aurobindo (b) Rabindranath Tagore
(c) Bankim Chandra Chatterjee (d) Sarojini Naidu

78. In which year was Tagore awarded the Nobel Prize for Literature?
(a) 1912 (b) 1913 (c) 1914 (d) 1915

79. Who translated Bengali version of *Gitanjali* into English?
(a) Gogonendranath (b) Abanindranath
(c) Rabindranath (d) Dwijendranath

80. Whose lines are these? "Into that heaven of Freedom my father let my country awake".
(a) Anita Desai (b) Sarojini Naidu
(c) Rabindranath Tagore (d) Kamala Markandaya

### 5. Sri Aurobindo

81. Which of the following writers was born in Calcutta on 15th August?
(a) Sri Aurobindo (b) Rabindranath Tagore
(c) Toru Dutt (d) Sarojini Naidu

82. Sri Aurobindo left Calcutta for Pondicherry in
(a) 1908 (b) 1910 (c) 1912 (d) 1914

83. Which work of Sri Aurobindo is a translation of Kalidasa's *Vikramorvasiya*?
(a) "Urvasie" (b) "Perseus the Deliverer"
(c) "Love and Death" (d) "The Hero and the Nymph"

84. *The Life Divine* is a well known work of
(a) Sarojini Naidu (b) Mahatma Gandhi
(c) Sri Aurobindo (d) Manmohan Ghose

85. In Sri Aurobindo's poetry which symbol is the supreme symbol of the essence and efflorescence of God?
(a) Rose (b) Light (c) Love (d) Nature

86. Which work is considered to be the most powerful artistic work in the world for expanding man's mind towards the Absolute?
(a) *Gitanjali* (b) *Savitri*
(c) *The Life Divine* (d) None of the above

87. "No one can write about my life because it has not been on the surface for men to see" Who wrote this?
(a) Sri Aurobindo (b) Rabindranath Tagore
(c) Toru Dutt (d) Sarojini Naidu

88. Who became editor of the "Bandemataram" a new English daily started by Bipin Chandra Pal, in 1906?
(a) Romesh Chunder Dutt (b) Manmohan Ghose
(c) Sri Aurobindo (d) Rabindranath Tagore

89. Which monthly philosophical journal devoted to the exposition of an integral view of life and existence was launched by Madame Mirra Richard (known as the Mother) and Sri Aurobindo on 15 August 1914?
(a) "The Arya" (b) "The Karmayogin"
(c) "The Bandemataram" (d) None of the above

90. Aurobindo's magnum opus the philosophical epic *Savitri* started appearing in instalments from
(a) 1945 onwards (b) 1946 onwards
(c) 1947 onwards (d) 1948 onwards

91. Aurobindo's masterpiece *Savitri* has been divided into .......... books.
(a) 11 (b) 12 (c) 13 (d) 14

92. "Her rapid fingers taught a flower song,/The stanzaed movement of a marriage hymn." These lines appear in which work of Aurobindo?
(a) "Rose of God" (b) *Savitri*
(c) *The Life Divine* (d) *Love and Death*

93. "The natural miracle was wrought once more/In the immutable ideal world/One human moment was eternal mode." These lines appear in
(a) "Revelation" (b) "Satyavan and Savitri"
(c) "Transformation" (d) "The Tiger and the Deer"

94. Which poet had a vision of Lord Krishna in the Alipore Jail?
(a) Sri Aurobindo (b) Tagore
(c) Toru Dutt (d) Sarojini Naidu

95. In Aurobindo's poem "The Bird of Fire" the bird symbolizes
(a) death (b) soul's asviation
(c) life (d) God

96. In which poem Aurobindo observes, "An unseen Hand controls my rudder"?
(a) "Rose of God" (b) *Savitri*
(c) "The Infinite Adventure" (d) "The Bird of Fire"

### 6. Sarojini Naidu

97. Which is Sarojini Naidu's first collection of poems?
(a) *The Bird of Time* (b) *The Golden Threshold*
(c) *The Broken Wing* (d) *The Feather of the Dawn*

98. "Life is a prism of My light/And Death the shadow of My face."
These lines have been uttered by
(a) Toru Dutt (b) Sri Aurobindo
(c) Sarojini Naidu (d) Rabindranath Tagore

99. Sarojini Naidu composed an English poem at the age of
(a) 12 (b) 13 (c) 14 (d) 15

100. Lightly, O lightly we bear her along,/She sways like a flower in the wind of our song ." These lines appear in
(a) "Indian Weavers" (b) "Palanquin Bearers"
(c) "Coromandel Fishers" (d) "Indian Dancers"

101. In 1906, at the Calcutta session of the Indian Social Conference which poet/poetess linked up the suppression of women's rights in India with the loss of the country's freedom?
(a) Toru Dutt (b) Sri Aurobindo
(c) Sarojini Naidu (d) Rabindranath Tagore

102. Sarojini Naidu's second volume of poems *The Bird of Time* came out in
(a) 1912 (b) 1913 (c) 1914 (d) 1915

103. Which poem of Sarojini Naidu is addressed to Gandhi?
(a) "Awake" (b) "The Lotus"
(c) "Indian Weavers" (d) None

104. Which is Sarojini Naidu's last collection of poems?
(a) *The Broken Wing* (b) *The Bird of Time*
(c) *The Golden Threshold* (d) None of the above

105. Sarojini Naidu presided over the Congress in
(a) 1923 (b) 1924 (c) 1925 (d) 1926

106. "Sarojini Naidu's work has a real beauty." Who said this?
(a) Tagore (b) Vivekananda
(c) Aurobindo (d) Gandhi

107. "Give me to drink each joy and pain/Which Thine eternal hand can mete ....."
These lines appear in
(a) "The Soul's Prayer" (b) "Caprice"
(c) "Village Song" (d) "Indian Weavers"

### 7. A.K. Ramanujan

108. Which of these has not been composed by A.K. Ramanujan?
(a) *The Striders* (b) *Selected Poems*
(c) *Relations* (d) *Draupadi and Jayadratha*

109. Which poem of Ramanujan is associated with the Hindu myth of Lord Vishnu?
(a) "The Striders" (b) "Still View of Another Grace"
(c) "Obituary" (d) "Breaded Fish"

110. "No, not only prophets / Walk on water ...." These lines have been taken from which of Ramanujan's poem?
(a) "Obituary" (b) "The Striders"
(c) "Breaded Fish" (d) "A Plant"

**8. Nissim Ezekiel**

111. Nissim Ezekiel was born into a Jewish family in
(a) Bombay (b) Bangalore
(c) Calcutta (d) New Delhi

112. Who has uttered this? "I like to make controlled meaningful statements avoiding extremes of thought and expresssion."
(a) Kamala Das (b) K.N. Darawallah
(c) Jayanta Mahapatra (d) Nissim Ezekiel

113. Which is Ezekiel's first book of poems?
(a) *A Time to Change* (b) *The Unifinished*
(c) *Hymns in Darkness* (d) *The Third Man*

114. Which poem of Nissim Ezekiel is a critique of the man-woman relationship in modern society?
(a) "Island" (b) "Woman and Child"
(c) "Philosophy" (d) "Poet, Lover, Birdwatcher"

115. Which poem of Ezekiel is an autobiographical poem?
(a) "Background, Casually" (b) "Poet, Lover, Birdwatcher"
(c) "Torso of a Woman" (d) "Island"

116. "To force the pace and never to be still
Is not the way of those who study birds
Or woman."
These lines have been taken from Ezekiel's poem
(a) "Background Casually" (b) "Poet, Lover, Birdwatcher"
(c) "Woman and Child" (d) "Philosophy"

### 9. Kamala Das

117. Which writer has won the PEN's Asian Poetry Prize?
(a) Shiv K. Kumar (b) Kamala Das
(c) Nissim Ezekiel (d) A.K. Ramanujan

118. Who has said this? "I am an Indian, very brown, born in Malabar".
(a) Kamala Das (b) Jayanta Mahapatra
(c) K.N. Daruwalla (d) Adil Jussawalla

119. *Summer in Calcutta is a poetical collection of*
(a) Sarojini Naidu (b) Amrita Pritam
(c) Kamala Das (d) Anita Desai

120. In which poem Kamala Das ironically provides a panacea for a happy married life? "Husbands and wives, here is my advice to you/Obey each other's crazy commands."
(a) "Composition" (b) "The Descendants"
(c) "An Introduction" (d) "In Love"

121. Who is the writer of *A Doll for the Child Prostitute and Other Stories*?
(a) Kamala Das (b) Bharati Mukherjee
(c) Jai Nimbkar (d) Anita Desai

122. In which story of Kamala Das lesbian relationship has been described?
(a) "Iqbal" (b) "The Guest"
(c) "A Doll for the Child Prostitute" (d) None of the above

123. "It was not to gather knowledge of yet another man that I came to you but to learn/What I was, and by learning, to learn to grow,/but every Lesson you gave was about yourself."
Who has written this?
(a) Kamala Das (b) Shiv K. Kumar
(c) A.K. Ramanujan (d) J. Mahapatra

124. *My Story* is the autobiography of
(a) Kamala Das (b) Tagore
(c) Sarojini Naidu (d) Vivekanand

### 10. Shiv K. Kumar

125. "In this triple-baked continent/women don't etch angry eyebrows/on mud walls." These lines have been written by
(a) Jayanta Mahapatra (b) Shiv K. Kumar
(c) Kamala Das (d) Nissim Ezekiel

126. Which is the latest book of verse of Shiv K. Kumar?
(a) *Articulate Silences* (b) *Cobwebs in the Sun*
(c) *Woolgathering* (d) *Woodpeckers*

127. Shiv K. Kumar has described sleeplessness caused by one's wife's infidelity in which poem?
(a) "Insomnia" (b) "Rape"
(c) "Bedroom" (d) "The Ring"

128. "I know where my wife's secrets/lie sealed. Each night I hear / the same tato in my skull's chamber." These lines appear in
(a) "Shadow Lines" (b) "Insomnia"
(c) "Sleep Walking" (d) "Blackout"

129. Death and resurrection are recurrent themes in which of Ramanujan's books?
(a) *Woolgathering* (b) *Woodpeckers*
(c) *Trapfalls in the sky* (d) *Subterfuges*

### 11. K.N. Daruwalla

130. In which year Daruwalla won the Sahitya Akademi Award?
(a) 1981 (b) 1982 (c) 1983 (d) 1984

131. Which poet has described his poetry as a 'totally impressionistic recording of subjective responses'?
(a) Adil Jussawalla (b) Keki N. Daruwalla
(c) A. K. Ramanujan (d) Kamala Das

132. Which poem of Daruwalla revolves around the experiences of hatred, violence and death?
(a) *Rumination* (b) *Death of a Bird*
(c) *The Ghaghra in Spate* (d) *The Professor Condoles*

133. "... Ten miles to her flank/peasants go fishing in rice-fields/and women in chauffer-driver cars/go looking for driftwood ...." These lines occur in
(a) *Death of a Bird* (b) *The Ghaghra in Spate*
(c) *The Professor Condoles* (d) None of the above

## 12. R. Parthasarthy

134. Which is the volume written by R. Parthasarthy?
(a) *Rough Passage* (b) *Subterfuges*
(c) *Articulate Silences* (d) *Woodpeckers*

135. "Cultivating an extreme austerity in style ..... his poems are so few but they are marble-images of integrity.." Here 'his' refers to
(a) Arun Kolatkar (b) R. Parthasarthy
(c) Nissim Ezekiel (d) A.K. Ramanujan

136. "To live in Tamil Nadu is to be conscious everyday of an importance."
This line appears in the poem
(a) "Homecoming" (b) "Delhi"
(c) "Dawn at Puri" (d) "The Mountain"

## 13. Adil Jussawalla

137. Who among the following poets was a Parsi educated at Anglian School in Bombay?
(a) Adil Jussawalla (b) R. Parthasarthy
(c) Jayant Mahapatra (d) Arun Kolatkar

138. In which year Jussawalla became the member of the International Writing Programme, Iowa
(a)1975 (b) 1976 (c) 1977 (d) 1978

139. The poem "The Waiters" has been taken from Jussawalla's volume
(a) *Land's End* (b) *New Writing in India*
(c) *Missing Person* (d) None of the above

140. "Behind our pasted smiles; their darkness grew/To insight in their day; they stand aloof." These lines appear in the poem
(a) "Sea Breeze, Bombay" (b) "The Waiters"
(c) "The Boatride" (d) None of the above

### 14. Gieve Patel

141. Who among the following poets is a doctor by profession?
(a) Arun Kolatkar (b) Gieve Patel
(c) R. Parthasarthy (d) K.N. Daruwalla

142. The poem "On Killing a Tree" has been composed by
(a) Gieve Patel (b) A.K. Ramanujan
(c) Adil Jussawalla (d) Kamala Das

143. "Then the matter/Of scorching and choking/In sun and air,/Browning, hardening/Twisting, withering." These lines appear in
(a) "Forensic Medicine" (b) "Hunger"
(c) "On Killing a Tree" (d) "The Mountain"

### 15. Jayanta Mahapatra

144. Jayanta Mahapatra is obsessed with the past and the present of
(a) Assam (b) West Bengal
(c) Orissa (d) Karnataka

145. "Thinking to escape his belief/I go to meet the spectre of belief"
These lines have been written by
(a) Jayanta Mahapatra (b) Nissim Ezekiel
(c) Kamala Das (d) A.K. Ramanujan

146. Which work of Mahapatra won him the Sahitya Akademi Award in 1981?
(a) "The False Start" (b) "Relationship"
(c) "Close the Sky" (d) "Waiting"

147. Which work of Mahapatra is an expansion of the private lyric voice into a chain of meditations?
(a) "Relationship" (b) "Ten by Ten"
(c) "Swayamvara" (d) "A Father's House"

148. "Late in the evening of life/an embarrassment prevents the world from speaking" These lines have been taken from
(a) "Dawn at Puri" (b) "The Mountain"
(c) "Hunger" (d) "Again one day walking by the river"

### 16. Arun Kolatkar

149. Arun Kolatkar is a bilingual poet who writes both in
   (a) Marathi and English (b) Bengali and English
   (c) English and Punjabi (d) Marathi and Punjabi

150. Which poem of Kolatkar has been considered as the poet's odyssey to the temple of Khandoba at Jejuri, a small town in western Maharashtra?
   (a) "The Boatride" (b) "Jejuri"
   (c) "The Bus" (d) None of the above

151. "... his wife has dismissed/the waves like a queen/a band of oiled acrobats."
   These lines have been composed by
   (a) Adil Jussawalla (b) Arun Kolatkar
   (c) Shiv K. Kumar (d) K.N. Daruwalla

152. In the poem "The Bus" each stanza is of how many lines?
   (a) 3 (b) 4 (c) 5 (d) 6

### 17. Mamta Kalia

153. The poem "Tribute to Papa" has been composed by
   (a) Mamta Kalia (b) Kamala Das
   (c) K.N. Daruwalla (d) Kolatkar

154. Who has authored the collection of poems *Khanti Gharelu Aurat?*
   (a) Kamala Das (b) Mamta Kalia
   (c) Shiv K. Kumar (d) Jayanta Mahapatra

## UNIT C: INDIAN WRITING IN ENGLISH: SHORT STORY

155. Kamala Satthianadhan has written the first collection of short stories
   (a) *Love and life Behind Purdah*
   (b) *Stories of Indian Christian Life*
   (c) *Sunbabies: Studies in the Child Life of India*
   (d) None of the above

156. Which collection of short stories of Cornelia Sorabji makes a study of legends, mythological and Puranic about Indian women?
   (a) *Sunbabies: Studies in the Child Life of Indian*
   (b) *Love and life Behind Purdha*

(c) *Between the Twilights: Being Studies of Indian Women by one of Themselves*
(d) *Indian Tales of the Great Ones*

157. The stories in which collection are in the direct tradition of *Panchatantra*
(a) Shovona Devi's *The Oriental Pearls: Indian Folklore*
(b) Sunity Devi's *Bengal Dacoits and Tigers*
(c) Kamala Satthianadhan's *Stories of Indian Christian Life*
(d) Cornelia Sorabji's *Love and Life behind Purdah*

158. *Tales of Bengal*, a collection of short stories has been written by
(a) Santa and Seeta Chatterjee (b) Svarna Kumari Ghosal
(c) C. Trikannad Ramobai (d) Ela Sen

159. Which author has written stories relating to Famine-stricken Bengal?
(a) *Sunity Devi* (b) *Cornelia Sorabji*
(c) *Ela Sen* (d) *C.T. Ramabai*

160. Attiah Hosain wrote a collection of short stories
(a) *Phoenix led and Other Stories* (b) *A Garland of Stories*
(c) *Shadow on the Wall* (d) *Gifts of Passage*

161. Who has written the story *Who Cares*?
(a) Attiah Hosain (b) Santha Rama Rau
(c) Cornelia Sorabji (d) Ela Sen

162. Who has portrayed two women characters, Janaki, a traditional Hindu housekeeper and the narrator, an emancipated foreign returned woman with her who cares attitude?
(a) Santha Rama Rau (b) Shovona Devi
(c) Santa Chatterjee (d) C.T. Ramabai

163. The collection *The House in the Hills and Other Stories*, has been authored by
(a) Sujata Bala Subramaniam (b) Dina Mehta
(c) Jai Nimbkar (d) Rita Singh Mathur

164. In which story of Sujata Bala the effect of over-dominance by parents on children is seen?
   (a) "The Zamindar of Pillapuram"
   (b) "Ants"
   (c) "A Time for Hunger"
   (d) "Betrayal"

165. Which author is a gifted story teller with a touch of humour?
   (a) Dina Mehta
   (b) Sujata Bala
   (c) Malathi Rao
   (d) Shashi Deshpande

166. Who has written the collection *The Other Woman and Other Stories*?
   (a) Nergis Dalal
   (b) Dina Mehta
   (c) Bharati Mukherjee
   (d) Kamala Das

167. Rita Singh Mathur has written the collection of stories
   (a) *Weeds*
   (b) *Shitfing Skies: A Collection of Short Stories*
   (c) *The House in the Hills and Other Stories*
   (d) *The Middleman and Other Stories*

168. Indrayani Sowkar's stories are collected in
   (a) *Weeds*
   (b) *The Old House and Other Stories*
   (c) *Coigns of Vantage*
   (d) *The House on the Hills and Other Stories*

169. Which work is a subtle delineation of the tragedy of partition?
   (a) *Green Parrots in a Cage*
   (b) *The White Dove*
   (c) *The Lotus Leaves*
   (d) *The Guest*

170. Monika Varma's "Those that Gifts" ... unveils the hypocrisy of a
   (a) teacher
   (b) priest
   (c) politician
   (d) doctor

171. The story "A Dead Wife" which is a pathetic story of a 17 year girl married to a widower of almost thrice her age, has been written by
   (a) Gopi Gauba
   (b) Monika Varma
   (c) Sunita Jain
   (d) Rita Singh Mathur

172. Who has written the collection of short stories *Came for a Coffee, Please*?
(a) Malathi Rao (b) Margaret Chatterji
(c) Juliette Banerjee (d) Vasantha Ravindran

173. In which story Malathi Rao has referred to the myth of Sisyphus?
(a) "The Crowd" (b) "The Metaphor of Stone"
(c) "The Masseuse" (d) "Retirement"

174. In which story of Malathi Rao there is a reference to an aged couple who get their fifth child at the age of 45?
(a) A Marriage is Performed (b) The Crowd
(c) Retirement (d) Come for a Coffee Please

175. Jayashree Chatterjee, living in Kuwait is a writer of
(a) *The Old House and Other Stories* (b) *Passion Fruit*
(c) *Where Oleanders Don't Grow* (d) *The Other Woman and Other Stories*

176. Vasanth Ravindran's story "Farewell" deals with evils of
(a) prostitution (b) arranged marriage
(c) dowry system (d) unemployment

177. Which story of Padma Hejmadi (Perera) is the story of the Kirits, a fisherfolk, who have sprung up the social ladder but are forced upon themselves mainly because of their birth?
(a) "Birthday Deathday" (b) "Monologue for Foreigners"
(c) "The School Master" (d) "Too late for Anger"

178. "Immersion" is a long story written by
(a) S.K. Chettur (b) Khwaja Ahmad Abbas
(c) Manjeri Isvaran (d) Khushwant Singh

179. Which story of Khwaja Ahmad Abbas describes the flight of pavement dwellers in Bombay?
(a) "Cartoon" (b) "One Thousand Nights"
(c) "Wheat and Roses" (d) "The Black Sun"

180. The recent collection of stories *A Bride for the Sahib* has been written by
(a) Mulk Raj Anand (b) R.K. Narayan
(c) Khushwant Singh (d) Raja Rao

181. *The Art of Dying*, a striking collection of short stories demonstrating the remarkable range of presenting Death of the Indian life has been written by
(a) Nergis Dalal (b) Githa Hariharan
(c) Geeta Mehta (d) Raji Narasimhan

182. Tagore's story ......... is a love story with political background.
(a) "Char Adhyay" (b) "Chaturanga"
(c) "Malancha" (d) None of the above

183. Which story of Tagore reflects his extraordinary understanding of a child's psychology?
(a) "Kabuliwallah" (b) "The Postmaster"
(c) "Atithi" (d) None of the above

184. Who has written the collection of short stories *The Thief of Nagarahalli and Other Stories*?
(a) Basavaraj Naikar (b) Tagore
(c) R.K. Narayan (d) Mulk Raj Anand

185. Who is the central character in the story "The Thief of Nagarahalli"?
(a) Bhalla (b) Malla
(c) Desai (d) Monappa

186. "Our life is like the balloon. We do not know when it bursts."
These lines occur in the story
(a) "All for Gold" (b) "Her Husband went to America"
(c) "The Thief of Nagarahalli" (d) "The Invisible Face"

187. In which story Basavaraj Naikar has tried to bring in the Oedipus myth with a slight twist?
(a) "She Wanted a Child" (b) "The Anonymous Letter"
(c) "Mother's Husband" (d) "Fulfilment"

188. In which story Naikar discusses campus conspiracy?
   (a) "The Anonymous Letter" (b) "When the News Came"
   (c) "Coffin in the house" (d) "The Invisible Face"

189. Who is the central character of the novel *The Sun Behind the Cloud?*
   (a) Madhavarao (b) Bhaskararao
   (c) Vilasarao (d) Ganesharao

190. In which story of Nergis Dalal the main character commits suicide in the end?
   (a) "The Intruder" (b) "The Connoisseur"
   (c) "The Exiles" (d) "The Sacrifice"

191. Whose stories are typically journalistic?
   (a) Bharati Mukherjee (b) Shashi Deshpande
   (c) Anita Desai (d) Nergis Dalal

## UNIT D: INDIAN WRITING IN ENGLISH: DRAMA

192. Which blank verse play of Aurobindo is a romance of Scandinavia, a tale of war and love?
   (a) *Perseus, the Deliverer* (b) *The Viziers of Bassora*
   (c) *Rodogune* (d) *Eric*

193. Which play of Aurobindo was posthumously published in 1858?
   (a) *Rodogune* (b) *The Viziers of Bassora*
   (c) *Eric* (d) *Perseus, the Deliverer*

194. Cleopatra is a character in Aurobindo's play
   (a) *Perseus, the Deliverer* (b) *Rodogune*
   (c) *Vasavadutta* (d) None of the above

195. In which play of Aurobindo there is a slave girl, Anice-al-jalice?
   (a) *The Viziers of Bassora* (b) *Vasavadutta*
   (c) *Eric* (d) *Rodogune*

196. The play entitled *Nala and Damayanti* has been written by
   (a) Sri Aurobindo (b) P.A. Krishnaswamy
   (c) Vasudeva Rao (d) None

197. "Millions dying and dead
In Europe
In Russia
In China"
These lines appear in Harindranath Chattopadhyaya's play
(a) *The Parrot* (b) *Siddharta: Man of Peace*
(c) *The Evening Lamp* (d) *The Coffin*

198. Whose plays are inspired by Puranic themes?
(a) Sri Aurobindo (b) Vasudeva Rao
(c) T.P. Kailasam (d) Harindranath Chattopadhyay

199. The play *Karna: the Brahmin's Curse* has been written by
(a) T.P. Kailasam (b) Tagore
(c) Vijay Tendulkar (d) Sri Aurobindo

200. Bharati Sarabhi's, the most distinguished of the women dramatists, first play is
(a) *Two Women* (b) *The Well of the People*
(c) *The Trial Celestial* (d) None of the above

201. *Hali* is a short poetic play written by
(a) A.S.P. Ayyar (b) Bharati Sarabhai
(c) T.P. Kailasam (d) G.V. Desani

202. Which play of Asif Currimbhoy is a powerful study of a Kathakali dancer?
(a) *The Doldrummers* (b) *The Dumb Dancer*
(c) *Thorns on a Canvas* (d) *The Restaurant*

203. Which play is a three-act play in verse on the controversial killing of Afzal Khan by Shivaji?
(a) *Tiger Claw* (b) *The Captives*
(c) *Om* (d) *The Clock*

204. Which play of Tagore is considered to be his first characteristic play?
(a) *Malini* (b) *Sacrifice*
(c) *The Ascetic* (d) *The King and the Queen*

205. Which play of Tagore has Prakriti, the untouchable girl as the central character?
(a) *The King and the Queen* (b) *Chandalika*
(c) *Sacrifice* (d) *The Ascetic*

206. Amal, the invalid child is a character in Tagore's play
(a) *The Post Office* (b) *The King of the Dark Chamber*
(c) *Mukta Dhara* (d) *Chitra*

207. 'Revenge is stronger than the thin wine of love. Revenge is freedom—freedom from the coils of cloying sweetness' These lines appear in Tagore's play
(a) *Sacrifice* (b) *The King and the Queen*
(c) *Chandalika* (d) *The Cycle of Spring*

208. Which play of Tagore is a succinct to Tagorean version of Kalidasa's *Sakuntala*?
(a) *Mukta-Dhara* (b) *Chandalika*
(c) *Chitra* (d) *Red Oleanders*

209. In Tendulkar's play *Kanyadan*, Arun Athavale, a young dalit boy falls in love with
(a) Jyoti (b) Seva (c) Savitri (d) Binny

210. "The seed's diseased. All else is good. But the vital core that takes root that's rotten."
Who is the speaker of this sentence taken from *Vulture*?
(a) Hari (b) Sakharam
(c) Umakant (d) Rajaninath

211. The two leading female characters in the play *Vulture* are
(a) Mani and Rani (b) Manik and Rama
(c) Rani and Manik (d) Rita and Rama

212. The play *Naga-Mandala* has been written by
(a) Rabindranath Tagore (b) Aurobindo
(c) Girish Karnad (d) Vijay Tendulkar

213. Which dramatist writes his plays first in Kannada and then translates them into English?
(a) Vijay Tendulkar (b) Girish Karnad
(c) Tagore (d) None of the above

214. Which play of Karnad is a commentary on our own society and its politicians and officials?
(a) *Naga-Mandala* (b) *Yayati*
(c) *Tughlaq* (d) *Hayavadana*

215. Which work of Karnad deals with the stigma of casteism?
(a) *Hayavadana* (b) *Tale Danda*
(c) *Yayati* (d) *Tughlaq*

216. Which play dramatizes the conflict between tradition and modernity?
(a) *Yayati* (b) *Naga-Mandala*
(c) *Tughlaq* (d) *Hayavadana*

217. Who is the wife of Appanna, the central character of the play *Naga-Mandala*?
(a) Sita (b) Rani (c) Mohini (d) Radha

218. Which play presents the psychological and emotional trauma of a mother who awakens one morning to the shattering news that her beloved son is lying dead in the police morgue?
(a) Mahasweta Devi's *Mother of 1084* (b) Grisish Karnad's *Naga Mandala*
(c) Tendulkar's *Kanyadan* (d) Tagore's *Chitra*

219. Which play of Nissim Ezekiel deals with the life of a painter?
(a) *Nalini: A Comedy* (b) *Marriage Poem: A Tragi Comedy*
(c) *The Sleepwalkers* (d) None of the above

220. Which play of Asif Currimbhoy centres round the Bengal naxalite movement?
(a) *The Refugee* (b) *Inquilab*
(c) *The Miracle Seed* (d) *Monsoon*

221. The play *Murder at the Prayer Meeting* which echoes the title of Eliot's *Murder in the Cathedral* has been written by
(a) Lakhan Deb (b) Gurcharan Das
(c) Gieve Patel (d) Girish Karnad

222. *Chidambaram*, a flashback chronicle play in 14 episodes has been written by
(a) K. Nagarajan (b) Girish Karnad
(c) M.V. Rama Sarma (d) Gurcharan Das

## UNIT E: INDIAN WRITING IN ENGLISH: PROSE

223. *The Story of My Experiments with Truth*, the autobiography of Mahatma Gandhi was published in the year
(a) 1924 (b) 1925 (c )1926 (d) 1927

224. Gandhi began his first Satyagraha campaign in
(a) 1906 (b) 1907 (c) 1908 (d) 1909

225. "Quit India, and leave us to God or anarchy."
Who has said this?
(a) Gandhi (b) Nehru
(c) Vivekananda (d) Radhakrishnan

226. *Kandan the Patriot* which was written after the occurrence of Gandhi on the Indian horizon was composed by
(a) Vivekananda (b) Mahatma Gandhi
(c) K.S. Venkataramani (d) K.M. Munshi

227. The killing of Afzal Khan by Shivaji has been depicted in the play
(a) *Tiger-Claw* (b) *Om*
(c) *The Dumb Dancer* (d) *The Captives*

228. Who gave the slogan 'Do and Learn'?
(a) Jawaharlal Nehru (b) Mahatma Gandhi
(c) Rabindranath Tagore (d) Vivekananda

229. 'Young India' (Later Harijan) has been written by
(a) S. Radhakrishnan (b) N.C. Chaudhuri
(c) Gandhi (d) K.M. Munshi

230. "Non-violence is the first article of my faith. It is also the last article of my creed..."
Who has said this?
(a) Jawaharlal Nehru (b) S. Radhakrishnan
(c) Gandhi (d) Vivekananda

231. The year of Gandhi-Irwin pact is
(a) 1931 (b) 1932 (c) 1933 (d) 1934

232. Who has authored the book *Mahatma?*
(a) Hiren Mukerjee (b) D.G. Tendulkar
(c) E.M.S. Namboodripad (d) P.A. Wadia

233. *Gita Rahasya* is a well known book written by
(a) Gandhi (b) Jawaharlal Nehru
(c) Lokamanya Tilak (d) K.M. Munshi

234. 'Meanwhile you sit in Anand Bhavan, and Mummie sits in Malacca Gaol, and I here in Naini prison – and we miss each other sometimes ...'
Who has said this?
(a) Gandhi (b) Nehru
(c) Vivekananda (d) Aurobindo

235. 'A university stands for humanism, for tolerance, for reason, for progress, for the adventure of ideas and for the search of truth.'
Who has said this?
(a) Bal Gangadhar Tilak (b) Gandhi
(c) Nehru (d) Vivekananda

236. Which political leader is known as the 'King of Poona'?
(a) Nehru (b) Bal Gangadhar Tilak
(c) Gandhi (d) Gopalkrishna Gokhale

237. Who gave the slogan – 'Swaraj is my birthright'?
(a) Tilak (b) Gokhale
(c) M.A. Jinnah (d) Nehru

238. Who was the editor of "The National Herald"?
(a) V.K. Narasimhan (b) M. Chalapathi Rau
(c) Kuldip Nayar (d) K. Rangaswami

239. Who among the following personalities has been the Vice Chancellor of Banaras Hindu University?
(a) S. Radhakrishnan (b) Nirad C. Chaudhuri
(c) M.G. Ranade (d) Jawaharlal Nehru

240. S. Radhakrishnan has been the ambassador to which country?
(a) France (b) America
(c) Soviet Russia (d) China

241. "Mother in one form Thou art in the street,
and in another form Thou art the Universe.
I salute Thee Mother, I salute Thee."
Who said this?
(a) Vivekananda (b) Tagore
(c) Aurobindo (d) Gandhi

242. In which work Radhakrishnan subjected the thought of Western thinkers-Bergson, William James and Bertrand Russell to a searching examination in the light of the absolute thought of the Upanishads?
(a) *The Reign of Religion in Contemporary Philosophy*
(b) *The Philosophy of Rabindranath Tagore*
(c) *The Hindu View of Life*
(d) *An Idealist View of Life*

243. Which one of the following English renderings has not been done by Radhakrishnan?
(a) *Bhagavad Gita* (b) *Dhammapada*
(c) *Upanishads* (d) *Ramayana*

244. Which of the following authors signed himself as 'Vighneswara'?
(a) N. Raghunathan (b) S. Radhakrishnan
(c) Jawaharlal Nehru (d) Sri Aurobindo

245. Who has written *Reason and Intuition in Indian Culture*?
(a) Mahatma Gandhi (b) N. Raghunathan
(c) S. Radhakrishnan (d) Vivekananda

246. 'May that divine forgiveness illumine India's heart. Then indeed will Gandhiji's great faith, his noble audacity be vindicated
Who has observed this?
(a) N. Raghunathan (b) Jawaharlal Nehru
(c) Rabindranath Tagore (d) Humayun Kabir

247. 'Chaudhuri writes the English language better than any Indian has done before and is much the most erudite writer in the country.'
Who has said this?
(a) Khushwant Singh (b) Aurobindo
(c) Gandhi (d) None of the above

248. Who is the author of *A Passage to England*?
(a) Khushwant Singh (b) Nirad C. Chaudhuri
(c) R. K. Narayan (d) Mahatma Gandhi

249. Which was the first book of N.C. Chaudhuri?
(a) *A Passage to England* (b) *The Autobiography of an Unknown Indian*
(c) *The Continent of Circe* (d) None of the above

250. Which book of Chaudhuri is described as 'an essay on the peoples of India'?
(a) *The Autobiography of an Unknown Indian*
(b) *The Continent of Circe*
(c) *To Live or Not to Live*
(d) *A Passage to England*

251. "I know I am extreme. It is like a tug-of -war: I cannot stand up straight, or the other side will pull me down. But I know my exaggerations."
Who has said this?
(a) Mulk Raj Anand (b) Jawaharlal Nehru
(c) N. C. Chaudhuri (d) Khushwant Singh

252. N.C. Chaudhuri's essay "The Objective Method in History" is a part of which book?
(a) *The Continent of Circe* (b) *The Autobiography of an Unknown Indian*
(c) *A Passage to England* (d) *To Live or Not to Live*

## UNIT F: INDIAN WRITING IN ENGLISH: NOVEL

253. The first novel written in Bengali was *Alalir Gharer Dulal* (Spoilt Son of a Rich Family) and it was published in
(a) 1858 (b) 1859 (c) 1860 (d) 1861

254. The first novel published in English was
(a) *The Hindu Wife* (b) *Rajmohan's Wife*
(c) *Bianca* (d) *Roshinara*

255. Which novel of Bankim Chandra Chatterjee gave the Indians their national anthem 'Vande Mataram?
(a) *Rajmohan's Wife* (b) *Durgesh Nandini*
(c) *Anand Math* (d) None of the above

256. Tagore's *Choker Bali* has been translated into English as
(a) *Srikanta* (b) *Binodini*
(c) *Dhaukhana* (d) None of the above

257. Who has observed that for the Anjans in India, the 'river cult' is a symbol of their pre Indian existence?
(a) N.C. Chaudhuri (b) Mahatma Gandhi
(c) Rabindranath Tagore (d) K.S. Venkataramani

258. The river 'Padma' has been in the background of which novel?
(a) *Murugan the Tiller* (b) *Men and Rivers*
(c) *Kanthapura* (d) *The Serpent and the Rope*

259. Plantation life in Assam comprises many linguistic and racial strands. In which novel there is no reference to the plantation life?
(a) *Two Leaves and a Bud* (b) *Kanthapura*
(c) *Combat of Shadows* (d) *The World of Nagaraj*

260. Which was the first historical novel in English?
(a) *Padmini* (b) *Nur Jahan*
(c) *The Slave Girl of Agra* (d) *Ushahkal*

261. In which novel, the protagonist rejects a king's love and prefers to enter the Buddha's fold?
(a) *Ambapali* (b) *Nur Jahan*
(c) *Padmini* (d) *Chanakya and Chandragupta*

262. Which novel does not portray the horrors of partition?
(a) *Train to Pakistan* (b) *The Dark Dancer*
(c) *A Bend in the Ganges* (d) *Waiting for the Mahatma*

263. Which novel is a picture of Muslim life in modern Delhi?
(a) *Twilight in Delhi* (b) *The Lake of Palms*
(c) *The Dive for Death* (d) *Nasrin*

264. Which novel exposes the life of some of the nawabs and taluqdars of yesterday?
(a) *The New Krishna* (b) *Nasrin*
(c) *Kamini* (d) *Scented Dust*

265. In which novel the history of a Maratha brahmin family in South India has been described?
(a) *A Daughter's Shadow* (b) *Thillai Govindan*
(c) *The Gong of Shiva* (d) *Athawar House*

266. *Chemmeen,* a poignant record of the life of the seafaring folk on the coast of Allepey fringing the Arabian Sea, has been written by
(a) Thakazhi Sivasankara (b) Vyankatesh Madgulkar
(c) S. Menon Marath (d) Krishna Baldev Vaid

267. Which of the following novels does not portray a sanyasi?
(a) *He who Rides a Tiger* (b) *The Guide*
(c) *A Silence of Desire* (d) *A Bend in the Ganges*

268. In which novel, there is a magnificent recreation of the Vedic and Epic ages?
(a) *Bhagwan Parashurama* (b) *Seasons of Jupiter*
(c) *The Serpent and the Rope* (d) *Swami and Friends*

269. S.K. Chettur's *Bombay Murder* is a ......... novel.
(a) social (b) detective
(c) political (d) satirical

270. Which work of Tagore is 'to Indian fiction what Tolstoy's *War and Peace* is to the Russian?'
(a) *The Wreck* (b) *The Post Office*
(c) *Hungry Stones* (d) *Gora*

271. Bimal is the central character in Tagore's novel
(a) *Gora* (b) *The Home and the World*
(c) *Broken Ties* (d) *The Wreck*

272. Which work of Tagore has been described as 'the epic of India in transition at the most crucially intellectual period of its modern history?'
(a) *Gora* (b) *The Wreck*
(c) *Gitanjali* (d) *The Home and the World*

273. 'You have no caste, you make no distinctions and have no hatred—you are the only image of our welfare.' These lines appear in Tagore's work
(a) *The Wreck* (b) *Gora*
(c) *Chitra* (d) *The Post Office*

274. Damini is a character in Tagore's work
   (a) *The Home and the World*  (b) *Gora*
   (c) *Chaturanga*  (d) *The Wreck*

275. Which novel of Tagore is considered to be the first modern novel in the history of Indian literature?
   (a) *Gora*  (b) *The Home and the World*
   (c) *The Wreck*  (d) *Choker Bali*

**1. R.K. Narayan**

276. Chandran is the central character of the novel
   (a) *Swami and Friends*  (b) *The Bachelor of Arts*
   (c) *The English Teacher*  (d) *Mr. Sampath*

277. Which character of Narayan teaches English in a college?
   (a) Krishnan  (b) Margayya
   (c) Raman  (d) Jagan

278. "I have never opposed my husband or argued with him at any time... What he does is right. It is a wife's duty to feel so." These lines appear in the novel *The Dark Room.* Who is the speaker?
   (a) Gangu  (b) Savitri
   (c) Janamma  (d) Ponni

279. Which female character of Narayan is a true disciple of Gandhi?
   (a) Daisy  (b) Rosie  (c) Bharati  (d) Sita

280. Name the novel in which Narayan has portrayed a foreign lady
   (a) *The Guide*  (b) *The Painter of Signs*
   (c) *The Man-Eater of Malgudi*  (d) *The Vendor of Sweets*

281. Which is the only novel of Narayan in which he has depicted a co-wife?
   (a) *Grandmother's Tale*  (b) *The World of Nagaraj*
   (c) *The Guide*  (d) *The Dark Room*

282. 'I belolng to a family traditionally dedicated to the temple as dancers ... I danced in the village temple ... we are viewed as public women.'

Here 'I' stands for

(a) Grace (b) Rosie
(c) Daisy (d) Malathi

283. In which novel of R.K. Narayan, Susila is the wife of a teacher?

(a) *Mr. Sampath* (b) *The English Teacher*
(c) *The World of Nagaraj* (d) *Garandmother's Talc*

284. Name the first recipient of the Sahitya Akademi Award for the best writing in English

(a) R.K. Narayan (b) Raja Rao
(c) Mulk Raj Anand (d) Khushwant Singh

285. On which novel of R.K. Narayan, a very popular film was made?

(a) *Waiting for the Mahatma* (b) *Malgudi Days*
(c) *The Guide* (d) *Mr. Sampath*

286. Identify the work of Narayan on which a very popular T.V. serial was made

(a) *Malgudi Days* (b) *Mr. Sampath*
(c) *The Bachelor of Arts* (d) *The Man - Eater of Malgudi*

287. Which is the first novel of R.K. Narayan?

(a) *The Bachelor of Arts* (b) *Swami and Friends*
(c) *The Dark Room* (d) *The English Teacher*

288. In which novel of Narayan the action strays out of Malgudi?

(a) *The Guide* (b) *Waiting for the Mahatma*
(c) *The English Teacher* (d) *The Vendor of Sweets*

289. Which novel of Narayan won the Sahitya Akademi Award in 1960?

(a) *Swami and Friends* (b) *The Guide*
(c) *The Financial Expert* (d) *The English Teacher*

290. 'A dose of prison life is not a bad thing. It may be just what he needs now'
Who is the speaker?

(a) Jagan in *The Vendor of Sweets* (b) Raju in *The Guide*
(c) Margayya in *The Financial Expert* (d) Chandran in *The Bachelor of Arts*

## 2. Mulk Raj Anand

291. Which is Anand's only novel in which a woman has been chosen as the central character?
(a) *The Village* (b) *Untouchable*
(c) *Coolie* (d) *The Old Woman and the Cow*

292. Who is the heroine of the novel *The Old Woman and the Cow*?
(a) Sajani (b) Gauri (c) Leila (d) Sohini

293. "The accumulated strength of his giant body glistened in him with the desire for revenge, while horror, rage, indignation swept over his frame."
Here Anand is talking about which character?
(a) Munoo (b) Lalu (c) Bakha (d) Gangu

294. Which novel of Anand discusses the theme of exploitation of coolies working in tea garden at the hands of British officials?
(a) *The Village* (b) *Across the Black Waters*
(c) *The Sword and the Sickle* (d) *Two Leaves and a Bud*

295. Lalu is the central character in the novel
(a) *The Big Heart* (b) *Untouchable*
(c) *The Village* (d) *The Death of a Hero*

296. Which is the earliest book of Mulk Raj Anand?
(a) *Curries and Other Indian Dishes* (b) *The Golden Breath*
(c) *Persian Painting* (d) *The Hindu View of Art*

297. Which is the first novel of Mulk Raj Anand?
(a) *Coolie* (b) *Two Leaves and a Bud*
(c) *Untouchable* (d) *The Village*

298. "Marg", a reputed journal devoted to the Arts has been edited by
(a) Raja Rao (b) Mulk Raj Anand
(c) R.K. Narayan (d) Bhabani Bhattacharya

299. In his novels Anand mainly deals with
(a) upper class (b) upper middle calss
(c) middle class (d) lower class

300. Sohini is the sister of which character?
(a) Ram Charan (b) Lalu
(c) Bakha (d) Chota

301. "I regard untouchability as the greatest blot on Hinduism." This sentence occurs in the novel
(a) *Coolie* (b) *Untouchable*
(c) *The Village* (d) *Two Leaves and a Bud*

302. In which novel the action is spread over some years and moves from village to town, from town to city and from city to Bombay and from Bombay to Simla?
(a) *The Village* (b) *Across the Black Waters*
(c) *Coolie* (d) *Untouchable*

303. Which novel has been called 'a character novel' by Edwin Muir?
(a) *Coolie* (b) *Untouchable*
(c) *Two Leaves and a Bud* (d) *The Village*

304. 'It actually proves to be a sort of madhouse and people are cruel because they cannot be happy.'
This line appears in the novel
(a) *Untouchable* (b) *Coolie*
(c) *The Village* (d) None of the above

305. In which novel there is a conflict between the thathiars (the hereditary coppersmiths) and the capitalists?
(a) *Two Leaves and a Bud* (b) *The Big Heart*
(c) *The Village* (d) *Private Life of an Indian Prince*

306. Which novelist sees life sometimes as a comedy sometimes as a tragedy and sometimes the two modes fuse distractingly ...?
(a) Raja Rao (b) R.K. Narayan
(c) Mulk Raj Anand (d) Bhabani Bhattacharya

**3. Raja Rao**

307. Which of the following books has not been written by Raja Rao?
(a) *The Serpent and the Rope* (b) *On the Ganga Ghat*
(c) *Swami and Friends* (d) *Kanthapura*

308. One of the following collections of short stories is not of Raja Rao. Identify it.
(a) *The Cat and Shakespeare* (b) *The Cow of the Barricades*
(c) *The Policeman and the Rose* (d) *On the Ganga Ghat*

309. Which is the first novel of Raja Rao?
(a) *Kanthapura* (b) *The Serpent and the Rope*
(c) *The Cat and Shakespeare* (d) None of the above

310. "What is a policeman before a Gandhi's man? Tell me, does a boar stand before a lion or a jackal before an elephant?
These lines appear in the novel
(a) *The Serpent and the Rope* (b) *Kanthapura*
(c) *The Financial Expert* (d) *The Man-Eater of Malgudi*

311. In which novel of Raja Rao, the story has been narrated by a brahmin widow?
(a) *Kanthapura* (b) *The Cat and Shakespeare*
(c) *The Serpent and the Rope* (d) None of the above

312. "... woman is the microcosm of the mind the articulations of space, the knowing in knowledge; the woman is fire ... the woman is that which seeks against that which is sought."
Who has said this?
(a) Mulk Raj Anand (b) Raja Rao
(c) R.K. Narayan (d) N.C. Chaudhuri

313. Which work of Raja Rao has been called 'a metaphysical comedy'?
(a) *The Serpent and the Rope* (b) *The Cat and Shakespeare*
(c) *Kanthapura* (d) *The Cow of the Barricades*

314. Ramakrishna Pai, a clerk is the narrator in the novel
(a) *Kanthapura* (b) *The Serpent and the Rope*
(c) *The Cat and Shakespeare* (d) None of the above

315. 'For me literature is sadhana—not a profession but a vocation.'
Here 'me' stands for
(a) Manohar Malgonkar (b) Raja Rao
(c) Mulk Raj Anand (d) N.C. Chaudhuri

316. *Kanthapura* is described to be a/an
(a) Purana (b) Upanishad
(c) epic (d) history

### 4. Bhabani Bhattacharya

317. Kajoli is the central character in Bhabani Bhattacharya's novel
(a) *So Many Hungers* (b) *Music for Mohini*
(c) *He Who Rides a Tiger* (d) *A Dream in Hawaii*

318. Bhabani Bhattacharya's first published book was
(a) *So Many Hungers* (b) *He Who Rides a Tiger*
(c) *Shadow from Ladakh* (d) *Music for Mohini*

319. In which novel Bhattacharya tells the story of a Calcutta-born Brahmin girl?
(a) *He Who Rides a Tiger* (b) *Music for Mohini*
(c) *So Many Hungers* (d) None of the above

320. "You are city-bred, village-wed. I am village bred, city-wed. We share one common lot, we've been pulled up by the roots"
These lines have been uttered by ......... in *Music for Mohini.*
(a) Mohini (b) Jayadev
(c) Rooplekha (d) Sudha

321. Which character is advised to offer a little of her heart's blood in the lotus-leaf bowl to the Virgin Goddess?
(a) Kajoli (b) Mohini
(c) Sudha (d) Lekha

322. In which novel, buckets of milk donated by the devotees are used for the idol's bath and then cast into the River Ganga?
(a) *He Who Rides a Tiger* (b) *So Many Hungers*
(c) *Music for Mohini* (d) *A Goddess Named Gold*

323. Which novel is described as 'a modern fable of India at the time of Independence'?
(a) *Music for Mohini* (b) *So Many Hungers*
(c) *A Goddess Named Gold* (d) None of the above

324. Bhattacharya got the Sahitya Akademi Award in the year
(a) 1965 (b) 1966 (c) 1967 (d) 1968

325. Which novel depicts the Chinese invasion of 1962?
(a) *Music for Mohini* (b) *Shadow from Ladakh*
(c) *So Many Hungers* (d) *He Who Rides a Tiger*

326. "The dark spaces between a man and woman have to be lit with sympathy and comprehension ..."
This line appears in the novel
(a) *Shadow from Ladakh* (b) *Music for Mohini*
(c) *He Who Rides a Tiger* (d) None of the above

**5. Manohar Malgonkar**

327. What is the central theme of Manohar Malgonkar's novel *A Bend in the Ganges?*
(a) The communal riots following the partition of India
(b) The Jallianwala massacre
(c) The martyrdom of Bhagat Singh
(d) The Sepoy Rebellion of 1857

328. Which is the first novel of Manohar Malgonkar?
(a) *Distant Drum* (b) *A Bend in the Ganges*
(c) *Combat of Shadows* (d) *The Princes*

329. In which novel there is a story of a 'Satpura' officer Kiran Garud?
(a) *A Bend in the Ganges* (b) *The Princes*
(c) *Distant Drum* (d) None of the above

330. "Desire and Aversion are opposite shadows..."
This statement appears in the novel
(a) *Combat of Shadows* (b) *Distant Drum*
(c) *The Princes* (d) *A Bend in the Ganges*

331. In which novel the scene, as in Mulk Raj Anand's *Two Leaves and a Bud* is set in a tea estate in Assam?
(a) *The Princes* (b) *Combat of Shadows*
(c) *A Bend in the Ganges* (d) *Distant Drum*

332. Abhay is the narrator in the novel
(a) *A Bend in the Ganges* (b) *The Princes*
(c) *Combat of Shadows* (d) None of the above

## UNIT G: INDIAN WRITING IN ENGLISH: WOMEN NOVELISTS

### 1. Anita Desai

333. Which is the first novel of Anita Desai?
(a) *Voices in the City* (b) *Cry, the Peacock*
(c) *Bye-Bye Blackbird* (d) *Fire on the Mountain*

334. Which novelist's serious concern is with 'the journey within' of her characters?
(a) Anita Desai (b) Kamala Markandaya
(c) Nayantara Sahgal (d) Ruth Prawer Jhabvala

335. Which Indo-English novelist was born in 1937 of a German mother and a Bengali father?
(a) Nayantara Sahgal (b) Anita Desai
(c) Shashi Deshpande (d) Kamala Markandaya

336. Which novel of Anita Desai depicts Maya, the central character who kills her husband Gautama and then herself commits suicide?
(a) *Voices in the City* (b) *Where Shall We Go This Summer?*
(c) *Cry, the Peacock* (d) *Clear Light of Day*

337. Which novel of Anita Desai is considered to be 'an epic on Calcutta'?
(a) *Bye-Bye Blackbird* (b) *Voices in the City*
(c) *The Village by the Sea* (d) *Fire on the Mountain*

338. Which novel is divided into three parts – Arrival, Discovery and Recognition?
(a) *Fire on the Mountain* (b) *Cry, the Peacock*
(c) *Baumgartner's Bombay* (d) *Bye-Bye Blackbird*

339. Anita Desai says, "If one opts for life one must compromise with it like Sita...." Sita is the central character in
   (a) *Where Shall We Go This Summer?* (b) *The Village by the Sea*
   (c) *Voices in the City* (d) *Clear Light of Day*

340. Which novel of Anita Desai is a fictional metaphor of existentialist philosophy?
   (a) *The Village by the Sea* (b) *Bye-Bye Blackbird*
   (c) *Fire on the Mountain* (d) *Voices in the City*

341. Anita Desai was awarded Sahitya Akademi for which novel?
   (a) *Clear Light of Day* (b) *Fire on the Mountain*
   (c) *The Village by the Sea* (d) *Cry, the Peacock*

342. Which novel of Anita Desai has been described as a 'four dimensional piece'?
   (a) *Cry, the Peacock* (b) *Clear Light of Day*
   (c) *Baumgartner's Bombay* (d) *Voices in the City*

343. The story of which novel unfolds against the backdrop of the Second World War?
   (a) *In Custody* (b) *The Village by the Sea*
   (c) *Baumgartner's Bombay* (d) *Fire on the Mountain*

344. The collection of short stories titled *Games at Twilight and Others Stories* has been written by
   (a) Rama Mehta (b) Nayantara Sahgal
   (c) Anita Desai (d) Shashi Deshpande

345. The city of Bombay is used as the backdrop in Anita Desai's novel
   (a) *Fire on the Mountain* (b) *Clear Light of Day*
   (c) *Voices in the City* (d) *Baumgartner's Bombay*

346. Which character of Anita Desai goes away to Manori, the magic island to achieve the miracle of not giving birth to her fifth child?
   (a) Sita (b) Maya (c) Manisha (d) Sarah

347. In which story of Anita Desai, a sensitive college student is let down, physically as well as psychologically by over insistence on his studies and the examination he is to take?
(a) "Sale" (b) "The Accompanist"
(c) "Studies in the Park" (d) "Scholar and Gipsy"

348. Manisha is the central character in Anita Desai's novel
(a) *Cry, the Peacock* (b) *Voices in the City*
(c) *Clear Light of Day* (d) *Where Shall We Go this Summer?*

349. Who is the central character of the novel *Fasting, Feasting*?
(a) Aruna (b) Uma
(c) Anamika (d) Uma's mother

350. The novel *Hullabaloo in the Guava Orchard* has been written by
(a) Anita Desai (b) Kiran Desai
(c) Shashi Deshpande (d) Nayantara Sahgal

351. In the novel *Hullabaloo in the Guava Orchard* the protagonist Sampath Chawla works in a
(a) post office (b) bank
(c) college (d) school

352. Which novel of Anita Desai has been considered 'more individual less generalized and conventional than her earliest fiction'?
(a) *Cry, the Peacock* (b) *In Custody*
(c) *Voices in the City* (d) *Clear Light of Day*

353. 'She had become nameless, she had shed her name as she had shed her ancestry and identity and she sat there, staring as though she watched them disappear ...'
Here 'she' refers to which character?
(a) Sarah (b) Sita (c) Maya (d) Manisha

354. "My religion forbids me to drink or smoke or touch a woman but here, in this country, what am I to do? I also do the things I see other men doing."
These lines appear in the novel
(a) *Bye-Bye Blackbird* (b) *Cry, the Peacock*
(c) *Voices in the City* (d) *Where Shall We Go This Summer?*

355. In *Journey to Ithaca* which character feels that all journeys to India mean frustration and disappointment?
(a) Matteo (b) Sophie (c) Paolo (d) Mother

## 2. Shashi Deshpande

356. For which novel Shashi Deshpande was awarded Sahitya Akademi Award?
(a) *That Long Silence* (b) *The Dark Holds No Terrors*
(c) *The Legacy* (d) *Roots and Shadows*

357. Which work of Shashi Deshpande has been translated into German and Russian?
(a) *The Dark Holds No Terrors* (b) *Come Up and Be Dead*
(c) *That Long Silence* (d) *The Legacy*

358. Jaya is the principal character in Shashi Deshpande's novel
(a) *The Legacy* (b) *That Long Silence*
(c) *Come Up and Be Dead* (d) None of the above

359. *The Legacy* is a collection of short stories written by
(a) Shashi Deshpande (b) Anita Desai
(c) Ruth Prawer Jhabvala (d) Bharati Mukherjee

360. Deshpande's stories mainly deal with
(a) woman's struggle (b) social struggle
(c) political struggle (d) economic struggle

361. In which novel of Shashi Deshpande the protagonist started living with her Muslim lover, her accompanist on tabala?
(a) *Small Remedies* (b) *Come Up and Be Dead*
(c) *That Long Silence* (d) *The Dark Holds No Terrors*

362. In which novel of Shashi Deshpande, the heroine leaves home unable to bear the animal-like behaviour of her husband in bed?
(a) *The Dark Holds No Terrors* (b) *That Long Silence*
(c) *Come Up and Be Dead* (d) *Roots and Shadows*

363. "Every thing in a girl's life was shaped to that single purpose of pleasing a male."
This line appears in the novel
(a) *Come Up and Be Dead* (b) *The Legacy*
(c) *The Dark Holds No Terrors* (d) *That Long Silence*

364. Which character of Shashi Deshpande becomes a famous doctor?
(a) Urmi (b) Sarita (c) Kalpana (d) Rita

365. Which is the first novel written by Shashi Deshpande?
(a) *The Dark Holds No Terrors* (b) *Roots and Shadows*
(c) *That Long Silence* (d) *Come Up and Be Dead*

366. Which is the last and most satisfying novel of Shashi Deshpande?
(a) *That Long Silence* (b) *The Dark Holds No Terrors*
(c) *Small Remedies* (d) *Come Up and Be Dead*

**3. Shobha De**

367. Karma is the central character in the novel
(a) *Sisters* (b) *Snapshots*
(c) *Socialite Evenings* (d) *Second Thoughts*

368. "I'd feel like a harlot self-consciously sneaking up to solicit customers"
Who has said this?
(a) Karma (b) Anjali (c) Ritu (d) Gul

369. *Selective Memory* is the autobiography of
(a) Shobha De (b) Anita Desai
(c) Manju Kapur (d) Nayantara Sahgal

370. Which character of Shobha De is married to a Bombay-based Bengali bank officer and is also a degree holder in textile designing?
(a) Ritu (b) Karma (c) Maya (d) Anjali

371. Which is the first novel of Shobha De?
(a) *Socialite Evenings* (b) *Sisters*
(c) *Snapshots* (d) *Strange Obsession*

372. Which novel of Shobha De deals with the story of a filmstar Asha Rani?
(a) *Starry Nights* (b) *Sisters*
(c) *Socialite Evenings* (d) *Sultry Days*

373. Shobha De's novel *Strange Obsession* revolves around the life and lustful relationship of two women
(a) Mallika and Alisha (b) Meenakshi and Amrita
(c) Aparna and Swati (d) Noor and Surekha

374. Which novel of Shobha De deals with a story of six women—Aparna, Rashmi, Swati, Reema, Surekha and Noor?
(a) *Sisters* (b) *Snapshots*
(c) *Sultry Days* (d) None of the above

375. Maya is the central character in Shobha De's novel
(a) *Starry Nights* (b) *Second Thoughts*
(c) *Strange Obsession* (d) *Sisters*

**4. Rama Mehta**

376. Who is the heroine of Rama Mehta's novel *Inside the Haveli*?
(a) Geeta (b) Jaya (c) Radha (d) Sita

377. "No one expressed their feelings here. They covered their emotions. Everyone moved cautiously, every word was weighed before it was spoken."
These lines appear in
(a) Anita Desai's *Cry the Peacock* (b) Rama Mehta's *Inside the Haveli*
(c) Shobha De's *Sisters* (d) Jhumpa Lahiri's *The Namesake*

**5. Kamala Markandaya**

378. Kamala Markandaya's first novel is
(a) *Nectar in a Sieve* (b) *Some Inner Fury*
(c) *Possession* (d) *Two Virgins*

379. Rukmani is the central character in
(a) *Some Inner Fury* (b) *Nectar in a Sieve*
(c) *A Silence of Desire* (d) *A Handful of Rice*

380. Which novel of Kamala Markandaya explores the evil and ugly nature of racial prejudice?
(a) *The Nowhere Man* (b) *Possession*
(c) *Some Inner Fury* (d) *Nectar in a Sieve*

381. Ravi and Nalini are the main characters in Markandaya's novel
(a) *A Handful of Rice* (b) *Nectar in a Sieve*
(c) *Some Inner Fury* (d) None of the above

382. The name of Rukmani's only daughter in *Nectar in a Sieve* is
(a) Kunthi (b) Irawaddy
(c) Sita (d) Nalini

383. In *A Handful of Rice,* Nalini is the daughter of Apu, who is by profession a
(a) tailor (b) carpenter
(c) blacksmith (d) cobbler

384. Which novel of Kamala Markandaya has been compared with Pearl S Buck's *The Good Earth* and K.S. Venkataramani's *Murugan, the Tiller*?
(a) *Some Inner Fury* (b) *Nectar in a Sieve*
(c) *A Handful of Rice* (d) *A Silence of Desire*

385. Which writer has observed that fear, hunger and despair are the constant companions of the peasant—"fear of the dark future; fear of the sharpness of hunger; fear of the blackness of death"?
(a) Anita Desai (b) Kamala Markandaya
(c) Nayantara Sahgal (d) Shashi Deshpande

386. Which character of Kamala Markandaya is symbolic of the Mother—Mother India who is compassion and sufferance, who must indeed suffer all hurts and survive all disasters?
(a) Premala (b) Mira
(c) Rukmani (d) Sarojini

387. In which novel, the scene shifts from India to England and America and again back to India?
(a) *A Silence of Desire* (b) *Possession*
(c) *A Handful of Rice* (d) *Nectar in a Sieve*

388. Kamala Markandaya's novel *Two Virgins* is about two village girls
(a) Lalitha and Manju (b) Lalitha and Saroja
(c) Saroja and Rewati (d) Asha and Manju

389. Which novel of Kamala Markandaya is considered to be a historical novel?
(a) *Nectar in a Sieve* (b) *The Nowhere Man*
(c) *The Golden Honeycomb* (d) *Some Inner Fury*

**6. Ruth Prawer Jhabvala**

390. Shakuntala is the central character in the novel
(a) *Esmond in India* (b) *The Nature of Passion*
(c) *Get Ready for Battle* (d) *A New Dominion*

391. Which woman in *Esmond in India* believes: 'it was a husband's right ... to do whatever he liked with his wife ... it was not her place to complain'?
(a) Betty (b) Gulab
(c) Shakuntala (d) None of the above

392. Which character of Ruth Prawer Jhabvala is a passionate woman longing for romantic adventures at forty?
(a) Asha in *A New Dominion* (b) Kusum in *Get Ready for Battle*
(c) Shakuntala in *Esmond in India* (d) Nimmi in *The Nature of Passion*

393. Which author, a Jewish German by origin, has married an Indian architect?
(a) Kamala Markandaya (b) Ruth Prawer Jhabvala
(c) Nayantara Sahgal (d) Anita Desai

394. Jhabvala won the Booker Prize for the novel
(a) *Heat and Dust* (b) *Esmond in India*
(c) *The Nature of Passion* (d) *A New Dominion*

395. In which story, Ruth Prawer Jhabvala using the stream of consciousness technique depicts the mind of an incompetent unemployed young graduate?
(a) "A Loss of Faith" (b) "A Star and Two Girls"
(c) "The Interview" (d) "Suffering Women"

396. East-West encounter is the dominant theme in the stories in the collection
(a) *A Stronger Climate* (b) *An Experience of India*
(c) *Like Birds, like Fishes and Other Stories* (d) *How I Became A Holy Mother and Other Stories*

397. Which collection of stories of Jhabvala is prefaced with an interesting essay "Myself in India"?
(a) *Like Birds, like Fishes and Other Stories* (b) *An Experience of India*
(c) *A Stronger Climate* (d) None of the above

398. Which story of Jhabvala of the latest collection *How I Became A Holy Mother and Other Stories* depicts the passion pain and self-deception of Sofia, 30 years younger to her husband, the Raja Sahib?
(a) "Bombay" (b) "On Bail"
(c) "Prostitutes" (d) "Desecration"

399. Who is the author of *The Sword and the Sickle?*
(a) Manohar Malgonkar (b) Ruth Prawer Jhabvala
(c) Kamala Das (d) Nayantara Sahgal

400. Which is the first novel of Ruth Prawer Jhabvala?
(a) *To Whom She Will* (b) *The Nature of Passion*
(c) *Esmond in India* (d) *The Householder*

401. "So like animals, like cows ... Beat them, starve them, maltreat them how you like, they will sit and look with animal eyes and never raise a hand to defend themselves..."
These lines appear in the novel
(a) *The Householder* (b) *Esmond in India*
(b) *The Nature of Passion* (d) *A Backward Place*

**7. Anita Nair**

402. Who is the central character in Anita Nair's novel *Ladies' Coupe*?
(a) Janaki (b) Akhilendeswari
(c) Margaret (d) Prabha

403. *The Better Man* is the first novel of
(a) Anita Nair (b) Shobha De
(c) Bharati Mukherjee (d) Shashi Deshpande

**8. Nayantara Sahgal**

404. Which character of Nayantara Sahgal confesses to her husand her pre-marital affair and looks forward to a clear break from the past?
(a) Sarojini in *Storm in Chandigarh* (b) Simrit in *The Day in Shadow*
(c) Nita in *This Time of Morning* (d) *A Time to be Happy*

405. In which novel of Sahgal, divorce actually takes place?
(a) *This Time of Morning* (b) *Storm in Chandigarh*
(c) *The Day in Shadow* (d) None of the above

406. Sanad is the main character in the novel
(a) *A Time to be Happy* (b) *Storm in Chandigarh*
(c) *This Time of Morning* (d) *The Day in Shadow*

407. Nayantara Sahgal in her novels as well as in her short stories portrays upper class characters of which city?
(a) Delhi (b) Bombay (c) Calcutta (d) Bangalore

408. In which story of Sahgal the narrator and protagonist is caught between two men her husband Naresh and her lover?
(a) "Martand" (b) "The Golden Afternoon"
(c) "Promising Young Woman" (d) None of the above

409. Simrit is a character in Nayantara Sahgal's
(a) *Storm in Chandigarh* (b) *The Day in Shadow*
(c) *This Time of Morning* (d) None of the above

410. *Prison and Chocolate Cake* is the autobiography of
(a) Nayantara Sahgal (b) Shashi Deshpande
(c) Anita Desai (d) Kamala Markandaya

411. Which is the first novel written by Nayantara Sahgal?
(a) *This Time of Morning* (b) *A Time to be Happy*
(c) *Storm in Chandigarh* (d) *The Day in Shadow*

412. Which is the last novel of Nayantara Sahgal?
(a) *Storm in Chandigarh* (b) *A Time to be Happy*
(c) *This Time of Morning* (d) None of the above

413. *Rich like Us* is a well known novel of
(a) Shobha De (b) Ruta Prawer Jhabvala
(c) Nayantara Sahgal (d) Manju Kapur

414. Which novel of Nayantara Sahgal has been written against the background of politics?
(a) *A Situation in New Delhi* (b) *Storm in Chandigarh*
(c) *The Day in Shadow* (d) None of the above

**9. Anees Jung**

415. *Unveiling India* is a well known work written by
(a) Manju Kapur (b) Anees Jung
(c) Geeta Mehta (d) Shobha De

416. Anees Jung is a muslim woman from
(a) Hyderabad (b) Lucknow
(c) Kashmir (d) Delhi

**10. Manju Kapur**

417. Who is the winner of the 1999 Commonwealth Writers' Prize for the Best First Book *Difficult Daughters*?
(a) Githa Hariharan (b) Arundhati Roy
(c) Manju Kapur (d) Shashi Deshpande

418. Which novel deals with the theme of lesbianism?
(a) *Difficult Daughters* (b) *A Married Woman*
(c) *Storm in Chandigarh* (d) *Roots and Shadows*

419. "Communal riot is a terrible disease that kills God in man." Who has observed this?
(a) Shobha De (b) Nayantara Sahgal
(c) Manju Kapur (d) Arundhati Roy

420. Who is the central character in the novel *A Married Woman*?
(a) Sita (b) Astha (c) Jaya (d) Maya

421. In which novel, the issue of Babri Masjid and Ram Janambhoomi has been referred to?
(a) *A Married Woman* (b) *Socialite Evenings*
(c) *That Long Silence* (d) *Storm in Chandigarh*

422. Which novelist thinks that there is a man within every woman and a woman in every man when manhood is questioned and womanhood is fragmented?
(a) Dina Mehta (b) Bharati Mukherjee
(c) Manju Kapur (d) Shobha De

423. Pipeelika, a Hindu Brahmin girl in *A Married Woman* marries whom?
(a) Aijaz Akhtar Khan (b) Ejaz Akhtar
(c) Haider Ahmed (d) Iqbal Haider

424. Virmati is a character portrayed by
(a) Shashi Deshpande (b) Manju Kapur
(c) Bharati Mukherjee (d) Arundhati Roy

425. *In Difficult Daughters,* Virmati falls in love with an Oxonian
(a) doctor (b) engineer (c) professor (d) banker

426. Ida, the narrator in *Difficult Daughters,* is the daughter of
(a) Ganga (b) Kasturi (c) Virmati (d) Indumati

### 11. Arundhati Roy

427. The setting of *The God of Small Things* is in India's southern state of
(a) Kerala (b) Karnataka
(c) Tamil Nadu (d) Andhra Pradesh

428. "Because of you! If it wasn't for you I wouldn't be here! ... I would have been free! I should have dumped you in an orphanage the day you were born! You're the millstones round my neck!" Who is the speaker of these lines?
(a) Sophie Mol (b) Rahel
(c) Ammu (d) Margaret Kochamma

429. Who is the untouchable in *The God of Small Things?*
(a) Esthappen (b) Velutha
(c) Father Mulligan (d) Pappachi

430. Which novel has won the English-speaking world's most prestigious award, The Booker Prize?
(a) *Train to Pakistan* (b) *The God of Small Things*
(c) *Interpreter of Maladies* (d) *So Many Hungers*

431. In *The God of Small Things* who is a high-ranking government official?
(a) Pappachi (b) Chacko (c) Rahel (d) Velutha

**12. Bharati Mukherjee**

432. *The Management of Grief* is a short story written by
(a) Bharati Mukherjee (b) Basavraj Naikar
(c) Santha Rama Rau (d) Cornelia Sorabji

433. Which book of Mukherjee bagged the 1988 National Book Critic's Award in America?
(a) *The Tiger's Daughter* (b) *Jasmine*
(c) *The Middleman and Other Stories* (d) None of the above

434. Tara, the heroine of *The Tiger's Daughter* is part and parcal of which city?
(a) Bombay (b) Madras (c) Calcutta (d) Delhi

435. "...... My characters are brash and spunky ... I'm writing about a kind of new pioneer." Who said this
(a) Bharati Mukherjee (b) Shashi Deshpande
(c) Anita Desai (d) Raji Narasimhan

436. *Jasmine* is a well known novel written by
(a) Shobha De (b) Bharati Mukherjee
(c) Shashi Deshpande (d) Nayantara Sahgal

437. What was Jasmine's name in New York?
(a) Jasmine (b) Jyoti (c) Jase (d) Jane

438. Hannah Easton is the heroine of Bharati Mukherjee's novel
(a) *The Tiger's Daughter* (b) *The Holder of the Word*
(c) *Wife* (d) *Jasmine*

439. The title of Bharati Mukherjee's novel *The Holder of the World* is after the name of a Mughal emperor. Who is he?
(a) Aurangzeb (b) Shahjahan
(c) Akbar (d) Humayun

440. Which heroine of Bharati Mukherjee kills her husband?
(a) Dimple (b) Jasmine (c) Swati (d) Nirmala

## 13. Jhumpa Lahiri

441. Who is the first Asian writer to win an individual Pulitzer Prize, America's ultimate literary accolade?
(a) Saul Bellow (b) Ernest Hemingway
(c) Jhumpa Lahiri (d) Pearl S. Buck

442. Which is the opening story in *Interpreter of Maladies*?
(a) "A Temporary Matter" (b) "Interpreter of Maladies"
(c) "A Real Durwan" (d) "The Treatment of Bibi Haldar"

443. Which story of Lahiri has Indo-Pak War of 1971 and the birth of Bangladesh as its backdrop?
(a) "The Third and Final Continent" (b) "A Real Durwan"
(c) "When Mr. Pirzada came to Dine" (d) "A Temporary Matter"

444. Miranda, a young American appears in Lahiri's story
(a) "A Real Durwan" (b) "Sexy"
(c) "The Third and Final Continent" (d) "The Treatment of Bibi Haldar"

445. According to Khushwant Singh which story of Jhumpa Lahiri is perhaps the best in the collection?
(a) "The Third and Final Continent" (b) "Interpreter of Maladies"
(c) "A Real Durwan" (d) "This Blessed House"

446. Jhumpa Lahiri's *Interpreter of Maladies* has how many stories?
(a) 8 (b) 9 (c) 10 (d) 11

## 14. Jai Nimbkar

447. Who inaugurated the emergence of women writers on the literary scene in the 1970's with her solitary collection *The Lotus Leaves and Other Stories*?
(a) Nayantara Sahgal (b) Jai Nimbkar
(c) Ruth Prawer Jhabvala (d) Cornelia Sorabji

448. In which story of Nimbkar, a young boy registers his heroic protest against his parents and meaningless rituals

by joining the picnic party on the day of his elder brother's death anniversary?
(a) "In Memorium" (b) "The Death of a Hero"
(c) "Unto Each Man His Due" (d) "Quit Yourself Like Men"

**15. Attia Hosain**

449. *Sunlight on a Broken Column* is the first novel written by
(a) Attia Hosain (b) Ruth Prawer Jhabvala
(c) Jhumpa Lahiri (d) Salman Rushdie

450. Who is the spokesperson of the novelist in *Sunlight on a Broken Column?*
(a) Zahid (b) Asad (c) Kemal (d) Saleem

451. *Phoenix Fled* is a collection of short stories written by
(a) Attia Hosain (b) Ruth Prawer Jhabvala
(c) Anita Desai (d) Shashi Deshpande

452. Who is the central character in the novel *Sunlight on a Broken Column?*
(a) Saleem (b) Laila (c) Kemal (d) Zahid

**16. Taslima Nasreen**

453. *Lajja* is a well known work of
(a) Shobha De (b) Taslima Nasreen
(c) Manju Kapur (d) Bharati Mukherjee

454. Which work of Taslima Nasreen was translated from Bangla to English by Rani Ray and was entitled *Getting Even?*
(a) *Shodh* (b) *Lajja*
(c) *Fera* (d) *Aurat Ke Haque Mein*

455. Which novel of Taslima is written in the loving memory of all who have left their nation and migrated to other countries like herself?
(a) *Lajja* (b) *Fera* (c) *Shodh* (d) None

456. Which novel is a recollection of Nasreen's real life incidents of her childhood days?
(a) *Mere Bachpan Ke Din* (b) *Aurat Ke Haque Mein*
(c) *Fera* (d) *Lajja*

457. Which award Taslima Nasreen won in 1992?
(a) Pulitzer Prize (b) Booker Prize
(c) The Anand Prize (d) Jnanpith Award

**17. Githa Hariharan**

458. Who is the heroine of Githa Hariharan's novel *The Thousand Faces of Night?*
(a) Devi (b) Jaya (c) Maya (d) Sarita

459. "Am I neurotic because I am a lazy woman who does not polish her floors everyday?"This line appears in
(a) *Second Thoughts* (b) *The Thousand Faces of Night*
(c) *The Dark Holds No Terrors* (d) *Disgrace*

**18. Raji Narasimhan**

460. *The Marriage of Bela* is the solitary collection of stories of
(a) Shashi Deshpande (b) Raji Narasimhan
(c) Anita Desai (d) Jai Nimbkar

461. Which story of Narasimhan deals with the problems of the working woman?
(a) "The Word" (b) "A Village Story"
(c) "End of Probation" (d) "Their Woman Colleague"

462. *Forever Free* is a novel written by
(a) Raji Narasimhan (b) Taslima Nasreen
(c) Jhumpa Lahiri (d) Geeta Mehta

463. Which of the following novels has been written by Raji Narasimhan?
(a) *The Heart of Standing is that You cannot Fly* (b) *Minari*
(c) *Two Virgins* (d) *Wife*

**19. Nergis Dalal**

464. Which is the first novel of Nergis Dalal?
(a) *The Sisters* (b) *Minari*
(c) *The Inner Door* (d) None of the above

465. Which of the following novels is located in Sukhananda Ashram, Rishikesh?
(a) *The Inner Door* (b) *The Sisters*
(c) *Narahari: Prophet of New India* (d) *This Alone is True*

## 20. Minor Novelists

466. The novel *The Little Black Box* in which the story is presented in the form of a diary, has been written by
(a) Shakuntala Shrinagesh (b) Anita Desai
(c) Anita Nair (d) Githa Hariharan

467. *Remember the House* is a novel written by
(a) Francois Mauriac (b) Santha Rama Rau
(c) Shakuntala Shrinagesh (d) Nayantara Sahgal

468. Francois Mauriac has written a novel
(a) *The Little Black Box* (b) *Remember the House*
(c) *The Knot of Vipers* (d) *This of Morning*

469. "I welcome you to darkness and despair Samrat of Magadh .....I bring to you the offering of the defeated and the humbled"
These lines appear in
(a) Vimala Raina's *Ambapali*
(b) Nayantara Sahgal's *Storm in Chandigarh*
(c) Anita Desai's *Voices in the City*
(d) Jhabvala's *The Householder*

470. *An Unfinished Autobiography* is a well known work of
(a) Nayantara Sahgal (b) Indira Goswami
(c) Shobha De (d) Jhumpa Lahiri

471. Which of the following authors has received the famous Jnanpith Award?
(a) Jhumpa Lahiri (b) Anita Nair
(c) Shashi Deshpande (d) Indira Goswami

472. *Lihaaf*, a popular novel, written before independence, is a work of
(a) Shobha De (b) Ismat Chugtai
(c) Anita Nair (d) Shashi Deshpande

473. *The Song for Anasuya* is a well known novel written by
(a) Raji Narasimhan (b) Uma Vasudev
(c) Geeta Mehta (d) Mahasweta Devi

## UNIT H: INDIAN WRITING IN ENGLISH: OTHER NOVELISTS OF POST-INDEPENDENCE PERIOD

### 1. Salman Rushdie

474. Salman Rushdie's fascination with Aesop's *Fables* and *Panchatantra* is evident from his novel
(a) *Midnight's Children* (b) *Grimus*
(c) *Shame* (d) *The Satanic Verses*

475. Salman Rushdie wrote his novels during
(a) 1970s (b) 1980s (c) 1960s (d) 1990s

476. Rushdie's first novel is
(a) *Grimus* (b) *Midnight's Children*
(c) *Shame* (d) *The Satanic Verses*

477. Rashid and Haroun are the protagonists in the novel
(a) *The Satanic Verses* (b) *Shame*
(c) *Grimus* (d) None of the above

478. Padma is the central character in the novel
(a) *Shame* (b) *The Satanic Verses*
(c) *Midnight's Children* (d) *Grimus*

479. For which of the following works was Salman Rushdie declared a Kafir by the Muslim world?
(a) *Midnight's Children* (b) *Grimus*
(c) *The Satanic Verses* (d) *Shame*

480. Which author has portrayed three Shakil sisters, Chunni, Munnee and Bunny in his novel?
(a) Chaman Nahal (b) Salman Rushdie
(c) Arun Joshi (d) Amitav Ghosh

481. Sufia Zinobia appears in Rushdie's novel
(a) *Shame* (b) *The Moor's Last Sigh*
(c) *Midnight's Children* (d) *Grimus*

482. Which novel of Salman Rushdie has won the Booker Prize as well as the James Tait Black Memorial Prize?
(a) *The Satanic Verses* (b) *Midnight's Children*
(c) *Shame* (d) *The Moor's Last Sigh*

483. The title of the novel *Midnight's Children* refers to the children born in the midnight hour of
(a) 15 August 1947 (b) 26 January 1950
(c) 22 June 1942 (d) 15 August 1950

**2. Khushwant Singh**

484. Name the author of *Train to Pakistan*
(a) Raja Rao (b) R. K. Narayan
(c) Khushwant Singh (d) Mulk Raj Anand

485. Who has translated Rajinder Singh Bedi's Urdu novel *Ek Chadar Maili Si* into English as *I Take This Woman*?
(a) Arun Joshi (b) Khushwant Singh
(c) Shashi Tharoor (d) Ruskin Bond

486. "Government! You expect the government to do anything? A government consisting of cowardly banian money lenders!"
These lines appear in
(a) *I Shall Not Hear the Nightingale* (b) *Train to Pakistan*
(c) *A Bride for the Sahib* (d) *The Mark of Vishnu and Other Stories*

487. The novel *I Shall Not Hear the Nightingale* concentrates on the inner tensions and external movements of a Sikh family in the Punjab during
(a) April 1942 – April 1943 (b) May 1942 – May 1943
(c) June 1943 – June 1944 (d) June 1942 – June 1943

488. In the novel *I Shall Not Hear the Nightingale*, 'I' stands for which character?
(a) Buta Singh (b) Sher Singh
(c) Sabhrai (d) Champak

489. In which novel, Khushwant Singh shows the ruthlessness of the mob against the Sikhs?
(a) *Train to Pakistan* (b) *Delhi*
(c) *I Shall Not Hear the Nightingale* (d) None of the above

490. The love story of Juggat Singh and Nooran is found in which novel of Khushwant Singh?
(a) *Train to Pakistan* (b) *Delhi*
(c) *The Company of Women* (d) None of the above

491. Mohan Kumar is the central character in which novel of Khushwant Singh?
(a) *Delhi* (b) *Train to Pakistan*
(c) *The Company of Women* (d) *I Shall Not Hear the Nightingale*

### 3. Rajendra Singh

492. *The Shirt of Flame* is a novel in verse written by
(a) Rajendra Singh (b) Khushwant Singh
(c) Vikram Seth (d) Mahip Singh

493. The title of which novel has been taken from T.S. Eliot's "Four Quartets"?
(a) *Train to Pakistan* (b) *The Golden Gate*
(c) *The Shirt of Flame* (d) *The Riot*

### 4. Chaman Nahal

494. *The Weird Dance* is a collection of short stories written by
(a) Chaman Nahal (b) Khushwant Singh
(c) Ved Mehta (d) Arun Joshi

495. Which novel won Chaman Nahal Sahitya Akademi Award?
(a) *The English Queens* (b) *Azadi*
(c) *Into Another Dawn* (d) *My True Faces*

496. The story of which novel of Chaman Nahal swings between India and U.S.A.?
(a) *Azadi* (b) *The Crown and the Loin Cloth*
(c) *My True Faces* (d) *Into Another Dawn*

497. Lala Kanshi Ram's family is at the centre of which novel?
(a) *Train to Pakistan* (b) *A Bend in the Ganges*
(c) *Azadi* (d) *So Many Hungers*

498. Which is the first novel of Chaman Nahal?
   (a) *The Crown and the Loin Cloth* (b) *My True Faces*
   (c) *The English Queens* (d) *Azadi*

**5. Vikram Seth**

499. *An Equal Music* is an absorbing novel written by
   (a) Amitav Ghosh (b) Vikram Seth
   (c) Vikram Chandra (d) Salman Rushdie

500. Which is the first novel of Vikram Seth?
   (a) *An Equal Music* (b) *A Golden Gate*
   (c) *A Suitable Boy* (d) None of the above

501. Which two authors have been described as 'Terrible Twins' of Indo-English fiction?
   (a) Salman Rushdie and Vikram Seth (b) Vikram Seth and Shashi Tharoor
   (c) Shashi Tharoor and Salman Rushdie (d) Arun Joshi and Vikram Seth

502. Vikram Chandra's *Love and Longing in Bombay* employs
   (a) 5 Stories (b) 6 Stories (c) 4 Stories (d) 7 Stories

**6. Ruskin Bond**

503. "Once you have lived with mountains, there is no escape. You belong to them."
   These lines have been spoken by
   (a) Arun Joshi (b) Ruskin Bond
   (c) Shiv K. Kumar (d) Vikram Seth

504. In Bond's work we get a glimpse of
   (a) rural life (b) town life (c) city life (d) urban life

505. *Our Trees Still Grow at Dehradun* is a work of
   (a) Ruskin Bond (b) Manohar Malgonkar
   (c) Chaman Nahal (d) Shashi Tharoor

506. Rusty is a creation of
   (a) Arun Joshi (b) Ruskin Bond
   (c) Vikram Seth (d) Rajendra Singh

507. *The Last Tiger is* a well known novel written by
(a) Ruskin Bond (b) Ved Mehta
(c) K.M. Munshi (d) Vikram Chandra

**7. Arun Joshi**

508. Which is the last novel of Arun Joshi?
(a) *The City and the River* (b) *The Strange Case of Billy Biswas*
(c) *The Apprentice* (d) *The Foreigner*

509. Ratan Rathor is a character in Joshi's novel
(a) *The Strange Case of Billy Biswas* (b) *The Apprentice*
(c) *The Last Labyrinth* (d) *The City and the River*

510. Who is the author of *The Strange Case of Billy Biswas*?
(a) Mulk Raj Anand (b) Chaman Nahal
(c) Arun Joshi (d) Bhabani Bhattacharya

511. Which novel of Arun Joshi is distantly inspired by Albert Camus' *The Outsider*?
(a) *The Foreigner* (b) *The Strange Case of Billy Biswas*
(c) *The Apprentice* (d) None of the above

512. Which is the first novel of Arun Joshi?
(a) *The Apprentice* (b) *The Foreigner*
(c) *The Strange Case of Billy Biswas* (d) *The Last Labyrinth*

**8. Ved Mehta**

513. *Delinquent Chacha* is the first novel by
(a) Shashi Tharoor (b) Ved Mehta
(c) Arun Joshi (d) Anand Lall

514. Which work of Ved Mehta is autobiographical?
(a) *Face to Face* (b) *Delinquent Chacha*
(c) *Fly and the Fly Bottle* (d) *The New Theologian*

515. "Here, ladies and gentlemen, is a building of milk-white marble ...... think not that the Taj belongs only to India. It belongs to you." These lines by have been spoken by
(a) Khushwant Singh (b) Rajendra Singh
(c) Chaman Nahal (d) Ved Mehta

### 9. Anand Lall

516. Which novel has been written by Anand Lall?
(a) *The House at Adampur* (b) *Seasons of Jupiter*
(c) Both (d) None

517. The protagonist of Anand Lall's second novel *Seasons of Jupiter,* Rai Gyan Chand belongs to which town?
(a) Amritsar (b) Hyderabad
(c) Udaipur (d) Bangalore

### 10. B. Rajan

518. *The Dark Dancer* is the first novel of
(a) Khushwant Singh (b) Vikram Seth
(c) Salman Rushdie (d) Balachandra Rajan

519. Krishnan and Kamala are the characters of the novel
(a) *The Dark Dancer* (b) *No Longer at Ease*
(c) *Just Flesh* (d) *There Lay the City*

520. "Mudalur isn't a place where things get too serious. What happens here deserves a sensible ending."
Who has observed this?
(a) Nalini (b) Krishnan (c) Kamala (d) Cynthia

### 11. Amitav Ghosh

521. Tridib is the central character in Amitav's novel
(a) *The Shadow Lines* (b) *The Circle of Reason*
(c) *The Calcutta Chromosome* (d) *The Countdown*

522. Which novel of Amitav Ghosh takes up the issue of Malaria?
(a) *The Calcutta Chromosome* (b) *The Countdown*
(c) *The Circle of Reason* (d) None of the above

523. Which is the first novel of Amitav Ghosh?
(a) *The Glass Palace* (b) *The Circle of Reason*
(c) *The Shadow Lines* (d) *The Calcutta Chromosome*

524. *The Shadow Lines* tell the story of three generations of the narrator's family spread over
(a) Calcutta, Dhaka and London (b) Delhi, Dhaka and London
(c) Calcutta, Dhaka and New York (d) Bombay, Dhaka, and London

525. The partition of India and the consequent trauma of the East Bengali psyche is focussed in Amitav Ghosh's
(a) *The Countdown* (b) *The Shadow Lines*
(c) *The Calcutta Chromosome* (d) *In an Antique Land*

**12. Shashi Tharoor**

526. *The Great Indian Novel* has been written by
(a) Amitav Ghosh (b) Shashi Tharoor
(c) Upamanyu Chatterjee (d) Arun Joshi

527. Which novel focuses on collisions of various sorts—between individuals, between cultures, between ideologies and between religions?
(a) *Train to Pakistan* (b) *A Bend in the Ganges*
(c) *The Riot* (d) *So Many Hungers*

528. The novel *The Riot* is divided into how many sections?
(a) 77 (b) 78 (c) 79 (d) 80

529. Who is the chief male character in *The Riot*?
(a) Lakshaman (b) Rama
(c) Iqbal (d) Bharat

530. "From dharma comes success, from dharma comes happiness, everything emerges from dharma, dharma is the essence of the world." Which character in Tharoor's book *Show Business* speaks it?
(a) Pranay (b) Ashok (c) Guru (d) Maya

531. "It is a beautiful amalgamation of all the nine elements—love, hate, joy, sorrow, pity, disgust, courage, and compassion which make a book great." Here it refers to which book?
(a) *Train to Pakistan* (b) *The Riot*
(c) *So Many Hungers* (d) *Azadi*

**13. Minor Novelists**

532. *Men and Rivers* is a well known novel written by
(a) Humayun Kabir (b) Sudhir N. Ghose
(c) Sivasankara Pillai (d) G.V. Desani

533. "Laughter is the gift of gods to man and not to the

wolves: a crowd that laughs is a crowd of brothers, a band of God's children."
Who has said this?

(a) Khushwant Singh (b) Arun Joshi
(c) Chaman Nahal (d) Sudhir N. Ghose

534. Which novel is not written by Sudhir N. Ghose?
(a) *Cradle of the Clonds* (b) *The Flame of the Forest*
(c) *The Vermilion Boat* (d) *Men and Rivers*

535. About the language of which book Anthony Burgess observes "a sort of creative chaos that grumbles at the restraining banks ... it is like the English of Shakespeare, Joyce and Kipling, gloriously impure"?
(a) *All About H Hatterr* (b) *The Living Mask*
(c) *The Upward Spiral* (d) *Miracles Do Still Happen*

536. The novel *Bhagwan Parashurama* has been written by
(a) Khushwant Singh (b) K.M. Munshi
(c) Khwaja Ahmad Abbas (d) Venu Chitale

537. Which novel covers the period from World War I to the coming of provincial autonomy in 1937?
(a) *In Transit* (b) *Inquilab*
(c) *Tapasvini or The Lure of Power* (d) *Sorrowing Lies My Land*

538. Which work of Dhan Gopal Mukherji is partly autobiographical?
(a) *Kari, the Elephant* (b) *My Brother's Face*
(c) *The Master Monkey* (d) *Gay-Neck*

539. *The Memory of Elephants*, which presents an honest account of the strengths and eccentricities of the Parsis, is the maiden novel of
(a) Boman Desai (b) Salman Rushdie
(c) Vikram Seth (d) Arun Joshi

540. Which is the only novel of S.Y. Krishnaswamy in which the protagonist Sekhar drifts from his wife to a woman of easy virtue?
(a) *The Wound of Spring* (b) *The Fisherman of Kerala*
(c) *Kalyani's Husband* (d) *Bond of Blood*

541. In which work, the theme is the communal frenzy that terrorized Calcutta in 1946?
(a) Jatindra Mohan Ganguli's *Bond of Blood*
(b) P.M. Nityananda's *The Long Long Days*
(c) S. Menon Marath's *The Wound of Spring*
(d) S.Y. Krishnaswamy's *Kalyani's Husband*

542. The *Blue Bedspread* is the debut novel of
(a) Raj Kamal Jha (b) Upamanyu Chatterjee
(c) Mahip Singh (d) Vikram Seth

543. *Freedom Song* is the famous novel of
(a) Upamanyu Chatterjee (b) Amit Chaudhari
(c) Amitav Ghosh (d) Vikram Seth

544. *English August* is the novel written by
(a) Arun Joshi (b) Vikram Chandra
(c) Upamanyu Chatterjee (d) Ved Mehta

545. Paul Scott's *Raj Quartet* comprises his four serial novels. Of the following novels which one is not written by him?
(a) *The Jewel in the Crown* (b) *The Day of the Scorpion*
(c) *The Towers of Silence* (d) *Combat of Shadows*

546. Which is the last novel of M.V. Rama Sarma?
(a) *The Stream* (b) *The Bliss of Life*
(c) *The Farewell Party* (d) *Look Homeward*

547. The novel *The Sword of Tipu Sultan* has been written by
(a) Manohar Malgonkar (b) Bhagwan S. Gidwani
(c) Vikram Chandra (d) Arun Joshi

548. *The Lesser Deities,* a novel firmly rooted in the history of Telangana, has been written by
(a) Amitav Ghosh (b) Dasarathi Rangacharya
(c) Arun Joshi (d) Ruskin Bond

## UNIT I: AFRICAN LITERATURE

### 1. Wole Soyinka

549. Who presents the African perspective in these lines?
"Let us as Africans/Define an African sanctity/A purity by which to live/And die."
(a) Wole Soyinka (b) Chinua Achebe
(c) Ngugi Wa Thiong'o (d) Mbella Sonne Dipok

550. What an African writer today has chosen to write about?
(a) reflect injustice and victimization
(b) hostility towards west
(c) freshness of African perception
(d) celebration of humanity in the African continent

551. What is significant factor of African writers opting for English language?
(a) to reach a wider audience
(b) for English is the language the writers are comfortable with
(c) the African writing in English is just like Indian writing in English
(d) the African writing in English are conscious of an ethnic betrayal yet the compulsion and desirability of English

552. African literature in English presents
(a) an awareness of racial and cultural divide
(b) an awareness of their own myths and their conflict with the Christian myths
(c) writings, the outcome of tension generated by co-existence of native God and Christ—the conflict of two myths
(d) wisdom of the ancients juxtaposed by Western knowledge

553. The African writings in English show an awareness of
(a) the post-colonial experience
(b) need of a language with wide reach
(c) socio-political conflict re-create their own myths
(d) African oral tradition, ancient wisdom, myths and racial pride

554. Wole Soyinka's first five significant writings were conceived in prison and published after his release in 1969. What factors kept him overcome 'shock-disorienation technique' and 'mind butchers'?
   (a) his faith in freedom
   (b) literary commitment
   (c) Christian preaching of hope and promise of salvation
   (d) a great reliance on African myths, images and symbols

555. In *Season of Anomy* Soyinka presents
   (a) African hope
   (b) suffering and torture
   (c) regeneration-renewal through rhythms of nature
   (d) human indebtedness to earth and sea

556. Who wrote these lines?
   "I do not/Dare to think these bones will bloom tomorrow"
   (a) Wole Soyinka (b) Ngugi Wa Thiong'o
   (c) Chinua Achebe (d) Nadine Gordimer

557. In "Idanare", a poem with epic dimensions Soyinka has employed ——
   (a) mythopoeic mode, Yoruba (b) mythic mode
   (c) national myth (d) the myth of Ogun

558. What is the length of "Idanare", a poem with epic dimensions?
   (a) 480 lines (b) 1000 lines
   (c) 535 lines (d) 435 lines

559. In "Idanare" the poet presents
   (a) unique primitive vitality in telling the story of Ogun
   (b) the story of Ogun in modern terms
   (c) freshness to the ancient African myth
   (d) the fact that primitive myth of Ogun does not work now

**2. J.P. Clark**

560. J.P. Clark is an African writer whose nationality is
   (a) South African (b) Ugandan
   (c) Nigerian (d) Namibian

561. Clark's *Reed in the Tide* is
    (a) a collection of poems (b) memoir
    (c) a story (d) a novel

562. The poet in *Reed in the Tide* presents
    (a) a conflict of cultures of different race
    (b) an encounter with the west
    (c) global consciousness
    (d) an encounter between the traditional Nigerian culture and modern Western culture in his life

563. J.P. Clark's use of English language was necessary because
    (a) Nigeria has more than 200 languages
    (b) English is the official language
    (c) many of the Nigerian languages in spite of their inherent poetical qualities are inadequate
    (d) English by choice in which nuances of African languages have been intertwined

564. J.P. Clark's *Ozidi* persents
    (a) the saga of the Ozidi
    (b) African experience of freedom
    (c) oral tradition of the Ozidi saga has been used
    (d) music, dance to accentuate the effect

565. The imagery in *Ozidi* shows
    (a) an awareness of the people; farming, fishing, hunting
    (b) use of the sound of drums
    (c) general life of Ijaw
    (d) people and the land

**3. Ayi Kwei Armah**

566. Ayi Kwei Armah's *Two Thousand Seasons* presents
    (a) African reality
    (b) African experience of eploitation and torture
    (c) the richness of native oral tradition
    (d) the triumph of truth over falsehood

567. Armah in his writings has used
    (a) communal consciousnes and racial memory
    (b) rich oral tradition

(c) understanding between man and nature
(d) ambiguity as a technique

568. Who is the griot?
(a) African parallel of Greek chorus
(b) the detached narrator as well as the sharer of collective life
(c) the voice of the people
(d) the consciousness enriched with African tradition

569. The *Healers* presents
(a) affirmation of the relevance of oral tradition
(b) oral tradition is effective in all ages
(c) Griot's voice is the authentic voice relevant even today
(d) African consciousness

570. In *The Healers* Armah presents
(a) the power of the community's collective voice
(b) the community's collective voice can bring the Nigerians together in their struggle against the white
(c) racial conflicts
(d) failure of the Whites to understand African way of life

**4. Chinua Achebe**

571. Which of the following descriptions of *Things Fall Apart* brings out the essence of the novel?
(a) a clash of religions, christian and pagan
(b) British hegemony, advancement of European culture over the innocent
(c) a clash of ideologies, traditional versus modern
(d) it brings many Nigerian issues together besides a clash between free will and predestination

572. Chinua Achebe presents the mythological concept of 'Chi' which means
(a) 'Chi' the spirit of human endeavour
(b) it has a central place in Igloo mythology, wherever something stands something else stands with it – like an alter ego

(c) if one grows too proud or too big for his shoes, he is overthrown by his 'Chi'
(d) it is conscience of man

573. What is the difference between the community burning down the church and Okonkwo killing the messenger?
(a) both are ghastly deeds
(b) the frenzy of the mass cannot be explained
(c) burning of the church has the sanction of the tradition but Okonkwo's action is personal. In the African eyes first deed is acceptable
(d) there is hardly any difference in the western perspective

574. Chinua Achebe weaves in his novel the concept of
(a) Karma
(b) rejection of self-styled tyranny of Okonkwo
(c) hubris
(d) free will

575. In the novels of Chinua Achebe 'Negro' stands for
(a) brand of socio-cultural inferiority, ignorant and immoral in the Western perception
(b) unspoiled child of nature, the noble savage in African perception
(c) noble savage, spontaneous and sexually uninhibited
(d) primitive wiseman.

576. For Achebe 'Negritude' is
(a) African myth of regeneration
(b) an attempt to liberate man from his colour
(c) cultural and political myth, he glorifies the African past but denounces the unhealthy traditions
(d) attitude of the West towards African people, generally with a negative stance

577. In *Things Fall Apart* reference to Okonkwo's age suggests
(a) the spirit of the Igloo system of telling time, though Achebe uses phraseology of Western time
(b) he was fifty
(c) no importance to dating as in the Western system
(d) in traditional African system time flows

578. *Things Fall Apart* suggests
   (a) collapse of the invaders, plunderers — the forces of colonialization
   (b) end of the West
   (c) end of the world
   (d) crumbling of the ancient order, the cultural charm

**5. Ngugi Wa Thiong'o**

579. Ngugi in *Weep Not, Child* calls the Kenyan youth to
   (a) rebel
   (b) protest
   (c) build the nation
   (d) identify and understand the features of their heritage
580. Ngotho in *Weep Not, Child* feels that protest against colonial situation should be based on
   (a) the idea of land as a heritage
   (b) individual
   (c) collective response
   (d) collective protest based on the knowledge of the heritage
581. Ngotho feels that
   (a) he has a specific call to lead
   (b) he is the living voice of the ancients
   (c) manifestation of the past was to be expressed through him
   (d) he was inseparable from his farms and land, his source of all strength
582. Ngugi has rejected English language and chosen to write in Gikuyu because
   (a) he was against linguistic colonialism
   (b) language is an important means of domination
   (c) he questions linguistic dependency, a type of slavery
   (d) pride of his own language
583. What is the subject matter of Ngugi's *Detained*?
   (a) history of Kenya
   (b) a Marxist approach
   (c) an academic study of ills in Kenyan society and government
   (d) prison experiences and incidents

### 6. Nadine Gordimer

584. Nadine Gordimer is a
(a) South African (b) White Nigerian
(c) Kenyan (d) White South African

585. Nadine is South African writer who writes with
(a) social responsibility and commitment to her craft
(b) an awareness of white man's encounter with black African tradition
(c) encounter between Christian west and African tradition in mind
(d) a desire to build a bridge between whites and native Africans

586. Which African writer talks about a writer's conscience?
(a) Soyinka (b) Ngugi
(c) Achebe (d) Gordimer

587. Who wrote this paradoxical phrase?
"To gain his freedom the writer must give up his freedom."
(a) Ngugi (b) J.P. Clark
(c) Achebe (d) Gordimer

588. In Gordimer's writings one finds
(a) a creative union between external motion and internal emotion
(b) the task of a writer a difficult act, of responsibility
(c) in a multi-racial society, the conflict is essential
(d) that passion must be balanced with perception

## UNIT J: MAJOR WRITERS OF OTHER COMMONWEALTH COUNTRIES

### 1. V.S. Naipaul

589. Who has written *The Pleasures of Exile*?
(a) V.S. Naipaul (b) Shiva Naipaul
(c) William Walsh (d) George Lamming

590. Who has written, *A Manifold Voices: Studies in Commonwealth Literature*?
(a) Landeg White (b) Patrick White
(c) George Lamming (d) William Walsh

591. Who has written, *Awakened Conscience: Studies in Commonwealth Literature*?
(a) William Walsh (b) George Lamming
(c) V.S. Naipaul (d) C.D. Narasimhaiah

592. 'Diaspora' means
(a) exile
(b) going away from home
(c) movement
(d) the movement of people or group to a country away from their own

593. The 'Diaspora' historically means
(a) return of Jews from different nations to Israel
(b) settlement of Israel after the Second World War
(c) the movement of the Jewish people away from their own country to live and work another countries, mainly exilement of Jews in Egypt
(d) none of these

594. The literature of Diaspora refers to the literature of
(a) any people who have moved away from their own country and settled elsewhere
(b) people in self-imposed exile
(c) banished people
(d) writers who have chosen to live in other countries

595. V.S. Naipaul born of Indian immigrants in Trinidad, educated in there and England and now has made London his home. He can be called
(a) an exile (b) free citizen of the world
(c) diasporic (d) multi-cultural modern writer

596. The travelogue in which Naipaul rejected India is named
(a) *An Area of Darkness* (b) *India: A Wounded Civilization*
(c) *A Land of Multiple Mutinies* (d) *A Bend in the River*

597. *The Mimic Men* presents Naipaul's encounter with
(a) Trinidadians (b) Indians
(c) Asians (d) English people

598. In which book Naipaul wrote these lines?
"It never occurred to me that writing of this book might have become an end in itself, that the recording of a life might become an extension of that life?"
(a) *The Mystic Masseur* (b) *Miguel Street*
(c) *A House for Mr. Biswas* (d) *The Mimic Men*

599. V.S. Naipaul in his writing moves from the 'Swiftean disgust of spinsterish finickiness'—it is brought out by his statement that
(a) I don't write about "poor hideous flesh but beyond flesh"
(b) I am interested in "art of writing".
(c) I believe in "order"
(d) I wish to establish "a relationship between writing and living"

600. What impression does Naipaul leave when he says?
"I cannot write sex ... my mother would be shocked"
(a) childish, unnecessarily finickiness
(b) unable to be honest
(c) shyness
(d) immaturity of an Indian middle class man

601. In *A House for Mr. Biswas* the reader comes across Naipaul's
(a) sense of rhythm and shape of letters
(b) craftsmanhip
(c) moods of 'R' and swing of 'S'
(d) the sensitivity to the physical shape of letters

602. The character of Mr. Biswas is derived from
(a) Indians in Trinidad (b) Asians
(c) Mulattos (d) Naipaul's own father

603. The house in *A House for Mr. Biswas* stands for
(a) recognizable location and identity
(b) an immigrant's need to have a living place, his own house
(c) Naipaul's search for identity
(d) a quest for permanence

604. Mr. Biswas calls 'Hanuman House' as
   (a) Mahavir House (b) Ram Sita Kutir
   (c) Ramayan House (d) Monkey House

605. Mr. Biswas in the novel presents
   (a) the ability of the creator's mind to order and interpret experiences
   (b) transmutation of anguish
   (c) overcoming tyrannical experiences
   (d) a comic view of human endeavour

606. Naipaul in his writings presents
   (a) cultural crisis (b) predicament of Indian immigrants
   (c) crisis in a multi-cultural society (d) problem of finding dignity and acceptance

607. The sense of exilement in Naipaul's writings is
   (a) physical (b) economic
   (c) political (d) more cultural than physical

608. The search for identity leads Naipaul to seek
   (a) meaning and dignity
   (b) purposefulness
   (c) amalgamation with other cultural groups
   (d) a place of importance

**2. Taslima Nasrin**

609. Taslima Nasrin's most well-known novel is
   (a) *Shame* (b) *Disgrace* (c) *Jwala* (d) *Lajja*

610. What does Taslima Nasrin present in *Lajja*?
   (a) ethnic crisis of a minority community in Bangladesh
   (b) Hindu-Muslim conflict in Bangladesh
   (c) subjugation of the minority Hindus by majority muslims in Bangladesh
   (d) lack of human consideration in the country even after establishment of Bangladesh

611. Sudhamoy resists
(a) conversion
(b) de-humanization
(c) economic deprivation
(d) treatment as a second-class citizen

612. Who asks this: "Are't Hindus human"?
(a) Kironmoyee
(b) Sudhamoy
(c) Suraujan
(d) Maya

613. What is so significant about *Lajja*?
(a) presentation and understanding the life of minority community, the Hindus in a pre-dominantly Muslim nation who are often not even aware of their predicament
(b) she voices the problems of Hindus in a Muslim state
(c) she rebels against the Muslim complacency
(d) herself a Muslim she writes about Hindus with commitment

**3. Carl Muller**

614. *The Jam Fruit Tree* is a symbol of
(a) the burghers of Sri Lanka
(b) the hard life of Sri Lanka
(c) the Sinhalese peasantry
(d) the ruthless burghers of Sri Lanka

615. What do these lines describe? "Oh, all in all a robust, brawny, bawdy family praising the Lord, churchgoing, singing their aves with the same gusto as they would eat, drink and fornicate."
(a) the burghers
(b) Von Bloss
(c) Fr. Romeil
(d) Sounaboy

616. What is the most important event in the life of burghers?
(a) Christmas
(b) quasi religious activities
(c) robust sexuality
(d) party – any occasion, any time, any place

617. Who has written *The Jam Fruit Tree*?
(a) Zulfikar Ghose
(b) William Walsh
(c) V.S. Naipaul
(d) Carl Muller

618. The style of Carl Muller is
(a) narrative
(b) historical
(c) psychological
(d) analytical

### 4. Patrick White

619. Patrick White is known for
   (a) dramatization of human isolation
   (b) concern for the personal life of an individual who is dis-satisfied and is marginalized
   (c) characters who are sansitive
   (d) characters who live a life of their own claustrophobic experience

620. Patrick White's *Voss* presents
   (a) concern for man in colonial Australia
   (b) experience of human suffering and isolation
   (c) aggresively romantic view of life
   (d) the vast deserts, the kangaroos and immigrants

621. Voss is
   (a) an explorer of life and land
   (b) in search for absolute truth
   (c) a crazy German trying to make Australian experience worthwhile
   (d) exploring his self

622. In *Voss* the great Australian desert is presented as
   (a) possibilities of exploration
   (b) unconquerable problems of the world
   (c) a symbol of futility
   (d) a symbol of man's harmony with the infinite cosmos

### 5. Judith Wright

623. In Australian poety the recurrent central theme is
   (a) the image of native land (b) the desert
   (c) the creatures (d) the immigrants/settlers

624. Who has written these lines?
   "Hunger and force his beauty made/and turned a Grid to a knife blade"
   (a) May Gilmore (b) Douglas Stewart
   (c) James Mcauley (d) Judith Wright

## 6. Writers of Pakistan

625. In recent times literature in Pakistan has registered the mood of the nation expressed by
   (a) protest against tyranny of dictatorship and imposition of martial law
   (b) sorrow at the demise of democracy
   (c) metaphoric expression of people in seige
   (d) mataphors of suffering and oppression

626. Suppression of democratic processes lead to imprisonment, torture and stifling of the voice of protest. Which great modern poet of Pakistan was imprisoned for a long period?
   (a) Habib Jalib (b) Ahsan Javed
   (c) Anwar Zahidi (d) Faiz Ahmad Faiz

627. Which poet was beaten publicly and also imprisoned?
   (a) Faiz Ahmad Faiz (b) Anwar Zahidi
   (c) Ilyas Ghumnam (d) Habib Jalib

628. Saeeda Gazdar has written a beautiful short story on dictators, its title is
   (a) "Death of Another Caesar" (b) "Cries of a Cat"
   (c) "The Lunatic" (d) "The Cuckoo and General"

629. Even natural and genuine love was not spared by the brutal regime, this is reflected in the writing of
   (a) Nawaz, and Sher Muhammad Masi (b) Parween Malik
   (c) Muhammad Mansha Yaad (d) Gohar Sultana Uzma

630. In the stories of Gohar Sultana Uzma, Ilyas Rahi, Ahmad Daud and Rasheed Amzad one finds
   (a) basic contradictions, between faith and the government
   (b) manifestation of fear and apprehension
   (c) a sense of timelessness, death of time
   (d) darkness in the morning

631. Women novelists in Pakistan have transcended the boundaries of feminism in the writings of
(a) Khadija Mastoor (b) Farkhanda Lodhi
(c) Bapsi Sidhwa (d) Zahida Hina

632. How has Nirupma Dutt brought contemporary writers of Pakistan to Indian readers?
(a) lectures (b) newspaper articles
(c) anthologies (d) seminars and conferences

633. *Half the Sky* and *Children of the Night* are collections of women writers and other writers respectively. These have been edited by
(a) R.K. Dhawan (b) M.L. Firdausi
(c) F. Zaman (d) Nirupma Dutt

634. Parween Malik in *The Tale of Hunger* writes about
(a) wretchedness in life: the doors of shop are shut, even the doors of human heart are shut and locked
(b) hunger
(c) curfew leading to starvation
(d) no food and solace possible in this world anymore total despair

635. Every where half the sky belongs to women yet they are oppressed, but in Pakistan they are twice-oppressed class as shown in these lines;"I am not mere dust to be trodden by all/I am the green grass on the ground/some what trampled/but still holding my head high".
Who has written these lines?
(a) Fakhar Zaman (b) Iftikhar Arif
(c) Yasmeen Hameed (d) Shaista Habib

636. Firdaus Haider in *The Cow* compares the life of a woman to
(a) harmless creature (b) a gentle being
(c) cattle (d) a person with no particular identity

637. Farkhanda Lodhi in *The Poor Thing* presents the predicament of a woman
(a) who is deserted (b) who is exploited

(c) who is abused
(d) who is de-humanized and passed from man to man in a loveless marriage

638. Rukshana Ahmad in *The Spell and the Ever-Changing Moon* presents a modern stance in which the woman
(a) breaks the social barriers
(b) runs away with another man
(c) deserts her husband
(d) walks out on a husband who does not love her or respect her

639. Who is the creator of Heer-Ranjha love legend?
(a) Zahida Parveen
(b) Shah Abdul Late Bhitai
(c) Mansoor Hallaj
(d) Waris Shah

640. Intizar Hussain, a well known Pakistani writer was born in
(a) Lahore
(b) Sind Province
(c) Bihar in India
(d) Uttar Pradesh in India

641. In his short stories Intizar Hussain has drawn on
(a) European art of story telling
(b) Buddha's stories
(c) art of Katha
(d) Panchatantra

642. About which writer it is said: "He wanders between Karbala and Ayodhya"?
(a) Sa'aat Hasan Manto
(b) Hasan Manzar
(c) Su Raa
(d) Intizar Hussain

643. What is the recurrent theme in Intizar Hussain's writings?
(a) freedom in Pakistan
(b) glorification of the Muslim state of Pakistan
(c) military dictatorship and common man's brutalization
(d) migration

## ANSWERS

### Unit A

| | | | | | | | |
|---|---|---|---|---|---|---|---|
| 1. | (b) | 2. | (b) | 3. | (b) | 4. | (b) |
| 5. | (b) | 6. | (a) | 7. | (c) | 8. | (a) |

| | | | | | | | |
|---|---|---|---|---|---|---|---|
| 9. | (b) | 10. | (a) | 11. | (a) | 12. | (b) |
| 13. | (c) | 14. | (c) | 15. | (a) | 16. | (a) |
| 17. | (b) | 18. | (d) | 19. | (c) | 20. | (a) |
| 21. | (c) | 22. | (a) | 23. | (c) | 24. | (b) |
| 25. | (c) | 26. | (c) | 27. | (a) | 28. | (b) |
| 29. | (c) | 30. | (b) | 31. | (a) | 32. | (b) |
| 33. | (d) | 34. | (a) | 35. | (b) | 36. | (a) |
| 37. | (a) | 38. | (b) | 39. | (c) | 40. | (a) |
| 41. | (b) | 42. | (b) | 43. | (a) | 44. | (c) |
| 45. | (b) | 46. | (a) | 47. | (b) | | |

**Unit B**

| | | | | | | | |
|---|---|---|---|---|---|---|---|
| 48. | (a) | 49. | (b) | 50. | (c) | 51. | (c) |
| 52. | (a) | 53. | (b) | 54. | (a) | 55. | (a) |
| 56. | (a) | 57. | (b) | 58. | (a) | 59. | (b) |
| 60. | (c) | 61. | (a) | 62. | (a) | 63. | (a) |
| 64. | (c) | 65. | (b) | 66. | (c) | 67. | (a) |
| 68. | (b) | 69. | (c) | 70. | (b) | 71. | (a) |
| 72. | (c) | 73. | (b) | 74. | (d) | 75. | (a) |
| 76. | (b) | 77. | (b) | 78. | (b) | 79. | (c) |
| 80. | (c) | 81. | (a) | 82. | (b) | 83. | (d) |
| 84. | (c) | 85. | (a) | 86. | (b) | 87. | (a) |
| 88. | (c) | 89. | (a) | 90. | (b) | 91. | (b) |
| 92. | (b) | 93. | (b) | 94. | (a) | 95. | (b) |
| 96. | (c) | 97. | (b) | 98. | (c) | 99. | (b) |
| 100. | (b) | 101. | (c) | 102. | (a) | 103. | (b) |
| 104. | (a) | 105. | (c) | 106. | (c) | 107. | (a) |
| 108. | (d) | 109. | (a) | 110. | (b) | 111. | (a) |
| 112. | (d) | 113. | (a) | 114. | (b) | 115. | (a) |
| 116. | (b) | 117. | (b) | 118. | (a) | 119. | (c) |
| 120. | (b) | 121. | (a) | 122. | (a) | 123. | (a) |
| 124. | (a) | 125. | (b) | 126. | (c) | 127. | (a) |

| | | | | | | | |
|---|---|---|---|---|---|---|---|
| 128. | (b) | 129. | (a) | 130. | (d) | 131. | (b) |
| 132. | (a) | 133. | (b) | 134. | (a) | 135. | (b) |
| 136. | (a) | 137. | (a) | 138. | (c) | 139. | (a) |
| 140. | (b) | 141. | (b) | 142. | (a) | 143. | (c) |
| 144. | (c) | 145. | (a) | 146. | (b) | 147. | (a) |
| 148. | (b) | 149. | (a) | 150. | (c) | 151. | (b) |
| 152. | (a) | 153. | (a) | 154. | (b) | | |

## Unit C

| | | | | | | | |
|---|---|---|---|---|---|---|---|
| 155. | (b) | 156. | (c) | 157. | (a) | 158. | (a) |
| 159. | (c) | 160. | (a) | 161. | (b) | 162. | (a) |
| 163. | (a) | 164. | (b) | 165. | (a) | 166. | (b) |
| 167. | (b) | 168. | (a) | 169. | (a) | 170. | (c) |
| 171. | (c) | 172. | (a) | 173. | (b) | 174. | (a) |
| 175. | (c) | 176. | (b) | 177. | (d) | 178. | (c) |
| 179. | (b) | 180. | (d) | 181. | (b) | 182. | (a) |
| 183. | (a) | 184. | (a) | 185. | (b) | 186. | (a) |
| 187. | (c) | 188. | (a) | 189. | (b) | 190. | (a) |
| 191. | (d) | | | | | | |

## Unit D

| | | | | | | | |
|---|---|---|---|---|---|---|---|
| 192. | (d) | 193. | (a) | 194. | (b) | 195. | (a) |
| 196. | (c) | 197. | (b) | 198. | (c) | 199. | (a) |
| 200. | (b) | 201. | (d) | 202. | (b) | 203. | (a) |
| 204. | (c) | 205. | (b) | 206. | (a) | 207. | (b) |
| 208. | (c) | 209. | (a) | 210. | (d) | 211. | (b) |
| 212. | (c) | 213. | (b) | 214. | (c) | 215. | (b) |
| 216. | (a) | 217. | (b) | 218. | (a) | 219. | (a) |
| 220. | (b) | 221. | (a) | 222. | (a) | | |

## Unit E

| | | | | | | | |
|---|---|---|---|---|---|---|---|
| 223. | (b) | 224. | (a) | 225. | (a) | 226. | (c) |
| 227. | (a) | 228. | (b) | 229. | (c) | 230. | (c) |
| 231. | (a) | 232. | (b) | 233. | (c) | 234. | (b) |

235. (c) 236. (b) 237. (a) 238. (b)
239. (a) 240. (c) 241. (a) 242. (a)
243. (d) 244. (a) 245. (b) 246. (a)
247. (a) 248. (b) 249. (b) 250. (b)
251. (c) 252. (b)

## Unit F

253. (a) 254. (b) 255. (a) 256. (b)
257. (a) 258. (b) 259. (c) 260. (a)
261. (a) 262. (d) 263. (a) 264. (b)
265. (d) 266. (a) 267. (d) 268. (a)
269. (b) 270. (d) 271. (b) 272. (a)
273. (b) 274. (c) 275. (d) 276. (b)
277. (a) 278. (c) 279. (c) 280. (d)
281. (a) 282. (b) 283. (b) 284. (a)
285. (c) 286. (a) 287. (b) 288. (b)
289. (b) 290. (b) 291. (d) 292. (b)
293. (c) 294. (d) 295. (c) 296. (a)
298. (b) 299. (d) 300. (c) 301. (b)
302. (c) 303. (a) 304. (b) 305. (b)
306. (c) 307. (c) 308. (c) 309. (a)
310. (b) 311. (a) 312. (b) 313. (b)
314. (c) 315. (b) 316. (a) 317. (a)
318. (a) 319. (b) 320. (c) 321. (b)
322. (a) 323. (b) 324. (c) 325. (b)
326. (b) 327. (a) 328. (a) 329. (c)
330. (a) 331. (b) 332. (b)

## Unit G

333. (b) 334. (a) 335. (b) 336. (c)
337. (b) 338. (d) 339. (a) 340. (c)
341. (b) 342. (b) 343. (c) 344. (c)
345. (d) 346. (a) 347. (c) 348. (b)

| | | | | | | | |
|---|---|---|---|---|---|---|---|
| 349. | (b) | 350. | (b) | 351. | (a) | 352. | (b) |
| 353. | (a) | 354. | (a) | 355. | (b) | 356. | (a) |
| 357. | (c) | 358. | (b) | 359. | (a) | 360. | (a) |
| 361. | (a) | 362. | (a) | 363. | (c) | 364. | (b) |
| 365. | (a) | 366. | (c) | 367. | (c) | 368. | (a) |
| 369. | (a) | 370. | (c) | 371. | (a) | 372. | (a) |
| 373. | (b) | 374. | (b) | 375. | (b) | 376. | (a) |
| 377. | (b) | 378. | (a) | 379. | (b) | 380. | (a) |
| 381. | (a) | 382. | (b) | 383. | (a) | 384. | (b) |
| 385. | (b) | 386. | (a) | 387. | (b) | 388. | (b) |
| 389. | (c) | 390. | (a) | 391. | (b) | 392. | (a) |
| 393. | (b) | 394. | (a) | 395. | (c) | 396. | (a) |
| 397. | (b) | 398. | (d) | 399. | (b) | 400. | (a) |
| 401. | (b) | 402. | (b) | 403. | (a) | 404. | (a) |
| 405. | (c) | 406. | (a) | 407. | (a) | 408. | (a) |
| 409. | (b) | 410. | (a) | 411. | (b) | 412. | (a) |
| 413. | (c) | 414. | (b) | 415. | (b) | 416. | (a) |
| 417. | (c) | 418. | (b) | 419. | (c) | 420. | (b) |
| 421. | (a) | 422. | (c) | 423. | (a) | 424. | (b) |
| 425. | (c) | 426. | (c) | 427. | (a) | 428. | (c) |
| 429. | (b) | 430. | (b) | 431. | (a) | 432. | (a) |
| 433. | (c) | 434. | (c) | 435. | (a) | 436. | (b) |
| 437. | (c) | 438. | (b) | 439. | (a) | 440. | (a) |
| 441. | (c) | 442. | (a) | 443. | (c) | 444. | (b) |
| 445. | (a) | 446. | (b) | 447. | (b) | 448. | (a) |
| 449. | (a) | 450. | (b) | 451. | (a) | 452. | (b) |
| 453. | (b) | 454. | (a) | 455. | (b) | 456. | (a) |
| 457. | (c) | 458. | (a) | 459. | (b) | 460. | (b) |
| 461. | (c) | 462. | (a) | 463. | (a) | 464. | (b) |
| 465. | (a) | 466. | (a) | 467. | (b) | 468. | (c) |
| 469. | (a) | 470. | (b) | 471. | (d) | 472. | (b) |
| 473. | (b) | | | | | | |

## Unit H

| | | | | | | | |
|---|---|---|---|---|---|---|---|
| 474. | (b) | 475. | (b) | 476. | (c) | 477. | (d) |
| 478. | (c) | 479. | (c) | 480. | (b) | 481. | (a) |
| 482. | (b) | 483. | (a) | 484. | (c) | 485. | (b) |
| 486. | (b) | 487. | (a) | 488. | (c) | 489. | (b) |
| 490. | (a) | 491. | (c) | 492. | (a) | 493. | (c) |
| 494. | (a) | 495. | (b) | 496. | (d) | 497. | (c) |
| 498. | (b) | 499. | (b) | 500. | (b) | 501. | (a) |
| 502. | (a) | 503. | (b) | 504. | (a) | 505. | (a) |
| 506. | (b) | 507. | (a) | 508. | (a) | 509. | (b) |
| 510. | (c) | 511. | (a) | 512. | (b) | 513. | (b) |
| 514. | (a) | 515. | (d) | 516. | (c) | 517. | (a) |
| 518. | (d) | 519. | (a) | 520. | (a) | 521. | (a) |
| 522. | (a) | 523. | (b) | 524. | (a) | 525. | (b) |
| 526. | (b) | 527. | (c) | 528. | (b) | 529. | (a) |
| 530. | (c) | 531. | (b) | 532. | (a) | 533. | (d) |
| 534. | (d) | 535. | (a) | 536. | (b) | 537. | (c) |
| 538. | (b) | 539. | (a) | 540. | (c) | 541. | (a) |
| 542. | (a) | 543. | (b) | 544. | (c) | 545. | (d) |
| 546. | (b) | 547. | (b) | 548. | (b) | | |

## Unit I

| | | | | | | | |
|---|---|---|---|---|---|---|---|
| 549. | (d) | 550. | (d) | 551. | (d) | 552. | (c) |
| 553. | (d) | 554. | (d) | 555. | (c) | 556. | (a) |
| 557. | (a) | 558. | (d) | 559. | (a) | 560. | (c) |
| 561. | (a) | 562. | (d) | 563. | (d) | 564. | (c) |
| 565. | (a) | 566. | (a) | 567. | (a) | 568. | (b) |
| 569. | (c) | 570. | (b) | 571. | (d) | 572. | (b) |
| 573. | (c) | 574. | (d) | 575. | (b) | 576. | (c) |
| 577. | (a) | 578. | (d) | 579. | (c) | 580. | (d) |
| 581. | (d) | 582. | (c) | 583. | (d) | 584. | (d) |
| 585. | (a) | 586. | (d) | 587. | (d) | 588. | (a) |

## Unit J

| | | | | | | | |
|---|---|---|---|---|---|---|---|
| 589. | (d) | 590. | (d) | 591. | (d) | 592. | (d) |
| 593. | (c) | 594. | (a) | 595. | (c) | 596. | (a) |
| 597. | (d) | 598. | (d) | 599. | (a) | 600. | (a) |
| 601. | (a) | 602. | (d) | 603. | (a) | 604. | (d) |
| 605. | (a) | 606. | (c) | 607. | (d) | 608. | (a) |
| 609. | (d) | 610. | (a) | 611. | (a) | 612. | (d) |
| 613. | (a) | 614. | (d) | 615. | (a) | 616. | (d) |
| 617. | (d) | 618. | (a) | 619. | (b) | 620. | (b) |
| 621. | (d) | 622. | (d) | 623. | (a) | 624. | (d) |
| 625. | (a) | 626. | (d) | 627. | (d) | 628. | (d) |
| 629. | (a) | 630. | (b) | 631. | (d) | 632. | (c) |
| 633. | (d) | 634. | (a) | 635. | (d) | 636. | (c) |
| 637. | (d) | 638. | (d) | 639. | (d) | 640. | (d) |
| 641. | (b) | 642. | (d) | 643. | (d) | | |

# Criticism from Beginning to Present

# 13

## UNIT A: THE ANCIENTS

### 1. Aristotle

1. Aristotle was a Greek philosopher and critic and belonged to
   (a) 384 - 322 B.C. (b) 360 - 302 B.C.
   (c) 394 - 333 B.C. (d) 400 - 338 B.C.
2. Aristotle was the son of
   (a) Nichomachus, the court physician to King Amyntas II of Macedonia
   (b) a Macedonian citizen
   (c) a nobleman of Athens
   (d) a common man of Macedonia
3. During Aristotle's period of Greek history virtues were
   (a) wisdom (b) religions
   (c) moral values (d) courage, heroism, magnificence and skill in the use of arms
4. According to Aristotle virtue stood for
   (a) excellence (b) goodness
   (c) performance of good deeds (d) moral mobility and performance of good deeds
5. Which man, according to Aristotle, does not unnecessarily expose himself to danger yet is ready to give his life?
   (a) a good man (b) the ideal man
   (c) a virtuous man (d) brave man

6. Aristotle said: "Neither one should do too little, nor too much". Which concept of the critic is implied?
   (a) moderation, the golden mean
   (b) to do what is right
   (c) carefully choose his actions
   (d) take moral responsibility and act carefully
7. Plato influenced Aristotle but what is the basic difference between the two giants?
   (a) Plato was an idealist and Aristotle a realist
   (b) they agreed in many issues but arrived at different conclusions
   (c) Plato rejected poetry and Aristotle defended it based on idealism of the former and realistic approach of the latter
   (d) there is no difference
8. What were the areas in literary criticism in which Plato and Aristotle agreed?
   (a) Poetry is an imitative art; poetry arouses emotions; poetry produces pleasure; poetry has an effect on human personality
   (b) they agreed in all major areas
   (c) they agreed on the Mimetic theory of creativity
   (d) Plato was the master and Aristotle the pupil agreement was unconditional acceptance
9. Is it correct to say that Aristotle was scientific and Plato was metaphysical?
   (a) true
   (b) partly true
   (c) false
   (d) both were metaphysical
10. Aristotle's *Poetics* is divided into how many chapters?
    (a) twenty six
    (b) thirty
    (c) twenty
    (d) sixteen
11. The first five chapters of Aristotle's *Poetics* deal with
    (a) discussion of poetry
    (b) different imitative arts, origin partly, its form comedy and tragedy
    (c) mimetic theory
    (d) tragedy

12. What is the topic of discussion in the next fourteen chapters (6-19)?
    (a) poetry, its origin (b) epic
    (c) diction (d) tragedy
13. What is Aristotle's definition of tragedy?
    (a) tragedy deals with the fall of a good man
    (b) tragic flaw is the cause of a good man's fall
    (c) catharsis is possible
    (d) tragedy is a serious drama in a form of action which through pity and fear leads to catharsis of such emotions
14. Aristotle defines tragedy: "an imitation of an action that is serious, complete and of certain magnitude,in language embellished with each kind of artistic ornament, the several kinds being found in several parts of the play in the form of action, not of narrative through pity and fear effecting its catharsis of such emotions." Is it complete and correct?
    (a) yes (b) partly correct
    (c) incomplete (d) no
15. There are six elements of tragedy according to Aristotle. These are: (i) imitation of a serious action with magnitude, (ii) complete in itself, (iii) language with rhythm and harmony, (iv) dramatic form, arousing pity and fear, and (v)
    (a) mimetic (b) poetic
    (c) sad ending (d) catharsis
16. What are six constituent elements in tragedy according to Aristotle?
    (i) plot, (ii) character, (iii) thought, (iv) diction, (v) melody and (vi)
    (a) incident (b) rhetorical brilliance
    (c) spectacle (d) grandeur
17. What unity a plot should have?
    (a) unity of purpose (b) unity of thought
    (c) unity of hero (d) unity of action

18. What factors are essential in a plot?
    (a) a grand opening (b) balanced in form
    (c) a beginning, middle and end (d) all
19. In a plot according to *Poetics* there should be self explanatory beginning, middle must follow naturally to the catastrophe and the end should be
    (a) naturally related to the beginning
    (b) related to the beginning and middle
    (c) causally related to something that
    (d) appropriate, went before beginning and middle
20. According to Aristotle, poetry is a form of imitation which does not present a photographic realism. A poet does not describe what has happened but what might happen. How correct is this statement?
    (a) imitation is copying
    (b) a poet copies life
    (c) poetry presents poetic truth, which based on probability and necessity leads to inevitability
    (d) poetry uses logical connections
21. According to Aristotle what points are important in a character? First goodness, secondly appropriateness, thirdly true to life and lastly
    (a) truthful (b) magnificent
    (c) powerful (d) consistency
22. Thought must have a
    (a) cause and effect relationship (b) nobility of expression
    (c) grandeur of presentation (d) dignity of the character
23. What are the proper emotions for a plot in tragedy?
    (a) pity and fear (b) tragic pleasure
    (c) horror (d) disaster
24. In a plot of tragedy the hero's fortunes move from happiness to misery because of
    (a) fate (b) tragic flaw
    (c) wrong judgement (d) human failings

25. Who can be a tragic hero?
    (a) a perfectly good man
    (b) a good man with human failings like error of judgement or a flaw
    (c) a good man with certain weaknesses over which he has no control
    (d) ill-fated man

**2. Horace**

26. Horace was a Roman poet who belonged to
    (a) 121 – 65 B.C. (b) 65 – 3 B.C.
    (c) 221 – 171 B.C. (d) 65 – 8 B.C.
27. Horace's views on Poetry are significant for he belonged to a glorious period of Roman rule. What was the period he represents?
    (a) Augustan age named after the Roman emperor Octavian Augustus
    (b) golden period of Roman poetry
    (c) the period which produced poets like Virgil
    (d) Augustus was interested in art and progress in literature was tremendous during his period
28. Horace's greatest works in criticism are contained in
    (a) odes (b) epistles
    (c) *Ars Poetica* (d) satires
29. *Ars Poetica* is Horace's treatise on art of poetry which contains
    (a) stray views on poetry
    (b) basically an epistle
    (c) significant deliberation on poetry
    (d) random observations on poetry but they are significant statements of a great poet.
30. Who advised the poets to choose a subject within his powers, to study the best models, to seek competent criticism and to revise his work with care?
    (a) Virgil (b) Horace (c) Ovid (d) Livy
31. Who said that perfection is not possible and small faults in a good piece will be tolerated?
    (a) Virgil (b) Livy (c) Horace (d) Aristotle

32. Which form of literature received greatest attention of Horace?
    (a) drama (b) poetry
    (c) satire (d) prose treatise
33. The discussion on importance of ancients and moderns received largest contribution from which critic?
    (a) Horace (b) Virgil (c) Ovid (d) Livy
34. The ancients in this discussion are
    (a) Greeks (b) early Romans
    (c) Greeks and Romans (d) all those who did not subscribe to Horace's concept of classical poetry
35. Which English writer made this discussion subject matter of his work?
    (a) Pope in Essays on Criticism (b) Matthew Arnold in Essays
    (c) Jonathan Swift in *The Battle of the Books* (d) John Dryden in his *Prefaces*
36. Horace's concept of poetry is based on
    (a) disenchantment with the Alexandrian and the old Latin models
    (b) the enlightened poets turned to revival of the ancient Greek tradition in place of Alexandria and old Roman models
    (c) the new-found splendour was great
    (d) there is a significant relationship between the theory and practice of the new-found splendour of ancient Greeks
37. Who said "the conquered Greece conquered her Roman Conqueror"?
    (a) Horace (b) Virgil (c) Tibullus (d) Ovid
38. Horace's discussion of poetry in *The Art of Poetry* includes his views on its nature, function, subject matter, kinds and language. But he nowhere calls poetry a

process of imitation as Plato and Aristotle did in their discussion. Is it correct?

(a) correct (b) incorrect
(c) partially correct (d) Horace agreed with the Greeks

39. Horace emphasized the nature of poetry and said it must be pleasure giving. Is it true?

(a) true (b) false
(c) true but didn't Plato also say the same (d) partially true

40. What was Horace's suggestion in the choice of subject matter?

(a) grand topic
(b) significant for the people
(c) any provided it was simple, familiar and uniform
(d) these should be within the power of the poet, to which he could do justice

41. For Horace what was of great importance in the choice of the subject matter and its rendering?

(a) appropriateness (b) natural affinity between the subject matter and metre
(c) harmony (d) balance

42. In his remarks on language Horace comes very close to Aristotle. He suggests

(a) right choice of words and their effective arrangement in a composition
(b) words and theme must match
(c) appropriate words
(d) words and style must match

43. Who examined the question of genius and art in the success of poetry?

(a) Plato (b) Aristotle (c) Virgil (d) Horace

44. What is the role of genius or talent in poetry?

(a) Horace is very candid on this topic. Natural gift must be subjected to the rigours of the craft to attain the desired result

(b) genius without hard work is inadequate
(c) natural gift is essential for success
(d) talent needs no schooling

45. What was the unique ability Horace possessed?
(a) boldness in rejection of what was inadequate—Alexandrian and old Roman models
(b) acceptance of tenets of great masters of Greece
(c) his natural poetic talent
(d) his ability to compromise between the conflicting claims of pleasure and profit

46. Horace said: "Mediocrity is forbidden to poets alike by gods and men and booksellers".
It suggests
(a) need of talent
(b) talent must be disciplined
(c) freak success or chance is not possible
(d) natural gift of genius must pass through hard work and training in the creative art for being successful

**3. Longinus**

47. Longinus, the Greek critic belonged to
(a) 1st century A.D. (b) 4th century A.D.
(c) 2nd century A.D. (d) 3rd century A.D.

48. Sublimity has been defined as
(a) excellence of language (b) uplifting effect
(c) intensity of thought (d) grandeur of thought and intensity of feeling expressed in appropriate language

49. What are the other requirements of sublimity according to Longinus?
(a) besides grandeur of thought and intensity of feeling, noble diction, skillful composition, appropriate rhetorical devices must be learned
(b) tools of language
(c) talent must be trained
(d) for genius without training may fail

50. According to Longinus can a genius succeed without skill?
   (a) No, for even a genius is prone to fall into bombast, frigidity or excess
   (b) training is always needed
   (c) even a genius has to be educated in subjecting himself to the discipline of the task
   (d) poetry is sacred and initiates and subjugation of the wild self is essential
51. Longinus considered the works of Homer and Sappho to be significant not only for instruction, delight and persuasion. What else did he find?
   (a) poetic charm
   (b) valuable treatise for cultural reasons
   (c) racial consciousness indomitable spirit of man
   (d) sublimity
52. How did Longinus explain the sublime?
   (a) as something more than what is good for instruction, delight and persuasion
   (b) more for the soul
   (c) uplifting spirit
   (d) a certain destination and consummate excellence in expression
53. Longinus says that "the effect of lofty passage is not to convince the reason of a reader but to transport him out of himself". What is this quality?
   (a) magic of great work
   (b) doesn't great poetry raise the dead from their grave
   (c) that certain beyond all writers attempt to reach but do not succeed.
   (d) admirable piece which costs a spell over us and eclipses that which merely aims at persuasion and pleasure
54. Do you feel that the concept of sublime is something like a sage's experience of the divine?
   (a) if sublime in a work grips as a true prayer or meditation does then they are alike

(b) sublimity in poetry and experience of divinity in prayer or meditation have similar nature
(c) Longinus here moves beyond the earlier masses who only aimed at utilitarian aspects of poetry
(d) Longinus here sets a purpose beyond the common one

55. What are the five sources of sublime according to Longinus?
(i) grandeur of the thought, (ii) capacity for strong emotion, (iii) appropriate use of figures, (iv) nobility of diction, (v)
(a) structure (b) pattern of the work
(c) form of the poem (d) dignity of composition

56. Longinus believed that stately thoughts belong to the
(a) stately minds (b) genius
(c) mind trained for the purpose (d) loftiest minds

57. Longinus believed sublimity is the echo of
(a) greatness of the soul (b) greatness of the mind
(c) greatness of art (d) committed mind

58. Sublimity brings out the
(a) nobility in man (b) value oriented experience
(c) great happiness (d) joy at discovery of something beyond

59. Longinus has emphasized which factor in the treatise on sublime?
(a) grandeur (b) figures of speech
(c) simplicity (d) powerful delivery

60. What are the chief figures which make for sublimity?
(a) rhetoric (b) emotion
(c) rapid flow (d) rhetorical question, asyndeton, hyperbaton and periphrasis

61. According to Longinus nobility of diction is one of the essential factors in sublimity. It comprises of
(a) way of speaking

(b) arrangement of words
(c) proper choice of words and use of metaphors and ornamental language
(d) ornamentation

62. What are the effects of suitable and striking words according to Longinus?
(a) effectiveness
(b) achieving the goal
(c) emotional effect
(d) a moving and seductive effect by their grandeur, beauty, mellowness, dignity, force, power and a sort of glittering charm

63. According to Longinus what is the power of suitable words?
(a) power to move
(b) power of emotional
(c) reaches the innermost recesses of listener's mind and heart
(d) they are so effective that they can breathe voice into dead things

64. What is the role of arrangement of words in a composition for sublimity?
(a) it blends thought, emotion and figures in a harmonious whole in which harmony plays a significant role
(b) harmony
(c) dignity
(d) logic and good taste

65. What is the value of Longinus' treatise on sublime for criticism?
(a) intimate connection between the greatness of the soul and greatness of speech
(b) his aesthetics are grounded in thoughts and emotions of noble mind
(c) noble mind alone can produce noble and dignified poetry
(d) excellence of thought and perfection of craft are essential

66. Longinus as a critic can be best defined as
    (a) a classicist
    (b) a classicist with moral bent of mind
    (c) seeker of perfection
    (d) a classicist in taste, romanticist in temper and an idealist at heart

**4. Plato**

67. Plato was a Greek philosopher who belonged to
    (a) 400 – 320 B.C.
    (b) 428 – 344 B.C.
    (c) 428 – 347 B.C.
    (d) 447 – 300 B.C.
68. Plato attacked poetry because he believed
    (a) poets had a bad influence on social morality
    (b) poetry is based on copy of the appearances and not reality
    (c) poets aroused emotions and desires which served no social purpose
    (d) poetry was based on irrational frenzy
69. Plato's dislike of poetry was based on the assumption and belief that
    (a) philosophy was superior to poetry
    (b) philosophy was a good guide
    (c) philosophy sees truth in its ideal or pure form
    (d) philosophy deals in truth and poetry only imitates shadow
70. What is Plato's concept of mimesis?
    (a) it means imitation, essential characteristic of art
    (b) in the process poetry could elevate human nature
    (c) copying life as it appears
    (d) the process is irrational
71. What is Plato's concept of organic unity?
    (a) one complete whole
    (b) complete in itself
    (c) a coherent whole in which every part is relevant
    (d) he believed that art is like a living organism, a complete coherent whole in which every part has relevance to each other and the whole

72. Plato desired that poetry should have
    (a) a structure (b) form and style
    (c) a moral purpose (d) austerity
73. Plato believed that poetry should have
    (a) decorum, order, austerity and restraint
    (b) a definite form
    (c) little experimentation
    (d) no deviation form the declared path of decorum
74. Who said that poetry must have a moral basis, an essential requirement for good art?
    (a) Aristotle (b) Socrates
    (c) Plato (d) Aristophanes
75. Plato's enjoyment of comedies of Aristophanes had a limitation. What was the reason?
    (a) laughter (b) laughter with instructions
    (c) he believed that laughter must be controlled (d) he was against excessive laughter
76. Do you find a basic flaw in Plato's rejection of poetry?
    (a) he said that poetry should not be away from moral teaching
    (b) poetry and morality should be linked
    (c) poetry is for delight and philosophy for instructions. Plato did not consider this basic difference between the two
    (d) he felt that purpose of poetry and philosophy were the same

## UNIT B: BRITISH CRITICS: SIDNEY TO JOHNSON

### 1. Sir Philip Sidney

77. Sidney's *An Apology for Poetry* is a defence of poetry against the charges brought against it by
    (a) Henry Howard (b) Roger Ascham
    (c) John Skelton (d) Stephen Gosson

78. What does Sidney say about the observance of the three dramatic unities in drama?
    (a) they must be observed
    (b) it is not necessary to observe them
    (c) only the unity of action should be observed
    (d) their observance depends upon the nature of the play concerned
79. "It is not rhyming and versing that maketh a poet, no more than a long gown maketh an advocate."
    Who has said this?
    (a) Shakespeare (b) Marlowe
    (c) Spenser (d) Sidney
80. Sidney was basically
    (a) a subjective critic (b) a critic
    (c) an objective critic (d) none of the above
81. According to Sir Philip Sidney 'poetry' consists in the art of
    (a) sublimity (b) imagination
    (c) imitation (d) expression
82. Sir Philip Sidney had a strong urge for reviving the canons of criticism of
    (a) Longinus (b) Aristotle
    (c) Dr. Johnson (d) Bacon
83. Which of the following works has not been written by Sidney?
    (a) *Arcadia* (b) *An Apology for Poetry*
    (c) *Astrophel and Stella* (d) *Shepherd's Calendar*
84. Which writer classed poets with pipers and jesters and called them caterpillars of the Commonwealth?
    (a) Stephen Gosson (b) Sir Philip Sidney
    (c) Ben Jonson (d) Dr. Johnson
85. In Sidney's *An Apology for Poetry* the Romans have a word for poets?
    (a) maker (b) creator (c) vates (d) prophets
86. According to Sidney, poetry can be divided into three broad divisions
    (a) religious, historical and moral poetry

(b) religious, philosophic and right kind of poetry
(c) moral, dramatic and philosophical poetry
(d) none of the above

87. Poetry is an imitation of nature and its function is to teach and delight. Who has said this?
(a) Sir Philip Sidney (b) Ben Jonson
(c) Dr. Johnson (d) John Dryden

88. Sidney is not in favour of
(a) comedy (b) tragedy
(c) tragi-comedy (d) all

89. In Greek literature, the word 'poet' means
(a) maker (b) prophet (c) teacher (d) all

90. Sidney's *An Apology for Poetry* is an epitome of
(a) Romantic criticism (b) Renaissance criticism
(d) Classical criticism (d) Modern criticism

91. Dramatic criticism in England began with
(a) Sidney (b) Ben Jonson
(c) Pope (d) Dr. Johnson

**2. Ben Jonson**

92. Which of the following is the critical work of Ben Jonson?
(a) *Discourse of English Poetrie* (b) *Discourses*
(c) *Art of English Poesie* (d) *An Apology for Poetry*

93. What does Ben Jonson mean by a 'humorous' character?
(a) a character who is always cheerful and gay
(b) a character who is by nature melancholy
(c) a character whose temper is determined by one of the four liquids in the human body
(d) an eccentric person

94. Who said this? "The judge of poets is only the faculty of poets."
(a) Sidney (b) Dryden
(c) Ben Jonson (d) Pope

95. Who appreciated the universal appeal of Shakespeare?
(a) Ben Jonson (b) Alexander Pope
(c) John Dryden (d) Dr. Johnson

96. The term 'comedy of humours' was popularized by Jonson through the titles of his comedies
    (a) *The Alchemist*
    (b) *Every Man in His Humour*
    (c) *Every Man Out of His Humour*
    (d) Both (b) and (c)
97. Which play of Ben Jonson constituted an important contribution to the art of comedy in England?
    (a) *Volpone*
    (b) *The Alchemist*
    (c) *Every Man in His Humour*
    (d) None of the above
98. Jonson gave to comedy
    (a) structure and coherence
    (b) a firm plot
    (c) clear characterization
    (d) all
99. Ben Jonson has talked about humours in the human body, they are
    (a) three (b) four (c) five (d) six
100. The Latin meaning of 'humours' is
    (a) mood (b) character (c) liquid (d) comedy
101. Which of the following does not come under four principal humours in the body?
    (a) phlegm (b) blood (c) choler (d) sweat
102. Which work of Jonson satirizes the humours of the court?
    (a) *Cynthia's Revels*
    (b) *The Poetaster*
    (c) *Every Man in His Humour*
    (d) *The Alchemist*
103. Jonson expounds his theory of 'Comedy of Humours' in the Introduction to his play
    (a) *Volpone*
    (b) *The Alchemist*
    (c) *Every Man in His Humour*
    (d) *The Silent Woman*
104. Which of the following humours is also called 'yellow bile'?
    (a) blood
    (b) choler
    (c) phlegm
    (d) melancholy

105. Which comedy of Ben Jonson has a similar story of quackery as is found in Chaucer's "The Canon's Yeoman's Tale"?
(a) *Volpone* (b) *Every Man in His Humour*
(c) *The Alchemist* (d) *The Poetaster*

### 3. John Dryden

106. In Dryden's *An Essay of Dramatic Poesy* there are four speakers representing four different ideologies. Which of them expresses Dryden's own views?
(a) Lisidius (b) Eugenius
(c) Neander (d) None of these

107. What does Dryden say about the observance of the three classical dramatic unities?
(a) he advocates their strict observance
(b) he does not advocate their strict observance
(c) every dramatist should decide it for himself
(d) he is silent regarding this issue

108. Dryden's *An Essay of Dramatic Poesy* is a work of
(a) interpretative criticism (b) legislative criticism
(c) comparative criticism (d) textual criticism

109. Who called Dryden the father of English criticism?
(a) Joseph Addison (b) Dr. Johnson
(c) Coleridge (d) Matthew Arnold

110. "They wholly mistake the nature of criticism who think, its business is principally to find fault. Criticism as it was first instituted by Aristotle was meant a standard of judging well." Who said this?
(a) Pope (b) Ben Jonson
(c) Dryden (d) Dr. Johnson

111. Dryden with all his critical allurement of classical love was unconsciously a forerunner of
(a) Romantic criticism (b) Neo-classicism
(c) Objective criticism (d) None of these

112. "What pleases the Greeks, would not satisfy an English audience."
Who has said this?
(a) Dryden (b) Pope
(c) Ben Jonson (d) Sidney

113. One of the most eminent critics of neo-classical school refused to abide by the rules of the classical masters. Who was he?
(a) Addison (b) Dr. Johnson
(c) Arnold (d) Dryden

114. Of the following works, which is not written by John Dryden?
(a) *Of Heroic Plays* (b) *Discourse on Satire*
(c) *An Essay of Dramatic Poesy* (d) *Essay on Criticism*

115. Dryden as a critic
(a) fovoured romantic qualities
(b) fovoured classical qualities
(c) synthesized classical and romantic qualities
(d) approved of neither classical nor romantic qualities

116. Who has defined drama "as a just and lively image of human nature, representing its passions and humours, and the changes of fortune to which it is subject for the delight and instruction of mankind"?
(a) Dr. Johnson (b) John Dryden
(c) Alexander Pope (d) None of the above

117. "Shakespeare was the man who of all modern and perhaps ancient poets had the largest and most comprehensive soul." Who has paid the tribute to Shakespeare in the above line?
(a) John Dryden (b) Ben Jonson
(c) S.T. Coleridge (d) T.S. Eliot

118. Who is the founder of descriptive criticism in English?
(a) Sidney (b) Ben Jonson
(c) Dryden (d) Dr. Johnson

119. Who has said this? "It is not enough that Aristotle has said so, for Aristotle drew his models of tragedy from

Sophocles and Euripides and of he had sear, ours, might have charged his mind."

(a) Dr. Johnson (b) Dryden
(c) Eliot (d) I.A. Richards

120. Dryden calls comedy "a representation of human life in inferior persons and low subjects". In this regard, he followed

(a) Horace (b) Aristotle (c) Plato (d) Longinus

**4. Alexander Pope**

121. "Be Homer's works your study and delight./Read them by day and meditate by night."
Who has given this advice to the poets?

(a) Sidney (b) Dryden
(c) Pope (d) Ben Jonson

122. Alexander Pope has an undying craving to conform to the laws of

(a) neo-classical tenacity (b) prose and reason
(c) nature (d) none of the above

123. Pope was a great critic of the age of

(a) prose (b) reason
(c) prose and reason (d) Augustan literature

124. In whose work did Pope find 'unequalled fire and rapture'?

(a) Aristotle (b) Virgil
(c) Homer (d) Dr. Johnson

125. Which poet has observed "Men not afraid of God, afraid of me"?

(a) Dr. Johnson (b) Dryden
(c) Pope (d) Addison

126. Which work of Pope is modelled on Horace's *Ars Poetica*?

(a) *Preface to the Works of Shakespeare* (b) *An Essay on Criticism*
(c) *Preface to the Translation of the Iliad* (d) *The Art of Sinking*

127. Pope's *Essay on Criticism* is divided into
(a) 3 parts (b) 2 parts (c) 4 parts (d) 5 parts

128. "A critic is born to judge as a poet is born to write. To be able to discharge this duty he has to be naturally gifted, properly trained and well versed in the rules of the ancients."
Who has observed this?
(a) Dr. Johnson (b) Arnold
(c) Pope (d) Eliot

129. Which poet was called in fondness the 'little Nightingale'?
(a) Dryden (b) Pope (c) Gray (d) Burns

130. Which poet was from his birth of constitution tender and delicate?
(a) Pope (b) Milton (c) Dryden (d) Collins

**5. Dr. Samuel Johnson**

131. Which of the following critics preferred Shakespeare's comedies to his tragedies?
(a) Dryden (b) Pope
(c) Dr. Johnson (d) Addison

132. 'The end of writing is to instruct, the end of poetry is to instruct by pleasing'
Who has said this?
(a) Wordsworth (b) Dr. Johnson
(c) Coleridge (d) Arnold

133. Regarding the observance of the three classical unities in a play Dr. Johnson observes that
(a) only the unity of time should be observed
(b) only the unity of place should be observed
(c) only the unity of action should be observed
(d) all the three unities should be observed

134. Dr. Johnson meticulously looked for the correctness of
(a) poetry (b) ideas
(c) form (d) none of the above

135. Who defined essay as "a loose sally of mind, an irregular undigested piece, not a regular and orderly performance?"
(a) Ben Jonson (b) Dr. Johnson
(c) Arnold (d) Dryden

136. Dr. Johnson gave a new interpretation to the term of
(a) imagination (b) fancy
(c) imitation (d) photographic reproduction

137. Which of the following critical works has not been written by Dr. Johnson?
(a) *Lives of the Poets* (b) *Preface to the Plays of Shakespeare*
(c) *Rasselas* (d) *Essay on Criticism*

138. Who is without doubt a neo-classical critic but it does not mean a 'blind surrender' to authority of ancient or modern, rather he is for liberty?
(a) Dryden (b) Dr Johnson
(c) Addison (d) Pope

139. Dr. Johnson observes: "Poetry is an imitation of particular, with which it deals, but, through it, the universal". This definition of poetry occurs in
(a) *Lives of the Poets* (b) *Preface to Shakespeare*
(c) *Rambler* (d) None of the above

140. Which of the unities Dr. Johnson found justified by reason?
(a) unity of time (b) unity of place
(c) unity of action (d) all

141. Who is the author of the famous biography *Life of Johnson*?
(a) Addison (b) Boswell (c) Pope (d) Gibbon

142. Johnson started the publication of two journals. They are
(a) "The Spectator and The Tatler" (b) "The Tatler and The Rambler"
(c) "The Rambler and The Idler" (d) "The Idler" and "The Tatler"

143. From which king Dr. Johnson received annual pension of three hundred pounds?
(a) George III (b) George II
(c) George I (d) None of the above

144. Who has written *Dictionary of English Language* the first ambitious attempt at an English lexicon?
(a) John Dryden (b) Dr. Johnson
(c) Joseph Addison (d) James Boswell

145. Johnson's Literary Club, which had Burke, Gibbon, Goldsmith and indeed all the great literary men and politicians of the time as members, was formed in the year
(a) 1761 (b) 1762 (c) 1763 (d) 1764

## UNIT C: BRITISH CRITICS: THE ROMANTICS AND THE VICTORIANS

### 1. William Wordsworth

146. Who for the first time discriminated between imagination and fancy?
(a) William Blake (b) William Wordsworth
(c) Samuel Taylor Coleridge (d) John Keats

147. Wordsworth's *Preface to The Lyrical Ballads* is a landmark because
(a) he makes a critical statement for the new romantic poetry
(b) he explains his own poetry
(c) he declares a departure from the classical mode of poetry
(d) presents the romantic ethics

148. Who said: "Imagination is the power of depicting, and fancy of yoking and combining"?
(a) Wordsworth (b) Keats
(c) Coleridge (d) Shelley

149. William Wordsworth believed that imagination is a creative faculty and fancy merely associative and decorative. Is it a correct description?
(a) true (b) false
(c) partly true (d) irrelevant

150. *Preface to The Lyrical Ballads* was published in
(a) 1795 (b) 1790 (c) 1798 (d) 1800

151. Wordsworth and Coleridge defined poetry as an "overflow of powerful feelings" but it was tempered by saying that it was
(a) emotion recollected in tranquillity
(b) assertion of emotion
(c) own feelings and personification of nature
(d) rationalization

152. Where has Wordsworth written the following? "I have never given way to my own feelings in personifying natural objects without bringing all that I have said to a rigorous after-test of good sense".
(a) *Preface* to *The Lyrical Ballads* (b) *Essays*
(c) "Letter" to W.R. Hamilton, December 23,1829 (d) *Prelude*

153. What idea is contained in the following lines of Wordsworth's verse?

"And then my heart with pleasure fills
And dances with the daffodils.
The music in my heart I bore
Long after it was heard no more."

(a) poetry must be subjected to rigorous after-test of good sense
(b) emotion is the guiding principle in creativity
(c) personal feelings play an important role in poetry
(d) poetry like life is beautiful and joyful so one should dance and celebrate

154. Who has written the following sentence?
"Humble and rustic life was generally chosen, because, in that condition, the essential passions of the heart find a better soil in which they can attain their maturity, are less under restraint, and speak a plainer and more emphatic language; because in that condition of their life our elementary feelings co-exist in a state of greater

simplicity, and, consequently, may be more accurately contemplated, and more forcibly communicated."

(a) Coleridge in *Biographia Literaria* (b) Wordsworth in *Preface to The Lyrical Ballads*
(c) *Essays* (d) *Letters*

155. Who has written these lines?
"Poetry sheds no tears 'such as Angels weep', but natural and human tears; she can boast of no celestial ichor that distinguishes her vital juices from those of prose; the same human blood circulates through the veins of them both."
(a) Wordsworth (b) Keats
(c) Coleridge (d) None

**2. Samuel Taylor Coleridge**

156. Who has said this? "The achievement of Coleridge is rightly held to be supreme among the English critics."
(a) D.J. Enright (b) George Watson
(c) Cleanth Brooks (d) T.S. Eliot

157. Who called Coleridge the 'mediator' between Germany and England?
(a) T.S. Eliot (b) Rene Wellek
(c) Cleanth Brooks (d) I.A. Richards

158. For Coleridge a poem is not a machine, and you cannot write it off. Who said this?
(a) George Watson (b) Rene Wellek
(c) F.R. Leavis (d) None of these

159. Coleridge was influenced in his critical thoughts by
(a) Immanuel Kant (b) Hegel
(c) Spinoza (d) German ethics

160. Coleridge's criticism is
(a) descriptive (b) textual
(c) legislative (d) idealistic

161. In terms of subjects Coleridge's descriptive criticism falls into three groups:

(i) Shakespearean, (ii) critique of Wordsworth, and (iii)

(a) seventeenth century poets
(b) miscellany of comments on various poets
(c) Milton
(d) notes

162. In which chapter of *Biographia Literaria* Coleridge examines and rejects Wordsworth's statement on 'real' life and language of rustics?

(a) XIV (b) XVII (c) XVIII (d) XIX

163. Who said this? "Imagination I hold to be the living and primary agent of all human perception, and as a repetition in the infinite mind of the eternal act of creation in the infinite I Am.—It dissolves, diffuses, dissipates, in order to recreate; or where this process is rendered impossible, yet at all events it struggles to idealize and to unify."

(a) Wordsworth
(b) Coleridge
(c) Keats
(d) Shelley

164. Who coined the term 'esemplastic' and what does it mean?

(a) Coleridge, it means unifying
(b) Wordsworth, it means fancy
(c) Coleridge, it means power of imagination
(d) Keats, it means negative capability

165. Whose poetry struck Coleridge as remarkable, what did he say?

(a) magnificent language
(b) harmony between theme and style
(c) delightful thought
(d) the union of deep feeling with profound

### 3. Percy Bysshe Shelley

166. Who has written this? "Poetry always contains a pinch of untruth. The philosophic spirit gives us the habit of noting this untruth, and goodbye poetic illusion, goodbye poetic effect."

(a) Macaulay
(b) Thomas Love Peacock
(c) Denis Diderot
(d) Plato

167. The charge that poetry corrupts is age old, even Plato condemned them. But who has written this line in the

19th century? "Perhaps no person can be a poet, or can even enjoy poetry, without a certain unsoundness of mind."

(a) Denis Diderot (b) Thomas Love Peacock
(c) Plato (d) Thomas Macaulay

168. Who condemned poetry and poets in derogatory terms in the heyday of romantic poetry in these words? "A poet in our times is a semi-barbarian in a civilized community. He lives in the days that are past.—The march of his intellect is like that of a crab, backward."

(a) Thomas Love Peacock (b) Thomas Macaulay
(c) Denis Diderot (d) Rousseau

169. "A Defence of Poetry" is an enthusiastic rebuttal to his friend's book *The four Ages of Poetry*. Who is this friend?

(a) John Keats (b) William Wordsworth
(c) Thomas Love Peacock (d) Thomas Macaulay

170. Who has defended poetry in these words? "Poetry is the record of the best and happiest moments of the happiest and best minds. ... It is as it were the interpenetration of a diviner nature through our own."

(a) Blake (b) Wordsworth
(c) Byron (d) Shelley

171. Who has written this? "Poetry is indeed something divine, ... for the mind in creation is like a fading coal, which some invisible influence, like an inconstant wind, awakens to transitory brightness; this power arises from within, like the colour of a flower which fades and changes as it developed, and the conscious portions of our natures are unprophetic either of its approach or its departure."

(a) Shelley (b) Coleridge
(c) Keats (d) Wordsworth

172. Who has written this in appreciation of poetry? "Poetry turns all things to loveliness; it exalts the beauty of that, which is beautiful, and it adds beauty that which is most

deformed; it marries exultation and horror. Grief and pleasure, eternity and change; it subdues to union under its light yoke all irreconcilable things. It transmutes all that it touches."

(a) Byron (b) Wordsworth
(c) Shelley (d) Keats

173. Shelley is inspired and enthusiastic in "A Defence of Poetry" just as he is in these lines of verse:
"Scatter, as from an extinguished hearth
Ashes and sparks, my words among mankind!
Be through my lips to awakened earth
The trumpet of a prophecy!"
These lines occur in which poem?
(a) "Ode to the Skylark" (b) "Queen Mab"
(c) "Ode to the West Wind" (d) "Prometheus Unbound"

174. Only one English poet of the era has presented a companion theory to Shelley's. He asserts, "Imagination is the real eternal World of which even this Vegetable Universe is but a faint shadow".
(a) William Blake (b) P.B. Shelley
(c) Robert Burns (d) George Gordon Byron

175. Shelley is in the tradition of
(a) Sidney (b) Plato
(c) Dryden (d) Dr. Johnson

**4. John Keats**

176. Choose that poet-critic who made significant contribution to Romantic criticism besides Blake, Wordsworth, Coleridge, Lamb, Hazlitt, De Quincey and Shelley?
(a) Burns (b) Southey (c) Scott (d) Keats

177. Who said that "imagination may be compared to Adam's dream, he awoke and found it truth"?
(a) Shelley (b) Burns (c) Keats (d) Lamb

178. Keats stated: "I mean Negative Capability, that is, when man is capable to be in uncertainties, mysteries, doubts,

without any irritable reaching after fact and reason". Where does this occur?

(a) "Letter to Benjamin Bailey, November 22, 1817"
(b) "Letter to Percy Bysshe Shelley, August 16, 1820"
(c) "Letter to John Taylor, February 27, 1818"
(d) "Letter to George and Tom Keats, December 21, 1817"

179. Who said this about poetry?

"Poetry should be great and unobtrusive, a thing which enters one's soul, and does not startle it or amaze it with itself, but with subject. How beautiful are the retired flowers! How would they lose their beauty were they to throng into the highway crying out, 'Admire me, I am violet! Dote upon me, I am primrose!"

(a) Shelley (b) Wordsworth
(c) Coleridge (d) Keats

180. Where did Keats write? "That if Poetry comes not naturally as the leaves to a tree, it had better not come at all"

(a) "The Eve of St Agnes" (b) "Endymion"
(c) "Letter to John Taylor, February 27, 1818" (d) "La Belle Dame Sans Merci"

**5. Matthew Arnold**

181. Arnold was opposed to

(a) romanticism (b) classicism
(c) sensuousness (d) philistinism

182. Arnold seeks to bring about a harmony between Hebraism and

(a) Hellenism (b) Romanticism
(c) Classicism (d) Medievalism

183. Who said? "Poetry is a criticism of life under curtains".

(a) Wordsworth (b) Coleridge
(c) Keats (d) Arnold

184. In which text does Arnold say that poetry is superior to history?

(a) "Keats" (b) "Milton"
(c) "Wordsworth" (d) "The Study of Poetry"

185. In "Wordsworth" Arnold collaborates on his idea of
(a) love (b) sin (c) poetry (d) nature

186. Who said that the greatness of Wordsworth as a poet lies in his shorter pieces?
(a) F.R. Leavis (b) I.A. Richards
(c) T.S. Eliot (d) Matthew Arnold

187. John Keats, according to Matthew Arnold was deficient in the area of
(a) moral interpretation (b) romance
(c) farsightedness (d) natural beauty

188. Arnold's high concept of poetry results from his
(a) moral bias (b) sharp intellect
(c) classicism (d) critical acumen

189. Arnold gives us a brief critical survey of English poetry in
(a) "Essays in Criticism" (b) "Dover Beach"
(c) "The Study of Poetry" (d) none

190. Arnold was the first English critic to insist on the necessity of
(a) dialectical criticism (b) comparative criticism
(c) functional criticism (d) classical criticism

191. Who said? Arnold's outlook is "honest and frank and often penetrating".
(a) Cazamian (b) Eliot
(c) Richards (d) Johnson

192. An important aspect of Arnold's classicism was his concept of
(a) love (b) sensuousness
(c) grand style (d) romance

193. There is plenty of ironic banter in
(a) "The Study of Poetry" (b) *Essays in Criticism*
(c) "The Functions of Criticism at the Present Time" (d) none

194. Who called Shelley "a beautiful and ineffectual angel, beating in the void his luminous wings in vain"?
(a) Richards (b) Arnold (c) Eliot (d) Yeats

195. Who called "a poet and philosopher, wrecked in the mist of opium"?
(a) Arnold (b) Wordsworth
(c) Hazlitt (d) Byron

**6. Walter Horatio Pater**

196. Pater's first essays appeared in book form in
(a) *Pall Mall* (b) *Appreciations*
(c) *Studies in the History of Renaissance* (d) *Imaginary Portraits*

197. Pater's *Imaginary Portraits* deals with
(a) love (b) artistes (c) romance (d) patriotism

198. Literary themes are dealt in Pater's
(a) *Appreciations* (b) *Pall Mall*
(c) *Guardian* (d) *Imaginary Portraits*

199. Pater's *Marius, the Epicurean* is a remarkable
(a) sonnet (b) essay
(c) ode (d) philosophical novel

200. In his essay on style in *Appreciations*, Pater gives importance to
(a) love (b) romance
(c) joy (d) beauty of expression

201. Pater in his writings is
(a) objective (b)subjective (c) satirical (d) romantic

202. Walter Pater believed that power of every word and phrase should be weighed in order to give a hard and proper shape to work. He treated words as
(a) precious metal (b) blue china
(c) marble (d) none of these

203. Did Pater move away from the mimetic theory and the concept of nature as the infallible goddess like Baudelaire?
(a) he was romantic in spirit
(b) in this period the concepts were changing from romantic to modern
(c) there was dominance of 'art for art's sake' and Poets like Baudelaire were influenced
(d) both accepted the need of a finished work of art

204. Who among English critics in the Victorian era appreciated this statement of Baudelaire?
"It is the right of woman and her duty to give herself a magical finish, a supernatural lustre. She is expected to astonish and charm us. She is a kind of idol, and she ought to gild herself until she is fit object of our adoration."
(a) Walter Pater (b) Tennyson
(c) Arnold (d) D.G. Rossetti

205. Who has written? "Not the fruit of experience, but experience itself is the end". And added: "Great passions may give us this quickened sense of life. ... Only be sure it is passion. ... Of such wisdom, the poetic passion, the desire of beauty, the love of art for its own sake, has most."
(a) D.G. Rossetti (b) Wordsworth
(c) Arnold (d) Walter Pater

## UNIT D: BRITISH CRITICS: THE MODERNS

### 1. D.H. Lawrence

206. "There is literary criticism in his travel sketches and philosophy in his criticism." This is true in the case of which modern British writer?
(a) James Joyce (b) George Eliot
(c) Kingsley Amis (d) D.H. Lawrence

207. Lawrence's *Twilight in Italy* and *Sea and Sardinia* are marked by
(a) a vivaciousness and descriptive brilliance of a Tolstoy, Dickens and George Eliot
(b) a true picture
(c) truthful travel sketches
(d) powerful language

208. Which travel sketch is considered Lawrence's best?
(a) *Twilight in Italy* (b) *Sea and Sardinia*
(c) *Morning in Mexico* (d) *Etruscan Places*

209. Lawrence's *Psychoanalysis and the Unconscious* (1920) and *Fantasia of the Unconscious* (1921) represent
   (a) an analysis of Freudian theory of sex and incest-motive
   (b) a reaction against and a rejection of theory based on sex
   (c) a reaction against Freudian theory of sex and incest-motive as the basis of human behaviour and prepared his own theory based on human physiology
   (d) a theory prepared by Lawrence based on the unconscious

210. According to Lawrence the basis of human sensuality was
   (a) Thoracic ganglion (b) The Lumbar ganglion
   (c) Cardiac plexus (d) Solar Plexus

211. Lawrence in his critical analysis of the unconscious and its role emphasizes on the role of solar plexus. What is solar plexus?
   (a) the solar plexus is the seat of creative knowledge more valuable than the cerebral knowledge—instinct is superior to intellect
   (b) it is a nerve centre which Lawrence believed to be responsible for human sensuality and creativity
   (c) solar plexus represents the ancestral knowledge, social and individual

212. In *Studies in Classic American Literature* what does Lawrence write about *Moby Dick*?
   (a) he is the deepest blood-being of the white race; he is our deepest blood nature
   (b) the whale is hunted, driven by the white mental consciousness
   (c) Moby Dick is the challenge to white race
   (d) it is the cerebral will hunting down the sensory instinct

213. These lines show his essential philosophy, what do they suggest?

"We are transmitter of life./And when we fail to transmit life,/Life fails to flow through us."

(a) life is instinctual

(b) life is instinctual and a flow onwards

(c) we have the responsibility to transmit what we receive

(d) life is not sexless dead end

214. Lawrence writes that "even the rainbow has a body made of the drizzling rain". What is the idea he is trying to present?

(a) Lawrence believed in the concept of instinct of the body being wiser than the knowledge of the intellect and he is celebrating the body, the instinct

(b) the rainbow delights the basic instinctual consciousness of man

(c) the mind the intellect cannot instant it

(d) body must exist and only then other areas of arguments may be taken up

215. In his major criticism Lawrence makes a distinction between

(a) knowledge and instinct

(b) sensitive mind and intellectual awareness

(c) education and ignorance

(d) intuition and the mind, instinct of the body and intellect of the mind

**2. T.S. Eliot**

216. Which one of the following phrases has been coined by T.S. Eliot?

(a) art for Art's sake (b) suspension of disbelief

(c) objective correlative (d) touchstone method

217. Which one of the following phrases has not been coined by T.S. Eliot?

(a) dissociation of sensibility (b) unified sensibility

(c) objective correlative (d) art for art's sake

218. The phrase 'Objective Correlative' was first used by Eliot in his
(a) *Essay on 'Hamlet'* (b) *Essay on 'Macbeth'*
(c) *Essay on 'King Lear'* (d) *Essay on 'Othello'*

219. "A set of objects, a situation, a chain of events, which shall be the formula for the poet's emotion so that when the external facts are given the emotion is at once evoked."
The above lines define which of the following phrases of T.S. Eliot?
(a) objective correlative (b) dissociation of sensibility
(c) unified sensibility (d) tradition and individual talent

220. The mental agony of Lady Macbeth has been expressed through the 'sleep walking scene' it (the mental agony) has not been expressed directly. This may be cited as an example of
(a) objective correlative (b) dissociation of sensibility
(c) unified sensibility (d) tradition and individual talent

221. The phrase 'dissociation of sensibility' was first used by Eliot in his
(a) *Essay on 'Hamlet'* (b) *Metaphysical Poets*
(c) *Frontiers of Criticism* (d) *Tradition and Individual Talent*

222. Which of the following statements may be true about Eliot's criticism?
(a) unification of sensibility means a fusion of thought and feeling
(b) unification of sensibility is a characteristic of bad poetry
(c) Eliot was a romanticist in literature, not classicist
(d) dissociation of sensibility is a characteristic of good poetry

223. The term 'new criticism' was first used by which of the following critics?
(a) Joel E. Spingarn (b) John Crowe Ransom
(c) T.S. Eliot (d) George Watson

224. Who is the author of *The Sacred Wood*?
(a) F.R. Leavis (b) T.S. Eliot
(c) I.A. Richards (d) James Wood

225. Which of the following critical opinions may be associated with T.S. Eliot?
(a) T.S. Eliot is against the Romantic critics like Coleridge, who judge a poet on the basis of their personal impressions and feelings. Such impressionism can never be a safe guide
(b) Poetry is an expression of personality, not an escape from personality
(c) Poetry is a spontaneous overflow of powerful feelings
(d) Inspiration is the safe guide for poets

**3. F.R. Leavis**

226. Which of the following critical works has been authored by F.R. Leavis?
(a) *The Principles of Literary Criticism* (b) *The Great Tradition*
(c) *The Sacred Wood* (d) *Poetics*

227. Which of the following critical works has not been authored by F.R. Leavis?
(a) *The Meaning of Meaning* (b) *The Great Tradition*
(c) *New Bearings in English Poetry* (d) *Revaluation*

228. Leavis' *The Great Tradition* provides us with his critical opinions on
(a) modern poetry (b) post-Shakespearean poetry
(c) drama (d) novel

229. Leavis' *Revaluation* provides us with his critical opinions on
(a) modern poetry (b) post-Shakespearean poetry
(c) drama (d) novel

230. Leavis' *New Bearings in English Poetry* provides us with his critical opinions on
(a) modern poetry (b) post-Shakespearean poetry
(c) drama (d) novel

231. Which of the following statements about F.R. Leavis may be true?
   (a) unlike the critics of the past Leavis nowhere lays down rules to judge the merit of a work
   (b) Leavis has certain rules and principles in his mind to judge the merit of a work
   (c) Leavis wrote the book *The Sacred Wood*
   (d) *The Principles of Literary Criticism* is a book authored by F.R. Leavis
232. Which of the following novelists has not been mentioned in Leavis' *The Great Tradition*?
   (a) Thomas Hardy (b) Joseph Conrad
   (c) Jane Austen (d) George Eliot
233. In which category can you keep the criticism of F.R. Leavis?
   (a) Ontological Criticism (b) Historical Criticism
   (c) Biographical Criticism (d) Comparative Criticism
234. Which of the following statements is true about the critical opinions of F.R. Leavis?
   (a) literature matters vitally to civilization
   (b) literature of the past is more valuable than the literature of the present
   (c) Leavis judges a work of art on the basis of rules and theories which he has framed
   (d) literature has nothing to do with the tastes and habits it fosters and its effect on the quality of living
235. Which of the following statements is true about the critical opinions of F.R. Leavis?
   (a) unlike the critics of the past Leavis nowhere lays down rules whereby to judge the merit of a work
   (b) Leavis judges a work of art on the basis of rules and theories which he has framed
   (c) Leavis in the evaluation of works lays much emphasis on the lives of the authors
   (d) none of these

## 4. I.A. Richards

236. The full name of I.A. Richards is
(a) Insle Anderson Richards (b) Ivor Armstrong Richards
(c) Iris Anderson Richards (d) Iris August Richards

237. Richards, *The Meaning of Meaning* was written in collaboration with whom?
(a) T.S. Eliot (b) C.K. Ogden
(c) R.P. Blackmur (d) William Empson

238. Who wrote the book *The Principles of Literary criticism*?
(a) William Empson (b) I.A. Richards
(c) T.S. Eliot (d) Cleanth Brooks

239. Which of the following has not been written by I.A. Richards?
(a) *The Principles of Literary Criticism* (b) *The Practical Criticism*
(c) *The Philosophy of Rhetoric* (d) *The Metaphysical Poets*

240. Who is the author of the book *Coleridge on Imagination*?
(a) I.A. Richards (b) F.R. Leavis
(c) L.K. Ogden (d) Games Wood

241. Which of the following books was written by I.A. Richards in collaboration with C.K. Ogden and James Wood?
(a) *The Foundation of Aesthetics* (b) *The Meaning of Meaning*
(c) *Coleridge on Imagination* (d) *The Principles of Literary Criticism*

242. According to I.A. Richards, there are two uses of language. What are they?
(a) referential or scientific and emotive
(b) communicative and suggestive
(c) referential and suggestive
(d) emotional and emotive

243. "There are two ways in which impulses may be organized by exclusion and by inclusion, by synthesis and by

elimination." The above lines are critical opinion of which of the following?

(a) T.S. Eliot (b) I.A. Richards
(c) F.R. Leavis (d) C.K. Ogden

244. "A poet in our time is a semi-barbarian in a civilized community." This line may be associated with which of the following critics?

(a) T.S. Eliot (b) I.A. Richards
(c) F.R. Leavis (d) Thomas Love Peacock

245. What does Richards mean by the term 'synaesthesis'?

(a) a harmony and equilibrium of our impulses
(b) a harmony between sound and rhythm
(c) a harmony between words and music
(d) a harmony between body and soul

**5. Jacques Derrida**

246. Of the following critics who is considered to be the most celebrated by the philosophers of the 20th century?

(a) F.R. Leavis (b) Jacques Derrida
(c) T.S. Eliot (d) I.A. Richards

247. Which theory was applied to the whole gamut of arts and social sciences, including linguistics, anthropology, political science, even architecture?

(a) Theory of Imagination (b) Theory of Poetry
(c) Theory of Deconstruction (d) Theory of Dramatic Pleasure

248. Which of the following books has not been written by Derrida?

(a) *Of Grammatology*
(b) *The Post Card: From Socrates to Freud and Beyond*
(c) *Ulysses Gramophone: Here Say Yes in Joyce*
(d) *Discoveries*

249. Jacques Derrida was an Algerian born intellectual.

(a) French (b) American
(c) British (d) Swiss

250. Who is known as the father of deconstruction?
(a) T.S. Eliot (b) F.R. Leavis
(c) I.A. Richards (d) Jacques Derrida

## UNIT E: AMERICAN CRITICS

### 1. Irving Babbitt

251. Irving Babbitt belongs to which period?
(a) 1865-1950 (b) 1869-1920
(c) 1855-1933 (d) 1865-1933

252. He was educated at
(a) Boston (b) Harvard
(c) New York (d) Washington

253. He was a Professor of French at
(a) Yale (b) Ohio (c) Nebraska (d) Harvard

254. He was an outstanding scholar, critic and leader of
(a) new humanist movement (b) aesthetics movement
(c) new Romantic movement (d) none of these

255. In *Literature and the American College* (1908) he presents
(a) humanist doctrine (b) aesthetic theory
(c) criticism of romantics (d) modern civilization

256. In *Democracy and Leadership* (1924) he presents
(a) plea for humanities (b) discussions on classical theory of imitation
(c) concepts of spontaneity (d) philosophy of modern civilization

257. Babbitt has presented a discussion on classical theories and remote concepts of spontaneity in
(a) *The New Laokoon* (b) *Democracy and Leadership*
(c) *On Being Creative* (d) *Spanish Character*

258. Babbitt expresses his views on romantic confusion in the arts in
(a) *Literature and the American College* (b) *The New Laokoon*
(c) *Rousseau and Romanticism* (d) *On Being Creative*

259. Which of his books is a posthumous collection of his works?
   (a) *On Being Creative* (b) *The New Laokoon*
   (c) *Spanish Character* (d) *Rousseau and Romanticism*

**2. Cleanth Brooks**

260. The "new criticism" in America was influenced by
   (a) T.S. Eliot and I.A. Richards (b) Coleridge
   (c) Irving Babbitt (d) None of these

261. Which books of criticism are almost the source of modern criticism?
   (a) *Preface to Lyrical Ballads* by Wordsworth and Coleridge
   (b) *Biographia Literaria* by Coleridge
   (c) *An Apology for Poetry* by Sidney
   (d) Eliot's *The Sacred Wood* and Richards' *Principles of Literary Criticism*

262. The tenets of "new critics" in America are
   (a) close examination of the texts themselves
   (b) close examination of the texts, analyzing style and imagery
   (c) a poem as an organic whole
   (d) technical criticism

263. The "New critics" like Yvor Winters and Cleanth Brooks believed that a poem can be "experienced" as a work of art by
   (a) the accurate sensibility of the critic
   (b) the integrity and knowledge of the critic
   (c) scholarly critic with the help of scientific methodology
   (d) the acuteness of the individual sensibility and knowledge of the semantics

264. What are the tools of criticism according to Cleanth Brooks?
   (a) acuteness of sensibility, knowledge of semantics to go to the analysis of the text and analyzing form, style, metrics, rhythm and imagery

(b) the poem is an organic whole and should not be subjected to dissection
(c) the best method is the historical approach
(d) literature is the revelation of the personality of the poet, therefore biographical approach is preferred

265. The function of a critic is to put the reader in possession of the work of art.
Who said this?
(a) I.A. Richards (b) T.S. Eliot
(c) Yvor Winters (d) Cleanth Brooks

266. What is Brook's contribution in *The Well Wrought Urn*?
(a) he has used his critical tools dexterously in analysis of a number of poems, especially Keats' odes
(b) his analysis is personal but very deep
(c) he has studied the imagery in these poems and highlighted its patterns
(d) he has discussed mostly the works of Augustan poets like Alexander Pope and John Dryden

267. Brooks has mainly used his critical tools on
(a) poetry (b) prose
(c) short stories (d) fiction

268. The southern movement was primarily agrarian but also included
(a) aesthetics (b) aesthetics and interpretation of difficult poetry
(c) political issues, like industrialization (d) a moral agenda

269. Brooks is associated with the southern movement which is manifested by
(a) his contribution to "Southern Review"
(b) his editorship of "Southern Review"
(c) his association with "Southern Review" and "The Kenyon Review"

270. Cleanth Brooks in *An Approach to Literature* presents
   (a) no concern
   (b) an academic concern by using 'new criticism' techniques
   (c) influence of southern movement
   (d) a moral approach

271. Cleanth Brooks wrote, *Understanding Poetry*, *Understanding Fiction* and *Understanding Drama.* Who is the co-author of these books?
   (a) Robert Penn Warren
   (b) Robert B. Heilman
   (c) the book on drama was written with R.B. Heilman and the other two with R.P. Warren
   (d) all the three books were written by Brooks, Warren and Heilman

272. Cleanth Brooks' works on poetry, fiction and drama became popular text book in a large number of universities globally because of
   (a) high level of quality
   (b) inclusion of typical pieces of literary writing of different genre
   (c) high level of quality and effectiveness in understanding the literary merit and value of pieces presented and analyzed
   (d) based on "new criticism"

273. Which book he wrote with W.K. Wimsatt during his days at Yale University?
   (a) *Literary Criticism: A Short History*
   (b) *An Approach to Literature*
   (c) *Understanding Fiction*
   (d) *Understanding Poetry*

274. What did Ransom declare about Brooks' *Modern Poetry and Tradition* (1939) and *The Well Wrought Urn* (1947)?
   (a) great works of criticism
   (b) a great modern critic
   (c) a true American critic
   (d) the best living interpreter of difficult verse

**3. R.P. Blackmur**

275. Who has written *The Double Agent*?
(a) R.P. Warren (b) Cleanth Brooks
(c) Kenneth Burke (d) R.P. Blackmur

276. Who has written *The Expense of Greatness*?
(a) Ezra Pound (b Yvor Winters
(c) William Empson (d) R.P. Blackmur

277. From whom did Blackmur derive the naturalistic motive?
(a) I.A. Richards (b) Allen Tate
(c) George Santayana (d) J.R. Ransom

278. In his analytical procedure Blackmur is indebted to whom?
(a) Allan Tate and J.C. Ransom (b) Cleanth Brooks and R.P. Warren
(c) Yvor Winters and John Crowe Ransom (d) I.A. Richards and William Empson

279. R.P. Blackmur combined in his criticism the techniques of George Santayana, I.A. Richards, William Empson, T.S. Eliot and Henry James. What was the result?
(a) aestheticism and a moral conception of literature
(b) a minute dissection of the style, form, diction and structure for proper evaluation of a literary work
(c) not much different from other critics
(d) destruction of a work of literature

**4. Lionel Trilling**

280. Lionel Trilling was associated with which university in America?
(a) Harvard (b) Yale (c) Chicago (d) Columbia

281. He was affiliated with
(a) the southern movement (b) "new criticism' like Brooks and Ransom
(c) Kenyon school of English (d) new humanist movement

282. Lionel Trilling was associated with literary magazine like
(a) *The Kenyon Review* and *Partisan Review* (b) *Southern Review*
(c) *Transition* (d) *The Literary Criterion*

283. Who has written *Matthew Arnold* (1939) and *E.M. Forster* (1943) with acumen?
(a) Cleanth Brooks (b) Yvor Winters
(c) Lionel Trilling (d) Allen Tate

284. *The Liberal Imagination* and *The Opposing Self* are Trilling's
(a) creative writings (b) essays
(c) critical writings (d) social writings expressing the need for moral climate

285. *Freud and the Crisis of our Culture* and *The Life and Works of Sigmund Freud* depict Lionel Trilling's concern with
(a) psychological approach to human problems
(b) the need for understanding human sexuality
(c) Freudian impact which was dominating mid twentieth century U.S.A.
(d) tribute to Freud's insight

286. In *The Opposing Self* Trilling highlights
(a) the basic problems of life and art
(b) the fundamental issues of life and art, the problem of self
(c) the kaleidoscopic view of Man's self
(d) the path of 'being' one's self

287. According to Trilling how many faces a man has?
(a) many
(b) two—inner and outer
(c) in the modern times attitude towards self has changed and developed resulting in various faces appearing with varying regularity in different situations
(d) As many as he chooses depending on his ability to let his self assert and develop

288. Trilling has written about Keats that: "He permitted nothing to be falsified". In which essay has he written this?
(a) in *The Opposing Self*
(b) in "The poet as Hero: Keats in his Letters" in *The Opposing Self*

(c) in "The Poet as Hero" in *The Liberal Imagination*
(d) in "The Kenyon Review"

289. A critic disagreed with Matthew Arnold's statement on *Anna Karenina* that it should be taken not as a work of art but as a piece of life. The critic said that art is art and life is life; we read novels and live life. Who is the critic?
(a) Cleanth Brooks (b) Yvor Winters
(c) Lionel Trilling in his essay on *Anna Karenina* (d) J.C. Ransom

**5. John Crowe Ransom**

290. John Crowe Ransom was a
(a) poet (b) critic of poetry
(c) critic (d) poet-critic

291. Ransom was a product of
(a) southern movement in literature
(b) agrarian movement
(c) the Vanderbilt circle who brought out *The Fugitive*
(d) various intellectual and political movement which were in force in the early 20th century America

292. The names of J.C. Ransom, Allen Tate and R.P. Warren are taken together in a particulate context
What is this context?
(a) members of the Fugitive-Agrarian group at Vanderbilt
(b) the group called New Critics
(c) southern literature
(d) mid west literature

293. John Crowe Ransom was in the thick of the southern movement but later on he placed more stress on
(a) New Criticism (b) New Criticism and not on regionalism
(c) good literature (d) good critical judgement

294. Ransom's *God without Thunder: An Unorthodox Defense of Orthodoxy* is an attack on
(a) politicalization of life
(b) moral collapse

(c) science for destroying the old mystery of God
(d) science for not bringing man the essential happiness

295. In *The World's Body* Ransom asserts
(a) failure of science to achieve the body that is in poetry
(b) poetry sustains more than science
(c) science has not lived up to man's expectations
(d) poetry is more real than the virtual reality of science

296. Ransom in *I'll Take My Stand* asserts that
(a) man must protest
(b) man must protest if situation so demands
(c) he contributed in this anthology which belongs to early Vanderbilt days
(d) a typical southerner's stand

297. In *The New Criticism* (1941) Ransom wrote about
(a) the writers of southern movement
(b) critics who belonged to the southern movement
(c) writers from the north
(d) his contemporaries

298. In *The New Criticism* what was the need of the times?
(a) a balanced critic
(b) adherence to the tenets of New Criticism
(c) giving importance to the tradition
(d) an ontological critic (based on the philosophy concerned with the nature of being)

299. Like his elegies Ransom in his criticism is
(a) witty and humorous (b) analytical
(c) witty and oblique (d) realistic and intelligible

## ANSWERS

### Unit A

| | | | |
|---|---|---|---|
| 1. (a) | 2. (a) | 3. (c) | 4. (d) |
| 5. (b) | 6. (a) | 7. (c) | 8. (a) |
| 9. (a) | 10. (a) | 11. (b) | 12. (d) |
| 13. (d) | 14. (a) | 15. (d) | 16. (c) |
| 17. (d) | 18. (d) | 19. (d) | 20. (c) |

| | | | | | | | |
|---|---|---|---|---|---|---|---|
| 21. | (d) | 22. | (b) | 23. | (a) | 24. | (b) |
| 25. | (b) | 26. | (d) | 27. | (a) | 28. | (c) |
| 29. | (d) | 30. | (b) | 31. | (c) | 32. | (a) |
| 33. | (a) | 34. | (a) | 35. | (d) | 36. | (b) |
| 37. | (a) | 38. | (a) | 39. | (a) | 40. | (c) |
| 41. | (b) | 42. | (a) | 43. | (d) | 44. | (a) |
| 45. | (d) | 46. | (d) | 47. | (d) | 48. | (d) |
| 49. | (a) | 50. | (a) | 51. | (d) | 52. | (d) |
| 53. | (d) | 54. | (b) | 55. | (d) | 56. | (d) |
| 57. | (a) | 58. | (a) | 59. | (b) | 60. | (d) |
| 61. | (c) | 62. | (d) | 63. | (d) | 64. | (a) |
| 65. | (b) | 66. | (d) | 67. | (c) | 68. | (a) |
| 69. | (a) | 70. | (a) | 71. | (d) | 72. | (b) |
| 73. | (a) | 74. | (c) | 75. | (c) | 76. | (c) |

## Unit B

| | | | | | | | |
|---|---|---|---|---|---|---|---|
| 77. | (d) | 78. | (a) | 79. | (d) | 80. | (b) |
| 81. | (c) | 82. | (b) | 83. | (d) | 84. | (a) |
| 85. | (c) | 86. | (b) | 87. | (a) | 88. | (c) |
| 89. | (a) | 90. | (b) | 91. | (a) | 92. | (b) |
| 93. | (c) | 94. | (c) | 95. | (a) | 96. | (d) |
| 97. | (c) | 98. | (d) | 99. | (b) | 100. | (c) |
| 101. | (d) | 102. | (a) | 103. | (c) | 104. | (b) |
| 105. | (c) | 106. | (c) | 107. | (b) | 108. | (b) |
| 109. | (b) | 110. | (c) | 111. | (a) | 112. | (a) |
| 113. | (d) | 114. | (d) | 115. | (c) | 116. | (b) |
| 117. | (a) | 118. | (c) | 119. | (b) | 120. | (b) |
| 121. | (c) | 122. | (c) | 123. | (c) | 124. | (c) |
| 125. | (c) | 126. | (a) | 127. | (a) | 128. | (c) |
| 129. | (b) | 130. | (a) | 131. | (c) | 132. | (b) |
| 133. | (c) | 134. | (c) | 135. | (b) | 136. | (c) |
| 137. | (d) | 138. | (b) | 139. | (b) | 140. | (c) |

| | | | | | | | |
|---|---|---|---|---|---|---|---|
| 141. | (b) | 142. | (c) | 143. | (a) | 144. | (b) |
| 145. | (d) | | | | | | |

## Unit C

| | | | | | | | |
|---|---|---|---|---|---|---|---|
| 146. | (b) | 147. | (a) | 148. | (a) | 149. | (a) |
| 150. | (d) | 151. | (a) | 152. | (c) | 153. | (a) |
| 154. | (b) | 155. | (a) | 156. | (b) | 157. | (b) |
| 158. | (a) | 159. | (a) | 160. | (a) | 161. | (b) |
| 162. | (b) | 163. | (b) | 164. | (a) | 165. | (c) |
| 166. | (c) | 167. | (d) | 168. | (a) | 169. | (c) |
| 170. | (d) | 171. | (a) | 172. | (c) | 173. | (c) |
| 174. | (a) | 175. | (a) | 176. | (d) | 177. | (c) |
| 178. | (d) | 179. | (d) | 180. | (c) | 181. | (d) |
| 182. | (a) | 183. | (d) | 184. | (d) | 185. | (c) |
| 186. | (d) | 187. | (a) | 188. | (a) | 189. | (a) |
| 190. | (b) | 191. | (a) | 192. | (c) | 193. | (c) |
| 194. | (b) | 195. | (a) | 196. | (c) | 197. | (b) |
| 198. | (a) | 199. | (d) | 200. | (d) | 201. | (b) |
| 202. | (a) | 203. | (c) | 204. | (a) | 205. | (d) |

## Unit D

| | | | | | | | |
|---|---|---|---|---|---|---|---|
| 206. | (d) | 207. | (a) | 208. | (c) | 209. | (c) |
| 210. | (d) | 211. | (a) | 212. | (d) | 213. | (b) |
| 214. | (a) | 215. | (d) | 216. | (c) | 217. | (d) |
| 218. | (a) | 219. | (a) | 220. | (a) | 221. | (b) |
| 222. | (a) | 223. | (a) | 224. | (b) | 225. | (a) |
| 226. | (b) | 227. | (a) | 228. | (d) | 229. | (b) |
| 230. | (a) | 231. | (a) | 232. | (a) | 233. | (a) |
| 234. | (a) | 235. | (a) | 236. | (b) | 237. | (b) |
| 238. | (b) | 239. | (d) | 240. | (a) | 241. | (a) |
| 242. | (a) | 243. | (b) | 244. | (b) | 245. | (a) |
| 246. | (b) | 247. | (b) | 248. | (d) | 249. | (a) |
| 250. | (d) | | | | | | |

## Unit E

| | | | | | | | |
|---|---|---|---|---|---|---|---|
| 251. | (d) | 252. | (b) | 253. | (d) | 254. | (a) |
| 255. | (a) | 256. | (d) | 257. | (c) | 258. | (b) |
| 259. | (c) | 260. | (a) | 261. | (d) | 262. | (b) |
| 263. | (d) | 264. | (a) | 265. | (d) | 266. | (a) |
| 267. | (a) | 268. | (b) | 269. | (c) | 270. | (b) |
| 271. | (c) | 272. | (c) | 273. | (a) | 274. | (d) |
| 275. | (d) | 276. | (d) | 277. | (c) | 278. | (d) |
| 279. | (b) | 280. | (d) | 281. | (c) | 282. | (a) |
| 283. | (c) | 284. | (c) | 285. | (c) | 286. | (b) |
| 287. | (c) | 288. | (b) | 289. | (c) | 290. | (d) |
| 291. | (d) | 292. | (a) | 293. | (a) | 294. | (c) |
| 295. | (a) | 296. | (c) | 297. | (b) | 298. | (d) |
| 299. | (c) | | | | | | |

# Classics of World Literature 14

## UNIT A: ANCIENT CLASSICS

### 1. *Aenid*

1. To which of the following period Virgil belongs?
   (a) 70 B.C. (b) 700 B.C. (c) 07 B.C. (d) 800 B.C.
2. *Aenid* is the great national epic of
   (a) classical Rome (b) Greece
   (c) England (d) France
3. *Aenid* was published after Virgil's death. When was it published?
   (a) 10 B.C. (b) 5 B.C. (c) 19 B.C. (d) 70 B.C.
4. Which of the following statements in the context of Virgil's *Aenid* may be correct?
   (a) Virgil took his story from the legend of the arrival in the west of the Trojan fugitive, Aeneas.
   (b) Virgil took his story from the legendary love between Aeneas and Helen
   (c) Virgil took his story from Aeneas's faithfulness to Dido
   (d) none of the above
5. In Virgil's *Aenid* Aeneas was the son of
   (a) Goddess Venus (b) Zeus
   (c) Mercury (d) Neptune
6. Which of the following characters in Virgil's *Aenid* has become a byword through the centuries for loyalty
   (a) Fidus Achates (b) Neptune
   (c) Juno (d) Mercury

7. Which of the following statements in the context of Virgil's *Aenid* is true?
   (a) Goddess Juno was an implacable enemy of Aeneas
   (b) Goddess Juno was the mother of Aeneas
   (c) Aeolus helped Aeneas in Trojan War
   (d) Neptune is the fire God
8. Which of the following statements in the context of Virgil's *Aenid* is not correct?
   (a) Goddess Juno persuades the wind God, Aeolus, to bring on a storm and scatter the Trojan fleet
   (b) God Neptune is persuaded by Venus to intervene and quells the storm.
   (c) Fidus Achates was a faithful follower of Aeneas
   (d) Dido, the Tyrian princess, does not accord a hospitable welcome to Aeneas
9. Which of the following statements is correct in the context of Virgil's *Aenid*?
   (a) in the Trojan War the Trojans were defeated
   (b) in the Trojan war the Greeks were defeated
   (c) Creusa was not the wife of Aeneas
   (d) none of these
10. In the context of Virgil's *Aenid*, who is the father of Aeneas?
    (a) Polydorus (b) Anchises (c) Achates (d) Dido
11. In the context of Virgil's *Aenid*, which of the following characters fell in love with Aeneas?
    (a) Dido (b) Venus (c) Helen (d) Juno
12. Which of the following statements is true about Dido's death in Virgils's *Aenid*?
    (a) Aeneas killed Dido
    (b) Dido takes her life in despair when Aeneas deserted her
    (c) Dido committed suicide after she became an unwed mother
    (d) Dido died on the funeral pyre of her husband
13. In how many books Virgil has written *Aenid*?
    (a) 5 (b) 2 (c) 8 (d) 12

14. In accordance with the wishes of which of the following emperors Virgil's *Aenid* was published?
    (a) Emperor Augustus (b) Alexander the Great
    (c) Julius Caesar (d) none of the above
15. In the context of Virgils's *Aenid*, who was Turnus?
    (a) Turnus, King of the Rutuliaus, was a friend of Aeneas
    (b) Turnus, king of the Rutuliaus, was a foe of Aeneas
    (c) Turnus was a mentor of Aeneas
    (d) Turnus vanquished Aeneas in a war

**2. *Iliad***

16. *Iliad* and *Odyssey* are based on
    (a) the legend of the Trojan War
    (b) the exploit of Hercules
    (c) the imperialism of Alexander the great
    (d) the love story of a Greek Goddess
17. Achilles is a character in which of the following great epics?
    (a) *The Ramayana* (b) *Iliad*
    (c) *Divine Comedy* (d) *Paradise Lost*
18. Homer, the Greek poet, belonged to
    (a) 8th or 9th B.C. (b) 115 B.C.
    (c) 323 B.C. (d) 415 B.C.
19. In Homer's *Iliad* Helew was the wife of which of the following characters?
    (a) Agamemnon (b) Menelaus
    (c) Acheles (d) Paris
20. Which of the following is the date of the fall of Troy to the Achaean Greeks?
    (a) 1230 B.C. (b) 1184 B.C.
    (c) 1064 B.C. (d) 1534 B.C.
21. In Homer's *Iliad*, who were the invaders that drove away the Achaens to the Aegean sea?
    (a) Aryans (b) Dravidians
    (c) Dorians (d) Russians

22. To which of the following places the Achaens established new settlements?
    (a) Rome (b) Ionia (c) Paris (d) London
23. Which of the following is referred to by the title *Iliad*?
    (a) the hero of the epic (b) Ilios, the capital of Troy
    (c) Helen (d) the Greeks
24. In *Iliad* who was Agamemnon?
    (a) commander-in-chief of the Achaens Army
    (b) the King of Troy
    (c) the Prince of Troy
    (d) the King of Greece
25. In *Iliad* who was the son of the Trojan?
    (a) Paris (b) Priam
    (c) Agamemnon (d) Achilles
26. In *Iliad* who was the Trojan king?
    (a) Paris (b) Priam
    (c) Agamemnon (d) Achilles
27. In *Iliad* who was Menelaus?
    (a) brother of Agamemnon (b) father of Agamemnon
    (c) sister of Agamemnon (d) mother of Agamemnon
28. Who had abducted Helen in Homer's *Iliad*?
    (a) Paris (b) Menelaus
    (c) Achilles (d) Agamemnon
29. Who seizes Briseis, the slave concubine of Achille, in Homer's *Iliad*?
    (a) Paris (b) Agamemnon
    (c) Menelaus (d) Priam
30. In Homer's *Iliad* Achilles refuses to take further part in a war. Which of the following may be the cause for it?
    (a) Achilles felt tired
    (b) Agamemnon, the commander-in-chief of the Achaean Army had seized Briseis, the slave concubine of Achilles
    (c) Achilles knew that the army was very strong
    (d) none of the above

31. In Homer's *Iliad* who was the commander-in-chief of the Achaeon Army?
    (a) Achilles (b) Agamemnon
    (c) Menelaus (d) Paris
32. Aphrodite in Greek mythology is the goddess of
    (a) war (b) love (c) wealth (d) anger
33. Which of the following may be the main cause for war between the Greeks and the Trojans?
    (a) the Greeks wanted to extend their empire
    (b) the Trojans wanted to extend their empire
    (c) to secure Helen
    (d) none of the above
34. In how many books *Iliad* has been written?
    (a) One (b) Five
    (c) Ten (d) More than ten
35. What was the conclusion of the Trojan war?
    (a) Greeks were defeated
    (b) the Trozans were defeated
    (c) it ended without the defeat of either
    (d) it ended without the victory of either

**3. Odyssey**

36. In Homer's epic *Odyssey*, Odysseus is the name of
    (a) the country (b) a town
    (c) the hero (d) the heroine
37. In which of the following epics, Polyphemus is a character?
    (a) *Iliad* (b) *Aenid*
    (c) *Odyssey* (d) *Paradise Lost*
38. If in Homer's *Iliad*, the wrath of Achilles is the main theme or subject, what is the main theme in Homer's *Odyssey*?
    (a) The homecoming of Odysseus after the fall of Troy
    (b) Odysseus's defeat and surrender
    (c) Odysseus's intrigue against the king
    (d) none of the above

39. In the context of Homer's *Odyssey* which of the following statements is not correct?
   (a) the *Iliad* and the *Odyssey* are epics describing the exploits of the heroes Achilles and Odysseus. But no attempt is made to tell everything about these heroes.
   (b) One specific action in the life of Odysseus is taken as the theme or subject
   (c) In *Odyssey* the homecoming of Odysseus after the fall of Troy is the theme
   (d) Odysseus does not possess enough courage to endure his manifold difficulties

40. Which of the statements about Homer's *Odyssey* is correct?
   (a) the charm of *Odyssey* arises from adventure and social life. It is less passionate than *Iliad*
   (b) Homer does not keep himself in the background as he tells his story
   (c) Penelope is not a character in Homer's *Odyssey*
   (d) there is no blending of divine and human action in Homer's *Odyssey*

**4. *Agamemnon***

41. In which century Aeschylus was born?
   (a) 6th century B.C. (b) 5th century B.C.
   (c) 4th century B.C. (d) 10th century B.C.

42. To which country did Aeschylus belong?
   (a) England (b) France (c) Germany (d) Greece

43. Which of the following is a play written by Aeschylus?
   (a) *The Play boy of the Western World* (b) *Antigone*
   (c) *Oedipus the King* (d) *The Persians*

44. Which of the following is not play written by Aeschylus?
   (a) *The Suppliants* (b) *Seven Against Thebes*
   (c) *Orestela* (d) *Medea*

45. In the context of Aeschylus' *Agamemnon* which of the following statement is true?
   (a) Agamemnon was the king of Argos. He married Clytemnestra and was elected commander of the Greek Host that went to Troy to recover Helen

(b) Helen was the wife of Agamemnon's brother Menelaus
(c) Helen was carried off by Paris
(d) all the above statements are true

### 5. *Oedipus, the King*

46. In which century Sophocles was born?
(a) 5th century B.C. (b) 6th century B.C.
(c) 15th century B.C. (d) 3rd century B.C.

47. To which country did Sophocles belong?
(a) England (b) France (c) Greece (d) America

48. Which of the following is a play authored by Sophocles?
(a) *Oedipus, the King* (b) *Dr. Faustus*
(c) *Hamlet* (d) *Arms and the Man*

49. Which of the following is a play not authored by Sophocles?
(a) *Oedipus, the King* (b) *Antigone*
(c) *Electra* (d) *The Persius*

50. Which of the following statements about Sophocles may be true?
(a) Sophocles is pre-eminently the dramatist of human character
(b) Sophocles differed from Euripides in representing men as they ought to be, while Euripides exhibited them as they are
(c) Sophocles was born at Colonus near Athens
(d) all the above statements may be true

51. In the context of Sophocles *Oedipus, the King* which of the following statements may be true?
(a) Oedipus was the son of Laius, king of Thebes and Jocasta
(b) Oedipus' father was informed by an oracle that he must perish at his son's hands
(c) in ignorance of his parentage, Oedipus slew Lais, his father and married his mother, Jocasta
(d) all the above statements may be true

52. Which of the following statements may not be true about *Antigone*?
    (a) Antigone is a tragedy by Sophocles
    (b) Antigone is a comedy by Sophocles
    (c) The story of Antigone is part of the Oedipus legend
    (d) Antigone was the daughter of King Oedipus

53. In the context of Sophocles' *Antigone*, who succeeded Oedipus as the king of Thebes?
    (a) Creon (b) Polynices (c) Eteocles (d) Ismene

54. In the tragedy *Antigone* what may be called the tragic flaw in the character of Antigone?
    (a) she was over-ambitious like Macbeth
    (b) she was too suspicious like Othelo
    (c) Antigone's tragic flaw lies in an uncalled for insolence towards civil authority, her determination not merely to do her duty for her brother but also to be put to death for it
    (d) she had a hesitant nature

### 6. *Bible* (*The Old Testament*)

55. Which of the following accomplished the first complete translation of the *Bible* in English?
    (a) Shakespeare (b) Milton
    (c) Dr. Johnson (d) Tyndale

56. *The Old Testament* is not a single book but a compendium of myths, historical records and writings by individuals which at various periods were collected by .......... priests and scholars as expressing the spirit of the nation and its peculiar message. Which one of the following words appropriately fill in the above blank space?
    (a) Hebrew (b) Greek (c) Roman (d) French

57. Abraham, a patriarch of the Hebrews, originally belonged to which of the following countries?
    (a) Mesopotamia (b) Germany
    (c) France (d) England

58. Some time around 1900 B.C., a small semitic clan, under a patriarch called Abraham moved from Ur of the

chaldies, in Mesopotamia towards which of the following countries?

(a) Palestine (b) Ineda (c) China (d) France

59. The *Bible* story shows that the descendants of Abraham in Cannan or Palestine suffered severely from famine and gradually migrated into which of the following countries?

(a) Egypt (b) Palestine
(c) Mesopotamia (d) England

60. When the Hebrews migrated to Egypt, they were at first well-received but later the Pharaoh began to enslave them. Around 14-1300 B.C., the Hebrew slaves escaped from Egypt led by a Hebrew born in Egypt. What is the name of this man who led the Hebrew slaves?

(a) Abraham (b) Moses (c) Nova (d) Achiles

61. Under the leadership of Moses, the Hebrews escaped from Egypt and came back to which of the following countries?

(a) Palestine (b) Egypt (c) England (d) France

62. As described in *The Old Testament*, who was David?

(a) the King of the Israelites (b) a brave warrior
(c) the King of Egypt (d) the general of the Egyptian army

63. As described in *The Old Testament* King David ruled during which of the following periods?

(a) 2000 B.C. to 1970 B.C. (b) 1000 B.C. to 961 B.C.
(c) 1000 AD to 961 AD (d) 2000 B.C. to 1970 B.C.

64. As described in *The Old Testament* who succeeded King David as the King of Israel?

(a) Moses (b) Solomon
(c) Goliath (d) Abraham

65. In 922 B.C. when King Solomon died, the kingdom of Israel split in two, into a northern realm called Israel or Ephrain and a smaller southern land called

(a) Judah (b) Mesopotamia
(c) Egypt (d) Syria

66. As described in *The Old Testament* what was the capital of Judah?
    (a) Nazareth (b) Jerusalem
    (c) Jehovah (d) Baghdad

67. Which of the following may be said to be the century in which the *Bible* was created?
    (a) 9 th Century B.C. (b) 10th Century B.C.
    (c) 11th Century B.C. (d) 12th Century B.C.

68. As described in *The Old Testament*, the Kingdom of Judah was conquered by which country?
    (a) Israel (b) Babylon (c) Egypt (d) England

69. As described in *The Old Testament,* which King allowed the Jews to return to Jerusalem?
    (a) King Cyrus (b) King David
    (c) King Solomon (d) King Alexander

### 7. *Bible* (*The New Testament*)

70. What is the meaning of the word 'testament'?
    (a) the word 'testament' comes from the Latin, and is a translation of the Greek word meaning covenant
    (b) the word 'testament' comes from the Greek language and it means a religious story
    (c) the word 'testament' means words of God
    (d) none of the above

71. How many books are there in *The New Testament*?
    (a) ten (b) twenty
    (c) twenty Seven (d) thirty

72. Originally all the 27 books of *The New Testament* were written in which language?
    (a) English (b) Latin
    (c) French (d) Hebrew later translated in a special form of Greek known as Koine

73. What is true about 'Koine'?
    (a) Koine is the name of a bird
    (b) Koine is the name of an extinct animal

(c) Koine was the common vernacular over the eastern parts of the Roman Empire
(d) None of the above

74. Which of the following statements may be correct?
(a) Koine language reflects the influence of Aramaic, the language that was the common tongue of the Palestinian Jews and which Jesus himself employed
(b) "Revelation" is the first book in *The Bible*
(c) Jesus Christ is the author of *The New Testament.*
(d) None of the above

**8. *Quran***

75. Which of the following statements may be true?
(a) *Quran* is an Arabic word meaning reading, lecture, or recitation or that which ought to be read
(b) *Quran* is a Latin word meaning a holy river
(c) *Quran* is an Arabic word which means a bright light
(d) None of these

76. Which of the following statements may be true?
(a) Islam means submission or surrender to the will of God or Allah
(b) Moslems worship Mohammad
(c) Mohammed is an Islamic God
(d) None of these

77. Which of the following statements may be true?
(a) Mohammad is the most authoritative of the prophets who have been commissioned by Allah to proclaim his message among men
(b) Mohammad is the prophet of Jews
(c) Mohammad wrote the *Quran*
(d) None of these

78. According to the beliefs of the Muslims who is the author of *Quran*?
(a) Mohammad wrote the *Quran*
(b) the author of *Quran* was none other than Allah himself
(c) Abu Bakre was the writer of *Quran*
(d) None of these

79. Which of the following statements may be true?
   (a) the original volume of *Quran* is believed to have rested, since the beginning of time, on a vast table placed beside the throne of Allah in heaven
   (b) a copy of *Quran* written on paper and bound in silk and adorned with gold and precious stones, was carried down from heaven by the angel, Gabriel
   (c) Gabriel, an angel, showed a copy of the *Quran* to Mohammad on a number of occasions generally once a year, but in the last year of the prophet's mission, twice
   (d) all the above statements are correct
80. *Quran* was originally written in which language?
   (a) Urdu (b) Arabic (c) Latin (d) Greek
81. Like *Bible*, *Quran* has been divided into chapters and verses. What are the chapters in *The Quran* called?
   (a) Suras (b) sutras (c) blocks (d) khandas
82. The opening chapter of the *Quran* is one of the shortest containing only half a dozen lines. It is the Moslem counterpart of the Lord's prayer, and it is repeated by the faithful Moslems everywhere a number of times each day. What is this chapter called?
   (a) fatwah (b) fatihah (c) wazoo (d) reyaj
83. Who was Abu Bakre?
   (a) Abu Bakre was the son of Prophet Mohammad
   (b) Abu Bakre was Mohammad's successor in the Moslem leadership
   (c) Abu Bakre was a famous Moghal historian
   (d) none of these
84. Where was Mohammad buried?
   (a) in the Mosque at Medina (b) in the Mosque at Mecca
   (c) in Basra (d) in Kufa

## 9. *Upanishada*

85. The number of *Upanishada* is
   (a) 10 (b) 9 (c) 11 (d) 12

86. The reference to Yama Nachiketa *samvad* is in
   (a) *Kathopanishada* (b) *Mundakopanishad*
   (c) *Prashnopanishada* (d) *Kenopanishada*

## 10. *Mahabharata*

87. The epic *Mahabharata* has been composed by
   (a) Ved Vyas (b) Bhasa
   (c) Valmiki (d) Kalidasa

88. *Mahabharata* was written during
   (a) 3000 B.C. (b) 4000 B.C.
   (c) 2000 B.C. (d) 1000 B.C.

89. *Mahabharata* has been divided into how many *parva*s (parts)?
   (a) 17 (b) 18 (c) 19 (d) 20

90. The name of the mother of Nakul-Sahdev is
   (a) Kunti (b) Madri (c) Gandhari (d) Draupadi

## 11. *Ramayana*

91. *Ramayana* has been written by
   (a) Valmiki (b) Ved Vyas
   (c) Bharavi (d) Ashvaghosh

92. *Ramayana* was composed around
   (a) 4000 B.C. (b) 3000 B.C.
   (c) 5000 B.C. (d) 1000 B.C.

93. The name of Lakshman's mother was
   (a) Kaikeyi (b) Kaushalya
   (c) Sumitra (d) Manthara

94. In the *Ramayana* Lav Kusha fought with
   (a) Rama (b) Lakshman
   (c) Bharat (d) Shatrughan

95. Lord Rama was exiled for how many years?
   (a) 13 (b) 14 (c) 15 (d) 16

## 12. *Srimadabhagavadgita*

96. The *Bhagavadgita* forms part of which book?
   (a) *Ramayana* (b) *Mahabharata*
   (c) *Upanishada* (d) *Puranas*

97. In the *Bhagavadgita*, the chief speaker is
   (a) Arjun (b) Karna
   (c) Krishna (d) Dhritarashtra
98. "Thou grievest where no grief should be! Thou speak'st words lacking wisdom!" Here 'Thou' stands for whom?
   (a) Krishna (b) Arjuna
   (c) Yudhisthira (d) Bhisma Pitamah
99. *Bhagavadgita* was written during
   (a) 4th century B.C. (b) 5th century B.C.
   (c) 6th century B.C. (d) 8th century B.C.
100. "I find a solace in the *Bhagavadgita* that I miss even in the Sermon on the Mount..." Who said this?
   (a) Mahatma Gandhi (b) S. Radhakrishnan
   (c) Jawaharlal Nehru (d) none of these
101. Which ancient work gives the messsage of *Karmayoga*?
   (a) *Ramayana* (b) *Mahabharata*
   (c) *Purana* (d) *Bhagavadgita*

## UNIT B: MODERN CLASSICS

### 1. *Utopia*

102. To which of the following countries, does Sir Thomas More belong?
   (a) France (b) America (c) Ireland (d) England
103. When was More's *Utopia* written?
   (a) 15th century (b) 16th century
   (c) 17th century (d) 18th century
104. What does the word 'Utopia' mean?
   (a) nowhere (b) everywhere
   (c) heaven (d) hell
105. The word 'Utopia' comes from the Greek word 'ou' and 'topos'; 'topos' means 'a place' what does 'ou' mean?
   (a) not (b) everywhere
   (c) all (d) some

106. Which of the following statements may be true about Thomas More?
   (a) More's *Utopia* was first written in English
   (b) More had been executed on Tower Hill for having refused to acknowledge Henry VIII as head of the English Church in place of the Pope of Rome
   (c) Thomas More was a physician by profession
   (d) none of these

107. Which of the following statements may not be true about Thomas More?
   (a) More's *Utopia* was first written in Latin
   (b) Sir Thomas More was a/an English scholar-statesman
   (c) More's *Utopia* is so famous that all similar imaginary commonwealth have been referred to as Utopias
   (d) More was executed on Tower Hill for having written a satire against king Henry VIII

108. What is the name of the capital city in More's *Utopia*?
   (a) Amravatti (b) Akola (c) Amaurot (d) Ankara

109. Which of the following statements is correct in the context of More's *Utopia*?
   (a) all the cities in *Utopia* are built on the same plan and are of about the same size
   (b) the streets are very dirty, not well-drained
   (c) the houses are built without any planning
   (d) in *Utopia* nobody is required to work on the farms or in trade

110. What idea is conveyed by More's *Utopia*?
   (a) no ideal society actually exists
   (b) all states must be ideal
   (c) man is perfect
   (d) man should prove himself to be the best creature on this earth

111. In which language originally *Utopia* was written?
   (a) English (b) Greek (c) Latin (d) German

## 2. *War and Peace*

112. In which of the following centuries Leo Tolstoy was born?
    (a) 17th century (b) 18th century
    (c) 19th century (d) 20th century

113. To which of the following countries did Tolstoy belong?
    (a) England (b) France (c) Russia (d) America

114. Which of the following statements about Tolstoy's *War and Peace* may not be correct?
    (a) *War and Peace* is a huge work, containing 7000,000 words and not less than 539 characters
    (b) Most of the novels that we read take a small slice of life present a handful or so of characters and pursue a recognizable plot, Tolstoy does nothing of these
    (c) *War and Peace* was written very late in the life of Tolstoy, when he was about to die
    (d) *War and Peace* is recognized as the greatest novel in world literature and it has been translated into dozens of languages

115. Which of the following statements about Tolstoy's *War and Peace* may be correct?
    (a) the book begins with a small scene: an evening reception given by a society lady in St. Petrsburg, in July, 1805
    (b) the book begins with a small scene: an evening reception given by a society lady in Moscow, in July, 1805
    (c) the book begins with a war between England and France
    (d) the book begins with the defeat of Napoleon

116. Which of the following incidents have not been mentioned in Tolstoy's *War and Peace*?
    (a) Napoleon had been proclaimed Emperor of the French
    (b) Napoleon had annexed Genoa, seized Hanover from the British
    (c) England was Napoleon's enemy
    (d) Russia was friend of Napoleon

117. Tolstoy's *War and Peace* begins with a small scene: an evening reception given by a society lady in St. Petersburg in July, 1805. What was happening in this reception?
   (a) in St. Petersburg tempers are raised against the barbarian who had murdered the Duc d' Enghien, heir to the Bourbons and now threatened the whole of Europe
   (b) in St. Petersburg, a great celebration was going on to mark the victory of a Napoleon, in recent wars
   (c) in St. Petersburg, a lady, who was one of the main conspirators against Napoleon, had invited a number of important people of France
   (d) none of these

118. Which of the following is a character in Leo Tolstoy's *War and Peace*?
   (a) Pierre (b) Samsung (c) Datsung (d) Tengsung

119. Which of the following statements may not be true about Tolstoy's *War and Peace*?
   (a) War has started between Russia and France
   (b) The Russian army has advanced into Austria to join hands with its ally
   (c) Tolstoy describes the movements of the army with the stress on individuals and their reactions to events
   (d) Tolstoy glorifies Napoleon, after the French Army had come to the help of Russia

120. Tolstoy had a double aim in *War and Peace*. On the one hand he depicts the whole flavour of the great patriotic war against Napoleon, on the other hand, Tolstoy pursues the threads of his domestic narrative by placing the young nobles in the Russian forces and by viewing the war through their eyes trace their own development in the midst of the national struggle.
   This statement is
   (a) true (b) false
   (c) partially correct (d) partially wrong

121. Which of the following statements may not be true about Tolstoy's *War and Peace*?
   (a) the scene shifts continually, from one family to another from a scintillating ball to a quiet conversation between two people, from love affairs to hunting scenes
   (b) the novel is full of apparently disjointed scenes all taking place in the interlocking aristocratic circles
   (c) the plot of the novel is loose and complex. It creates a facsimile of real life: its untidiness its disjointedness, its extreme variety, its crowd of struggling, lonely human beings and its seemingly lack of purpose
   (d) the novel is very compact. The plot of the novel is organic. There is a causal relationship between the incidents of the novel

122. What breaks the peace in Tolstoy's *War and Peace*?
   (a) Russian soldiers invade France
   (b) Napoleon invades Russia
   (c) England and Austria attack Russia
   (d) Austria attacks Russia

123. In Tolstoy's *War and Peace* when Napoleon invaded Russia, who was the commander-in-chief of the Russian army?
   (a) Kutozov (b) Chekhov
   (c) Dostoyevsky (d) Turgnev

124. Which one of the following is not a character in Tolstoy's *War and Peace*?
   (a) Prince Andrew (b) Kutozov
   (c) Pierre (d) Turgnev

125. Which of the following comments about Tolstoy's *War and Peace* may not be correct?
   (a) For modern readers accustomed to taut plots and strenuous efforts by authors to claim and sustain their interest *War and Peace* is a difficult book to read
   (b) In *War and Peace* there are no cheap effects. Melodrama is entirely absent

(c) this book is full of life, variety and memorable characters and in the last resort it is not the great battle scenes which one remembers, but an eager young girl at her first ball, an old man dying, a declaration of love, the shouts of children

(d) Tolstoy's *War and Peace* is nothing but battles and wars

126. Which of the following statements is true about Tolstoy's *War and Peace*?

(a) It is about the destructive effects of war in general

(b) *War and Peace* presents a picture of Russian life, set against the background of Napoleon's invasion

(c) *War and Peace* has been set against the background of World War II

(d) the message of the novel is War and Peace are two aspects of life, which cannot be avoided

### 3. *The Prince*

127. Who wrote the book *The Prince*?

(a) Niccolo Machiavelli (b) Bertrand Russel
(c) Voltaire (d) Rousseau

128. In which language originally *The Prince* was written?

(a) English (b) Greek (c) French (d) Italian

129. Which of the following statements may be true about *The Prince?*

(a) *The Prince* is a biography of a lustful prince in Italy

(b) *The Prince* is a book on private lives of princes

(c) *The Prince* is a treatise on political power, dealing in particular with how states are established in the modern world and how they may be preserved and aggrandized

(d) none of these

130. When was *The Prince* written?

(a) 16th century (b) 15th century
(c) 14th century (d) 18th century

131. Which of the following statements may be true about Machiavelli?

(a) Machiavelli had been sacked from his important position of Chief Secretary to the Government of the Florentine Republic

(b) Machiavelli was born in England
(c) Machiavelli was a prince and *The Prince* is his autobiography
(d) none of these

132. Which of the following sentences may be an extract from Machiavellis's *The Prince*?
(a) the truly capable ruler must combine the qualities of the lion and the fox, striving to be as brave as the one and as crafty as the other
(b) now the Lord had said unto Abraham get thee out of the country and from thy kindred and from thy father's house unto land that I will show thee
(c) Ful wel she sang the services divine, Entuned in her nose ful seemly; And French she spake ful faire and sweetly
(d) none of these

133. *The Prince* advocates that
(a) a state should run strictly on the principles of truth and non-violence
(b) a state is free to do anything necessary to strengthen itself
(c) a state should perish but never adopt unfair means even though the unfair means may be for the welfare of the state
(d) none of these

134. Which of the following statements may be correct about Machiavelli's *The Prince*?
(a) the book assembles a number of shrewd maxims and methods by which a ruler may eliminate his rivals
(b) the book emphasizes upon the divine right of princes to rule
(c) morality is very important for princes
(d) none of these

135. Which of the following statements may not be true in the context of *The Prince*?
(a) a good ruler must be a good man
(b) precepts of morality played little part in the practical politics

(c) a good prince is moral rather to benefit his people than to obey the laws of God
(d) none of these

136. What does the term 'Machiavellian' mean?
(a) honesty, integrity (b) firm determination
(c) cunningness (d) bravery

4. *Pierre Et Jean*

137. In which century Maupassant was born?
(a) 17th century (b) 18th century
(c) 19th century (d) 20th century

138. To which country did Maupassant belong?
(a) England (b) France (c) Spain (d) America

139. Maupassant is known for his
(a) dramas (b) poems
(c) novels (d) short stories and novels

140. Maupassant was an exponent of
(a) romanticism (b) classicism
(c) realism (d) psychological novels

141. When was *Pierre Et Jean* written?
(a) 18th century (b) 19th century
(c) 20th century (d) 21st century

142. In Maupassant's *Pierre Et Jean* who is the father of Pierre?
(a) Monsieur Roland (b) Monsieur Donald
(c) Mr. Marechal (d) Jean

143. In Maupassant's *Pierre Et Jean* what is the relationship between Pierre and Jean?
(a) husband and wife (b) wife and husband
(c) brothers (d) cousins

144. Which of the following statements may be true in the context of Maupassant's *Pierre Et Jean*?
(a) Madame Rosenilly is a neighbour of Monsieur Roland
(b) Monsieur Marechal of Paris is a former friend of the Rolands

(c) Monsieur Marechal has died and has left all his money to Jean
(d) all the above statements are true

145. In Maupassant's *Pierre Et Jean* what was the suspicion in the mind of Pierre?
(a) his younger brother Jean was conspiring to kill him
(b) his younger brother Jean was conspiring to kill his father
(c) his younger brother was not his father's son
(d) none of these

146. In Maupassant's *Pierre Et Jean* who was suspected to be the father of Jean?
(a) Monsieur Roland (b) Monsieur Marechal
(c) Pierre (d) none of these

**5. *Don Quixote***

147. Mignel de Cervantes belonged to which of the following countries?
(a) England (b) France (c) Spain (d) America

148. In which century Miguel de Cervantes was born?
(a) 15th century (b) 16th century
(c) 17th century (d) 18th century

149. Which statement about *Don Quixote* may be true?
(a) it is a historical novel (b) it is an adventure story
(c) it is a biography of a Spanish king (d) it is a comic drama

150. What was the name of the village in which Don Quixote lived?
(a) Behula (b) La Mancha
(c) Sancho Panja (d) Quixote

151. In the context of Cervantes' *Don Quixote* which of the following statements may be true?
(a) Don Quixote had decided to become a great philosopher and preacher
(b) Don Quxote was moving about here and there to preach his religious beliefs

(c) Don Quixote had decided to become a knight-errant, He would travel the globe in shining armour, mounted on a steed, in search of adventure
(d) none of these

152. What was the name of the horse of Don Quixote?
(a) Chetak (b) Brutus
(c) Julius (d) Rocinnate

153. In the content of Cervantes' *Don Quixote* what is true about Dulcinea Del Toboso?
(a) Dulcinea Del Toboso is a supposed giant with whom Don Quixote fought
(b) Duclinea Del Toboso is a brawny farm-girl whom Don Quixote admired
(c) Dulcinea Del Toboso is a beautiful lake in Quixote's village
(d) none of these

154. Who is the character in Cervantes' *Don Quixote* who accompanies him as a Squire?
(a) Sancho Panza (b) La Mancha
(c) Rocinnate (d) Dulcinea

155. In Cervantes' *Don Quixote* which of the following was mistaken for giants?
(a) wind mills (b) wild elephants
(c) a powerful storm (d) primitive tribal people

156. Which of the following, statements may be true in the context of Cervantes' *Don Quixote*?
(a) Don Quixote is one of the most pathetic, laughable and lovable characters in all fiction
(b) Don Quixote would travel the globe in shining armour, mounted on a mettlesome steed, in search of adventure righting wrongs rescuing maids in distress
(c) in Don Quixote adventure succeeds adventure and in almost all of them Quixote is the loser
(d) all the above statements may be true

### 6. *Doctor Zhivago*

157. In which of the following centuries Boris Pasternak was born?
(a) 17th century (b) 18th century
(c) 19th century (d) 20th century

158. To which of the following countries did Boris Pasternak belong?
(a) Russia (b) England (c) France (d) America

159. Which of the following writers was awarded the Nobel Prize for literature?
(a) Boris Pasternak (b) R.K. Narayan
(c) Karl Marx (d) none of these

160. Which of the following statements is true about Pasternak's *Doctor Zhivago*?
(a) the novel gives an account of the Crimean War
(b) the novel presents a graphic panorma of life in Russia during the Russian Revolution, the Provisional Government and the Civil War
(c) the novel presents the discoveries of a scientist Doctor Zhivago
(d) none of these

161. The main thread of *Doctor Zhivago* is provided by
(a) the political events during the Russian Revolution and after it
(b) the private world of two characters—Yuri Zhivago and Larissa Guishar
(c) the story of the two characters—Yuri Zhivago and Larissa Guishar runs parallel to and is influenced by political events of the Russian revolution
(d) none of these

162. Which one of the following is not a character in *Doctor Zhivago*?
(a) Yuri Gagrin (b) Yuri Zhivago
(c) Kamarovsky (d) Larissa Guishar

163. Which of the following statements may not be true about Boris Pasternak's *Doctor Zhivago*?
   (a) readers first meet Yuri Zhivago as a child weeping at his mother's funeral outside Moscow
   (b) Zhivago's father, once a millionaire, has long since abandoned his family
   (c) Zhivago's father has been compelled to commit suicide by an unscrupulous lawyer named Kamarovsky
   (d) all the above statements are wrong

164. In the context of Pasternak's *Doctor Zhivago* which of the following statements may not be true?
   (a) the orphaned Yuri goes to live in Moscow with the Gromekos, a cultured family of intellectuals
   (b) the Gromekos have a daughter Lara, who is of the same age as Yuri
   (c) the Gromekos have a daughter Tonya, who is of the same age as Yuri
   (d) Gromekos are wealthy people, but in a poor part of the city another much impoverished family of a widow Amalia Guishar has come to live with them with her young daughter Lara

165. In the context of Pasternak's *Doctor Zhivago* which of the following statements may be correct?
   (a) Komarovsky, who was a close friend of Amalia's husband, becomes Amalia's lover
   (b) Komarovsky becomes Lara's lover
   (c) Komarovsky becomes Amalia's lover but his eyes are on her beautiful daughter Lara
   (d) Komarovsky was a lawyer who always helped Yuri's father

166. Which one of the following is not a character in Pasternak's *Doctor Zhivago*?
   (a) Paul (b) Antipov
   (c) Amalia (d) Komarovsky

167. In Pasternak's *Doctor Zhivago* who is the father of Pasha?
   (a) Antipov (b) Komarovsky
   (c) M. Gromeko (d) Yuri Zhivago

168. In Pasternak's *Doctor Zhivago* who seduces Lara?
   (a) Antipov (b) Komarovsky
   (c) Mr. Gromeko (d) Yuri Zhivago

169. In Pasternak's *Doctor Zhivago* Lara was married to whom?
   (a) Yuri Zhivago (b) Pasha Antipov
   (c) Komarovsky (d) none of these

170. Doctor Zhivago in the novel *Doctor Zhivago* was married to which of the following characters?
   (a) Lara (b) Tonya
   (c) Amalia (d) none of these

171. In *Doctor Zhivago* Strelnikov is a character who returned from a German prison camp after the war and made himself useful to the reds. Strelnikov is none other than
   (a) Pasha Antipov (b) Yuri Zhivago
   (c) Komarovsky (d) Mr. Gromeko

### 7. *The Playboy of the Western World*

172. In which century Synge was born?
   (a) 19th century (b) 18th century
   (c) 20th century (d) 16th century

173. To which country did Synge belong?
   (a) England (b) France (c) Ireland (d) Germany

174. Which of the following is a play not written by Synge?
   (a) *Riders to the Sea* (b) *The Playboy of the Western World*
   (c) *Deirdre of the Sorrows* (d) *Antigone*

175. Who is the main character in Synge's *The Playboy of the Western World?*
   (a) Christy (b) Sir Arthur (c) Claudius (d) Deborah

176. In the context of Synge's *The Playboy of the Western World* which of the following statements may be correct?
   (a) Christy is a young weakling who flees away to an isolated public house after a family quarrel
   (b) Christy is accepted as a dashing figure by all the country folk, on the basis of his boast that he had just killed his father

(c) Christy becomes the local hero, centre of female admiration and attention, especially pursued by a widow
(d) all the above statements are correct

177. Christy in Synge's *The Playboy of the Western World* is engaged to whom?
(a) Peregrine (b) Pegeen (c) Tiara (d) Shamela

178. In which category would you keep Synge's *The Playboy of the Western World*?
(a) comedy (b) tragedy (c) epic (d) mock-epic

179. Who is the father of Christy in Synge's *The Playboy of the Western World*?
(a) Damien (b) Mahon
(c) Gabriel (d) Agamemnon

180. Which of the following statements in Synge's *The Playboy of the Western World* may not be true?
(a) Christy said that he had killed his father, but his father appeared alive
(b) Christy had killed his father
(c) Christy was engaged to Pegeen
(d) Mahon, Christy's father, is proud to be led off by the son who has become a man

181. Which of the following statements is true about Christy in Synge's *The Playboy of the Western World*?
(a) Christy is a fugitive who has murdered the King
(b) Christy is a stout, brave hero in the play
(c) Christy gives out that he is a fugitive from justice who in a quarrel has killed his bullying father
(d) Christy has really murdered his father

**8. *The Divine Comedy***

182. *The Divine Comedy* was written by
(a) Alighieri Dante (b) Lamartine
(c) Victor Hugo (d) Emile Zola

183. The original title of Dante's epic was
(a) *The Comedy* or *La Commedia* (b) *The Divine Comedy*
(c) *La Vita Nuova* (d) *Paradise*

184. *Inferno, Purgatory* and *Paradiso* are the three parts of
(a) *The Divine Comedy* (b) *La Vita Nuova*
(c) *The Ancient Mariner* (d) *Ethics*

185. Who leads Dante through spiritual journey of *The Divine Comedy*?
(a) Virgil (b) Beatrice (c) St. Bernard (d) God

186. Dante meets Belaequa in
(a) Paradise (b) Purgatory
(c) Hell (d) None of these

187. *The Divine Comedy* narrates Dante's journey from
(a) hell to paradise (b) life on earth to life in the other world
(c) birth to death (d) purgatory to paradise

188. In which century Dante was born?
(a) 10th (b) 11th (c) 13th (d) 14th

189. To which of the following countries Dante belongs?
(a) England (b) France (c) Italy (d) America

190. With which of the following works, Dante gained a reputation as a poet?
(a) Vita Nuova (b) Life Divine
(c) The Odyssey (d) The Aenid

191. Dante had love for which of the following women?
(a) Helen (b) Beatrice (c) Dorothy (d) Rebecca

192. Which of the following statements may be true in the context of Dante's *The Divine Comedy*?
(a) *The Divine Comedy* is a description of the Trojan War
(b) *The Divine Comedy* is a description of heaven, hell and purgatory
(c) *The Divine Comedy* is a mock epic presenting the war between man and woman
(d) *The Divine Comedy* is a mock epic presenting the war between man and women

193. Which of the following, statements is not correct in the context of Dante's *The Divine Comedy*?
(a) *The Divine Comedy*, is a description of heaven, hell and purgatory

(b) *The Divine Comedy* is version of the state of men's soul after death
(c) *The Divine Comedy* is an allegory demonstrating man's need of spiritual illumination and guidance.
(d) *The Divine Comedy* is a mockery of God

194. In the context of *The Divine Comedy*, Dante meets which of the following in hell?
(a) Virgil (b) Homer (c) Plato (d) Aristotle

195. Which of the following statements is true about Dante?
(a) Dante married Beatrice
(b) Dante married a Florentine lady, Gemma Donati
(c) Dante was an Elizabethan poet
(d) None of these

196. In the context of Dante's *The Divine Comedy* who is the ferryman, ferrying across the river Acheron?
(a) Judas (b) Charon (c) Cassiust (d) Zeus

197. In the context of Dante's *The Divine Comedy* where is the river Acheron?
(a) hell (b) heaven
(c) the earth (d) a river between earth and heaven

198. What does Limbo refer to in Dante's *The Divine Comedy*?
(a) name of a character (b) a river
(c) the first circle of hell (d) heaven

199. Who is Minos in Dante's *The Divine Comedy*?
(a) the Infernal Judge (b) a God
(c) a Goddess (d) a Poet

200. Who is Cerberus in Dante's *The Divine Comedy*?
(a) The infernal judge
(b) A giant dog, who barks and snarls at the gluttons
(c) A ferryman taking the people across the river Acheron
(d) none of these

201. Which of the following poets showed Dante the punishments of hell?
(a) Homer (b) Virgil (c) Plutarch (d) Chaucer

202. Which of the following characters Dante meets in *The Divine Comedy*?
   (a) Helen (b) Beatrice
   (c) Charon (d) Gemma Donati

**9. *Gone with the Wind***

203. *Gone with the Wind* was written by
   (a) Pearl S. Buck (b) Somerset Maugham
   (c) Margaret Mitchell (d) none of these

204. It was published in
   (a) 1930 (b) 1936 (c) 1939 (d) 1935

205. *Gone with the Wind* was awarded
   (a) Nobel Prize (b) Booker's Prize
   (c) Pulitzer Prize (d) Book of the Year award

206. *Gone with the Wind* narrates the adventures of
   (a) Scarlet, the willful daughter of General O'Hara, an Irish immigrant
   (b) Melanie Hamilton
   (c) Honey Wilkes
   (d) General O'Hara

207. *Gone with the Wind* presents
   (a) civil war and reconstruction (b) war of independence
   (c) world war I (d) the great depression

208. *Gone with the Wind* shows
   (a) futility of romantic love
   (b) how true love is nearby while one struggles to find it elsewhere as scarlet realized that Rhett was her true love while she thought it to be Ashley
   (c) human relationship is supreme
   (d) romantic love completes the mission of life

**10. *The Good Earth***

209. *The Good Earth* was written by
   (a) Margret Mitchell (b) Pearl S. Buck
   (c) William Gordon (d) Emile Zola

210. *The Good Earth* was published in
(a) 1930 (b) 1931 (c) 1936 (d) 1940

211. *The Good Earth* narrates
(a) a poor man becoming rich
(b) Wang Lung's rise from a Chinese peasant to a rich landowner
(c) transformation and social ascendancy is possible
(d) life has rules that must be followed

212. *The Good Earth* shows
(a) Wang Lung's rise to wealth and power through reverence for the soil
(b) Wang Lung's rise through hard work
(c) Wang Lung's rise through speculation
(d) Wang Lung's wealth and power are inherited

213. What happens after Wang Lung's death in *The Good Earth*?
(a) the sons remain wealthy and powerful through inheritance
(b) the sons divorce their lives from the soil and lose their pre-eminence for they lacked the vigour and intensity
(c) the sons join other ways of livelihood and lose contact with reality
(d) the good earth is neglected

### 11. *Kim*

214. *Kim* was written by
(a) Paul Scot (b) E.M. Forster
(c) Rudyard Kipling (d) Madame Kaye

215. Rudyard Kipling was
(a) an Englishman's son who has written about British experience of India
(b) Irish
(c) half Irish, half Indian
(d) Anglo Indian

216. *Kim* was written when the British empire was at its peak. It was published in
(a) 1898 (b) 1901 (c) 1910 (d) 1921

217. Kim started life as a street Arab in Lahore and was known as
    (a) an Irish sergeant's son (b) friend of the Stars or friend of all the world
    (c) black Indian (d) swami

218. *Kim* presents
    (a) a complex world
    (b) the immortal boy, the uncontaminated by schooling
    (c) friendship of Kim and Lama
    (d) Indian life and its beauty during the British rule

### 12. *The Second Sex*

219. Simone De Beauvoir is known
    (a) as an existentialist writer (b) as a friend of Jean Paul Sartre
    (c) as a modern French novelist (d) as a fashionable Parisian

220. *The Second Sex* was written by
    (a) Simone De Beauvoir (b) Jean Paul Sartre
    (c) Samuel Beckett (d) James Joyce

221. The theme of *The Second Sex* is
    (a) individuality and independence of women
    (b) emancipation of women
    (c) freedom of women
    (d) women as women, most precious creation of God

### 13. *Lolita*

222. Who has written *Lolita*?
    (a) Henry Miller (b) Vladimir Nabokov
    (c) Simone De Beauvoir (d) Edna O'Brien

223. Nabokov by nymphet means
    (a) an adolescent girl
    (b) a young girl who looks like a nymph
    (c) a girl who grips the imagination of men
    (d) a girl almost like a goddess

224. What is the theme of *Lolita*?
   (a) it tells of a fatal attraction of a 56 year old man for an adolescent gril who also happens to be his step daughter
   (b) an old man's attraction for a very young woman
   (c) a 56 years old man's sexual fantasy
   (d) a 56 years old man's sexual fantasy for a girl-child

225. *Lolita* became famous because
   (a) it presents an unusual sexual story
   (b) it presents a story of a mature man's sexual fantasy—which attracts as well as repels
   (c) it tells of Humbert seducig his own step daughter
   (d) a unique story of love and sex between 13 year old girl and her step father of 56 years

226. *Lolita* does not repel because
   (a) Nabokov has told the unusual sex-related story very aesthetically, in an exemplary manner
   (b) it is a poem on the theme of unusual sexuality
   (c) the adulterous affair is shorn off grossness
   (d) it is a fantasy

### 14. *A Doll's House*

227. Henrik Ibsen's period is
   (a) 1830 - 1906 (b) 1828 - 1905
   (c) 1820 - 1880 (d) 1828 - 1906

228. As in his life so in his works Ibsen was a
   (a) rebel (b) rebel and self assertive
   (c) a symbolist playwright (d) social reformer

229. In his dramas he is pre-occupied with a desire to
   (a) change the social condition prevailing in Norway
   (b) transform the political system in Norway
   (c) change the way human life has been degraded
   (d) make his country rich and powerful

230. Ibsen's greatest contribution to modern drama is
   (a) realistic prose drama (b) social drama
   (c) drama of ideas (d) cause of woman

231. What happens in *A Doll's House* (1879)?
(a) a woman declares independence
(b) Nora awakens to her responsibility and leaves her husband to be herself
(c) it deals with woman emancipation
(d) new-world order

232. *The Wild Duck* presents
(a) a conflict between illusion and reality
(b) a conflict between love and romance
(c) robust thoughts opposed to pretencious
(d) none

233. *The Wild Duck* is based on
(a) the idea of a wild a goose chase
(b) the legend that when a wild duck is wounded it does not return to the flock but dives deep and fastens itself to seaweed.
(c) the belief that a wild duck can never be tamed or caged
(d) the spirit of wilderness, freedom

**15. *Tropics of Capricon***

234. Who has written *Tropics of Capricon*?
(a) Arthur Miller (b) Henry Miller
(c) Jonathan Swift (d) Samuel Butler

235. In *Tropics of Cancer* Henry Miller has narrated
(a) seemy life of Singapore (b) sleazy night life of New York
(c) promiscuous life style of Paris (d) sex-life of people in power

236. *Tropics of Cancer* and *Tropics of Capricon* are works of
(a) satire (b) pure imagination
(c) pornography (d) autobiography

237. Henry Miller has written
(a) *The Second Sex* (b) *Lolita*
(c) *Sexus and Plexus* (d) *The Naked Ape*

238. Henry Miller has been at times labelled as a writer of pornography because he
   (a) has presented cheap sex
   (b) has written about free sex
   (c) franky confronts and exposes human sexuality
   (d) has shown mid-twentieth century attitude towards sex

### 16. *Faust*

239. *Faust* was a drama written by
   (a) Johann Wolfgang Von Goethe
   (b) Jean Giradoux
   (c) Henrik Ibsen
   (d) Christopher Marlowe

240. What is the main theme of *Faust*?
   (a) human desire for knowledge
   (b) spiritual transcendence
   (c) man's desire to transcend his physical limitations and gain answer to the eternal questions of the meaning of life
   (d) overt knowledge was within man's reach and for this even black magic was acceptable

241. What is God's plan for man in *Faust*?
   (a) man may be tempted and beguiled but he cannot be misled forever because he retains the instinct for the one true divine way
   (b) man errs
   (c) man falls but is capable of arising
   (d) man created in the image of God, so basically he is good

242. What are the characteristics of Mephistopheles in *Faust*?
   (a) a destructive and nihilistic force
   (b) master of worldly knowledge
   (c) feeds on man's discontent and desire
   (d) anti-God

243. Faust's desire for the intellectual and the beautiful are
   (a) beyond the comprehension of Mephistopheles
   (b) earth bound though Mephistopheles understands Faust

(c) human desires and devil's plan are opposed to each other
(d) interesting but not plausible

### 17. *The Cherry Orchard*

244. *The Cherry Orchard* was written by
(a) Turgnev (b) Ibsen
(c) Pirandello (d) Anton Chekhov

245. Anton Chekhov's characters are unique, marked by
(a) a subtle sympathy
(b) characters not as they should be but as they really are. A subtle touch
(c) playwright as a judge
(d) playwright as a creator

246. *The Cherry Orchard* is a symbol of
(a) complicated social, economic and cultural problems in Russia
(b) change in Russian society
(c) cherry blossom in spring
(d) possibilities

247. Who is the chief protagonist of the play *The Cherry Orchard*?
(a) Madame Revensky (b) Trophimof
(c) Lopakhin (d) Firs

### 18. *Magic Mountain*

248. Who has written *Magic Mountain*?
(a) Thomas Mann (b) James Joyce
(c) Herman Hesse (d) Marcel Proust

249. Thomas Mann added a new dimension to the novel by
(a) exploring the inner man
(b) searching inquiry into the history and civilization of man
(c) moving from the present to the unfathomable deep past
(d) anthropological approach

250. The period of Thomas Mann is
(a) 1875 - 1965 (b) 1875 - 1955
(c) 1860 - 1955 (d) 1875 - 1945

251. In *Magic Mountain* Mann is preoccupied with
(a) beauty (b) narrative technique
(c) time (d) none

252. One of the interesting references in *The Magic Mountain* is
(a) clockless time in the sanatorium (b) timeless time
(c) imaginative time (d) none

## ANSWERS

### Unit A

| | | | | | | | |
|---|---|---|---|---|---|---|---|
| 1. | (a) | 2. | (a) | 3. | (c) | 4. | (a) |
| 5. | (a) | 6. | (a) | 7. | (a) | 8. | (d) |
| 9. | (a) | 10. | (b) | 11. | (a) | 12. | (b) |
| 13. | (d) | 14. | (a) | 15. | (b) | 16. | (a) |
| 17. | (b) | 18. | (a) | 19. | (b) | 20. | (b) |
| 21. | (c) | 22. | (b) | 23. | (b) | 24. | (a) |
| 25. | (a) | 26. | (b) | 27. | (a) | 28. | (a) |
| 29. | (b) | 30. | (b) | 31. | (b) | 32. | (b) |
| 33. | (c) | 34. | (c) | 35. | (b) | 36. | (c) |
| 37. | (c) | 38. | (a) | 39. | (d) | 40. | (a) |
| 41. | (a) | 42. | (d) | 43. | (d) | 44. | (d) |
| 45. | (d) | 46. | (a) | 47. | (c) | 48. | (a) |
| 49. | (d) | 50. | (d) | 51. | (d) | 52. | (b) |
| 53. | (a) | 54. | (c) | 55. | (d) | 56. | (a) |
| 57. | (a) | 58. | (a) | 59. | (a) | 60. | (b) |
| 61. | (a) | 62. | (a) | 63. | (b) | 64. | (b) |
| 65. | (a) | 66. | (b) | 67. | (a) | 68. | (b) |
| 69. | (a) | 70. | (a) | 71. | (c) | 72. | (d) |
| 73. | (c) | 74. | (a) | 75. | (a) | 76. | (a) |